Student Workbook to Accompany

USING COMPUTERS IN THE

LAW OFFICE

SIXTH EDITION

Student Workbook to Accompany

USING COMPUTERS IN THE

LAW OFFICE

SIXTH EDITION

Matthew S. Cornick, J.D.
Clayton State University

DELMAR
CENGAGE Learning™

Australia • Brazil • Japan • Korea • Mexico • Singapore • Spain • United Kingdom • United States

DELMAR
CENGAGE Learning

Student Workbook to Accompany Using Computers in the Law Office, Sixth Edition
Matthew S. Cornick

Vice President, Career and Professional Editorial: Dave Garza

Director of Learning Solutions: Sandy Clark

Senior Acquisitions Editor: Shelley Esposito

Managing Editor: Larry Main

Senior Product Manager: Melissa Riveglia

Editorial Assistant: Danielle Klahr

Vice President, Career and Professional Marketing: Jennifer Baker

Marketing Director: Deborah Yarnell

Marketing Manager: Erin Brennan

Marketing Coordinator: Erin DeAngelo

Production Director: Wendy Troeger

Production Manager: Mark Bernard

Content Project Manager: Christopher Chien

Senior Art Director: Joy Kocsis

Senior Technology Product Manager: Joe Pliss

For product information and technology assistance, contact us at
Cengage Learning Customer & Sales Support, 1-800-354-9706
For permission to use material from this text or product,
submit all requests online at **www.cengage.com/permissions**
Further permissions questions can be e-mailed to
permissionrequest@cengage.com

Library of Congress Control Number: 2010938512

ISBN-13: 978-1-4390-5712-4

ISBN-10: 1-4390-5712-5

Delmar
5 Maxwell Drive
Clifton Park, NY 12065-2919
USA

Cengage Learning is a leading provider of customized learning solutions with office locations around the globe, including Singapore, the United Kingdom, Australia, Mexico, Brazil, and Japan. Locate your local office at: **international.cengage.com/region**

Cengage Learning products are represented in Canada by Nelson Education, Ltd.

To learn more about Delmar, visit **www.cengage.com/delmar**

Purchase any of our products at your local college store or at our preferred online store **www.ichapters.com**

Notice to the Reader
Publisher does not warrant or guarantee any of the products described herein or perform any independent analysis in connection with any of the product information contained herein. Publisher does not assume, and expressly disclaims, any obligation to obtain and include information other than that provided to it by the manufacturer. The reader is expressly warned to consider and adopt all safety precautions that might be indicated by the activities described herein and to avoid all potential hazards. By following the instructions contained herein, the reader willingly assumes all risks in connection with such instructions. The reader is notified that this text is an educational tool, not a practice book. Since the law is in constant change, no rule or statement of law in this book should be relied upon for any service to any client. The reader should always refer to standard legal sources for the current rule or law. If legal advice or other expert assistance is required, the services of the appropriate professional should be sought. The publisher makes no representations or warranties of any kind, including but not limited to, the warranties of fitness for particular purpose or merchantability, nor are any such representations implied with respect to the material set forth herein, and the publisher takes no responsibility with respect to such material. The publisher shall not be liable for any special, consequential, or exemplary damages resulting, in whole or part, from the readers' use of, or reliance upon, this material.

Printed in the United States of America
2 3 4 5 6 7 14 13 12 11

For Renda, Peter, and Julia

BRIEF CONTENTS

CONTENTS

CHAPTER 3

Spreadsheet Software | 109

CHAPTER 4

Legal Timekeeping and Billing Software | 174

CHAPTER 5

Databases, Case Management, and Docket Control Software | 198

CHAPTER 6

Electronic Discovery | 240

CHAPTER 7

Litigation Support Software | 241

CHAPTER 8

The Internet, Computer-Assisted Legal Research, and Electronic Mail | 308

CHAPTER 9

The Electronic Courthouse, Automated Courtroom, and Presentation Graphics | 364

Overview of Computers in the Law Office

There are no Hands-On Exercises for Chapter 1.

CHAPTER 2

Word Processing, PDF File Creation, and Document Assembly

FEATURED SOFTWARE
Microsoft Word 2007
Microsoft Word 2003
Adobe Acrobat
HotDocs

WORD PROCESSING HANDS-ON EXERCISES

 ## READ THIS FIRST!

1. Microsoft Word 2007
2. Microsoft Word 2003

I. DETERMINING WHICH TUTORIAL TO COMPLETE

To use the Word Processing Hands-On Exercises, you must already own or have access to Microsoft Word 2007 or Microsoft Word 2003. If you have one of the programs but do not know the version you are using, it is easy to find out (e.g., to discover whether your version is Word 2007 or Word 2003 or some other version of this program).

1. For Word 2003, load your word processor; then click on Help from the menu bar and then on "About [name of the program]" (e.g., "About Microsoft Office Word). It should then tell you exactly what version of the program you are using.

2. For Word 2007, click on the Office button; then click on Word Options and look under the title "Resources."

You must know the version of the program you are using and select the correct tutorial version, or the tutorials will not work correctly. For example, if you have Word 2003 but try to use the Word 2007 tutorial, the tutorial will not work correctly.

II. USING THE WORD-PROCESSING HANDS-ON EXERCISES

The Word-Processing Hands-On Exercises in this section are easy to use and contain step-by-step instructions. They start with basic word-processing skills and proceed to intermediate and advanced levels. If you already have a good working knowledge of your word processor, you may be able to proceed directly to the intermediate and advanced exercises. To be truly ready for word processing in a legal environment, you must be able to accomplish the tasks and exercises in the advanced exercises.

III. ACCESSING THE HANDS-ON EXERCISE FILES ON THE DISK THAT COMES WITH THE TEXT

Some of the intermediate and advanced Word-Processing Hands-On Exercises use documents on the disk that comes with the text. On some computers, all you need to do to access the files is put the disk in the drive and close the drive drawer; the directory will load automatically. If the directory does not load automatically, follow these directions:

To access these files in Windows XP, put the disk in your computer. Select Start, then My Computer; then select the appropriate drive and double-click on the Word-Processing Files folder. To access the exercise files, double-click on the appropriate folder (e.g., Word). You should then see a list of word-processing files that are available for each lesson.

To access these files in Windows Vista, put the disk in your computer, select the Start button, select Computer, and then double-click on the appropriate folder (e.g., Word). You should then see a list of word-processing files that are available for each lesson.

IV. INSTALLATION QUESTIONS

If you have questions regarding installation or loading the word-processing files from the data disk, you may contact Technical Support at 800-648-7450.

Number	Lesson Title	Concepts Covered
BASIC LESSONS		
Lesson 1	Typing a Letter	Using word wrap, Tab key, cursor keys, underline, bold, italics; saving and printing a document
Lesson 2	Editing a Letter	Retrieving a file, block moving/deleting, and spell/grammar checking
Lesson 3	Typing a Pleading	Centering, changing margins, changing line spacing, adding a footnote, double indenting, and automatic page numbering
Lesson 4	Creating a Table	Creating a table, entering data in a table, using automatic numbering, adjusting columns in a table and using the Table AutoFormat command
INTERMEDIATE LESSONS		
Lesson 5	Tools and Techniques	Editing an employment policy using the Format Painter tool, revealing document formatting, using the Beginning of Document command, clearing formatting, changing case, using Search and Replace, using the Go To command, creating a section break, and changing the orientation of the page to Landscape
Lesson 6	Using Styles	Using, modifying, and creating styles to maintain consistent and uniform formatting of documents
Lesson 7	Creating a Template (office letterhead/letter)	Finding ready-made templates in Word, creating a new office letterhead and letter template, filling in/completing a template, and adding a command to the Quick Access toolbar

(continued)

HANDS-ON EXERCISES

Number	Lesson Title	Concepts Covered
Lesson 8	Comparing Documents (multiple versions of an employment contract)	Comparing documents using the simultaneous viewing method and merging the documents into a separate annotated blacklined document
Lesson 9	Using Track Changes	Turning on Track Changes, making revisions, and accepting and rejecting revisions
ADVANCED LESSONS		
Lesson 10	Creating a Mail-Merge Document	Creating and entering a list of recipients for a mail merge, creating a mail-merge document, and merging the list with the document
Lesson 11	Creating a Table of Authorities	Finding and marking cases in a brief and generating an actual table of authorities for the brief
Lesson 12	Creating a Macro (pleading signature block)	Creating and executing a pleading signature block macro
Lesson 13	Drafting a Will	Using Word to draft a will
Lesson 14	The Pleading Wizard	Using the Pleading Wizard

GETTING STARTED

Introduction

Throughout these lessons and exercises, information you need to type into the program will be designated in several different ways:

- Keys to be pressed on the keyboard are designated in brackets, in all caps, and in bold (e.g., press the **[ENTER]** key). A key combination, where two or more keys are pressed at once, is designated with a plus sign between the key names (e.g., **[CTRL]+[BACKSPACE]**). You should not type the plus sign.
- Movements with the mouse are designated in bold and italics (e.g., ***point to File on the menu bar and click***).
- Words or letters that should be typed are designated in bold (e.g., type **Training Program**).
- Information that should display on your computer screen is shown in the following style: ***Press ENTER to continue.***

OVERVIEW OF MICROSOFT WORD 2007

The following tips on using Microsoft Word will help you complete these exercises.

I. General Rules for Microsoft Word 2007

A. *Word Wrap*—You do not need to press the **[ENTER]** key after each line of text, as you would with a typewriter.

B. *Double Spacing*—If you want to double-space, do not hit the **[ENTER]** key twice. Instead, change the line spacing (***click on the Home ribbon tab, then click on the Line spacing icon in the Paragraph group and select 2.0***). See Word 2007 Exhibit 1.

C. *Moving Through Already-Entered Text*—If you want to move the cursor to various positions within already-entered text, use the cursor (arrow) keys, or ***point and click.***

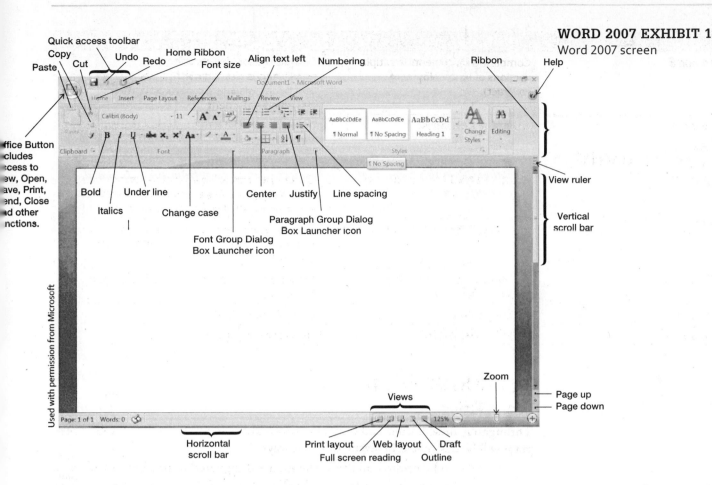

HANDS-ON EXERCISES

D. *Moving the Pointer Where No Text Has Been Entered*—You cannot use the cursor keys to move the pointer where no text has been entered. Said another way, you cannot move any further in a document than where you have typed text or pressed the **[ENTER]** key. You must use the **[ENTER]** key or first type text.

E. *Saving a Document*—To save a document, **click the Office button in the upper left corner of the screen and then click Save** (see Word 2007 Exhibit 1).

F. *New Document*—To get a new, clean document, **click the Office button, then click New, then double-click on Blank document** (see Word 2007 Exhibit 1).

G. *Help*—To get help, press **[F1]** or **click on the ? icon in the upper right corner of the screen** (see Word 2007 Exhibit 1).

II. Editing a Document

A. Pointer Movement

One space to left	**[LEFT ARROW]**
One space to right	**[RIGHT ARROW]**
Beginning of line	**[HOME]**
End of line	**[END]**
One line up	**[UP ARROW]**
One line down	**[DOWN ARROW]**
One screen up	**[PAGE UP]**
One screen down	**[PAGE DOWN]**
Beginning of document	**[CTRL]+[HOME]**
End of document	**[CTRL]+[END]**

B. Deleting Text

Delete the text under the cursor or to the right of it	[DEL]
Delete the text to the left of the cursor	[BACKSPACE]
Delete the whole word to the left of the cursor	[CTRL]+[BACKSPACE]
Delete the whole word to the right of the cursor	[CTRL]+[DEL]

C. *Delete Blocked Text*—**Drag the mouse pointer to select or highlight text,** and then press **[DEL]**; or ***drag the mouse pointer to select or highlight text, and then from the Home ribbon tab, select the Cut icon from the Clipboard group*** (see Word 2007 Exhibit 1). Another way to select or highlight text is to press and hold the **[SHIFT]** key while using the cursor keys to mark/highlight the desired text.

D. *Undoing/Undeleting Text*—If you delete text and immediately want it back, ***click the Undo icon on the Quick Access toolbar.*** This can also be done by pressing **[CTRL]+[Z]**. Press **[CTRL]+[Z]** or ***click the Undo icon*** until your desired text reappears. The Undo feature also works on many other activities in Word, but not all. So, if something goes wrong, at least try pressing **[CTRL]+[Z]** to undo whatever you did.

E. *Moving Text*—***Drag the mouse pointer to highlight or select the text. Then, from the Home ribbon tab, select the Cut icon from the Clipboard group*** (see Word 2007 Exhibit 1). ***Move the cursor to where the text should be inserted, and, from the Home ribbon tab, select Paste from the Clipboard group.*** Another way to do this is to ***drag the mouse pointer to highlight the area and then right-click.*** This brings up a menu that includes the Cut, Copy, and Paste commands. Yet another way to do this is to use the drag-and-drop method: ***Drag the mouse pointer to highlight the area, release the mouse button, click the highlighted area, drag the text to the new location, and release the mouse button.***

F. *Copying Text*—***Drag the mouse pointer to highlight or select the area. From the Home ribbon tab, click the Copy icon from the Clipboard group*** (see Word 2007 Exhibit 1). ***Move the cursor to where the text should be copied, and, from the Home ribbon tab, click Paste.*** Another way to do this is to ***drag the pointer to highlight the area and then right-click Copy. Then move the cursor to where you want to copy the text and right-click Paste.*** Still another way to do this is to use the drag-and-drop method: ***Drag the cursor to highlight the area, release the mouse button, click the highlighted area*** while pressing **[CTRL]**, ***drag the text to the new location, and release the mouse button.*** The text is then copied to the new location.

III. Formatting

A. *Centering Text*—***Move the pointer to the line where the text should be centered. From the Home ribbon tab, click the Paragraph Group Dialog Box Launcher icon*** (see Word 2007 Exhibit 1). ***In the Indents and Spacing tab, click on the down arrow key next to Alignment and select Centered; then click on OK and begin typing.*** If the text has already been typed, move the pointer to the paragraph where the text is and then issue the command. Alternatively, ***from the Home ribbon tab, click the Center icon in the Paragraph group*** (see Word 2007 Exhibit 1).

B. *Bold Type*—To type in bold, ***from the Home ribbon tab, click the Font Group Dialog Box Launcher icon*** (see Word 2007 Exhibit 1); ***in the Font tab, click Bold under Font style. Click on OK.*** Alternatively, ***from the Home ribbon tab, click the Bold icon in the Font group.*** Another way is to press **[CTRL]+[B]**.

C. *Underlining*—To underline, ***from the Home ribbon tab, click the Font Group Dialog Box Launcher icon*** (see Word 2007 Exhibit 1); ***in the Font tab, click the down arrow under Underline style, select the underline style you would like, then click OK.*** Alternatively, ***from the Home ribbon tab, click the Underline icon in the Font group.*** Another way is to press **[CTRL]+[U]**.

D. *Margins*—Margins can be set by ***clicking the Page Layout ribbon tab and then clicking on Margins from the Page Setup group.***

E. *Line Spacing*—Line spacing can be changed by ***clicking the Home ribbon tab, then clicking the Line spacing icon in the Paragraph group*** (see Word 2007 Exhibit 1).

F. *Justification*—***Move the pointer to the line where the text should be justified.*** Then, ***from the Home ribbon tab, click the Paragraph Group Dialog Box Launcher icon*** (see Word 2007 Exhibit 1). ***In the Indents and Spacing tab, click the down arrow key next to Alignment and select Justified; then click on OK and begin typing.*** If the text has already been typed, move the cursor to the paragraph where the text is and then issue the command. Alternatively, ***from the Home ribbon tab, click the Justify icon in the Paragraph group*** (see Word 2007 Exhibit 1).

G. *Header/Footer*—***From the Insert ribbon tab, click Header or Footer from the Header & Footer group.***

H. *Hard Page Break*—To force the addition of a new page in the current document by using the Hard Page Break command, press **[CTRL]+[ENTER]**, or ***from the Insert ribbon tab, click Blank Page from the Pages group.*** Page breaks also occur automatically when the current page is full of text.

I. *Indent*—***From the Home ribbon tab, click the Paragraph Group Dialog Box Launcher icon*** (see Word 2007 Exhibit 1). ***In the Indents and Spacing tab under Indentation, click the up arrow next to Left or Right to set the indentation amount; then click on OK and begin typing.*** Alternatively, ***from the Home ribbon tab, point to the Decrease Indent or Increase Indent icon in the Paragraph group.***

IV. Other Functions

A. *Printing*—To print, ***click the Office button, and then click Print*** (see Word 2007 Exhibit 1).

B. *Spell Check*—To turn on the spell-checking function, ***from the Review ribbon tab, click Spelling & Grammar in the Proofing group.*** Additionally, a red squiggly line will appear under each word that the computer's dictionary does not recognize. If you right-click the word, the program will suggest possible spellings.

C. *Open Files*—To open a file, ***click the Office button, and then click Open*** (see Word 2007 Exhibit 1).

D. *Tables*—***From the Insert ribbon tab, click Table from the Tables group.*** You can move between cells in the table by pressing the **[TAB]** and the **[SHIFT]+[TAB]** keys.

HANDS-ON EXERCISES

▶ BASIC LESSONS

LESSON 1: TYPING A LETTER

This lesson shows you how to type the letter shown in Word 2007 Exhibit 2. It explains how to use the word wrap feature; the [TAB] key; the cursor (or arrow) keys; the underline, bold, and italics features; the save document function; and the print document function. Keep in mind that if you make a mistake in this lesson at any time, you may press [CTRL]+[Z] to undo what you have done. Also remember that any time you would like to see the name of an icon on the ribbon tabs, just *point to the icon for a second or two* and the name will be displayed.

WORD 2007 EXHIBIT 2
Letter

1. Open Windows. After it has loaded, *double-click on the Microsoft Office Word 2007 icon on the desktop* to open Word 2007 for Windows. Alternatively, *click the Start button, point to Programs or All Programs, then click on the Microsoft Word 2007 icon,* or *point to Microsoft Office and then click Microsoft Office Word 2007.* You should now be in a new, clean, blank document. If you are not in a blank document, *click the Office button, click New, then double-click Blank document.*

2. At this point you cannot move the pointer around the screen by pressing the cursor keys (also called arrow keys). This is because text must first be entered; the pointer can only move through text, so the cursor keys will not function if no text exists. *On the Home ribbon tab, click the Paragraph Group Dialog Launcher icon. In the "Paragraph" window, click the down arrow below Line spacing and select Single.* Make sure the "Before" and "After" spacing boxes are both 0 point. *Click OK.*

3. Press the [ENTER] key four times. Watch the status line in the lower left-hand corner of the screen, which tells you what page of your document you are on.

4. Type the date of the letter as shown in Word 2007 Exhibit 2. Notice that as you type the word "October," AutoText may anticipate that you are typing "October" and give you the following prompt: **October (Press ENTER to Insert)**. If you press the [**ENTER**] key, AutoText will finish typing the word for you. You can also ignore it and just continue typing the word yourself.

5. Press the [**ENTER**] key three times.

6. Type the inside address as shown in Word 2007 Exhibit 2. Press the [**ENTER**] key after each line of the inside address. When you finish the line with "Boston, MA 59920," press the [**ENTER**] key three times.

7. Press the [**TAB**] key one time (Word automatically sets default tabs every five spaces). The pointer will move five spaces to the right.

8. Type **Subject:** and then press the [**TAB**] key. ***On the Home ribbon tab, click on the Underline icon in the Font group*** (it looks like a "U" with a thin line under it). Alternatively, you can press [**CTRL**]+[**U**] to turn the underline feature on and off, or ***point to the Font Group Dialog Box Launcher icon*** (see Word 2007 Exhibit 1) and ***select the Underline style***. Then, type **Turner v. Smith**. ***On the Home ribbon tab in the Font group, click the Underline icon*** to turn the underline feature off.

9. Press the [**ENTER**] key one time.

10. Press the [**TAB**] key three times, and then type **Case No. CV-11-0046**.

11. Press the [**ENTER**] key three times.

12. Type the salutation **Dear Mr. Matthews:**

13. Press the [**ENTER**] key twice.

14. Type **In line with our recent conversation, the deposition of the defendant, Jonathan R. Smith, will be taken in your office on**. *Note:* You should not press the [**ENTER**] key at the end of a line. Word will automatically "wrap" the text down to the next line. Be sure to press the [**SPACEBAR**] once after the word "on."

15. Turn on the bold feature by ***clicking the Bold icon*** (a capital "B") ***in the Font group in the Home ribbon tab*** (see Word 2007 Exhibit 1). Alternatively, you can press [**CTRL**]+[**B**] to turn bold on and off. Type **November 15 at 9:00 a.m.** Turn off the bold feature either by pressing [**CTRL**]+[**B**], or ***by clicking the Bold icon in the Font group in the Home ribbon tab.*** Press the [**SPACEBAR**] twice.

16. Type **Please find enclosed a** and then press [**SPACEBAR**].

17. Turn on the italics feature by ***clicking the Italics icon*** (it looks like an "I") ***in the Font group in the Home ribbon tab*** (see Word 2007 Exhibit 1). Alternatively, you can press [**CTRL**]+[**I**] to turn italics on and off. Type "**Notice of Deposition.**" Turn off the italics feature either by pressing [**CTRL**]+[**I**], or ***by clicking the Italics icon in the Font group in the Home ribbon tab.***

18. Press the [**ENTER**] key twice.

19. Type the second paragraph of the letter and then press the [**ENTER**] key twice.

20. Type the third paragraph of the letter and then press the [**ENTER**] key twice.

21. Type the fourth paragraph of the letter and then press the [**ENTER**] key twice.

22. Type **Kindest regards,** and then press the [**ENTER**] key four times.

23. Type **Mirabelle Watkinson** and then press the [**ENTER**] key.

24. Type **For the Firm** and then press the [**ENTER**] key twice.

25. Finish the letter by typing the author's initials, enclosures, and copy abbreviation (cc) as shown in Word 2007 Exhibit 2.

26. To print the document, *click the Office button, then click Print, then click on OK.*

27. To save the document, *click the Office button and then click Save.* Type **Letter1** next to File name:. *Click Save* to save the letter to the default directory. *Note*: You will edit this letter in Lesson 2, so it is important that you save it.

28. *Click the Office button and then Close* to close the document, or, to exit Word 2007, *click the Office button and then click Exit Word.*

This concludes Lesson 1.

LESSON 2: EDITING A LETTER

This lesson shows you how to retrieve and edit the letter you typed in Lesson 1. It explains how to retrieve a file, perform block moves and deletes, and spell/grammar check your document. Keep in mind that if you make a mistake in this lesson at any time, you may press [**CTRL**]+[**Z**] to undo what you have done. Also remember that any time you would like to see the name of an icon on the ribbon tab, just *point to the icon for a second or two* and the name will be displayed.

1. Open Windows. *Double-click on the Microsoft Office Word 2007 icon on the desktop* to open Word 2007 for Windows. Alternatively, *click the Start button, point to Programs or All Programs, then click the Microsoft Word 2007 icon.* (You can also *point to Microsoft Office and then click Microsoft Office Word 2007).* You should now be in a new, clean, blank document. If you are not in a blank document, *click the Office button, click New, then double-click Blank document.*

2. In this lesson, you will begin by retrieving the document you created in Lesson 1. To open the file, *click the Office button and click Open.* Then type **Letter1** and *click Open.* Alternatively, *scroll using the horizontal scroll bar until you find the file, then click on it, then click Open.*

3. Notice in Word 2007 Exhibit 3 that some editing changes have been made to the letter. You will spend the rest of this lesson making these changes.

4. Use your cursor keys or mouse to go to the salutation line, "Dear Mr. Matthews:" With the pointer to the left of the "M" in "Mr. Matthews," press the [**DEL**] key 12 times until "Mr. Matthews" is deleted.

5. Type **Steve**. The salutation line should now read "Dear Steve:"

WORD 2007 EXHIBIT 3
Corrections to a letter

October 1, 2011

Steven Matthews
Matthews, Smith & Russell
P.O. Box 12341
Boston, MA 59920

Subject: Turner v. Smith
            Case No. CV-11-0046

~~Steve~~
Dear ~~Mr. Matthews:~~   of September 30

In line with our recent conversation, the deposition of the defendant, Jonathan R. Smith, will be taken in your office on **November 15 at 9:00 a.m.** Please find enclosed a *"Notice of Deposition."*

I expect that I will be able to finish this deposition on November 15 and that discovery will be finished, in line with the Court's order by December 15.

I will be finishing answers to your interrogatories ~~this week and will have them to you by early next week.~~   next

If you have any questions, please feel free to contact me.

Kindest regards,

Mirabelle Watkinson
For the Firm

MW:db
Enclosures (As indicated)
cc

6. Using your cursor keys or mouse, ***move the pointer to the left of the comma following the word "conversation" in the first paragraph.*** Press the **[SPACEBAR]**, then type **of September 30**. The sentence now reads:

In line with our recent conversation of September 30, the deposition of the defendant, ...

7. The next change you will make is to move the second paragraph so that it becomes part of the first paragraph. Although this can be accomplished in more than one way, this lesson uses the **Cut** command.

8. Using your cursor keys or mouse, ***move the pointer to the beginning of the second paragraph of Word 2007 Exhibit 3.***

9. ***Click and drag the cursor*** (hold the left mouse button down and move the mouse) ***until the entire second paragraph is highlighted, and then release the mouse button.***

10. ***From the Home ribbon tab, click the Cut icon in the Clipboard group*** (see Word 2007 Exhibit 1). An alternative is to ***right-click anywhere in the highlighted area and then click Cut.*** The text is no longer on the screen, but it is not deleted—it has been temporarily placed on the Office Clipboard.

11. Move the pointer to the end of the first paragraph. Press the **[SPACEBAR]** twice. If the pointer appears to be in italics mode, ***from the Home ribbon tab, click the Italics icon in the Font group,*** or press **[CTLR]+[I]** to turn the italics feature off.

12. ***From the Home ribbon tab, click Paste from the Clipboard group*** (see Word 2007 Exhibit 1). Notice that the text has now been moved. Also, you may notice that a small icon in the shape of a clipboard has appeared where you pasted the text. Click the down arrow of the Paste Options icon. Notice that you are given the option to keep the source formatting or change the formatting so that the text matches the destination formatting (i.e., the formatting of the place you are copying it to). In this example, both formats are the same, so it does not matter, but if the text you are copying is a different format, you can choose whether or not to change it to the destination format. Press the **[ESC]** key to make the Paste Options menu disappear.

13. Move the pointer to the line below the first paragraph, and use the **[DEL]** key to delete any unnecessary blank lines.

14. Using your cursor keys or mouse, ***move the pointer to what is now the second paragraph and place the pointer to the left of the "t" in "this week."***

15. Use the **[DEL]** key to delete the word "this," and then type **next**.

16. We will now delete the rest of the sentence in the second paragraph. ***Drag the pointer until "and will have them to you by early next week." is highlighted.*** Press the **[DEL]** key. Type a period at the end of the sentence.

17. You have now made all of the necessary changes. To be sure the letter does not have misspelled words or grammar errors, you will use the Spelling and Grammar command.

18. ***Point on the Review ribbon tab, then click Spelling & Grammar in the Proofing group.***

19. If an error is found, it will be highlighted. You have the options of ignoring it once, ignoring it completely, accepting one of the suggestions listed, or changing/correcting the problem yourself. Correct any spelling or grammar errors. When the spell and grammar check is done, ***click OK.***

20. To print the document, ***click on the Office button, click Print, then click on OK.***

21. To save the document, *click the Office button and then select Save As.* Type **Letter2** in the "File name:" box, *then click Save* to save the document in the default directory.

22. *Click the Office button and then click Close* to close the document, or *click the Office button and then click Exit Word* to exit the program.

This concludes Lesson 2.

LESSON 3: TYPING A PLEADING

This lesson shows you how to type a pleading, as shown in Word 2007 Exhibit 4. It expands on the items presented in Lessons 1 and 2. It also explains how to center text, change margins, change line spacing, add a footnote, double-indent text, and use automatic page numbering. Keep in mind that if you make a mistake at any time, you may press **[CTRL]+[Z]** to undo what you have done.

WORD 2007 EXHIBIT 4
A pleading

IN THE DISTRICT COURT OF
ORANGE COUNTY, MASSACHUSETTES

JIM TURNER,

        Plaintiff,

vs.   Case No. CV-11-0046

JONATHAN R. SMITH,

        Defendant.

NOTICE TO TAKE DEPOSITION

COMES NOW, the plaintiff and pursuant to statute[1] hereby gives notice that the

deposition of Defendant, Jonathan R. Smith, will be taken as follows:

      Monday, November 15, 2012, at 9:00 a.m. at the law offices of Matthews,

      Smith & Russell, 17031 W. 69th Street, Boston, MA.

Said deposition will be taken before a court reporter and is not expected to take more than

one day in duration.

_____
Mirabelle Watkinson
Attorney for Plaintiff

_____
[1] Massachusetts Statutes Annotated 60-2342(a)(1).

Page 1

1. Open Windows. ***Double-click the Microsoft Office Word 2007 icon on the desktop*** to open Word 2007 for Windows. Alternatively, ***click the Start button, point to Programs or All Programs, then click the Microsoft Word 2007 icon.*** (You can also ***point to Microsoft Office and then click Microsoft Office Word 2007***). You should now be in a new, clean, blank document. If you are not in a blank document, ***click the Office button, click New, then double-click on Blank document.*** Remember, any time you would like to see the name of an icon on the ribbon tabs, just ***point to the icon for a second or two*** and the name will be displayed.

2. You will be creating the document shown in Word 2007 Exhibit 4. The first thing you will need to do is change the margins so that the left margin is 1-1/2 inches and the right margin is 1 inch. To change the margins, ***click the Page Layout ribbon tab and then click Margins in the Page Setup group. Next, click Custom Margins at the bottom of the drop-down menu. In the "Page Setup" window in the Margins tab, change the left margin to 1.5 inches and the right margin to 1 inch. Click OK.*** Also, ***on the Home ribbon tab, click the Paragraph Group dialog launcher. In the "Paragraph" window in the Indents and Spacing tab, click the down arrow below Line spacing and select Single.*** Make sure the "Before" and "After" spacing boxes are both 0 point; then ***click OK.***

3. Notice in Word 2007 Exhibit 4 that there is a page number at the bottom of the page. Word will automatically number your pages for you.

4. ***Click the Insert ribbon tab, then click Page Number in the Header & Footer group*** (see Word 2007 Exhibit 5).

5. ***Point to Bottom of Page*** (see Word 2007 Exhibit 5) and notice that a number of options are displayed. ***Click the down arrow in the lower right for additional options*** (see Word 2007 Exhibit 5). Notice that many page number options are available. ***Scroll back up to the top of the option list and click the second option, Plain Number 2.***

WORD 2007 EXHIBIT 5
Adding a page number

6. Your pointer should now be in the area marked "Footer." Specifically, your pointer should be to the left of the number 1. Type **Page** and then press **[SPACEBAR].**

7. *Click the Home ribbon tab. Then, click the vertical scroll bar* (see Word 2007 Exhibit 1) *or use the [UP ARROW] key to go back to the beginning of the document.*

8. *Point and double-click just below the header.*

9. On the first line of the document, *from the Home ribbon tab, click the Center icon in the Paragraph group*. Type **IN THE DISTRICT COURT OF**. Press the **[ENTER]** key. Type **ORANGE COUNTY, MASSACHUSETTS.**

10. Press the **[ENTER]** key five times. *From the Home ribbon tab, click the Align Text Left icon in the Paragraph group.*

11. Type **JIM TURNER,** and press the **[ENTER]** key twice.

12. Press the **[TAB]** key three times and type **Plaintiff,** then press the **[ENTER]** key twice.

13. Type **vs**. Then press the **[TAB]** key six times, and type **Case No. CV-11-0046**.

14. Press the **[ENTER]** key twice.

15. Type **JONATHAN R. SMITH,** and press the **[ENTER]** key twice.

16. Press the **[TAB]** key three times and type **Defendant.** Press the **[ENTER]** key four times.

17. *From the Home ribbon tab, click the Center icon in the Paragraph group.*

18. *From the Home ribbon tab, click the Bold icon and the Underline icon, both found in the Font group.* Type **NOTICE TO TAKE DEPOSITION**. *Click the Bold and Underline icons to turn them off.*

19. Press the **[ENTER]** key three times. *From the Home ribbon tab, click the Align Text Left icon in the Paragraph group.*

20. *From the Home ribbon tab, click the Line spacing icon from the Paragraph group* (see Word 2007 Exhibit 1), *then click on 2.0.* This will change the line spacing from single to double.

21. Type **COMES NOW, the plaintiff and pursuant to statute**. Notice that a footnote follows the word *statute* in Word 2007 Exhibit 4.

22. With the pointer just to the right of the e in "statute," *from the References ribbon tab, click Insert Footnote from the Footnotes group.* The cursor should now be at the bottom of the page in the footnote window.

23. Type **Massachusetts Statutes Annotated 60–2342(a)(1).**

24. To move the pointer back to the body of the document, simply *click to the right of the word "statute" and the superscript number 1 in the body of the document.* Now, continue to type the rest of the first paragraph. Once the paragraph is typed, press the **[ENTER]** key twice.

25. To double-indent the second paragraph, *from the Home ribbon tab, click the Paragraph Group Dialog Box Launcher icon* (see Word 2007 Exhibit 1). The "Paragraph" window should now be displayed. *In the Indents and Spacing tab under Indentation, add a 0.5-inch left indent and a 0.5-inch right indent using the up arrow icons* (or you can type in **.5**). *Click OK in the "Paragraph" window.*

26. Type the second paragraph.

27. Press the **[ENTER]** key twice.

28. *From the Home ribbon tab, click the Paragraph Group dialog launcher and, under Indentation, change the left and right indents back to 0. Click OK.*

29. Type the third paragraph.

30. Press the **[ENTER]** key three times.

31. The signature line is single spaced, so *from the Home ribbon tab, click the Line spacing icon from the Paragraph group, then click 1.0.* This will change the line spacing from double to single.

32. Press **[SHIFT]+[-]** (the key to the right of the zero key on the top row of the keyboard) 30 times to draw the signature line. Press the **[ENTER]** key. *Note*: If Word automatically inserts a line across the whole page, press **[CTRL]+[Z]** to undo the AutoCorrect line. Alternatively, you can *click the down arrow in the Auto Correct Options icon* (it looks like a lightning bolt and should be just over the line that now runs across the page) *and select Undo Border Line.*

33. Type **Mirabelle Watkinson** and then press the **[ENTER]** key.

34. Type **Attorney for Plaintiff.**

35. To print the document, *click the Office button, click Print, then click OK.*

36. To save the document, *click the Office button and then select Save As.* Type **Pleading1** in the "File name:" box, *then click Save* to save the document in the default directory.

37. *Click the Office button and then click Close* to close the document, or *click the Office button and then click Exit Word* to exit the program.

This concludes Lesson 3.

LESSON 4: CREATING A TABLE

This lesson shows you how to create the table shown in Word 2007 Exhibit 6. It expands on the items presented in Lessons 1, 2, and 3 and explains how to change a font size, create a table, enter data into a table, add automatic numbering, adjust column widths, and use the Table AutoFormat command. Keep in mind that if you make a mistake at any time, you may press **[CTRL]+[Z]** to undo what you have done.

WORD 2007 EXHIBIT 6
Creating a table

Used with permission from Microsoft.

Average Hourly Billing Rates for Paralegals

Number	Region	Paralegals
1.	California	$120
2.	West	$110
3.	South Central	$88
4.	West Central	$88
5.	East Central	$95
6.	South	$87
7.	Northeast	$95

Dragging the vertical column line left and right expands or reduces the size of the column.

HANDS-ON EXERCISES

1. Open Windows. *Double-click the Microsoft Office Word 2007 icon on the desktop* to open Word 2007 for Windows. Alternatively, *click the Start button, point to Programs or All Programs, then click the Microsoft Word 2007 icon,* or *point to Microsoft Office and then click on Microsoft Office Word 2007.*) You should be in a new, clean, blank document. If you are not in a blank document, *click the Office button, click on New, then double-click on Blank document.*

2. *From the Home ribbon tab, click the Center icon in the Paragraph group, and then click the Bold icon in the Font group.*

3. *From the Home ribbon tab, click the Font Size icon in the Font group* and change the font size to 14 by either typing **14** in the box or *choosing 14 from the drop-down menu.* Alternatively, you can both turn on bold and change the font size by *clicking the Font Group Dialog Box Launcher icon from the Home ribbon tab* (see Word 2007 Exhibit 1).

4. Type **Average Hourly Billing Rates for Paralegals** (see Word 2007 Exhibit 6). Press the **[ENTER]** key once, and then *click the Font Size icon and change the type back to 12 point. Click the Bold icon to turn bold off.*

5. Press the **[ENTER]** key once.

6. *From the Insert ribbon tab, click Table from the Tables group.* Notice that a number of columns and rows of boxes are displayed. This allows you to choose the graphic style of your table.

7. *Point within the Table menu so that three columns are highlighted, then point and click so that eight rows are highlighted* (e.g., 3 x 8 Table). Notice that as you point, the table is temporarily shown in your document. This is called a *live preview.* When you point and click on the cell that is three columns over and eight cells down, the table (as opposed to the live preview) will be displayed permanently in your document.

8. The blank table should now be displayed and the cursor should be in the first column of the first row of the table. If the cursor is not in the first column of the first row, *click in this cell to place the cursor there. From the Home ribbon tab, click on the Bold icon on the Font group.* Type **Number** and then press the **[TAB]** key once to go to the next cell in the table.

9. *Click on the Bold icon.* Type **Region** and then press the **[TAB]** key once to go to the next cell in the table. *Note*: If you need to go back to a previous cell, you can use either the mouse or the cursor keys, or you can press **[SHIFT]+[TAB]**. Also, if you accidentally hit the **[ENTER]** key instead of the **[TAB]** key, you can either press the **[BACKSPACE]** key to delete the extra line, or you can press **[CTRL]+[Z]** to undo it.

10. *Click on the Bold icon.* Type **Paralegals** and then press the **[TAB]** key to go to the next cell.

11. You will now use the automatic paragraph numbering feature to number the rows. *From the Home ribbon tab, click on the Numbering icon in the Paragraph group* (see Word 2007 Exhibit 1—it is the icon that has the numbers 1, 2, 3 in a column, with a short line next to each number). Notice that the number 1 was automatically entered in the cell. *From the Home ribbon tab, point on the down arrow next to the Numbering icon in the Paragraph group.* Under Numbering Library, look at the different formats that are available. The default format is fine, so press **[ESC]** to make the menu disappear.

12. Press the **[TAB]** key to go to the next cell.

13. Type **California** and then press the **[TAB]** key to go to the next cell.

14. Type **$120** and then press the **[TAB]** key to go to the next cell.

15. *From the Home ribbon tab, click on the Numbering icon in the Paragraph group,* and then press the **[TAB]** key to go to the next cell.

16. Continue entering all of the information shown in Word 2007 Exhibit 6 into your table.

17. *Put the pointer in the uppermost left cell of the table and drag the pointer to the lowest cell at the right of the table to completely highlight the table. Then, from the Home ribbon tab, click on the Align Text Left icon in the Paragraph group.* Now the whole table is left-aligned.

18. *Put the pointer on the vertical column line that separates the Number column and the Region column, and then drag the line to the left* (see Word 2007 Exhibit 6). Notice that by using this technique you can completely adjust each column width as much as you like. Press **[CTRL]+[Z]** to undo the column move, because the current format is fine.

19. *Click on any cell in the table.* Notice that just above the ribbon tab, new options are now shown; two more tabs, Design and Layout, appear under the new heading "Table Tools." *Click on the Design ribbon tab.* Notice that the ribbon tab now shows seven table styles. *Point (don't click) on one of the tables;* notice that the Live Preview feature shows you exactly what your table will look like with this design. *Point and click on the down arrow in the Table Styles group and browse to see many more table styles. Point and click on a table style that you like.* The format of the table changes completely.

20. To print the document, *click on the Office button, click on Print, then click on OK.*

21. To save the document, *click on the Office button and then select Save As.* Type **Table1** in the "File name:" box, *then point and click on Save* to save the document in the default directory.

22. *Click on the Office button and then on Close* to close the document, or *click on the Office button and then on Exit Word* to exit the program.

This concludes Lesson 4.

▶ INTERMEDIATE LESSONS

LESSON 5: TOOLS AND TECHNIQUES

This lesson shows you how to edit an employment policy (from the data disk supplied with this text), use the Format Painter tool, reveal formatting, clear formatting, change the case of text, use the Find and Replace feature, use the Go To command, create a section break, and change the orientation of a page from portrait to landscape. This lesson assumes that you have completed Lessons 1 through 4 and that you are generally familiar with Word 2007.

1. Open Windows. *Double-click on the Microsoft Office Word 2007 icon on the desktop* to open Word 2007 for Windows. Alternatively, *click on the Start button, point the pointer to Programs or All Programs, then click on the Microsoft Word 2007 icon.* (You also may *point to Microsoft Office and then click on Microsoft Office Word 2007*). You should be in a new, clean, blank document. If you are not in a blank document, *click on the Office button, click on New, then double-click on Blank document.*

2. The first thing you will do is open the "Lesson 5" file from the disk supplied with this text. Ensure that the disk is inserted in the disk drive,

point and click on the Office button, then point and click on Open. The "Open" window should now be displayed. *Point and click on the down arrow to the right of the white box next to "Look in:" and select the drive where the disk is located. Point and double-click on the Word Processing Files folder. Double-click on the Word 2007 folder. Double-click on the "Lesson 5" file.*

3. The file entitled "World Wide Technology, Inc. alcohol and drug policy" should now be displayed on your screen. In this lesson, you will be editing this policy for use by another client. The next thing you need to do is to go to section 3, "Definitions," and change the subheadings so that they all have the same format. You will use the Format Painter tool to do this.

4. Use the cursor keys or the mouse and the scroll bars to scroll to section 3, "Definitions" (see Word 2007 Exhibit 7). Notice that the first definition, "Alcohol or alcoholic beverages:," is bold and in a different font from the rest of the definitions in section 3. You will use the Format Painter tool to quickly copy the formatting from "Alcohol or alcoholic beverages:" to the other four definitions in section 3.

5. *Point and click anywhere in the text "Alcohol or alcoholic beverages:"* This tells the Format Painter tool the formatting you want to copy.

6. Next, *from the Home ribbon tab, point and click on the Format Painter icon in the Clipboard group.* It looks like a paintbrush (see Word 2007 Exhibit 7). Remember, if you hover your cursor over an icon for a second or two, the name of the icon will appear.

7. Notice that your cursor now turns to a paintbrush. *Drag the pointer* (hold the left mouse button down and move the mouse) *until the heading "Legal drugs:" is highlighted* (see Word 2007 Exhibit 7), *then let go of the mouse button.* Notice that the paintbrush on your cursor is now gone. *Click the left mouse button once anywhere in the screen to make the highlight go away.* Notice that "Legal drugs:" now has the same formatting as "Alcohol or alcoholic

WORD 2007 EXHIBIT 7
The Format Painter tool

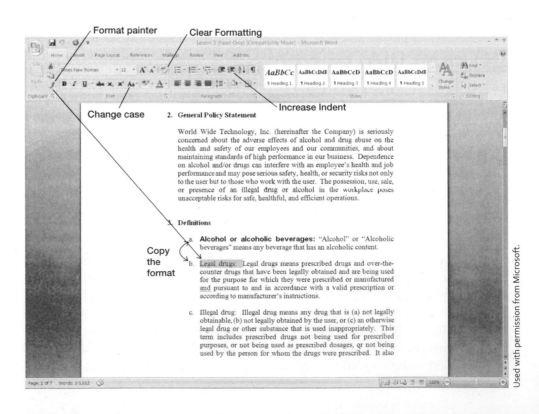

beverages:" The Format Painter command is a quick way to make formatting changes.

8. You will now use the Format Painter command to copy the formatting to the remaining three definitions, with one additional trick. ***Point and click anywhere in the text "Legal drugs:"***

9. Next, ***from the Home ribbon tab, double-click on the Format Painter icon in the Clipboard group.*** (Your pointer should now have a paintbrush attached to it.) The double-click tells Format Painter that you are going to copy this format to multiple locations, instead of just one location. This is a great time-saving feature if you need to copy formatting to several places, because it keeps you from having to click the Format Painter icon each time you copy the same formatting to a new location.

10. ***Drag the pointer until the heading "Illegal drug:" is highlighted, then let go of the mouse button.*** Notice that the paintbrush is still attached to your pointer.

11. ***Drag the pointer until the heading "Controlled substance:" is highlighted, then let go of the mouse button.***

12. ***Drag the pointer until the heading "Prescription drug:" is highlighted, then let go of the mouse button.***

13. To turn the Format Painter off, press the **[ESC]** button on the keyboard. ***Click the left mouse button once, with the cursor anywhere in the document, to make the highlight go away.*** Notice that all of the headings are now uniform.

14. You will now learn to use the Reveal Formatting command. ***Point and click on the heading "Prescription drug:"***

15. Press **[SHIFT]+[F1]** on the keyboard. Notice that the Reveal Formatting task pane opened on the right side of the screen. The Reveal Formatting task pane lists all format specifications for the selected text. The items are divided into several groups, including Font, Paragraph, Bullets and Numbering, and Section. You can make formatting changes to the text directly from the Reveal Formatting task pane simply by clicking on the format setting you want to change (the links are shown in blue, underlined text). For example, ***point and click on the blue underlined word*** Font ***in the Reveal Formatting task pane.*** Notice that the "Font" window opens. You can now select a new font if you so desire. The Reveal Formatting task pane allows you to quickly see all formatting attached to specific text and, if necessary, to change it.

16. ***Point and click on Cancel in the "Font" window.*** To close the Reveal Formatting task pane, ***point and click on the "x" (the Close button) at the top of the Reveal Formatting task pane.*** It is just to the right of the words "Reveal Formatting." The Reveal Formatting task pane should now be gone.

17. Press **[CTRL]+[HOME]** to go to the beginning of the document.

18. You will now learn how to use the Clear Formats command. Notice under the heading "1. Objectives" that the sentence "The objectives of this policy are as follows:" is bold and italics; this is a mistake. ***Drag the pointer until this text is highlighted.***

19. ***From the Home ribbon tab, point and click on the Clear Formatting icon in the Font group*** (see Word 2007 Exhibit 7). This icon looks like an eraser next to a capital "A" and a lowercase "a." Then, ***move the pointer to anywhere in the sentence and click the left mouse button once to make the highlight go away.*** Notice that all of the formatting is now gone. The "Clear Formats" command is a good way to remove all text formatting quickly and easily.

20. To move the text to the right so it is under "1. Objectives," *from the Home ribbon tab, point and click three times on the Increase Indent icon in the Paragraph group* (see Word 2007 Exhibit 7). This is the icon with a right arrow and some lines on it. The line should now be back in its place.

21. You will now learn how to use the Change Case command. Press **[CTRL]+[HOME]** on the keyboard to go to the beginning of the document.

22. *Drag the pointer until "World Wide Technology, Inc." in the document's title is highlighted.*

23. *From the Home ribbon tab, point and click on the Change Case icon in the Font group. Point and click on UPPERCASE.* Notice that the text is now in all capitals. *Point and click the left mouse button once anywhere in the document to make the highlighting disappear.*

24. *Drag the pointer until the subtitle "alcohol and drug policy" is highlighted. From the Home ribbon tab, point and click on the Change Case icon in the Font group. Point and click on "Capitalize Each Word."* Notice that the text is now in title case. *Click the left mouse button once anywhere in the document to make the highlighting go away.* The Change Case command is a convenient way to change the case of text without having to retype it. *Note:* Retyping always increases the risk of introducing errors!

25. Notice that the *A* in *and* in "Alcohol And Drug Policy" is now capitalized, and that a green squiggly line is underneath it. This tells you that Word believes there is a grammar error. *Point and right-click on the word "And" in the title.* A menu will be displayed. *Point and click on* **and** *(this is what Word is suggesting the correction should be).* The word "and" in the title is now lowercase.

26. Press **[CTRL]+[HOME]** on the keyboard to go to the beginning of the document.

27. You will now learn how to use the Find and Replace command. *From the Home ribbon tab, point and click on the Replace icon in the Editing group.* Alternatively, you could press **[CTRL]+[H]**, then *click on Replace.*

28. In the "Find and Replace" window, in the white box next to "Find what:" type **World Wide Technology, Inc.** Then, in the white box next to "Replace with:" type **Johnson Manufacturing.** *Point and click on the Replace All button in the "Find and Replace" window.* The program will respond by stating that it made four replacements. *Click on OK in that notification window.*

29. *Point and click on the Close button in the "Find and Replace" window to close the window.* Notice that "World Wide Technology, Inc." has now been changed to "Johnson Manufacturing."

30. You will now learn how to use the Go To command. The Go To command is an easy way to navigate through large and complex documents. Press **[F5].** Notice that the "Find and Replace" window is again displayed on the screen, but this time the Go To tab is selected. In the white box directly under "Enter page number:" type **7** using the keyboard and then *point and click on Go To in the "Find and Replace" window.* Notice that page 7, "Reasonable Suspicion Report," is now displayed. (*Note:* If the "Find and Replace" window blocks your view of the text of the document, point at the blue box in the "Find and Replace" window and drag the window lower so you can see the document.) *Point and click on Close in the "Find and Replace" window.*

31. Suppose that you would like to change the orientation of only one page in a document from Portrait (where the length is greater than the width) to

Landscape (where the width is greater than the length). In this example, you will change the layout of only the Reasonable Suspicion Report to Landscape while keeping the rest of the document in Portrait orientation. To do this in Word, you must enter a section break.

32. Your cursor should be on page 7, just above "Johnson Manufacturing Reasonable Suspicion Report." *From the Page Layout ribbon tab, point and click on Breaks in the Page Setup group.*

33. *Under Section Breaks, point and click on Next Page.*

34. *Point and click on the Draft icon* in the lower right area of the screen (see Word 2007 Exhibit 7). *Press the [UP] arrow key two times.* Notice that a double dotted line that says "Section Break (Next Page)" is now displayed.

35. The Word 2007 interface allows you to switch views by clicking on one of the view layouts in the lower right of the screen (see Word 2007 Exhibit 7). Print and Draft are two of the most popular layouts. In addition, the Zoom tool just to the right of the Draft view allows you to zoom in or out (increase or decrease the magnification) of your document.

36. With the section break in place, you can now change the format of the page from Portrait to Landscape without changing the orientation of previous pages.

37. *With the cursor on the "Johnson Manufacturing Reasonable Suspicion Report" page, from the Page Layout ribbon tab, point and click on Orientation in the Page Setup group. Point and click on Landscape.* Notice that the layout of the page has changed.

38. *Point and click on the Print Layout icon* in the lower right of the screen (see Word 2007 Exhibit 7).

39. To confirm that the layout has changed, *point and click on the Office button, then point to Print, then click on Print Preview.* Notice that the layout is now Landscape (the width is greater than the length). Press the **[PAGE UP]** key until you are back to the beginning of the document. Notice that all of the other pages in the document are still in Portrait orientation.

40. *From the Print Preview ribbon tab, point and click on the Close Print Preview icon in the preview group* (this icon is a red X at the far right of the ribbon tab).

41. To print the document, *click on the Office button, click on Print, then click on OK.*

42. To save the document, *click on the Office button, point to Save As, then click on Word 97—2003 Document. Under Save in, select the drive or folder* you would like to save the document in. Then, next to File name:, type **Done—Word 2007 Lesson 5 Document** *and point and click on Save to save the document.*

43. *Click on the Office button, then click on Close* to close the document, or *click on the Office button and then on Exit Word* to exit the program.

This concludes Lesson 5.

LESSON 6: USING STYLES

This lesson gives you an introduction to styles. Styles are particularly helpful when you are working with long documents that must be formatted uniformly.

1. Open Windows. *Double-click on the Microsoft Office Word 2007 icon on the desktop* to open Word 2007 for Windows. Alternatively, *click on the Start button, point the cursor to Programs or All Programs, then click on the Microsoft Word 2007 icon.* (You may also *point to Microsoft Office and then click on Microsoft Office Word 2007.*) You should now be in a new,

HANDS-ON EXERCISES

clean, blank document. If you are not in a blank document, ***click on the Office button, click on New, then double-click on Blank document.***

2. The first thing you will do is open the "Lesson 6" file from the disk supplied with this text. Ensure that the disk is inserted in the drive, ***point and click on the Office button, then point and click on Open.*** The "Open" window should now be displayed. ***Point and click on the down arrow to the right of the white box next to "Look in:" and select the drive where the disk is located. Point and double-click on the Word Processing File folder. Double-click on the Word 2007 folder. Point and double-click on the "Lesson 6" file.***

3. The text "SARBANES-OXLEY ACT OF 2002" should now be displayed on your screen (see Word 2007 Exhibit 8). In this lesson you will use styles to add uniform formatting to this document. In the Home ribbon tab, notice the Styles group. ***Point and click on any text on the page.*** Notice in the Styles group on the Home ribbon tab that the Normal box is highlighted in yellow (see Word 2007 Exhibit 8). Currently, all text in this document is in the Normal style.

4. Using your cursor keys or the scroll bar, scroll down through the document. Notice that all of the paragraphs are left-aligned and that the right edge of all the paragraphs is ragged (not justified).

5. ***From the Home ribbon tab, point and click on the Styles Group Dialog Box Launcher icon.*** Notice that the Styles task pane now appears on the right side of the screen (see Word 2007 Exhibit 8). In the Styles task pane, ***if the white box next to Show Preview is not marked, click on the box so that a green check mark appears*** (see Word 2007 Exhibit 8). Notice that a few styles in the Styles task pane are currently being displayed (*e.g.,* Heading 1, Heading 2, and Normal). Also notice that the Normal style has a blue box around it, indicating that your cursor is on text with the Normal style. Finally, notice that there is a paragraph sign after each of these heading names, indicating that these are paragraph styles.

WORD 2007 EXHIBIT 8
Styles

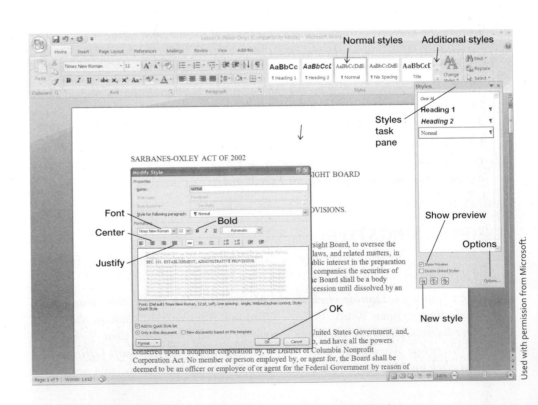

6. Notice at the bottom of the Styles task pane the word Options… in blue; *point and click on Options.* The "Style Pane Options" window should now be displayed.

7. *In the "Style Pane Options" window under Select styles to show, click the down arrow next to "In current document" and click on "All styles." Then, in the "Style Pane Options" window, click on OK.*

8. Notice that the Styles task pane is now full of additional styles. These are all of the styles that are automatically available in Word 2007. *Point and click on the down arrow in the Styles task pane to see the full list of styles.*

9. To return to the list of just a few styles, *point and click on Options in the lower right of the Styles task pane. Under Select styles to show: click on the down arrow and click on "In current document." Then, in the "Style Pane Options" window, click on OK.*

10. Notice that the short list of styles is again displayed. To access a longer list of styles from the Styles group on the Home ribbon tab, *point and click on the down arrow in the Styles group.* If you select the More icon (the icon that shows a down arrow with a line over it) in the Styles group, you can see all of the styles at one time. Press the **[ESC]** key to close the list.

11. Styles are extremely useful. Assume now that you would like to have all of the text in the document justified. *Point and right-click on Normal in the Styles task pane. Point and left-click on Modify.* The Modify Style task pane should now be displayed (see Word 2007 Exhibit 8). Using the Modify Style task pane, you can completely change the formatting for any style.

12. *Point and click on the Justify icon in the Modify Style task pane* to change the Normal style from left-aligned to fully justified (see Word 2007 Exhibit 8).

13. *Point and click on the down arrow in the "Font" box in the Modify Style task pane and point and click on Arial* (you may have to scroll through some fonts to find it). *Point and click on the OK button in the Modify Style task pane.* Notice that Word quickly changed the alignment of all of the text to fully justified and changed the font to Arial.

14. *Drag the pointer until the full title of the document is highlighted* (SARBANES-OXLEY ACT OF 2002 TITLE I—PUBLIC COMPANY ACCOUNTING OVERSIGHT BOARD).

15. *Point and click on Heading 1 in the Styles task pane.*

16. *Point and right-click on Heading 1 in the Styles task pane and select Modify. Then, point and click on the Center icon. Select the OK button in the Modify Style task pane.*

17. *Click the left mouse button anywhere in the title to make the highlight disappear.* Notice that the text of the title shows as Heading 1 in the Styles task pane.

18. *Point and click anywhere in "SEC. 101. ESTABLISHMENT; ADMINISTRATIVE PROVISIONS." Point and click on Heading 2 in the Styles task pane.* Notice that the heading has now changed.

19. *Point and click anywhere in the subheading "(a) ESTABLISHMENT OF BOARD." Point and click on the New Style icon at the bottom of the Styles task pane* (see Word 2007 Exhibit 8).

20. The "Create New Style from Formatting" window should now be displayed. Under Properties, next to Name, type **Heading 3A**; then, *under Formatting, point and click on the Bold icon. Point and click on OK in the "Create New Style from Formatting" window.*

21. Now, go to the following subheadings and format them as Heading 3A by clicking on them and selecting Heading 3A from the Styles task pane:

   (b) STATUS.

   (c) DUTIES OF THE BOARD.

   (d) COMMISSION DETERMINATION.

   (e) BOARD MEMBERSHIP.

   (f) POWERS OF THE BOARD.

   (g) RULES OF THE BOARD.

   (h) ANNUAL REPORT TO THE COMMISSION.

Press **[CTRL]+[HOME]** to go to the beginning of the document. Your document is now consistently formatted. Using styles, your documents can also easily be uniformly changed. For example, if you read in your local rules that subheadings for pleadings must be in 15-point Times New Roman font, you could quickly change the subheadings in your document by modifying the heading styles, rather than highlighting each subheading and changing the format manually.

22. To print the document, ***click on the Office button, click on Print, then click on OK.***

23. To save the document, ***click on the Office button and point to Save As. Then click on Word 97—2003 Document. Under Save in, select the drive or folder in which you would like to save the document.*** Then, next to File name:, type **Done—Word 2007 Lesson 6 Document** *and point and click on Save* to save the document.

24. ***Click on the Office button and then on Close*** to close the document, or ***click on the Office button and then on Exit Word*** to exit the program.

This concludes Lesson 6.

LESSON 7: CREATING A TEMPLATE

This lesson shows you how to create the template shown in Word 2007 Exhibit 9. It explains how to create a template of a letter, how to insert fields, and how to fill out

WORD 2007 EXHIBIT 9
Office Letter template

and use a finished template. You will also learn how to add a command to the Quick Access toolbar. The information that will be merged into the letter will be entered from the keyboard. Keep in mind that if you make a mistake at any time, you may press **[CTRL]+[Z]** to undo what you have done.

1. Open Windows. ***Double-click on the Microsoft Office Word 2007 icon on the desktop*** to open Word 2007 for Windows. Alternatively, ***click on the Start button, point the cursor to Programs or All Programs, then click on the Microsoft Word 2007 icon.*** (You can also ***point to Microsoft Office and then click on Microsoft Office Word 2007.***) You should be in a new, clean, blank document. If you are not in a blank document, ***click on the Office button, click on New, then double-click on Blank document.***

2. ***Click on the Office button, then click on New. Under Templates, click on My templates.***

3. ***Click on Template under the Create New field in the lower right of the "New" window*** (see Word 2007 Exhibit 10).

4. ***Click on Blank Document.*** Blank Document should now be highlighted. ***Click on OK*** (see Word 2007 Exhibit 10).

5. You should now have a blank template on your screen. The Windows title should say ***Template1—Microsoft Word*** in the upper middle of the screen. You will now build the template shown in Word 2007 Exhibit 9.

6. ***Also, on the Home ribbon tab, click the Paragraph Group dialog launcher. In the "Paragraph" window, in the Indents and Spacing tab click the down arrow below Line spacing and select Single.*** Make sure the Before and After spacing are both 0 point. Then, ***click OK.***

7. ***From the Home ribbon tab, click on the Center icon in the Paragraph group. From the Home ribbon tab, click on the Bold icon in the Font group.***

8. ***From the Home ribbon tab, click on the Font Size icon from the Font group and select 14 from the list. Click on Font and select Times New Roman.***

HANDS-ON EXERCISES

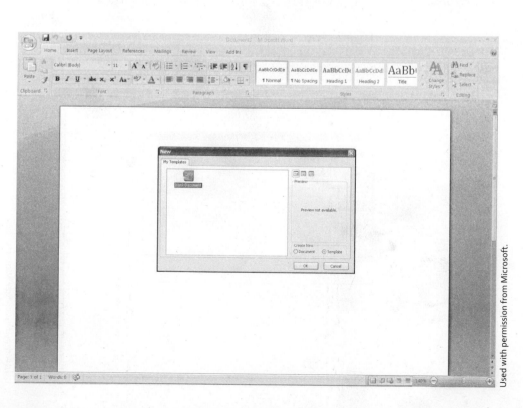

WORD 2007 EXHIBIT 10
Creating a new template

Used with permission from Microsoft.

9. Type **Watkinson & Associates** and then, *from the Home ribbon tab, click on the Font Size icon and select 12 from the list. Click on the Bold icon from the Font group* to turn off bolding.

10. Press the **[ENTER]** key.

11. Type **55 Marietta Street, Suite 1000** and press the **[ENTER]** key.

12. Type **Atlanta, GA, 30303** and press the **[ENTER]** key.

13. Type **(404) 555–3244; Fax (404) 555–3245** and press the **[ENTER]** key.

14. *From the Home ribbon tab, click on the Align Text Left icon in the Paragraph group.*

15. Press the **[ENTER]** key three times.

16. *From the Insert ribbon tab, point and click on Quick Parts from the Text group and then click Field.*

17. The "Field" window should now be displayed (see Word 2007 Exhibit 11). The "Field" window has several sections, including Categories: and Field names:. Under Categories:, (All) should be selected.

18. *Point and click on the down arrow on the Field names: scroll bar until you see the field name Date* (see Word 2007 Exhibit 11). *Click on it.*

19. *From the Field properties list, click on the third option from the top (the month spelled out, the date, and the year).* Notice that the current date is displayed. This field will always display the date on which the template is actually executed, so if the template is executed on January 1, January 1 will be the date shown on the letter. *Click on OK in the "Field" window.*

20. Press the **[ENTER]** key three times.

21. *From the Insert ribbon tab, point and click on Quick Parts from the Text group and then click Field.*

22. *Point and click on the down arrow on the Field names: scroll bar until you see "Fill-in" in the Field names: area* (see Word 2007 Exhibit 11). *Click on Fill-in.*

WORD 2007 EXHIBIT 11
Inserting fields in a template

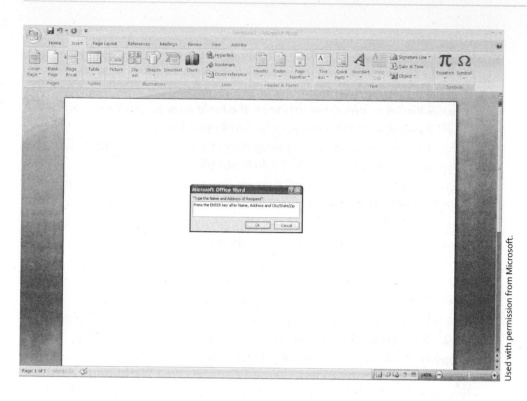

Used with permission from Microsoft.

23. In the Prompt: box under Field properties:, type **"Type the Name and Address of the Recipient."** *Note:* You must include the quotation marks.

24. *Point and click on OK in the "Field" window.*

25. You will now see a window on your screen that says "Type the Name and Address of Recipient." ***Press the ENTER key after Name, Address and City/ State/Zip*** (see Word 2007 Exhibit 12). ***Click on OK.***

26. Press the [**ENTER**] key three times.

27. Press the [**TAB**] key.

28. Type **Subject:**.

29. Press the [**TAB**] key.

30. *From the Insert ribbon tab, point and click on Quick Parts from the Text group and then click on Field.*

31. *Point and click on the down arrow on the Field names: scroll bar until you see "Fill-in" in the Field names: area. Click on Fill-in.*

32. In the "Prompt:" box under Field properties:" type **"Type the Subject of the Letter."** *Note:* You must include the quotation marks. *Point and click on OK.*

33. You will now see a window on your screen that says "Type the Subject of the Letter." Type **Enter the Subject of the Letter.** *Click on OK.*

34. Press the [**ENTER**] key three times.

35. Type **Dear** and press the [**SPACEBAR**]. Then, *from the Insert ribbon tab, point and click on Quick Parts from the Text group, then click Field.*

36. *Point and click on the down arrow on the Field names: scroll bar until you see "Fill-in" in the Field names: area. Click on Fill-in.*

37. In the "Prompt:" box under Field properties:, type **"Salutation"** (*Note:* You must include the quotation marks). *Point and click on OK.*

38. You will now see a window on your screen that says "Salutation." Type **Enter the Salutation.** *Click on OK.*

39. Type **:** [a colon].

40. Press the [**ENTER**] key twice.

41. *From the Insert ribbon tab, point and click on Quick Parts from the Text group and then click Field.*

42. *Point and click on the down arrow on the Field names: scroll bar until you see "Fill-in" in the Field names: area. Click on Fill-in.*

43. In the "Prompt:" box under Field properties:, type **"Body of Letter."** *Note:* You must include the quotation marks. *Click on OK.*

44. You will now see a window on your screen that says "Body of Letter." Type **Enter the Body of the Letter**. *Click on OK.*

45. Press the [**ENTER**] key twice.

46. Type **If you have any questions, please do not hesitate to contact me.** Press the [**ENTER**] key three times.

47. Type **Kindest regards,** and press the [**ENTER**] key four times.

48. Type **Mirabelle Watkinson** and press the [**ENTER**] key once.

49. Type **For the Firm**.

50. *Click on the Office button, then point to Save As and click on Word Template.* (*Note:* If you do not save this as a Word Template, you will not be able to finish the lesson.) Then, next to File name:, type **Watkinson Letter Template**. Word will save the template to a special template folder; if you save it to another folder, you will not be able to run the template in the next portion of this exercise. *Next to "Save as type:" point and click on the down arrow button, select Word 97–2003 Template(*.dot), then point and click on Save* to save the document.

51. *Click on the Office button and then on Close.* You are now ready to type a letter using the template.

52. *Click on the Office button, then click on New. Under Templates, click on My templates. In the "New" window, under the My Templates tab, double-click on Watkinson Letter Template.*

53. The template letter is now running. You will see the "Type the Name and Address of the Recipient" field on the screen. You will also see the prompt that reminds you to press ENTER after the name, address, and city/state/zip. Type over this prompt.

54. Type **Steven Matthews, Esq.** and press the [**ENTER**] key.

55. Type **Matthews, Smith & Russell** and press the [**ENTER**] key.

56. Type **P.O. Box 12341** and press the [**ENTER**] key.

57. Type **Boston, MA 59920** and then *click on OK.*

58. You will see the "Type the Subject of the Letter" field on the screen. You will also see the prompt that reminds you to enter the subject of the letter. Type over this prompt.

59. Type **Turner v. Smith, Case No. CV-11-0046** and then *click on OK.*

60. You will now see the "Salutation" field on the screen. You will also see the prompt that reminds you to enter the salutation. Type over this prompt.

61. Type **Steve** and then *click on OK.*

62. You will now see the "Body of Letter" field on the screen. You will also see the prompt that reminds you to enter the body of the letter. Type over this prompt.

63. Type **This will confirm our conversation of this date. You indicated that you had no objection to us requesting an additional ten days to respond to your**

Motion for Summary Judgment. *Click on OK.* You are now through typing the letter. The completed letter should now be displayed. (*Note:* If another window is displayed prompting you for the name and address of the recipient, simply *click Cancel*; the completed letter should then be displayed.)

64. You are now ready to print the document. First, you will create a Quick Print icon on the Quick Access toolbar. Instead of going to the Office button each time to print, you will be able to print a document from the Quick Access toolbar (see Word 2007 Exhibit 12).

65. *Point and right-click anywhere in the ribbon. Point and click on Customize Quick Access Toolbar....*

66. The "Word Options" window should now be displayed. *Point and double-click on Quick Print on the left side of the screen (under Popular Commands), then click Add.   Point and click on OK in the "Word Options" window.*

67. Notice that a Quick Print icon is now displayed in the Quick Access toolbar.

68. *Point and click on the Quick Print icon on the Quick Access toolbar,* or *click on the Office button, click on Print, then click on OK.*

69. To save the document, *click on the Office button, point to Save As, then click on Word 97—2003 Document. Under Save in, select the drive or folder in which you would like to save the document.* Next to File name:, type **Done—Word 2007 Lesson 7 Document** and *point and click on Save* to save the document. *Note:* You just saved the output of your template to a separate file named "Done—Word Lesson 7 Document." Your original template ("Watkinson Letter Template") is unaffected by the Lesson 7 document, and is still a clean template ready to be used again and again for any correspondence.

70. *Click on the Office button and then on Close* to close the document, or *click on the Office button and then on Exit Word* to exit the program.

This concludes Lesson 7.

LESSON 8: COMPARING DOCUMENTS

This lesson shows you how to compare documents by simultaneously viewing two documents and by creating a separate blacklined document with the changes. In your law-office career, you will often send someone a digital file for revision, only to find that when the file is returned, the revisions are not apparent. Using the comparison tools in Word 2007, you can see what has changed in the document.

1. Open Windows. *Double-click on the Microsoft Office Word 2007 icon on the desktop* to open Word 2007 for Windows. Alternatively, *click on the Start button, point the cursor to Programs or All Programs, then click on the Microsoft Word 2007 icon.* (You can also *point to Microsoft Office and then click on Microsoft Office Word 2007.*) You should now be in a new, clean, blank document. If you are not in a blank document, *click on the Office button, click on New, then double-click on Blank document.*

2. For the purpose of this lesson, we will assume that your firm drafted an employment contract for a corporate client named Bluebriar Incorporated. Bluebriar is in negotiations with an individual named John Lewis, whom they would like to hire as their vice president of marketing. Your firm is negotiating with John Lewis's attorney regarding the terms and language of the employment contract. The "Lesson 8A" file on the disk supplied with this text is the original document you sent to John Lewis's attorney. The "Lesson 8B" file on the disk is the new file sent back to you by John Lewis's attorney.

3. You will now open both of these files from the disk supplied with this text and then compare them side by side. Ensure that the disk is inserted in the drive, *point and click on the Office button, then point and click on Open.* The "Open" window should now be displayed. *Point and click on the down arrow to the right of the white box next to "Look in:" and select the drive where the disk is located. Point and double-click on the Word Processing Files folder. Double-click on the Word 2007 folder. Point and double-click on the "Lesson 8A" file.*

4. Follow the same directions to open the "Lesson 8B" file.

5. *From the View ribbon tab, point and click on View Side by Side in the Window group.* Both documents should now be displayed side by side (see Word 2007 Exhibit 13).

6. Push the [**DOWN ARROW**] key to scroll down through the document. Notice that both documents simultaneously scroll.

7. From the View ribbon tab, notice that the Synchronous Scrolling icon in the Window group is highlighted (see Word 2007 Exhibit 13). To turn this feature off, you would click on this icon. The Synchronous Scrolling icon toggles synchronous scrolling on and off. If you turn off synchronous scrolling and wish to turn it back on, simply realign the windows where you want them, and *point and click on the Synchronous Scrolling icon.* (*Note:* If the View ribbon tab looks like Word 2007 Exhibit 13, with the Window group collapsed, *point and click on the Window group, and click Synchronous Scrolling.*)

8. You will now learn how to merge the changes into one document. *Point and click anywhere in Lesson 8A.doc, then point and click on the Office button and then on Close.*

9. *Do the same to close Lesson 8B.doc.*

10. You should now have no documents open.

WORD 2007 EXHIBIT 13
Comparing documents side-by-side

Compare
documents

11. *From the Review ribbon tab, point and click on Compare in the Compare group. Then, point and click on "Compare..."*

12. The "Compare Documents" window should now be displayed (see Word 2007 Exhibit 14). *Under Original document, point and click on the down arrow; use the Browse... feature to find Lesson 8A.doc, then double-click on it* (see Word 2007 Exhibit 14).

13. *Next, under Revised document, point and click on the down arrow; use the Browse feature to find "Lesson 8B.doc" and then double-click on it* (see Word 2007 Exhibit 14).

14. Next to "Label changes with," type **John Lewis' Attorney** and then *point and click on OK in the "Compare Documents" window.*

15. Notice that a new document has been created that merges the documents (see Word 2007 Exhibit 15). Scroll through the new document and review all of the changes.

16. The Compare and Merge Document feature is extremely helpful when you are comparing multiple versions of the same file. By right-clicking on any of the additions or deletions, you can accept or reject the change. This is called Track Changes, and you will learn how to do this in more detail in Lesson 9.

17. To print the document, *point and click on the Quick Print icon on the Quick Access toolbar,* or *click on the Office button, click on Print, then click on OK.*

18. To save the document, *click on the Office button, point to Save As, and then click on Word 97—2003 Document. Under Save in, select the drive or folder in which you would like to save the document.* Next to File name:, type **Done—Word 2007 Lesson 8 Merged Document** and then *click on Save to* save the document.

19. *Click on the Office button and then on Close to close the document, or click on the Office button and then on Exit Word to exit the program.*

This concludes Lesson 8.

WORD 2007 EXHIBIT 15
Completed blackline
document

Used with permission from Microsoft.

LESSON 9: USING TRACK CHANGES

In this lesson, you will learn how to use the Track Changes feature by editing a will, and then accepting and/or rejecting the changes.

1. Open Windows. ***Double-click on the Microsoft Office Word 2007 icon on the desktop*** to open Word 2007 for Windows. Alternatively, ***click on the Start button, point the cursor to Programs or All Programs, then click on the Microsoft Word 2007 icon.*** (You can also ***point to Microsoft Office and then click on Microsoft Office Word 2007***). You should now be in a new, clean, blank document. If you are not in a blank document, ***click on the Office button, click on New, then double-click on Blank document.***

2. The first thing you will do is open the "Lesson 9" file from the disk supplied with this text. Ensure that the disk is inserted in the drive, ***click on the Office button, then click on Open.*** The "Open" window should now be displayed. ***Point and click on the down arrow to the right of the white box next to "Look in:" and select the drive where the disk is located. Point and double-click on the Word Processing Files folder. Double-click on the Word 2007 folder. Double-click on the "Lesson 9" file.***

3. The text "LAST WILL AND TESTAMENT" should now be displayed on your screen (see Word 2007 Exhibit 16). Notice in Word 2007 Exhibit 16 that several revisions have been made to this document. Your client, William Porter, has asked you to use the Track Changes feature to show your supervising attorney the changes he would like to make. Mr. Porter is rather leery of the legal process and wants to make sure your supervising attorney approves of the changes.

4. ***From the Review ribbon tab, point and click on Track Changes from the Tracking group. Point and click on Track Changes from the drop-down menu*** to turn on Track Changes.

5. Make the changes shown in Word 2007 Exhibit 16. Everything that should be added is in red and underlined, and everything that should be deleted is in red and has a line through it.

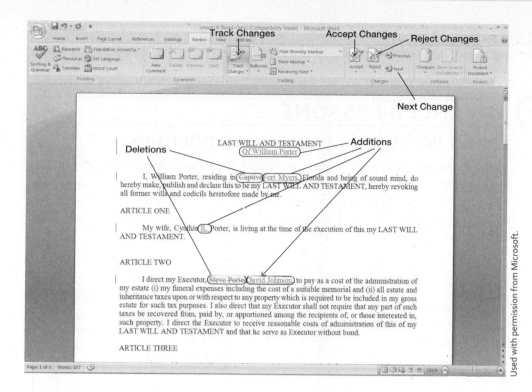

WORD 2007 EXHIBIT 16
Using Track Changes

6. Assume now that you have shown the changes to your supervising attorney. *From the Review ribbon tab, click on Track Changes, then click on Track Changes on the drop-down menu* to turn off Track Changes (see Word 2007 Exhibit 16). This allows you to make changes to the document without having them show up as revisions.

7. *Point and right-click anywhere on the text, "Of William Porter," which you added just under "LAST WILL AND TESTAMENT."* Notice that a menu is displayed that allows you to accept or reject the insertion, among other actions. *Point and click on Accept Change.* The revision has now been accepted.

8. *From the Review ribbon tab, point and click on Next in the Changes group.* This should take you to the next change. *From the Review ribbon tab, point and click on Accept in the Changes group, then click on Accept and Move to Next to accept the change.* Notice that one of the options is "Accept All Changes in Document." This is a quick way to accept all changes in a document without going through each one of them. However, do not select it; we do not want to accept all the changes in this document.

9. Use the Next feature to continue to go to each change and accept the revisions. The only revision you will *not* accept is changing the executor from Steve Porter to David Johnson; reject this change. Assume that the supervising attorney has learned that Mr. Johnson is terminally ill and most likely will not be able to serve as executor, so the client has decided to keep Steve Porter as the executor.

10. To print the document, *point and click on the Quick Print icon on the Quick Access toolbar,* or *click on the Office button, click on Print, then click on OK.*

11. To save the document, *click on the Office button, then point to Save As, then click on Word 97—2003 Document. Under Save in, select the drive or folder in which you would like to save the document.* Next to File name:, type **Done—Word 2007 Lesson 9 Document** *and then click on Save* to save the document.

12. *Click on the Office button and then on Close* to close the document, or *click on the Office button and then on Exit Word* to exit the program.

This concludes Lesson 9.

▶ ADVANCED LESSONS

LESSON 10: CREATING A MAIL-MERGE DOCUMENT

In this lesson, you will create a merge document for an open house that you will send to three clients (see Word 2007 Exhibit 17). First, you will create the data file that will be merged into the letter. Then, you will create the letter itself, and finally, you will merge the two together. Keep in mind that if you make a mistake at any time, you may press **[CTRL]+[Z]** to undo what you have done.

WORD 2007 EXHIBIT 17
Mail-merge letter

Used with permission from Microsoft.

1. Open Windows. *Double-click on the Microsoft Office Word 2007 icon on the desktop* to open Word 2007 for Windows. Alternatively, *click on the Start button, point the cursor to Programs or All Programs, then click on the Microsoft Word 2007 icon.* (You may also *point to Microsoft Office and then click on Microsoft Office Word 2007.*) You should now be in a new, clean, blank document. If you are not in a blank document, *click on the Office button, click on New, then double-click on Blank document.*

2. *From the Mailings ribbon tab, point and click on Start Mail Merge from the Start Mail Merge group. From the drop-down menu, select Step by Step Mail Merge Wizard....* The Mail Merge task pane is now shown to the right of your document.

3. The bottom of the Mail Merge task pane shows that you are on Step 1 of 6. You are asked to "Select document type." You are typing a letter, so the default selection, "Letters," is fine. To continue to the next step, *click on Next: Starting document at the bottom of the Mail Merge task pane under Step 1 of 6.*

4. The bottom of the Mail Merge task pane shows that you are on Step 2 of 6. You are asked to "Select starting document." You will be using the current document

to type your letter, so the default selection, "Use the current document," is fine. To continue to the next step, *click on Next: Select recipients at the bottom of the Mail Merge task pane under Step 2 of 6.*

5. The bottom of the Mail Merge task pane shows that you are on Step 3 of 6. You are asked to "Select recipients." You will be typing a new list, so *click on Type a new list.*

6. *Under the "Type a new list" section of the Mail Merge task pane, click on Create....*

7. The "New Address List" window is now displayed. You will now fill in the names of the three clients to whom you want to send your open house letter.

8. Type the following. (*Note:* You can use the [**TAB**] key to move between the fields, or you can use the mouse.) Only complete the fields below; skip the fields in the "New Address List" window that we will not be using.

TITLE	
First Name	Jim
Last Name	Woods
Company Name	
Address Line 1	2300 Briarcliff Road
Address Line 2	
City	Atlanta
State	GA
ZIP Code	30306
Country	
Home Phone	
Work Phone	
Email Address	

9. When you have entered all of the information for Jim Woods, *click on the New Entry button in the "New Address List" window.*

10. Enter the second client in the blank "New Address List" window.

TITLE	
First Name	Jennifer
Last Name	John
Company Name	
Address Line 1	3414 Peachtree Road
Address Line 2	
City	Atlanta
State	GA
ZIP Code	30314
Country	
Home Phone	
Work Phone	
Email Address	

HANDS-ON EXERCISES

11. When you have entered all of the information for Jennifer John, ***click on the New Entry button in the "New Address List" window.***

12. Enter the third client in the blank "New Address List" window.

TITLE	
First Name	Jonathan
Last Name	Phillips
Company Name	
Address Line 1	675 Clifton Road
Address Line 2	
City	Atlanta
State	GA
ZIP Code	30030
Country	
Home Phone	
Work Phone	
Email Address	

13. **When you have entered all of the information for Jonathan Phillips, *click on OK in the "New Address List" window.***

14. The "Save Address List" window is now displayed. You need to save the address list so that it can later be merged with the open-house letter. In the "Save Address List" window, next to File name:, type **Open House List** and then ***click on Save in the "Save Address List" window*** to save the file to the default directory.

15. The "Mail Merge Recipients" window is now displayed (see Word 2007 Exhibit 18). ***Click on the Last Name field in the "Mail Merge Recipients" window*** to sort the list by last name (see Word 2007 Exhibit 18). Notice that the order of the list is now sorted by last name.

16. ***Click on OK in the "Mail Merge Recipients" window.*** You are now back at a blank document with the Mail Merge task pane open to the right. The bottom of the Mail Merge task pane indicates that you are still at Step 3 of 6. ***Click on Next: Write your letter at the bottom of the Mail Merge task pane under Step 3 of 6*** to continue to the next step.

17. The bottom of the Mail Merge task pane indicates that you are on Step 4 of 6. In the Mail Merge task pane, "Write your letter" is displayed. You are now ready to write the letter. ***On the Home ribbon tab, click the Paragraph Group dialog launcher. In the "Paragraph" window in the Indents and Spacing tab, click the down arrow below Line spacing and select Single.*** Make sure the Before and After spacing are both 0 point. Then, ***click OK.***

18. Press the **[ENTER]** key four times.

19. Type the current date and press the **[ENTER]** key three times.

20. ***Click on Address block… in the Mail Merge task pane under "Write your letter."***

21. The "Insert Address Block" window is now displayed. You will now customize how the address block will appear in the letters.

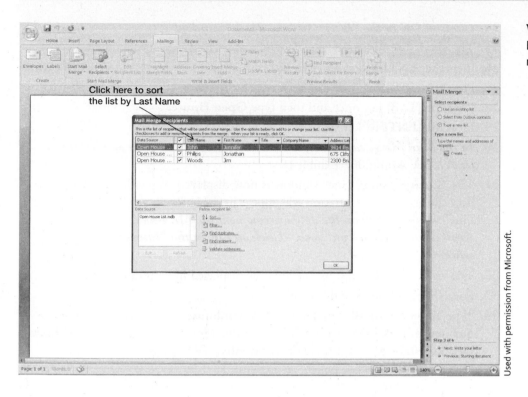

WORD 2007 EXHIBIT 18
Entering mail-merge recipients

22. *In the "Insert Address Block" window, under Insert recipient's name in this format:, click on the second entry, "Joshua Randall Jr." Click on "Insert company name" to deselect it,* because we did not include company names in our data list (see Word 2007 Exhibit 19).

23. *Under Insert postal address:, click on "Never include the country/region in the address"* (see Word 2007 Exhibit 19).

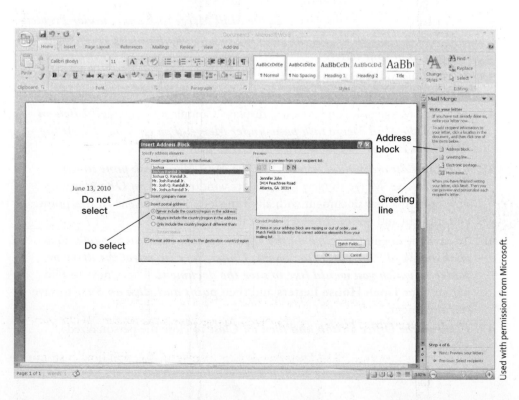

WORD 2007 EXHIBIT 19
Insert address block

HANDS-ON EXERCISES

24. ***Click on OK in the "Insert Address Block" window.***
25. The words "<<AddressBlock>>" are now displayed in your document.
26. Press the [**ENTER**] key three times.
27. Press the [**TAB**] key once and then type **Subject:**.
28. Press the [**TAB**] key once and then type **Open House.**
29. Press the [**ENTER**] key twice.
30. ***In the Mail Merge task pane, under Write your letter, click on Greeting line...*** (see Word 2007 Exhibit 19).
31. The "Insert Greeting Line" window is now displayed. You will now customize how the greeting or salutation will appear in the letter. In the "Insert Greeting Line" window, ***click on the down arrow next to "Mr. Randall" and then scroll down and click on "Josh." Click on OK in the "Insert Greeting Line" window.***
32. The words "<<GreetingLine>>" are now displayed in your document.
33. Press the [**ENTER**] key three times.
34. Type **You are cordially invited to our open house, which will take place in our new offices at 1414 Pine Street, on the 28th of this month, at 7:00 p.m. Drinks will be served. Please dress casually. We hope you will attend.**
35. Press the [**ENTER**] key twice.
36. Type **Kindest Regards,**.
37. Press the [**ENTER**] key four times.
38. Type **Mirabelle Watkinson**.
39. Press the [**ENTER**] key once and type **For the Firm**.
40. You are now done typing the letter. Your letter should look similar to Word 2007 Exhibit 17. The only thing left to do is merge the recipient list with the form.
41. Under "Step 4 of 6" at the bottom of the Mail Merge task pane, ***click on Next: Preview your letters*** to continue to the next step.
42. Your first letter is now displayed. ***In the Mail Merge task pane, under Preview your letters, click on the button showing two arrows pointing to the right to see the rest of your letters.***
43. To continue to the next step, ***click on "Next: Complete the merge" at the bottom of the Mail Merge task pane under Step 5 of 6.***
44. The Mail Merge task pane now will display "Complete the merge." ***Click on Print in the Mail Merge task pane under Merge, then click on OK. At the "Merge to Printer" window, click on OK*** to print your letters.
45. ***Click on Edit individual letters... in the Mail Merge task pane under Merge.*** In the "Merge to New Document" window, ***click on OK.*** Word has now opened a new document with all of the letters in it. (*Note:* At this point, you can edit and personalize each letter if you so desire).
46. To save the document, ***click on the Office button, point to Save As, then click on Word 97—2003 Document. Under Save in, select the drive or folder in which you would like to save the document.*** Then, next to File name:, type **Open House Letters** and then ***point and click on Save*** to save the document.
47. ***Click on the Office button and then on Close*** to close the personalized letters.

48. You should be back at the mail-merge letter. *Click on the Office button and point to Save As. Click on Word 97—2003 Document. Under Save in, select the drive or folder in which you would like to save the document.* Next to File name:, type **Open House Mail Merge** and then *point and click on Save* to save the document.

49. *Click on the Office button and then on Close* to close the document, or *click on the Office button and then on Exit Word* to exit the program.

This concludes Lesson 10.

LESSON 11: CREATING A TABLE OF AUTHORITIES

In this lesson, you will prepare a table of authorities for a reply brief (see Word 2007 Exhibit 22). You will learn how to find cases, mark cases, and then automatically generate a table of authorities.

1. Open Windows. *Double-click on the Microsoft Office Word 2007 icon on the desktop* to open Word 2007 for Windows. Alternatively, *click on the Start button, point the cursor to Programs or All Programs, then click on the Microsoft Word 2007 icon.* (You may also *point to Microsoft Office and then click on Microsoft Office Word 2007*). You should now be in a new, clean, blank document. If you are not in a blank document, *click on the Office button, click on New, then double-click on Blank document.*

2. The first thing you will do is open the "Lesson 11" file from the disk supplied with this text. Ensure that the disk is inserted in the disk drive, *point and click on the Office button, then point and click on Open.* The "Open" window should now be displayed. *Point and click on the down arrow to the right of the white box next to "Look in:" and select the drive where the disk is located. Point and double-click on the Word Processing Files folder. Double-click on the Word 2007 folder. Point and double-click on the "Lesson 11" file.*

3. The text *In the Supreme Court of the United States–Ted Sutton, Petitioner, v. State of Alaska, Respondent* should now be displayed on your screen.

4. In this exercise you will build the case section of the table of authorities for this reply brief. There are five cases to be included and they are all shown in bold so that you can easily identify them. Your first task will be to mark each of the cases so that Word knows they are to be included; you will then execute the command for Word to build the table.

5. If you are not at the beginning of the document, press **[CTRL]+[HOME]** to go to the beginning.

6. You will now mark the cases. *From the References ribbon tab, click on Mark Citation from the Table of Authorities group.*

7. The "Mark Citation" window should now be displayed (see Word 2007 Exhibit 20). Notice next to Category: that "Cases" is displayed. This indicates that you will be marking case citations. *Point and click on the down arrow next to Cases to see that you can also mark citations to be included for statutes, rules, treatises, regulations, and other sources.*

8. *Point and click on Cases again,* because you will now start marking cases to be included in the table of authorities.

9. *In the "Mark Citation" window, click on Next Citation.* Word looks for terms such as "vs" or "v." when finding citations. The cursor should now be on the "v." in *Ted Sutton, Petitioner, v. State of Alaska.* Because this is the caption

WORD 2007 EXHIBIT 20
Marking a citation for inclusion in a table of authorities

Used with permission from Microsoft.

of the current case, we do not want to mark it for inclusion in the table. *Note:* If the "Mark Citation" window gets in the way and prevents you from seeing the brief, ***put the cursor on the blue title bar of the "Mark Citation" window and drag it out of your way.***

10. ***Click on Next Citation in the "Mark Citation" window.*** Again, this is the caption of the current case, *Ted Sutton, Petitioner, v. State of Alaska,* so we do not want to mark it.

11. ***Click again on Next Citation in the "Mark Citation" window.*** Word has now found the case *Carey v. Saffold.* We want to mark this case so that it is included in the table of authorities.

12. ***Click once on the*** **Carey v. Saffold** *case.*

13. ***Drag the pointer to highlight Carey v. Saffold, 536 U.S. 214 (2002), then click in the white box under Selected text: in the "Mark Citation" window.*** The case is automatically copied there (see Word 2007 Exhibit 20).

14. ***Click on Mark in the "Mark Citation" window.*** *Note:* When you mark a citation, Word changes your view to the Show/Hide paragraph view. It shows you that you have embedded table-of-authorities formatting codes in the document. To switch out of Show/Hide view, ***from the Home ribbon tab, point on the Show/Hide icon in the Paragraph group.*** (It looks like a paragraph sign.)

15. ***Click on Next Citation in the "Mark Citation" window.***

16. ***Click once on the*** **Duncan v. Walker** *case.*

17. ***Drag the mouse to highlight*** **Duncan v. Walker, 533 U.S. 167, 174 (2001)** and then ***click in the white box under Selected text: in the "Mark Citation" window.*** The case is automatically copied there.

18. ***Click on Mark in the "Mark Citation" window.*** Notice that, under Short citation: in the "Mark Citation" window, the *Carey* and *Duncan* cases are listed.

Again, if at any time the "Mark Citation" window prevents you from seeing the case you need to highlight, just click on the blue bar at top of the "Mark Citation" window and drag to the left or right to move the window out of your way.

19. To switch out of Show/Hide view, *from the Home ribbon tab, point and click on the Show/Hide icon in the Paragraph group.*

20. *Click on Next Citation in the "Mark Citation" window.*

21. *Click once on the* Bates v. United States *case.*

22. *Drag the pointer to highlight* Bates v. United States, 522 U.S. 23, 29–30 (1997) *and then click in the white box under Selected text: in the "Mark Citation" window.* The case is automatically copied there.

23. *Click on Mark in the "Mark Citation" window.*

24. *Click on Next Citation in the "Mark Citation" window.*

25. *Click once on the* Abela v. Martin *case.*

26. *Drag the pointer to highlight* Abela v. Martin, 348 F.3d 164 (6th Cir. 2003) *and then click in the white box under Selected text: in the "Mark Citation" window.* The case is automatically copied there.

27. *Click on Mark in the "Mark Citation" window.*

28. *Click on Next Citation in the "Mark Citation" window.*

29. *Click once on the* Coates v. Byrd *case.*

30. *Drag the pointer to highlight* Coates v. Byrd, 211 F.3d 1225, 1227 (11th Cir. 2000) *and then click in the white box under Selected text: in the "Mark Citation" window.* The case is automatically copied there.

31. *Click on Mark in the "Mark Citation" window.*

32. *Click on Close in the "Mark Citation" window* to close it.

33. *Point and click on the Show/Hide paragraph icon on the Home ribbon tab* make the paragraph marks disappear.

34. Using the cursor keys or the scroll bar, *place the cursor on page 3 of the document two lines under the title "TABLE OF AUTHORITIES"* (see Word 2007 Exhibit 21). You are now ready to generate the table.

35. *From the References ribbon tab, click on the Insert Table of Authorities icon in the Table of Authorities group* (see Word 2007 Exhibit 21).

36. *The "Table of Authorities" window should now be displayed* (see Word 2007 Exhibit 21). *Click on Cases under Category and then click on OK.*

37. Notice that the table of authorities has been prepared and completed, and that the cases and the page numbers where they appear in the document have been included (see Word 2007 Exhibit 22).

38. To print the document, *point and click on the Quick Print icon on the Quick Access toolbar,* or *click on the Office button, click on Print, then click on OK.*

39. To save the document, *click on the Office button and point to Save As, then click on Word 97—2003 Document. Under Save in, select the drive or folder in which you would like to save the document.* Next to File name:, type Done—Word 2007 Lesson 11 Document and *click on Save* to save the document.

40. *Click on the Office button and then on Close* to close the document, or *click on the Office button and then on Exit Word* to exit the program.

This concludes Lesson 11.

HANDS-ON EXERCISES

WORD 20

Inserting a
authorities

Insert
Table of
Authorities

WORD 2007 EXHIBIT 22

Completed table of
authorities

LESSON 12: CREATING A MACRO

In this lesson you will prepare a macro that will automatically type the signature
block for a pleading (see Word 2007 Exhibit 23). You will then execute the macro to
make sure that it works properly.

1. Open Windows. ***Double-click on the Microsoft Office Word 2007 icon on
the desktop*** to open Word 2007 for Windows. Alternatively, ***click on the Start
button, point to Programs or All Programs, then click on the Microsoft***

WORD 2007 EXHIBIT 23
Creating a pleading
signature block macro

Word 2007 icon. (You can also *point to Microsoft Office and then click on Microsoft Office Word 2007.)* You should now be in a new, clean, blank document. If you are not in a blank document, *click on the Office button, click on New, then double-click on Blank document.*

2. The first thing you need to do to create a new macro is to name the macro and then turn on the Record function. *From the View ribbon tab, point and click on the down arrow under Macros in the Macros group* (see Word 2007 Exhibit 23).

3. *Point and click on Record Macro … on the drop-down menu.*

4. The "Record Macro" window should now be displayed (see Word 2007 Exhibit 23). In the "Record Macro" window, under Macro name:, type **Pleadingsignblock** *and then point and click on OK* (see Word 2007 Exhibit 23).

5. Notice that your cursor looks like a cassette tape. The cassette-tape cursor indicates that Word is now recording all of your keystrokes and commands.

6. Type the information in Word 2007 Exhibit 23. When you have completed typing the information, *from the View ribbon tab, point and click on the down arrow under Macros in the Macros group* (see Word 2007 Exhibit 23).

7. *Point and click on Stop Recording on the drop-down menu.*

8. You will now test your macro to see if it works properly. *Click on the Office button and then on Close* to close the document. At the prompt "Do you want to save the changes to document?," *click on No.*

9. To open a blank document, *click on the Office button, click on New, then double-click on Blank document.*

10. To run the macro, *from the View ribbon tab, point and click on the down arrow under Macros in the Macros group* (see Word 2007 Exhibit 23).

11. *Point and click on View Macros.*

12. *In the "Macros" window, point and click on* **Pleadingsignblock** *and then point and click on Run.* Your pleading signature block should now be in your document.

13. To print the document, *point and click on the Quick Print icon on the Quick Access toolbar,* or *click on the Office button, click on Print, then click on OK.*

14. To save the document, *click on the Office button, point to Save As, then click on Word 97—2003 Document. Under Save in, select the drive or folder in which you would like to save the document.* Then, next to File name:, type **Done—Word 2007 Lesson 12 Document** *and point and click on Save* to save the document.

15. *Click on the Office button and then on Close to close the document, or click on the Office button and then on Exit Word* to exit the program.

This concludes Lesson 12.

LESSON 13: DRAFTING A WILL

Using the websites at the end of Chapter 2 in the main text, or using a form book from a law library, draft a simple will that would be valid in your state. You will be drafting the will for Thomas Mansell, who is a widower. The will should be dated July 1 of the current year. Mr. Mansell requests the following:

- That his just debts and funeral expenses be paid.
- That his lifelong friend, Elizabeth Smith, receive $50,000 in cash.
- That his local YMCA receive his 100 shares of stock in Google.
- That all of his remaining property (real or personal) descend to his daughter Sharon Mansell.
- That in the event Mr. Mansell and his daughter die simultaneously, for all of his property to descend to Sharon's son Michael Mansell.
- That Elizabeth Smith be appointed the executor of the will; if Ms. Smith predeceases Mr. Mansell, that Mr. Stephen Dear be appointed executor.

Mr. Mansell has also requested that his will be double-spaced and have one-inch margins. He would like the will to look good and be valid in his state.

- Three witnesses will watch the signing of the will: Shelley Stewart, Dennis Gordon, and Gary Fox.
- You will notarize the will.

Print out a hard copy of the will and email it to your instructor.

LESSON 14: THE PLEADING WIZARD

Use the Pleading Wizard in Microsoft Word 2007 to create the motion in Exhibit 2–11 of Chapter 2 of the main text. To bring up the Pleading Wizard, *click on the Office button, then click on New. Under Templates, click on My templates.... Click on the Legal Pleadings tab, click on "Pleading Template 1," and under Create New click on Template. Finally, click on OK.* (*Note*: If you are unable to find the Pleading Wizard, it may not have been installed. If this is the case, move to the next lesson.) The Pleading Wizard will guide you through creating a pleading form and completing the form. Use Exhibit 2–11 as a guide, but do not try to copy the format exactly. When the document is completed, print out a hard copy and email the file to your instructor.

HANDS-ON EXERCISES

MICROSOFT WORD 2003 FOR WINDOWS

Number	Lesson Title	Concepts Covered
BASIC LESSONS		
Lesson 1	Typing a Letter	Using word wrap, Tab key, cursor keys, underline, bold, italics; saving and printing a document.
Lesson 2	Editing a Letter	Retrieving a file, Insert mode, Overtype mode, block moving/deleting, and spell/grammar checking
Lesson 3	Typing a Pleading	Centering, changing margins, changing line spacing, adding a footnote, double indenting, and automatic page numbering
Lesson 4	Creating a Table	Creating a table, entering data in a table, using automatic numbering, adjusting columns in a table and using the Table AutoFormat command
INTERMEDIATE LESSONS		
Lesson 5	Tools and Techniques	Editing an employment policy using the Format Painter tool, revealing document formatting, using the Beginning of Document command, clearing formatting, changing case, using Find and Replace, using the Go To command, creating a section break, and changing the orientation of the page to landscape
Lesson 6	Using Styles	Using, modifying, and creating styles to maintain consistent and uniform formatting of documents
Lesson 7	Creating a Template (office letterhead/ letter)	Finding ready-made templates in Word, creating a new office letterhead and letter template, and filling in and completing a template
Lesson 8	Comparing Documents	Comparing documents using the simultaneous viewing method and merging the documents into a separate annotated blacklined document
Lesson 9	Using Track Changes	Turning on Track Changes, making revisions, and accepting and rejecting revisions
ADVANCED LESSONS		
Lesson 10	Creating a Mail-Merge Document	Creating and entering a list of recipients for a mail merge, creating a mail-merge document, and merging the list with the document
Lesson 11	Creating a Table of Authorities	Finding and marking cases in a brief and generating an actual table of authorities for the brief
Lesson 12	Creating a Macro (pleading signature block)	Creating and executing a pleading signature block macro
Lesson 13	Drafting a Will	Using Word to draft a will
Lesson 14	The Pleading Wizard	Using the Pleading Wizard

GETTING STARTED

Introduction

Throughout these lessons and exercises, information you need to type into the program will be designated in several different ways:

- Keys to be pressed on the keyboard are designated in brackets, in all caps, and in bold (e.g., press the [ENTER] key). A key combination, where two or more keys are pressed at once, is designated with a plus sign between the key names (e.g., [CTRL]+[BACKSPACE]). You should not type the plus sign.
- Movements with the mouse are designated in bold and italics (e.g., *point to File on the menu bar and click*).
- Words or letters that should be typed are designated in bold (e.g., type **Training Program**).
- Information that should display on your computer screen is shown in the following style: *Press ENTER to continue.*

OVERVIEW OF MICROSOFT WORD

The following tips on using Microsoft Word will help you complete these exercises.

I. General Rules for Microsoft Word 2003

A. *Word Wrap*—You do not need to press the [ENTER] key after each line of text, as you would with a typewriter.

B. *Double Spacing*—If you want to double-space, do not hit the [ENTER] key twice. Instead, change the line spacing (*click on Format from the menu bar, then click on Paragraph)*. In the Indents and Spacing tab under Spacing— Line Spacing, *click on the down arrow key, select Double, then click on OK.*

C. *Moving Through Already-Entered Text*—If you want to move the cursor to various positions within already-entered text, use the cursor (arrow) keys, or *point and click.*

D. *Moving the Cursor Where No Text Has Been Entered*—You cannot use the cursor keys to move the cursor where no text has been entered. Said another way, you cannot move any further in a document than where you have typed text or pressed the [ENTER] key. You must use the [ENTER] key or first type text.

E. *Saving a Document*—To save a document, *click on File from the menu bar, then click on Save.*

F. *New Document*—To get a new, clean document, *click on File from the menu bar, then click on New, and click on Blank document* (or choose another document).

G. *Help*—To get help, *click on Help from the menu bar, then click on Microsoft Office Word Help.* In the "Search for" box, type the subject you would like to search for, and then *click on the green "Start searching" arrow to execute the search.*

II. Editing a Document

A. Cursor Movement

One space to left	[LEFT ARROW]
One space to right	[RIGHT ARROW]
Beginning of line	[HOME]

End of line	[END]
One line up	[UP ARROW]
One line down	[DOWN ARROW]
One screen up	[PAGE UP]
One screen down	[PAGE DOWN]
Beginning of document	[CTRL]+[HOME]
End of document	[CTRL]+[END]

B. *Insert v. Overtype*—The **[INSERT]** key toggles from Insert mode to Overtype mode. When text is added in Overtype mode, the new text is typed over the existing text, in effect deleting the existing text. In Insert mode, the text is added to the existing text.

C. *Deleting Text*

Delete the text under the cursor or to the right of it	[DEL]
Delete the text to the left of the cursor	[BACKSPACE]
Delete the whole word to the left of the cursor	[CTRL]+[BACKSPACE]
Delete the whole word to the right of the cursor	[CTRL]+[DEL]

D. *Delete Blocked Text*—**Drag the mouse to select or highlight text,** then press the **[DEL]** key, or **drag the mouse, select Edit from the menu bar, and then choose Cut,** or **drag the mouse, then right-click the mouse and select Cut.** Another way to select or highlight text is to press and hold the **[SHIFT]** key while using the cursor keys to mark/highlight the desired text.

E. *Undo/Undeleting Text*—If you delete text and immediately want it back, **click on Edit from the menu bar, then select Undo Typing.** This can also be done by pressing **[CTRL]+[Z].** Press **[CTRL]+[Z]** or **click on Undo typing** until your desired text reappears. The Undo feature also works on many other activities in Word, but not all. So, if something goes wrong, at least try pressing **[CTRL]+[Z]** to undo whatever you did.

F. *Moving Text (Cutting and Pasting)*—**Drag the mouse to highlight or select the text. Click on Edit from the menu bar and then click on Cut.** Next, **move the cursor to where the text should be inserted, click on Edit from the menu bar, then click on Paste.** Another way to do this is to **drag the mouse to highlight the area and then right-click.** This brings up a menu that includes the commands to Cut, Copy, and Paste text. Yet another way to do this is to use the drag-and-drop method: **Drag the mouse to highlight the area, release the mouse button, click on the highlighted area, drag the text to the new location, and release the mouse button.**

G. Copying Text—**Drag the mouse to highlight or select the area. Click on Edit from the menu bar, then click on Copy.** Next, **move the cursor to where you want the copied text to appear, click on Edit on the menu bar, then click on Paste.** Another way to do this is to **drag the mouse to highlight the area, then right-click and click on Copy.** Next, **move the cursor to where you want the copied text to appear, right-click, and click on Paste.** Still another way to do this is to use the drag-and-drop method: **Drag the mouse to highlight the area, release the mouse button, click on the highlighted area while pressing the [CTRL] key, drag the text to the new location, and release the mouse button.** With any of these techniques, the text will be copied to the new location.

HANDS-ON EXERCISES

III. Formatting

A. *Centering Text*—Move the cursor to the line where the text should be centered, **click on Format from the menu bar, then click on Paragraph.** In the Indents and Spacing tab, **click on the down arrow next to Alignment, select Centered, then click on OK** and begin typing. If the text has already been typed, move the cursor to the paragraph where the text is and then issue the command. Alternatively, you can use the Center icon on the toolbar.

B. *Bold Type*—To type in bold, **click on Format from the menu bar, then click on Font. In the Font tab, click on Bold under Font Style. Click on OK.** Alternatively, you can use the Bold icon on the toolbar or press **[CTRL]+[B]** using the keyboard.

C. *Underlining*—To underline, **click on Format from the menu bar, then click on Font. In the Font tab, click on the down arrow under Underline Style and click on the type of underline you would like. Click on OK.** Alternatively, you can use the Underline command on the toolbar or press **[CTRL]+[U]** using the keyboard.

D. *Margins*—Margins can be set by **clicking on File on the menu bar and then in Page Setup click on the Margins tab.**

E. *Line Spacing*—Line spacing can be changed by **clicking on Format on the menu bar and then on Paragraph.** In the Indents and Spacing tab under Spacing—Line spacing, change the line spacing.

F. *Justification*—Move the cursor to the line where the text should be justified. **Click on Format from the menu bar, then click on Paragraph. In the Indents and Spacing tab, click on the down arrow next to Alignment and select Justified. Click on OK.** Alternatively, you can use the Justify icon on the toolbar.

G. *Header/Footer*—**Click on View from the menu bar, then click on Header and Footer.**

H. *Hard Page Break*—To start a new page of text in the current document by using the hard page command, press **[CTRL]+[ENTER]**. A soft page break occurs when the program automatically creates a new page because the current page is full of text.

I. *Indent*—To indent a paragraph, **click on Format from the menu bar, then select Paragraph.** Change the indentation in the Indents and Spacing tab under Indentation.

IV. Other Functions

A. *Printing*—To print, **click on File from the menu bar, then on Print, then on OK.** Alternatively, you can select the Printer icon from the toolbar.

B. *Spell Check*—To turn on the spell-checking function, **click on Tools from the menu bar, then click on Spelling and Grammar.** Alternatively, a red squiggly line appears under a word that the computer's dictionary does not recognize. You can **right-click on the word** to get the program to suggest possible spellings.

C. *Open Files*—To open a file, **click on File from the menu bar, then select Open.**

D. *Tables*—To insert a table, **click on Table from the menu bar, then on Insert, then on Table.** You can move between cells in the table by pressing the **[TAB]** and the **[SHIFT]+[TAB]** keys.

BEFORE STARTING LESSON 1—SETTING THE TOOLBAR AND MENU BAR

Before starting Lesson 1, complete the following exercise to adjust the toolbar and menu bar so that they are consistent with the instructions in the lessons.

1. Load Windows. After it has finished loading, ***double-click on the Microsoft Office Word 2003 icon on the desktop*** to load Word 2003 for Windows. Alternatively, ***click on the Start button, point with the cursor to Programs or All Programs, and then click on the Microsoft Word icon (or point to Microsoft Office, then click on Microsoft Office Word 2003).*** You should be in a new, clean, blank document. If you are not in a clean document, ***click on File on the menu bar, then click on New, then click on Blank document.***

2. ***Click on View from the menu bar, then point the cursor to Toolbars.***

3. Only the Standard and Formatting toolbars should be checked (see Word 2003 Exhibit 1). If the Standard and Formatting toolbars are not checked, ***click on them to select them*** (the check mark indicates that they have been selected). If another toolbar has been selected (marked with a check mark), click on it to deselect it. Note that you can only make one change to the toolbar at a time, so it may take you a few steps to have only Standard and Formatting selected.

WORD 2003 EXHIBIT 1
Setting the toolbar

Used with permission from Microsoft.

Your computer may already be set for this and you may not have to make any changes. If you do not have to make changes, just press the **[ESC]** key to exit the View menu.

4. We also want to make sure that the full menus display when you select an item from the menu bar (Word normally shows only the most recent/commonly used selections), and that the toolbars are shown on two rows so that you can see all the icons.

5. ***Click on View from the menu bar, then point to Toolbars, then click on Customize.***

6. ***Click on the Options tab.*** Then, under Personalized Menus and Toolbars, make sure that check marks appear next to "Show Standard and Formatting Toolbars

WORD 2003 EXHIBIT 2
Customizing the toolbar

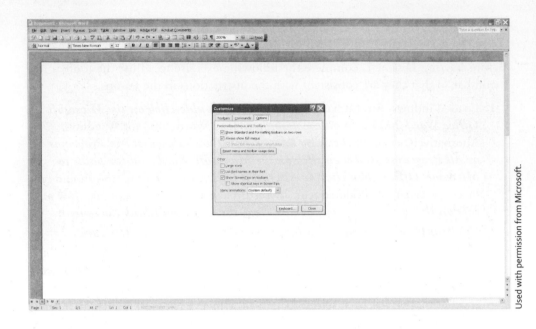

Used with permission from Microsoft.

on two rows" and "Always show full menus" (see Word 2003 Exhibit 2). *Note:* If there is an option under Personalized Menus and Toolbars that says "Standard and Formatting Toolbars share one row," do not check the box (the toolbars are already on two rows). If there is an option that says "Menus show recently used commands first," again, do not check the box (full menus will already be displayed). ***Click on Close.***

You are now ready to begin Lesson 1.

▶ BASIC LESSONS

LESSON 1: TYPING A LETTER

This lesson shows you how to type the letter in Word 2003 Exhibit 3. It explains how to use the word wrap feature; the [TAB] key; the cursor (or arrow) keys; the underline, bold, and italics commands; the save document function; and the print document function. Keep in mind that if you make a mistake in this lesson at any time, you may press [CTRL]+[Z] to undo what you have done.

1. Open Windows. After it has loaded, ***double-click on the Microsoft Office Word 2003 icon on the desktop*** to open Word 2003 for Windows. Alternatively, ***click on the Start button, point the cursor to Programs or All Programs, then click on the Microsoft Word icon*** (or ***point to Microsoft Office, then click on Microsoft Office Word 2003***). You should be in a new, clean, blank document. If you are not in a clean document, ***click on File on the menu bar, then click on New, then click on Blank document.***

2. You cannot yet move the cursor around the screen by pressing the cursor keys (also called arrow keys). This is because text must first be entered; the cursor can only move through text, so the cursor keys will not function if no text exists.

3. Press the [**ENTER**] key four times. Watch the status line in the lower left-hand corner of the screen. The status line tells you what page of your document you are on, and the line number and position where your cursor is.

4. Type the date of the letter as shown in Word 2003 Exhibit 3. Notice that as you type the word "October," Auto Text may anticipate that you are typing the word "October" and give you the following prompt: October (Press ENTER to Insert). If you press the **[ENTER]** key, Auto Text will finish typing the word for you. You can also ignore it and just continue typing the word yourself.

5. Press the **[ENTER]** key three times.

6. Type the inside address as shown in Word 2003 Exhibit 3. Press the **[ENTER]** key after each line of the inside address. When you finish the line with "Boston, MA 59920," press the **[ENTER]** key three times.

7. Press the **[TAB]** key one time (Word automatically sets default tabs every five spaces). The cursor moves five spaces to the right.

8. Type **Subject:** and then press the **[TAB]** key. ***Click on the Underline icon on the toolbar*** (it looks like a *U* with a thin line under it). *Note*: If you hover the cursor over any single icon on the toolbar for a few seconds, Word will show you a description of what the icon does. Alternatively, to turn the underline feature on and off, you can press **[CTRL]+[U]**, or ***select Format from the menu bar and click on Font. Then click on the down arrow under Underline style, click on the type of underline you want, and click on OK.***

9. Type **Turner v. Smith**. ***Click on the Underline icon on the toolbar again.*** This will turn the underline feature off.

10. Press the **[ENTER]** key one time.

11. Press the **[TAB]** key three times, and then type **Case No. CV-11-0046**.

12. Press the **[ENTER]** key three times.

13. Type the salutation **Dear Mr. Matthews:**

14. Press the **[ENTER]** key twice. *Note*: If the animated assistant appears, ***right-click on it and click on Hide*** to make it go away.

15. Type the first paragraph of the letter. Do not press the **[ENTER]** key at the end of each line. Word will automatically "wrap" the text down to the next line. *Note*: To turn on the bold feature (e.g., for **November 15 at 9:00 a.m.**), press **[CTRL]+[B]** on the keyboard, or ***click the Bold icon on the toolbar***. To turn on the italics feature (e.g., for ***"Notice of Deposition."***), press **[CTRL]+[I]** on the keyboard, or ***click the Italics icon on the toolbar***.

16. After you have typed the first paragraph, press the **[ENTER]** key twice.

17. Type the second paragraph of the letter, then press the **[ENTER]** key twice.

18. Type the third paragraph of the letter, then press the **[ENTER]** key twice.

19. Type the fourth paragraph of the letter, then press the **[ENTER]** key twice.

20. Type **Kindest regards**, then press the **[ENTER]** key four times.

21. Type **Mirabelle Watkinson** and then press the **[ENTER]** key.

22. Type **For the Firm** and then press the **[ENTER]** key twice.

23. Finish the letter by typing the author's initials, enclosures, and copy abbreviation (cc) as shown in Word 2003 Exhibit 3.

24. To print the document, *click on File from the menu bar, click on Print, then click on OK.* Alternatively, *click the Printer icon on the toolbar.*

25. To save the document so that you can retrieve it later (you will need to retrieve this letter to complete Lesson 2), *click on File on the menu bar, then select Save.* Type **Letter1** in the "File name" box, *then click on Save* to save the document in the default directory.

26. To close the document, *click on File on the menu bar and then on Close*, or *click on File from the menu bar and then on Exit* to exit Word.

This concludes Lesson 1.

LESSON 2: EDITING A LETTER

This lesson shows you how to retrieve and edit the letter you typed in Lesson 1. It explains how to retrieve a file, use the Insert and Overtype modes, perform block moves and deletes, and spell/grammar check your document. Keep in mind that if you make a mistake in this lesson at any time, you may press **[CTRL]+[Z]** to undo what you have done.

1. Open Windows. After it has loaded, *double-click on the Microsoft Office Word 2003 icon on the desktop* to open Word 2003 for Windows. Alternatively, *click on the Start button, point the cursor to Programs or All Programs, then click on the Microsoft Word icon* (or *point to Microsoft Office and then click on Microsoft Office Word 2003*). You should be in a new, clean, blank document. If you are not in a clean document, *click on File on the menu bar, then click on New, then click on Blank document.*

2. In this lesson, you will begin by retrieving the document you created in Lesson 1. To open the file, *click on File from the menu bar and select Open.* Then type **Letter1** and *click on Open.* Alternatively, *scroll until you find the file, using the horizontal scroll bar, then click on Open.*

3. Notice in Word 2003 Exhibit 4 that some editing changes have been made to the letter. You will spend the rest of this lesson making these changes.

4. Use your cursor keys or mouse to go to the salutation line, "Dear Mr. Matthews:" With the cursor left of the "M" in "Mr. Matthews," press the **[DEL]** key 12 times until "Mr. Matthews" is deleted.

5. Type **Steve**. The salutation line should now read "Dear Steve:"

6. Using your cursor keys or mouse, *move the cursor to the left of the comma following the word "conversation" in the first paragraph.* Press the **[SPACE BAR]**, then type **of September 30**. The sentence now reads:

In line with our recent conversation of September 30, the deposition of the defendant,

Because Word is in the Insert mode (i.e., the default mode) when it is loaded, it allows you to add the words **of September 30** automatically. *Note:* When Word is in

October 1, 2011

Steven Matthews
Matthews, Smith & Russell
P.O. Box 12341
Boston, MA 59920

Subject: Turner v. Smith
             Case No. CV-11-0046

Steve
Dear Mr. Matthews: *of September 30*

In line with our recent conversation, the deposition of the defendant, Jonathan R. Smith,
will be taken in your office on **November 15 at 9:00 a.m.** Please find enclosed a
"Notice of Deposition."

I expect that I will be able to finish this deposition on November 15 and that discovery
will be finished, in line with the Court's order by December 15.

I will be finishing answers to your interrogatories this week and will have them to you by
early next week.   *next*

If you have any questions, please feel free to contact me.

Kindest regards,

Mirabelle Watkinson
For the Firm

MW:db
Enclosures (As indicated)
cc

Insert mode, it is not specifically indicated on the screen. However, when Word is in the Overtype mode, the letters OVR appear in the center of the status line at the bottom of the screen.

7. The next change you will make is to move the second paragraph so that it becomes part of the first paragraph. Although this can be accomplished in more than one way, this lesson uses the opportunity to show you the Cut command.

8. Using your cursor keys or mouse, ***move the cursor to the beginning of the second paragraph of Word 2003 Exhibit 3.***

9. ***Click and drag the mouse*** (i.e., hold the left mouse button down and move the mouse) ***until the entire second paragraph is highlighted, and then release the mouse button.***

10. ***Click on Edit from the menu bar, then click on Cut.*** An alternative is to ***right-click the mouse anywhere in the highlighted area and then select Cut.*** The text is no longer on the screen, but it is not deleted—it has been temporarily placed on the Office Clipboard.

11. Move the cursor to the end of the first paragraph. Press the **[SPACEBAR]** twice. If the cursor appears to be in Italics mode, click on the Italics icon on the toolbar to turn it off.

12. ***Click on Edit from the menu bar, then select Paste.*** Notice that the text has now been moved. Also, you may notice that a small icon in the shape of a clipboard has appeared where you pasted the text. ***Click on the down arrow of the Paste Options icon.*** Notice that you are given the option to keep the source formatting or change the formatting so that the text matches the destination formatting (the formatting of the place you are copying it to). In this example, both formats are the same, so it does not matter, but if the text you are copying is a different format, you can choose whether or not to change it to the destination format. Press the **[ESC]** key to make the Paste Options menu disappear.

13. Move the cursor to the line below the first paragraph and use the **[DEL]** key to delete any unnecessary blank lines.

14. Using your cursor keys or mouse, *move the cursor to what is now the second paragraph and place the cursor to the left of the t in "this week."* You will change "this week" to "next week," using the Overtype mode.

15. Press the [**INS**] key. Notice that on the status line at the bottom of the screen, the letters OVR appear. This indicates that Word is now in Overtype mode. In Overtype mode, any characters entered will replace existing characters.

16. Type **next**. Notice how the word *this* is replaced with the word *next*. Press the [**INS**] key to return to Insert mode.

17. You will now delete the rest of the sentence in the second paragraph. *Drag the mouse until "and will have them to you by early next week." is highlighted.* Press the [**DEL**] key.

18. Type a period at the end of the sentence.

19. You have now made all of the necessary changes. To be sure the letter does not have misspelled words or grammar errors, you will use the Spelling and Grammar command.

20. *Click on Tools from the menu bar, then click on Spelling and Grammar.*

21. If an error is found, it will be highlighted. You have the options to ignore it once, ignore it completely, accept one of the suggestions listed, or change/correct the problem yourself. Correct any spelling or grammar errors. When the spell and grammar check is done, *click on OK.*

22. To print the document, *click on File from the menu bar, click on Print, then click on OK.* Alternatively, click on the Printer icon on the toolbar.

23. To save the document, *click on File from the menu bar and then select Save As....* Type **Letter2** in the "File name" box, *then point and click on Save* to save the document in the default directory.

24. *Click on File on the menu bar and then on Close* to close the document, or *click on File from the menu bar and then on Exit* to exit Word.

This concludes Lesson 2.

LESSON 3: TYPING A PLEADING

This lesson shows you how to type a pleading, as shown in Word 2003 Exhibit 5. It expands on the items presented in Lessons 1 and 2. It also explains how to center

WORD 2003 EXHIBIT 5
Pleading

text, change margins, change line spacing, add a footnote, double-indent text, and use automatic page numbering. Keep in mind that if you make a mistake at any time, you may press **[CTRL]+[Z]** to undo what you have done.

1. Open Windows. After it has loaded, ***double-click on the Microsoft Office Word 2003 icon on the desktop*** to open Word 2003 for Windows. Alternatively, ***click on the Start button, point the cursor to Programs or All Programs, then click on the Microsoft Word icon*** (or ***point to Microsoft Office, then click on Microsoft Office Word 2003).*** You should be in a new, clean, blank document. If you are not in a clean document, ***click on File on the menu bar, then click on New, then click on Blank document.***

2. You will be creating the document in Word 2003 Exhibit 5. The first thing you will need to do is to change the margins so that the left margin is 1-1/2 inches and the right margin is 1 inch. To change the margins, ***click on File on the menu bar, then click on Page Setup. Change the left margin to 1.5" and the right margin to 1". Click on OK.***

3. Notice in Word 2003 Exhibit 5 that there is a page number at the bottom of the page. Word will automatically number your pages for you.

4. ***Click on View from the menu bar, then on Header and Footer.*** The Header and Footer toolbar is then displayed (see Word 2003 Exhibit 6).

Center

Insert Page Number

Footer

Page 1

Used with permission from Microsoft.

WORD 2003 EXHIBIT 6
Creating a footer

5. ***Click on the fourth item from the right (the Switch Between Header and Footer icon) in the Header and Footer bar*** (see Word 2003 Exhibit 6). *Note:* If you point at an icon with your cursor for a second, the description of the icon will be displayed. Notice that the screen moved from the page header (at the top of the page) to the page footer (at the bottom of the page).

6. ***Click on the Center icon on the toolbar*** (see Word 2003 Exhibit 6). Notice that the line in the footer is now centered.

7. Type **Page** and press the **[SPACEBAR]** key.

8. ***Click on the Insert Page Number icon*** (it is the second item from the left, just to the right of the Insert AutoText icon) in the Header and Footer toolbar (see Word 2003 Exhibit 6). A "1" is then displayed on the screen. The footer should now read "Page 1."

HANDS-ON EXERCISES

9. Before closing the Header and Footer bar, *click on Insert AutoText.* Notice that Word can automatically print additional information in your header and footer, including the file name, the author, the path, the last printed date, Page X of Y, and much more. We do not need any of these selections for this document, so press the [ESC] key to exit the Insert AutoText field.

10. *Click on Close in the Header and Footer bar* to close it.

11. On the first line of the document, *click on the Center icon on the toolbar.* Type **IN THE DISTRICT COURT OF**. Press the [ENTER] key. Type **ORANGE COUNTY, MASSACHUSETTS**.

12. Press the [ENTER] key five times. *Click on the Align Left icon on the toolbar* (it is just to the left of the Center icon).

13. Type **JIM TURNER**, then press the [ENTER] key twice.

14. Press the [TAB] key three times and type **Plaintiff,** then press the [ENTER] key twice.

15. Type **vs**. Then press the [TAB] key six times and type **Case No. CV-11-0046**.

16. Press the [ENTER] key twice.

17. Type **JONATHAN R. SMITH,** then press the [ENTER] key twice.

18. Press the [TAB] key three times and type **Defendant.** Press the [ENTER] key four times.

19. *Click on the Center icon on the toolbar.*

20. *Click on the Bold icon on the toolbar, then click on the Underline icon on the toolbar.* Type **NOTICE TO TAKE DEPOSITION**. *Click on the Bold and Underline icons on the toolbar* to turn them off.

21. Press the [ENTER] key three times and *click on the Align Left icon on the toolbar.*

22. *Click on Format on the menu bar, then on Paragraph. In the Indents and Spacing tab, under Spacing—Line spacing, click on the down arrow and select Double. Click on OK.* This will change the line spacing from single to double.

23. Type **COMES NOW, the plaintiff and pursuant to statute**. Notice that a footnote follows the word *statute* in Word 2003 Exhibit 5.

24. With the cursor just to the right of the e in "statute," *click on Insert from the menu bar, point to Reference, then click on Footnote.* The "Footnote and Endnote" window is now displayed; the default options are fine, so *click on Insert in the "Footnote and Endnote" window.*

25. Type **Massachusetts Statutes Annotated 60–2342(a)(1).**

26. To move the cursor back to the body of the document, simply *click just to the right of the word "statute" and footnote number 1 in the body of the document.* Now, continue to type the rest of the first paragraph. Once the paragraph is typed, press the [ENTER] key twice.

27. To double-indent the second paragraph, *click on Format in the menu bar, then click on Paragraph. In the Indents and Spacing tab, under Indentation, add a .5" left indent and a .5" right indent using the up arrow icons* (or you can type it in). *Click on OK.*

28. Type the second paragraph.

29. Press the [ENTER] key twice.

30. *Click on Format from the menu bar, then click on Paragraph.* In the Indents and Spacing tab, under Indentation, change the left and right indents back to 0″. *Click on OK.*

31. Type the third paragraph.

32. Press the [ENTER] key.

33. The signature line is single-spaced, so *click on Format from the menu bar, then click on Paragraph.* In the Indents and Spacing tab, under Spacing—Line spacing, *click on the down arrow and select Single, then click OK.* Press the [ENTER] key.

34. Press [SHIFT]+[-] (the "_" is the underscore; it is the key to the right of the zero key on the top row of the keyboard) 30 times to draw the signature line. Press the [ENTER] key. *Note:* If Word automatically inserts a line across the whole page, press [CTRL]+[Z] to undo the AutoCorrect action.

35. Type **Mirabelle Watkinson** and then press the [ENTER] key.

36. Type **Attorney for Plaintiff.**

37. To print the document, *click on File from the menu bar, click on Print, then click on OK.* Alternatively, *click on the Printer icon on the toolbar.*

38. To save the document, *click on File from the menu bar and then select Save As....* Type **Pleading1** in the "File name" box, *then point and click on Save* to save the document in the default directory.

39. *Click on File on the menu bar, then on Close* to close the document, or *click on File from the menu bar, then on Exit* to exit Word.

This concludes Lesson 3.

LESSON 4: CREATING A TABLE

This lesson shows you how to create the table shown in Word 2003 Exhibit 7. It expands on the items presented in Lessons 1, 2, and 3. It explains how to change a font size, create a table, enter data into a table, add automatic numbering, adjust column widths, and use the Table AutoFormat command. Keep in mind that if you make a mistake at any time, you may press [CTRL]+[Z] to undo what you have done.

1. Open Windows. After it has loaded, *double-click on the Microsoft Office Word 2003 icon on the desktop* to open Word 2003 for Windows. Alternatively, *click on the Start button, point the cursor to Programs or All Programs, then click on the Microsoft Word icon* (or *point to Microsoft Office, then click on Microsoft Office Word 2003*). You should be in a new,

WORD 2003 EXHIBIT 7
Creating a table

clean, blank document. If you are not in a clean document, *click on File on the menu bar, then click on New, then click on Blank document.*

2. *Click on the Center icon on the toolbar. Click on the Bold icon on the toolbar. Click on the Font Size icon on the toolbar* (just to the left of the Bold icon) and change the font size to 14 by either typing **14** in the box or *choosing 14 from the drop-down menu.* Alternatively, you can turn on bold and change the font size by *clicking on Format on the menu bar, then on Font, and then selecting these options in the "Font" window. Then click on OK.*

3. Type **Average Hourly Billing Rates for Paralegals** (see Word 2003 Exhibit 7). Press the [**ENTER**] key once, then *click back on the Font size icon on the toolbar and change the type back to 12 point. Click on the Bold icon to turn bold off.*

4. Press the [**ENTER**] key once.

5. *Click on Table from the menu bar, then point to Insert, then click on Table.* The "Insert Table" window is now displayed. Under Table size, make the Number of columns **3** and the Number of rows **8**. *Click on OK.*

6. The blank table should now be displayed; the cursor should be in the first column and the first row of the table (that is, in the uppermost lefthand cell). If the cursor is not in the first column of the first row, *click into this cell to place the cursor there. Click on the Bold icon on the toolbar.* Type **Number** and then press the [**TAB**] key once to go to the next cell in the table.

7. *Click on the Bold icon on the toolbar.* Type **Region** and then press the [**TAB**] key once to go to the next cell in the table. *Note:* If you need to go back to a previous cell, you can either use the mouse or press [**SHIFT**]+[**TAB**]. Also, if you accidentally hit the [**ENTER**] key instead of the [**TAB**] key, you can either press the [**BACKSPACE**] key to delete the extra line, or you can press [**CTRL**]+[**Z**] to undo it.

8. *Click on the Bold icon on the toolbar.* Type **Paralegals** and then press the [**TAB**] key to go to the next cell.

9. You will now use the automatic paragraph numbering feature to number your rows. *Click on the Numbering icon on the toolbar* (see Word 2003 Exhibit 7—it is the icon that has the numbers 1, 2, 3 in a column, with a short line next to each number). Notice that the number 1 was automatically entered in the cell. *Click on Format on the menu bar, then on Bullets and Numbering, then on Customize.* You can completely customize your numbering if you wish. The default format is fine for the purposes of this lesson, so *click on Cancel twice* to make the "Bullets and Numbering" window disappear.

10. Press the [**TAB**] key to go to the next cell.

11. Type **California** and then press the [**TAB**] key to go to the next cell.

12. Type **$120** and then press the [**TAB**] key to go to the next cell.

13. *Click on the Numbering icon on the toolbar* and then press the [**TAB**] key to go to the next cell.

14. Continue entering all of the information shown in Word 2003 Exhibit 7 into your table.

15. *Point the cursor to the upper left cell of the table and drag the mouse to the lower right cell of the table to completely highlight the table. Then, click on the Align left icon on the toolbar.* Now the whole table is left-aligned.

16. *Point the cursor to the vertical column line that separates the Number column and the Region column. Click on it and hold the mouse button down, then drag the line to the left.* Notice that by using this technique you

can adjust each column width as much as you like. Press **[CTRL]+[Z]** to undo the column move, because the current format is fine.

17. ***Click the mouse on any cell in the table. Next, click on Table in the menu bar, then on Table AutoFormat, then click on Table Colorful 1*** (or any of the other options). ***Click on Apply.***

18. The format of the table completely changes. Experiment with some of the other formats using the Table AutoFormat command. Press **[CTRL]+[Z]** to undo the format changes—if you tried a number of formats, just keep pressing **[CTRL]+[Z]** until your table is back to its original format.

19. To print the document, ***click on File from the menu bar, click on Print, then click on OK.*** Alternatively, ***click on the Printer icon on the toolbar.***

20. To save the document, ***click on File from the menu bar and then select Save As....*** Type **Table1** in the "File name" box, ***then point and click on Save*** to save the document in the default directory.

21. ***Click on File on the menu bar and then on Close*** to close the document, or ***click on File from the menu bar and then on Exit*** to exit Word.

This concludes Lesson 4.

▶ INTERMEDIATE LESSONS

LESSON 5: TOOLS AND TECHNIQUES

This lesson shows you how to edit an employment policy (from a file on the disk supplied with this text), use the Format Painter tool, reveal formatting, clear formatting, change the case of the text, use the Find and Replace feature, use the Go To command, create a section break, and change the orientation of a page from portrait to landscape. This lesson assumes you have completed Lessons 1 through 4 and that you are generally familiar with Word 2003.

1. Open Windows. ***Double-click on the Microsoft Office Word 2003 icon on the desktop*** to open Word 2003 for Windows. Alternatively, ***click on the Start button, point the cursor to Programs or All Programs, then click on the Microsoft Word icon*** (or ***point to Microsoft Office and then click on Microsoft Office Word 2003).*** You should be in a new, clean, blank document. If you are not in a clean document, ***click on File on the menu bar, then click on New, then click on Blank document.***

2. The first thing you will do is open the "Lesson 5" file from the disk supplied with this text. Ensure that the disk is inserted in the disk drive, ***point and click on File on the menu bar, then point and click on Open.*** The "Open" window should now be displayed. ***Point and click on the down arrow to the right of the white box next to "Look in:" and select the drive where the disk is located. Point and double-click on the Word-Processing Files folder. Double-click on the Word 2003 folder. Point and double-click on the "Lesson 5" file.***

3. The file entitled "World Wide Technology, Inc. alcohol and drug policy" should now be displayed on your screen. In this lesson, you will be editing this policy for use by another client. The next thing you need to do is to go to section 3, "Definitions," and change the subheadings so that they have all have the same format. You will use the Format Painter tool to do this.

4. Use the cursor keys or the mouse and the scroll bars to scroll to Section 3, "Definitions" (see Word 2003 Exhibit 8). Notice that the first definition, "Alcohol or alcoholic beverages:" is bold and in a different font from the rest

WORD 2003 EXHIBIT 8
The Format Painter tool

Print Preview

Format Painter

Increase Indent

Used with permission from Microsoft.

of the definitions in section 3. You will use the Format Painter tool to quickly copy the formatting from "Alcohol or alcoholic beverages" to the other four definitions in section 3.

5. *Point and click anywhere in the text "Alcohol or alcoholic beverages:"* This tells the Format Painter tool what formatting you want to copy.

6. Next, *point and click on the Format Painter icon on the toolbar.* It looks like a paintbrush (see Word 2003 Exhibit 8—remember, if you hover your pointer over an icon for a second or two, the name of the icon will appear).

7. Notice that your pointer now turns to a paintbrush. *Drag the mouse* (hold the left mouse button down and move the mouse) *until the heading "Legal drugs:" is highlighted* (see Word 2003 Exhibit 8), *then let go of the mouse button.* Notice that the paintbrush on your cursor is now gone. *Click the left mouse button once anywhere to make the highlight go away.* Notice that "Legal drugs:" now has the same formatting as "Alcohol or alcoholic beverages:" The Format Painter command is a quick way to make formatting changes.

8. You will now use the Format Painter tool to copy the formatting to the remaining three definitions, with one additional trick. *Point and click anywhere in the text "Legal drugs:"*

9. Next, *point and double-click on the Format Painter icon on the toolbar.* (*Your cursor should now have a paintbrush attached to it.*) The double-click tells Format Painter that you are going to copy this format to multiple locations, instead of just one location. This is a great time-saving feature if you need to copy the formatting to several places, because it keeps you from having to click the Format Painter icon each time you copy the same formatting to a new location.

10. *Drag the pointer until the heading "Illegal drug:" is highlighted, then let go of the mouse button.* Notice that the paintbrush is still attached to your mouse pointer.

11. *Drag the pointer until the heading "Controlled substance:" is highlighted, then let go of the mouse button.*

12. *Drag the pointer until the heading "Prescription drug:" is highlighted, then let go of the mouse button.*

13. To turn the Format Painter off, press the [ESC] button on the keyboard. *Click the left mouse button once, with the cursor anywhere, to make the highlight go away.* Notice that all of the subheadings are now uniform.

14. You will now learn to use the Reveal Formatting command. *Point and click with the mouse on the subheading "Prescription drug:"*

15. *Point and click on Format on the menu bar, then on Reveal Formatting….* (Alternatively, you can press [SHIFT]+[F1] on the keyboard.)

16. Notice that the Reveal Formatting task pane opened on the right side of the screen. The Reveal Formatting task pane lists all format specifications for the selected text. The items are divided into several groups, including Font, Paragraph, Bullets and Numbering, and Section. You can make formatting changes to the text directly from the Reveal Formatting task pane by clicking on the format setting you want to change. (The links are shown in blue, underlined text.) For example, *point and click on the blue underlined word* Font *in the Reveal Formatting task pane.* Notice that the "Font" window opens. You could now select a new font if you so desired. The Reveal Formatting task pane allows you to quickly see all formatting attached to specific text, and gives you the ability to change it.

17. *Point and click on Cancel in the "Font" window.* To close the Reveal Formatting task pane, *point and click on the "x" (the Close button) at the top of the Reveal Formatting task pane.* It is just to the right of the words "Reveal Formatting." The Reveal Formatting task pane should now be gone.

18. Press [CTRL]+[HOME] on the keyboard to go to the beginning of the document.

19. You will now learn how to use the Clear Formats command. Notice under the heading "1. Objectives" that the sentence "The objectives of this policy are as follows:" is bold and italics; this is a mistake. *Drag the pointer until this text is highlighted.*

20. Next, *point and click on Edit on the menu bar, then point to Clear, then to Formats. Click the left mouse button once anywhere in the sentence* to make the highlight go away. Notice that all of the formatting is now gone. The Clear Formats command is a good way to remove all text formatting quickly and easily.

21. To move the text to the right so that it is under "1. Objectives," *point and click on the Increase Indent Icon three times* (see Word 2003 Exhibit 8). Then, using whatever method you choose, put the line back in its original place.

22. You will now learn how to use the Change Case command. Press [CTRL]+[HOME] on the keyboard to go to the beginning of the document.

23. *Drag the pointer until the title "World Wide Technology, Inc." is highlighted.*

24. *Point and click on Format on the menu bar, then click on Change Case.* UPPERCASE should already be selected, but if it is not, *click on UPPERCASE, then click on OK in the "Change Case" window.* Notice that the text is now in all capitals.

25. *Drag the pointer until the subtitle "alcohol and drug policy" is highlighted. Point and click on Format on the menu bar, then click on Change Case.* Title Case should already be selected, but if it is not, *go ahead and click on Title Case and then click on OK in the "Change Case" window.* Notice that the text is now in title case. *Click the left mouse button once anywhere* to make the highlight go away. The Change Case command is a convenient way

to change the case of text without having to retype it. *Note:* Retyping always increases the risk of introducing errors!

26. Press **[CTRL]+[HOME]** on the keyboard to go to the beginning of the document.

27. You will now learn how to use the Find and Replace command. ***Point and click on Edit on the menu bar, then click on Replace.*** Alternatively, you could press **[CTRL]+[H]**, or **[F5]** and then ***click on Replace.***

28. In the "Find and Replace" window, in the white box next to "Find what:" type **World Wide Technology, Inc.** Then, in the white box next to "Replace with:" type **Johnson Manufacturing.** Now, ***click on the Replace All button in the "Find and Replace" window.*** The program responds by stating that it made four replacements. ***Point and click on OK in the notification window.***

29. ***Point and click with the mouse on the Close button in the "Find and Replace" window to close the window.*** Notice that "World Wide Technology, Inc." has now been changed to "Johnson Manufacturing."

30. You will now learn how to use the Go To command. Press **[F5]** on the keyboard. Notice that the Find and Replace window is again displayed on the screen, but this time the Go To tab is selected. In the white box directly under "Enter page number," type **7** from the keyboard and then ***point and click on Go To in the "Find and Replace" window.*** Notice that page 7, "Reasonable Suspicion Report," is now displayed. The Go To command is an easy way to navigate through large and complex documents. ***Point and click on Close in the "Find and Replace" window.***

31. Suppose that you would like to change the orientation of only one page in a document from Portrait (meaning the length is greater than the width) to Landscape (meaning the width is greater than the length). In this example you will change the layout of only the Reasonable Suspicion Report to Landscape while the rest of the document remains in Portrait. To do this in Word, you must enter a section break.

32. Your cursor should be on page 7, just above "Johnson Manufacturing Reasonable Suspicion Report." ***Point and click on View from the menu bar, then on Normal. Point and click on Insert from the menu bar, then on Break. Under Section break types, point and click on Next page, then click on OK in the "Break" window.*** A double dotted line that says "Section Break (Next Page)" is now displayed. You can now change the format of the page from Portrait to Landscape without changing the orientation of preceding pages.

33. With the cursor on the "Johnson Manufacturing Reasonable Suspicion Report" page, ***point and click on File from the menu bar, then on Page Setup. Under the Margins tab, point and click on Landscape under Orientation, then on OK in the "Page Setup" window.*** Notice that the layout of the page has changed.

34. To confirm that the layout has changed, ***point and click on the Print Preview icon on the toolbar*** (see Word 2003 Exhibit 8). Notice that the layout is now Landscape (the width is greater than the length). Press the **[PAGE UP]** key on the keyboard until you are back to the beginning of the document. Notice that all of the other pages in the document are still in Portrait orientation.

35. ***Point and click on Close from the Print Preview toolbar.*** (It is the word "Close" just under "Table" on the menu bar).

36. To print the document, ***click on File on the menu bar, click on Print, then click on OK.*** Alternatively, ***click on the Printer icon on the toolbar.***

37. To save the document, *click on File from the menu bar and then select Save As…. Under Save in, select the drive or folder where you would like to save the document. Next to "File name"* type **Done—Word 2003 Lesson 5 Document** *and then point and click on Save* to save the document.

38. *Click on File on the menu bar and then on Close* to close the document, or *click on File on the menu bar and then on Exit* to exit Word.

This concludes Lesson 5.

LESSON 6: USING STYLES

This lesson gives you an introduction to styles. Styles are particularly helpful when working with long documents that must be formatted uniformly.

1. Open Windows. *Double-click on the Microsoft Office Word 2003 icon on the desktop* to open Word 2003 for Windows. Alternatively, *click on the Start button, point the cursor to Programs or All Programs, then click on the Microsoft Word icon* (or *point to Microsoft Office and then click on Microsoft Office Word 2003*). You should be in a new, clean, blank document. If you are not in a clean document, *click on File on menu bar, then click on New, then click on Blank document.*

2. The first thing you will do is open the "Lesson 6" file from the disk supplied with this text. Ensure that the disk is inserted in the disk drive, *point and click on File on the menu bar, then point and click on Open.* The "Open" window should now be displayed. *Point and click on the down arrow to the right of the white box next to "Look in:" and select the drive where the disk is located. Point and double-click on the Word-Processing Files folder. Double-click on the Word 2003 folder. Point and double-click on the "Lesson 6" file.*

3. The text "SARBANES-OXLEY ACT OF 2002" should now be displayed on your screen (see Word 2003 Exhibit 9). In this lesson you will use styles to add uniform formatting to this document. Notice the Style box on your toolbar (see Word 2003 Exhibit 9); it should say "Normal" in the box. This is telling you that the text where your cursor is located is formatted in the Normal style.

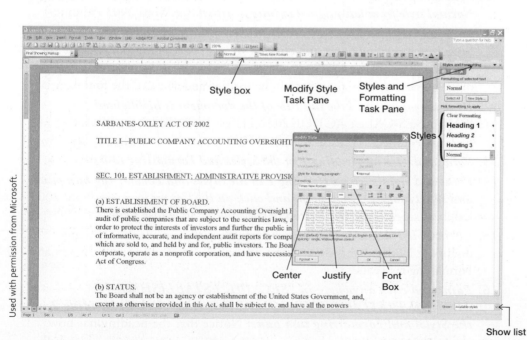

WORD 2003 EXHIBIT 9
Style

HANDS-ON EXERCISES

4. *Point and click on any text on the page.* Notice that "Normal" continues to be displayed in the Style box on the toolbar. Currently, all text in this document is in the Normal style.

5. Using your cursor keys or the scroll bar, scroll down through the document. Notice that all of the paragraphs are left-aligned and that the right edge of all the paragraphs is ragged (not justified).

6. *Point and click on Format on the menu bar, then on Styles and Formatting.* Notice that the Styles and Formatting task pane now appears on the right side of the screen (see Word 2003 Exhibit 9). Notice that a few styles are currently being displayed (Heading 1, Heading 2, Heading 3, and Normal). Also, notice that "Normal" has a blue box around it, indicating that your cursor is on text with the Normal style. Finally, notice that there is a paragraph sign after each of these heading names, indicating that these are paragraph styles.

7. At the bottom of the Styles and Formatting task pane, there is an option to "Show: Available Styles" (see Word 2003 Exhibit 9). *Point and click on the down arrow next to "Available styles." Point and click with the mouse on "All styles."* Notice that the Styles and Formatting task pane is now full of additional styles. These are all of the styles that are automatically available in Word. *Point and click on the down arrow next to the styles in the Styles and Formatting task pane to see the full list of styles.*

8. *Point and click on the down arrow next to "Show: All styles." Then point and click on "Available styles."* Notice that the short list of styles is again displayed. To access the longer list of styles from the toolbar, press the [SHIFT] key while *pointing and clicking on the down arrow on the Style box* (press the [ESC] key to close the list).

9. Styles are extremely useful. Assume now that you would like to have all of the text in the document justified. *Right-click on Normal in the Styles and Formatting task pane. Then left-click on Modify.* The Modify Style task pane should now be displayed (see Word 2003 Exhibit 9). Using the Modify Style task pane, you can completely change the formatting for any style.

10. *Point and click on the Justify icon in the Modify Style task pane to switch the Normal style from left-aligned to fully justified* (see Word 2003 Exhibit 9).

11. *Point and click on the down arrow in the Formatting box in the Modify Style task pane and point and click on Arial. Then, point and click on the OK button in the Modify Style task pane.* Notice that Word quickly changed the alignment of all of the text to fully justified and changed the font to Arial.

12. *Drag the mouse until the full title of the document is highlighted* (SARBANES-OXLEY ACT OF 2002 TITLE I—PUBLIC COMPANY ACCOUNTING OVERSIGHT BOARD).

13. *Point and click on Heading 1 in the Styles and Formatting task pane.*

14. *Point and right-click on Heading 1 in the Styles and Formatting task pane and select Modify. Then, point and click on the Center icon* (see Word 2003 Exhibit 9). *Select the OK button in the Modify Style task pane.*

15. *Click the left mouse button anywhere in the title* to make the highlight disappear. Notice that the text of the title shows "Heading 1" in the Styles and Formatting task pane.

16. *Point and click anywhere in "SEC. 101. ESTABLISHMENT; ADMINISTRATIVE PROVISIONS." Point and click on Heading 2 in the Styles and Formatting task pane.* Notice that the heading has now changed.

17. *Point and click anywhere in the subheading "(a) ESTABLISHMENT OF BOARD." Point and click on Heading 3 in the Styles and Formatting task pane.*

18. Now, go to the following subheadings and format them as Heading 3:

   (b) STATUS.

   (c) DUTIES OF THE BOARD.

   (d) COMMISSION DETERMINATION.

   (e) BOARD MEMBERSHIP.

   (f) POWERS OF THE BOARD.

   (g) RULES OF THE BOARD.

   (h) ANNUAL REPORT TO THE COMMISSION.

19. You will now create your own style. Press **[CTRL]+[END]** on the keyboard to go to the end of the document. *Point and click on New Style … in the Styles and Formatting task pane.*

20. The New Style task pane is now displayed. "Style1" is currently highlighted in blue next to "Name." Type **Statutory Heading.** This will be the name of the new style that you are creating. Next, change the font to Times New Roman, change the font size to 14 point, and change the color to red (the color icon is the letter A with a line under it).

21. *Point and click on OK in the New Style task pane.* Notice that the Statutory Heading style has now been added.

22. *Point and click anywhere on "15 U.S.C. 7201" and then point and click on Statutory Heading in the Styles and Formatting task pane.* The text is now displayed in the Statutory Heading style.

23. Press **[CTRL]+[HOME]** on the keyboard to go to the beginning of the document. Your document is now consistently formatted. Using styles, your documents can also easily be uniformly changed. For example, if you read in your local rules that subheadings for pleadings must be in 15-point Times New Roman font, you could quickly change the subheadings in your document by modifying the heading styles, rather than highlighting each subheading and changing the format manually.

24. To print the document, *click on File on the menu bar, click on Print, then click on OK.* Alternatively, *click on the Printer icon on the toolbar.*

25. To save the document, *click on File from the menu bar and then select Save As…. Under Save in, select the drive or folder you would like the document in. Next to "File Name"* type **Done—Word 2003 Lesson 6 Document** *and then click on Save* to save the document.

26. *Click on File on the menu bar and then on Close* to close the document, or *click on File from the menu bar and then on Exit* to exit Word.

This concludes Lesson 6.

LESSON 7: CREATING A TEMPLATE

This lesson shows you how to create the template in Word 2003 Exhibit 10. It explains how to create a template of a letter, how to insert fields, and how to fill out and use a finished template. The information that will be merged into the letter will be entered from the keyboard. Keep in mind that if you make a mistake at any time, you may press **[CTRL]+[Z]** to undo what you have done.

WORD 2003 EXHIBIT 10
Office Letter template

Used with permission from Microsoft.

1. Open Windows. After it has loaded, *double-click on the Microsoft Office Word 2003 icon on the desktop* to open Word 2003 for Windows. Alternatively, *click on the Start button, point the cursor to Programs or All Programs, then click on the Microsoft Word icon* (or *point to Microsoft Office and then click on Microsoft Office Word 2003).* You should be in a new, clean, blank document. If you are not in a clean document, *click on File on the menu bar, then click on New, then click on Blank document.*

2. *Click on File on the menu bar and then click on New. Under Templates (to the right of the screen), click on On my computer...*

3. Notice that Word automatically provides you with a number of ready-made templates. *Click on the Letters & Faxes tab*; notice that there are a number of different letter styles, fax cover pages, and other documents. *Click on the Memos tab*; note that there are a number of different memo styles. *Click on the Other Documents tab*; note that several different resume styles are presented. *Click on the General tab.*

4. *Click on Template under Create New field in the lower right of the Templates task pane* (see Word 2003 Exhibit 11).

5. Under the General tab, *click on Blank Document.* "Blank Document" should now be highlighted. *Click on OK* (see Word 2003 Exhibit 11).

6. You should now have a blank template on your screen. The Windows title should say "Template1—Microsoft Word" in the upper left of the screen. You will now build the template shown in Word 2003 Exhibit 10.

7. *Click on the Center icon on the toolbar, then click on the Bold icon on the toolbar. Click on the Font Size icon and select 14 from the list.*

8. Type **WATKINSON & ASSOCIATES** and then *click on the Bold icon on the toolbar* to turn off Bold. *Click on the Font Size icon and select 12 from the list.*

9. Press the **[ENTER]** key.

10. Type **55 Marietta Street, Suite 1000** and press the **[ENTER]** key.

11. Type **Atlanta, GA 30303** and press the **[ENTER]** key.

12. Type **(404) 555-3244; Fax (404) 555-3245** and press the **[ENTER]** key.

13. *Click on the Align Left icon on the toolbar.*

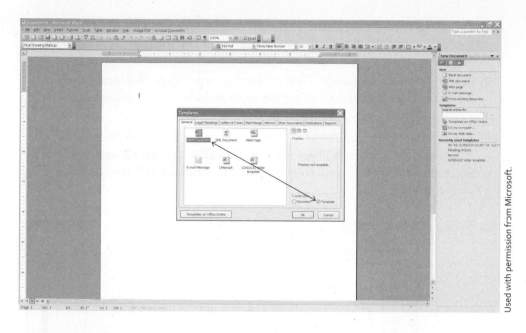

WORD 2003 EXHIBIT 11
Creating a new template

14. Press the **[ENTER]** key three times.
15. *Point and click on Insert on the menu bar and then select Field.*
16. The Field task pane should now be displayed (see Word 2003 Exhibit 12). The Field pane has several sections, including Categories and Field names. Under Categories, "(All)" should be selected.
17. *Point and click on the down arrow on the Field names: scroll bar until you see the field name "Date"* (see Word 2003 Exhibit 12). *Click on it.*
18. *From the Field properties: list, click on the third option from the top (the one with month, day of the month spelled out, and year).* Notice that the current date is displayed. (This field will always display the date on which the template is actually executed, so if the template is executed on January 1, "January 1" will be the date shown on the letter.) *Click on OK in the Field task pane.*
19. Press the **[ENTER]** key three times.
20. *Click on Insert on the menu bar and then on Field.*

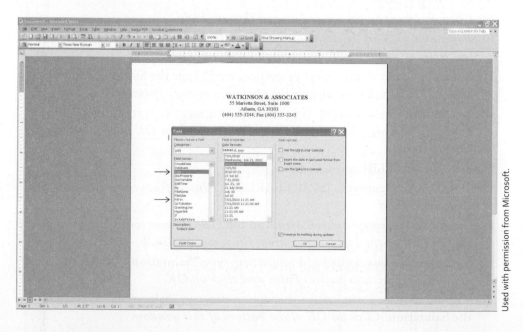

WORD 2003 EXHIBIT 12
Inserting a field in a template

HANDS-ON EXERCISES

21. *Point and click on the down arrow on the Field names: scroll bar until you see "Fill-in" in the Field name: area* (see Word 2003 Exhibit 12). *Click on Fill-in.*

22. In the "Prompt:" box under Field properties:, type "**Type the Name and Address of the Recipient.**" *Note*: You must include the quotation marks.

23. *Click on OK in the Field task pane.*

24. You will now see a window on your screen that says "Type the Name and Address of the Recipient." Type **Press the ENTER key after Name, Address and City/St/Zip** (see Word 2003 Exhibit 13). *Click on OK in the bottom of this window.*

WORD 2003 EXHIBIT 13
Inserting a "fill-in" field

25. Press the [**ENTER**] key three times.

26. Press the [**TAB**] key.

27. Type **Subject:**

28. Press the [**TAB**] key.

29. *Click on Insert on the menu bar and then on Field.*

30. *Point and click on the down arrow on the Field names: scroll bar until you see "Fill-in" in the Field name: area. Click on "Fill-in."*

31. In the prompt box under Field properties:, type "**Type the Subject of the Letter.**" (*Note*: You must include the quotation marks.) *Point and click on OK.*

32. You will now see a window on your screen that says "Type the Subject of the Letter." Type **Enter the Subject of the Letter.** *Click on OK in the bottom of this window.*

33. Press the [**ENTER**] key three times.

34. Type **Dear** and press the [**SPACEBAR**], select *Insert from the menu bar, and then select Field.*

35. *Point and click on the down arrow on the Field names: scroll bar until you see "Fill-in" in the Field name: area. Click on "Fill-in."*

36. In the prompt box under Field properties:, type "**Salutation.**" (*Note*: You must include the quotation marks.) *Point and click on OK.*

37. You will now see a window on your screen that says "Salutation." Type **Enter the Salutation.** *Click on OK at the bottom of this window.*

38. Type **:** [a colon].

39. Press the **[ENTER]** key twice.

40. *Click on Insert on the menu bar and then on Field.*

41. *Point and click on the down arrow on the Field names: scroll bar until you see "Fill-in" in the Field name: area. Click on "Fill-in."*

42. In the prompt box under Field properties:, type **"Body of Letter."** (*Note*: You must include the quotation marks.) *Point and click on OK.*

43. You will now see a window on your screen that says "Body of Letter." Type **Enter the Body of the Letter.** *Click on OK in the bottom of this window.*

44. Press the **[ENTER]** key twice.

45. Type **If you have any questions, please do not hesitate to contact me.** Press the **[ENTER]** key three times.

46. Type **Kindest Regards,** and press the **[ENTER]** key four times.

47. Type **Mirabelle Watkinson** and press the **[ENTER]** key once.

48. Type **For the Firm**.

49. *Click on File on the menu bar, then on Save.* Type **Watkinson Letter Template** and then *click on Save.*

50. *Click on File on the menu bar, then on Close.* You are now ready to type a letter using the template.

51. *Click on File on the menu bar, then click on New.* Under Templates, *click on On my computer….*

52. In the "Templates" window, under the General tab, *double-click on "Watkinson Letter Template."*

53. The template letter is now running. You will see the "Type the Name and Address of the Recipient" field on the screen. You will also see the prompt that reminds you to press ENTER after the name, address and city/state/zip. Type over this prompt.

54. Type **Steven Matthews** and press the **[ENTER]** key.

55. Type **Matthews, Smith & Russell** and press the **[ENTER]** key.

56. Type **P.O. Box 12341** and press the **[ENTER]** key.

57. Type **Boston, MA 59920** and then *click on OK.*

58. You will see the Type the Subject of the Letter field on the screen. You will also see the prompt that reminds you to enter the subject of the letter. Type over this prompt.

59. Type **Turner v. Smith, Case No. CV-11-0046** and then *click on OK.*

60. You will now see the Salutation field on the screen. You will also see the prompt that reminds you to enter the salutation. Type over this prompt.

61. Type **Steve** and then *click on OK.*

62. You will now see the Body of Letter field on the screen. You will also see the prompt that reminds you to enter the body of the letter. Type over this prompt.

63. Type **This will confirm our conversation of this date. You indicated that you had no objection to us requesting an additional ten days to respond to your Motion for Summary Judgment.** *Click on OK.* You are now through typing the letter. The completed letter should now be displayed. (*Note:* If another window is displayed prompting you for the name and address of the recipient, simply *click Cancel*; the completed letter should then be displayed.)

64. To print the document, *click on File on the menu bar, click on Print, then click on OK.* Alternatively, *click on the Printer icon on the toolbar.*

65. To save the document, *click on File from the menu bar and then select Save As....* Type **Matthews Letter** in the "File name" box. *Click on the down arrow next to the "Save as type:" box and choose "Word document (*.doc)." Point and click on Save to save the document in the default directory.* *Note:* You saved the output of your template to a separate file named "Matthews Letter." Your original template ("Watkinson Letter Template") is unaffected by the Matthews letter, and is still a clean template ready to be used again and again for any case.

66. *Click on File on the menu bar and then on Close* to close the document, or *click on File from the menu bar and then on Exit* to exit Word.

This concludes Lesson 7.

LESSON 8: COMPARING DOCUMENTS

This lesson shows you how to compare documents by simultaneously viewing documents and by creating a separate blacklined document with the changes. In your law-office career, you will often send someone a digital file for revision, only to find that when the file is returned, the revisions are not apparent. Using the comparison tools in Word, you can see what has changed in the document.

1. Open Windows. *Double-click on the Microsoft Office Word 2003 icon on the desktop* to open Word 2003 for Windows. Alternatively, *click on the Start button, point the cursor to Programs or All Programs, then click on the Microsoft Word icon* (or *point to Microsoft Office and then click on Microsoft Office Word 2003*). You should be in a new, clean, blank document. If you are not in a clean document, *click on File on the menu bar. then click on New, then click on Blank document.*

2. For the purpose of this lesson, we will assume that your firm drafted an employment contract for a corporate client named Bluebriar Incorporated. Bluebriar is in negotiations with an individual named John Lewis, whom they would like to hire as their vice president of marketing. Your firm is negotiating with John Lewis's attorney regarding the terms and language of the employment contract. The "Lesson 8A" file on the disk for this text is the original document you sent to John Lewis's attorney. The "Lesson 8B" file on the disk for this text is the new file sent back to you by John Lewis's attorney.

3. You will now open both of these files from the disk supplied with this text and then compare them side by side. Ensure that the disk is inserted in the drive, *point and click on File on the menu bar, then point and click on Open.* The Open task pane should now be displayed. Point and *click on the down arrow to the right of the white box next to "Look in:" and select the drive where the disk is located. Point and double-click on the Word-Processing Files folder. Double-click on the Word 2003 folder. Double-click on the "Lesson 8A" file.*

4. Follow the same directions to open the "Lesson 8B" file. Then, *point and click on Window from the menu bar and click on "Lesson 8A.doc (Read Only)."*

5. *Point and click on Window from the menu bar, then click on "Compare Side by Side with Word Lesson 8B.doc."* Both documents should now be displayed side by side (see Word 2003 Exhibit 14).

6. Push the [**DOWN ARROW**] key on the keyboard to scroll down through the document. Notice that both documents simultaneously scroll. Also, notice the small "Compare Side by Side" window (see Word 2003 Exhibit 14). The Synchronous Scrolling icon toggles synchronous scrolling on and off. If you turn off synchronous scrolling and wish to turn it back on, simply realign the windows where you want them, *point and click on the Reset Window Position icon on the "Compare Side by Side" window* (see Word 2003 Exhibit 14), *and then select the Synchronous Scrolling icon in the "Compare*

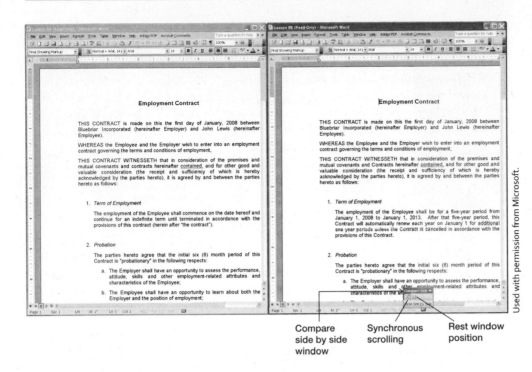

WORD 2003 EXHIBIT 14
Comparing documents side-by-side

Compare side by side window

Synchronous scrolling

Rest window position

Side by Side" window. Using the Compare Side by Side feature, you can see the changes to the document paragraph by paragraph.

7. You will now learn how to merge the changes into one document. *Point and click on Close Side by Side in the "Compare Side by Side" window.*

8. *Point and click on Window on the menu bar, then point and click on Lesson 8A.doc.*

9. *Click on File from the menu bar and then on Close* to close this document.

10. Lesson 8B.doc should still be open. You will now create a separate file with the changes merged into one document so you can see everything that has been modified.

11. *Point and click on Tools on the menu bar, then on Compare and Merge Documents. Point and click on Lesson 8A.doc. Make sure there are check marks next to "Legal blackline" and "Find formatting" in the Compare and Merge Documents task pane in the lower portion of the window.*

12. *Click on Compare in the Compare and Merge Documents pane.* Notice that a new document has been created that merges the documents (see Word 2003 Exhibit 15). Scroll through the new document and review all the changes.

13. The Compare and Merge Documents feature is extremely helpful when comparing multiple versions of the same file. By right-clicking on any of the additions or deletions, you can accept or reject the change. This is part of the feature called Track Changes, which you will learn about in Lesson 9.

14. To print the document, *click on File on the menu bar, click on Print, then click on OK.* Alternatively, *click on the Printer icon on the toolbar.*

15. To save the document, *click on File from the menu bar and then select Save As.... Under Save in, select the drive or folder where you would like to save the document. Next to "File name"* type **Done—Word 2003 Lesson 8 Merged Document,** *then click on Save to save the document.*

16. *Click on File on the menu bar and then on Close* to close the document.

17. *Click on File on the menu bar and then on Close* to close Lesson 8B.doc.

18. *Click on File on the menu bar and then on Exit* to exit Word.

This concludes Lesson 8.

WORD 2003 EXHIBIT 15
Compare and merge
documents—Legal blackline

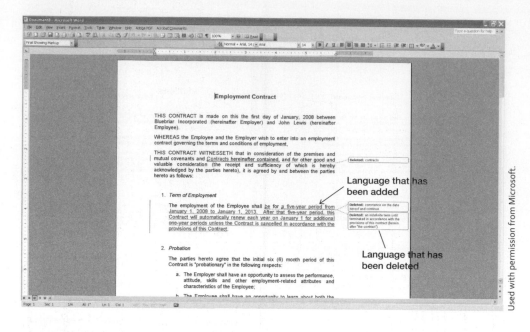

LESSON 9: USING TRACK CHANGES

In this lesson, you will learn how to use the Track Changes feature by editing a will and then accepting and/or rejecting the changes.

1. Open Windows. *Double-click on the Microsoft Office Word 2003 icon on the desktop* to open Word 2003 for Windows. Alternatively, *click on the Start button, point the cursor to Programs or All Programs, then click on the Microsoft Word icon* (or *point to Microsoft Office and then click on Microsoft Office Word 2003).* You should be in a new, clean, blank document. If you are not in a clean document, *click on File on the menu bar, click on New, then click on Blank document.*

2. The first thing you will do is open the "Lesson 9" file from the disk supplied with this text. Ensure that the disk is inserted in the drive, *point and click on File on the menu bar, then point and click on Open.* The "Open" window should now be displayed. *Point and click on the down arrow to the right of the white box next to "Look in:" and select the drive where the disk is located. Point and double-click on the Word-Processing Files folder. Double-click on the Word 2003 folder. Point and double-click on the "Lesson 9" file.*

3. The text "Last Will and Testament" should now be displayed on your screen (see Word 2003 Exhibit 16). Notice in Word 2003 Exhibit 16 that several revisions have been made to this Last Will and Testament. Your client, William Porter, has asked you to use the Document Review feature to show your supervising attorney the changes he would like to make. Mr. Porter is rather leery of the legal process and wants to make sure your supervising attorney approves of the changes.

4. *Point and click on Tools on the menu bar and then on Track Changes.*

5. Notice that, on the status line at the bottom of the screen, the letters "TRK" (standing for Track Changes) are shown. This tells you that the Track Changes feature is now on (see Word 2003 Exhibit 16). Notice also at the top of the screen that the Review toolbar has now been displayed (see Word 2003 Exhibit 16). This toolbar displays the commands to control Track Changes.

Used with permission from Microsoft.

6. Make the changes shown in Word 2003 Exhibit 16. Everything that should be added is circled, and everything that should be deleted is shown at the right.

7. Assume now that you have shown the changes to your supervising attorney. *Point and click on the Track Changes icon on the Review toolbar* to turn off Track Changes (see Word 2003 Exhibit 16). It is the second icon from the right on the Review toolbar. *Note:* Remember that you can hover your cursor over an icon on the toolbar and the name will appear after a second or two. Turning off Track Changes allows you to make changes to the document without them showing up as revisions.

8. *Point and right-click anywhere on the revised text you added—"Of William Porter"—just under "LAST WILL AND TESTAMENT."* Notice that a menu is displayed that allows you to accept or reject the insertion, among other things. *Point and click on Accept Insertion.* The revision has now been accepted.

9. *Point and click on the Next icon on the Review toolbar* (see Word 2003 Exhibit 16). This should take you to the insertion of "Fort Myers." *Point and click on the Accept Change icon on the Review toolbar* (see Word 2003 Exhibit 16) to accept the change.

10. *Point and click on the down arrow next to "Accept Change" on the toolbar* (see Word 2003 Exhibit 16). Notice that one of the options is "Accept All Changes in Document." (Do not select it now.) This is a quick way to accept all changes in a document without going through each one of them. Press the **[ESC]** key on the keyboard to close this menu.

11. Use the Next feature to continue to go to each change and to accept the revision. The only revision you will not accept is changing the executor from Steve Porter to David Johnson; reject this change. Assume that the supervising attorney has learned that Mr. Johnson is terminally ill and most likely will not be able to serve as executor, so the client has decided to stay with Steve Porter as the executor.

12. To print the document, *click on File from the menu bar, click on Print, then click on OK.* Alternatively, *click on the Printer icon on the toolbar.*

13. To save the document, *click on File from the menu bar and then select Save As.. ..* Type **Done—Word 2003 Lesson 9 Document** in the "File

HANDS-ON EXERCISES

name" box, **then point and click on Save** to save the document in the default directory.

14. **Click on File on the menu bar and then on Close** to close the document, or **click on File on the menu bar and then on Exit** to exit Word.

This concludes Lesson 9.

▶ ADVANCED LESSONS

LESSON 10: CREATING A MAIL-MERGE DOCUMENT

In this lesson, you will create a merge document for an open house that you will send to three clients (see Word 2003 Exhibit 17). First, you will create the data file that will be merged into the letter. Then, you will create the letter itself, and finally, you will merge the two together. Keep in mind that if you make a mistake at any time, you may press **[CTRL]+[Z]** to undo what you have done.

1. Open Windows. **Double-click on the Microsoft Office Word 2003 icon on the desktop** to open Word 2003 for Windows. Alternatively, **click on the Start button, point the cursor to Programs or All Programs, then click on the Microsoft Word icon** (or **point to Microsoft Office and then click on Microsoft Office Word 2003).** You should be in a new, clean, blank document. If you are not in a clean document, **click on File on the menu bar, click on New, then click on Blank document.**

2. **Click on Tools on the menu bar, then point to Letters and Mailings and then click on Mail Merge.** The Mail Merge task pane is now shown to the right of your document.

3. The bottom of the Mail Merge task pane shows that you are on Step 1 of 6. You are asked to "Select document type." You will be typing a letter, so the default selection, "Letters," is fine. To continue to the next step, **click on "Next: Starting document" at the bottom of the Mail Merge task pane under Step 1 of 6.**

4. The bottom of the Mail Merge task pane shows that you are on Step 2 of 6. You are asked to "Select starting document." You will be using the current document to type your letter, so the default selection, "Use the current document," is fine.

WORD 2003 EXHIBIT 17
Mail-merge letter

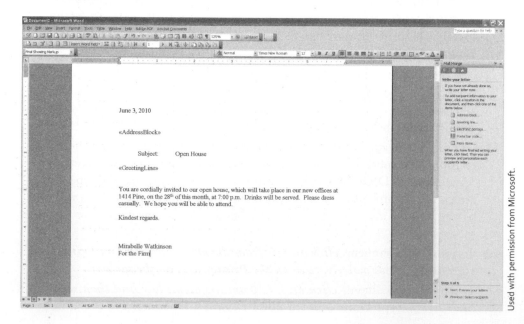

Used with permission from Microsoft.

To continue to the next step, **click on "Next: Select recipients" at the bottom of the Mail Merge task pane under Step 2 of 6**.

5. The bottom of the Mail Merge task pane shows that you are on Step 3 of 6. You are asked to "Select recipients." You will be typing a new list, so **click on "Type a new list."**

6. **Under the "Type a new list" section of the Mail Merge task pane, click on "Create...."**

7. The "New Address List" window is now displayed. You will now fill in the names of the three clients to whom you want to send your open-house letter.

8. Type the following. (*Note:* You can use the **[TAB]** key to move between the fields, or you can use the mouse pointer.) Only complete the fields below (skip the fields in the "New Address List" window; we will not be using this).

TITLE	
First Name	Jim
Last Name	Woods
Company Name	
Address Line 1	2300 Briarcliff Road
Address Line 2	
City	Atlanta
State	GA
ZIP Code	30306
Country	
Home Phone	
Work Phone	
Email Address	

9. When you have entered all of the information for Jim Woods, **click on the New Entry button in the "New Address List" window.**

10. Enter the second client in the blank "New Address List" window.

TITLE	
First Name	Jennifer
Last Name	John
Company Name	
Address Line 1	3414 Peachtree Road
Address Line 2	
City	Atlanta
State	GA
ZIP Code	30314
Country	
Home Phone	
Work Phone	
Email Address	

11. When you have entered all of the information for Jennifer John, *click on the New Entry button in the "New Address List" window.*

12. Enter the third client in the blank "New Address List" window.

TITLE	
First Name	Jonathan
Last Name	Phillips
Company Name	
Address Line 1	675 Clifton Road
Address Line 2	
City	Atlanta
State	GA
ZIP Code	30030
Country	
Home Phone	
Work Phone	
Email Address	

13. When you have entered all of the information for Jonathan Phillips, *click on Close in the "New Address List" window.*

14. The "Save Address List" window is now displayed. You need to save the address list so that it can later be merged with the open-house letter. In the "Save Address List" window, next to File name:, type **Open House List** and then *click on Save.*

15. The "Mail Merge Recipients" window is now displayed (see Word 2003 Exhibit 18). *Click on the Last Name field in the "Mail Merge Recipients" window to sort the list by last name* (see Word 2003 Exhibit 18). Notice that the order of the list is now sorted by last name.

WORD 2003 EXHIBIT 18
Entering mail-merge recipients

16. **Click on OK in the "Mail Merge Recipients" window.** You are now back at your blank document with the Mail Merge task pane open at the right. The bottom of the Mail Merge task pane indicates that you are still at Step 3 of 6. **Click on "Next: Write your letter" at the bottom of the Mail Merge task pane under Step 3 of 6.**

17. The bottom of the Mail Merge task pane indicates that you are on Step 4 of 6. In the Mail Merge task pane, "Write your letter" is displayed. You are now ready to write the letter.

18. Press the [ENTER] key four times.

19. Type the current date and press the [ENTER] key three times.

20. **Click on "Address block…" in the Mail Merge task pane under "Write your letter."**

21. The "Insert Address Block" window is now displayed. You will now customize how the address block will appear in the letters.

22. **In the "Insert Address Block" window, click on the second entry, "Joshua Randall Jr." Click on "Insert company name" to deselect it,** because we did not include company names in our data list (see Word 2003 Exhibit 19). Under "Insert postal address:," **click on "Never include the country/region in the address"** (see Word 2003 Exhibit 19).

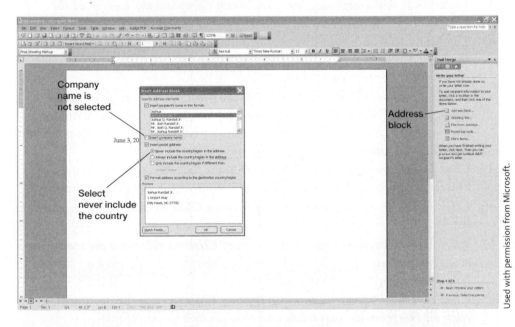

WORD 2003 EXHIBIT 19
Insert address block

23. **Click on OK in the "Insert Address Block" window.**

24. The words "<<AddressBlock>>" are now displayed in your document.

25. Press the [ENTER] key three times.

26. Press the [TAB] key once and then type **Subject.**

27. Press the [TAB] key and then type **Open House.**

28. Press the [ENTER] key twice.

29. **Under "Write your letter" in the Mail Merge task pane, click on "Greeting line…."**

30. The "Greeting Line" window is now displayed. You will now customize how the greeting or salutation will appear in the letter. In the "Greeting Line" window, **click on the down arrow next to "Mr. Randall" and then scroll down and click on "Josh." Click on OK in the "Greeting Line" window.**

31. The words "<<GreetingLine>>" are now displayed in your document.

32. Press the [ENTER] key three times.

33. Type **You are cordially invited to our open house, which will take place in our new offices at 1414 Pine, on the 28th of this month, at 7:00 p.m. Drinks will be served. Please dress casually. We hope you will be able to attend.**

34. Press the [ENTER] key twice.

35. Type **Kindest regards.**

36. Press the [ENTER] key four times.

37. Type **Mirabelle Watkinson**.

38. Press the [ENTER] key once and type **For the Firm**.

39. You are now done typing the letter. The only thing left to do is merge the recipient list with the form.

40. Under "Step 4 of 6" at the bottom of the Mail Merge task pane, *click on "Next: Preview your letters"* to continue to the next step.

41. Your first letter is now displayed. In the Mail Merge task pane, under "Preview your letters," *click on the button showing two arrows pointing to the right to see the rest of your letters.*

42. To continue to the next step, *click on "Next: Complete the merge" at the bottom of the Mail Merge task pane under "Step 5 of 6."*

43. The Mail Merge task pane displays "Complete the Merge." *Click on Print in the Mail Merge task pane under Merge. At the "Merge to Printer" window, click on OK to print your letters.*

44. *Click on "Edit individual letters…" in the Mail Merge task pane under Merge. In the "Merge to New Document" window, click on OK.* Word has now opened a new document with all of the letters in it. *Note:* At this point you can edit and personalize each letter if you so desire.

45. *Click on File from the menu bar and then on Save.* Type **Open House Letters** and then *click on Save* to save the document in the default directory.

46. *Click on File from the menu bar and then on Close* to close the personalized letters.

47. You should be back at the mail-merge letter. *Click on File from the menu bar and then on Save.* Type **Open House Mail Merge** and then *click on Save* to save the document in the default directory.

48. *Click on File on the menu bar and then on Close* to close the document, or *click on File from the menu bar and then on Exit* to exit Word.

This concludes Lesson 10.

LESSON 11: CREATING A TABLE OF AUTHORITIES

In this lesson, you will prepare a table of authorities for a reply brief (see Word 2003 Exhibit 22). You will learn how to find cases, mark cases, and then automatically generate a table of authorities.

1. Open Windows. *Double-click on the Microsoft Office Word 2003 icon on the desktop* to open Word 2003 for Windows. Alternatively, *click on the Start button, point the cursor to Programs or All Programs, then click on the Microsoft Word icon* (or *point to Microsoft Office and then click on Microsoft Office Word 2003*). You should be in a new, clean, blank document. If you are not in a clean document, *click on File on the menu bar, click on New, then click on Blank document.*

2. The first thing you will do is open the "Lesson 11" file from the disk supplied with this text. Ensure that the disk is inserted in the disk drive, ***point and click on File on the menu bar, then point and click on Open.*** The "Open" window should now be displayed. ***Point and click on the down arrow to the right of the white box next to "Look in:" and select the drive where the disk is located. Point and double-click on the Word-Processing Files folder. Double-click on the Word 2003 folder. Point and double-click on the "Lesson 11" file.*** The text "In the Supreme Court of the United States" and "TED SUTTON, *Petitioner* v. STATE OF ALASKA, *Respondent*" should now be displayed on your screen.

3. In this exercise you will build the case section of the table of authorities for this reply brief. There are five cases to be included and they are all shown in bold so that you can easily identify them. Your first task will be to mark each of the cases so that Word knows they are to be included; you will then execute the command for Word to build the table.

4. If you are not at the beginning of the document, press **[CTRL]+[HOME]** on the keyboard to go to the beginning.

5. You will now mark the cases. ***Click on Insert from the menu bar, point to Reference, then click on Index and Tables….***

6. ***Click on the Table of Authorities tab in the Index and Tables pane.***

7. ***Click on "Cases" under Category: and then click on the Mark Citation… button*** (see Word 2003 Exhibit 20). This tells Word that you are going to mark a case, as opposed to a statute, rule, or other data type, because those other materials go in their own separate tables.

8. The "Mark Citation" window is now displayed. ***Click on Next Citation in the "Mark Citation" window.*** Word looks for words such as "vs" or "v." when finding citations. The cursor should now be on "v." in *Ted Sutton v. State of Alaska.* Because this is the caption of the current case, we do not want to mark it for inclusion in the table.

9. ***Click on Next Citation in the "Mark Citation" window.*** Again, this is the caption of the current case, *Ted Sutton v. State of Alaska,* so we do not want to mark it.

WORD 2003 EXHIBIT 20
Building a table of authorities

WORD 2003 EXHIBIT 21
Marking a citation for inclusion in a table of authorities

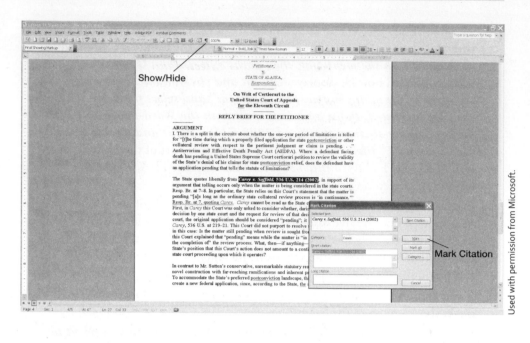

Show/Hide

Mark Citation

10. *Click on Next Citation in the "Mark Citation" window.* Word has now found the case *Carey v. Saffold.* We want to mark this case so that it will be included in the table of authorities.

11. *Click once on the* **Carey v. Saffold** *case.*

12. *Drag the cursor to highlight "***Carey v. Saffold***, 536 U.S. 214 (2002)," then click in the white box under Selected text: in the "Mark Citation" window;* the case is automatically copied there (see Word 2003 Exhibit 21).

13. *Click on Mark in the "Mark Citation" window. Note:* When you mark a citation, Word changes your view to the Show/Hide paragraph view. It shows you that you have embedded table-of-authorities formatting codes in the document. To switch out of Show/Hide view, click on the Show/Hide icon on the toolbar (it looks like a paragraph symbol and is just to the left of the Zoom view, which typically says "100%"; see Word 2003 Exhibit 21).

14. *Click on Next Citation in the "Mark Citation" window.*

15. *Click once on the* **Duncan v. Walker** *case.*

16. *Drag the pointer to highlight "***Duncan v. Walker***, 533 U.S. 167, 174 (2001)," and then click in the white box under "Selected text" in the "Mark Citation" window.* The case is automatically copied there.

17. *Click on Mark in the "Mark Citation" window.* Notice under <u>S</u>hort citation: in the "Mark Citation" window that the *Carey* and *Duncan* cases are listed.

18. If at any time the "Mark Citation" window prevents you from seeing the case you need to highlight, just click on the blue bar at the top of the "Mark Citation" window and drag the pointer to the left or the right to move the window out of your way.

19. *Click on Next Citation in the "Mark Citation" window.*

20. *Click once on the* **Bates v. United States** *case.*

21. *Drag the cursor to highlight "***Bates v. United States***, 522 U.S. 23, 29–30 (1997)," then click in the white box under Selected text: in the "Mark Citation" window.* The case is automatically copied there.

22. *Click on Mark in the "Mark Citation" window.*

23. *Click on Next Citation in the "Mark Citation" window.*

24. *Click once on the* **Abela v. Martin** *case.*

25. *Drag the pointer to highlight* **"Abela v. Martin, 348 F.3d 164 (6th Cir. 2003),"** *then click in the white box under Selected text: in the "Mark Citation" window.* The case is automatically copied there.

26. *Click on Mark in the "Mark Citation" window. Click on Next Citation in the "Mark Citation" window.*

27. *Click once on the* **"Coates v. Byrd"** *case.*

28. *Drag the mouse to highlight* **"Coates v. Byrd, 211 F.3d 1225, 1227 (11th Cir. 2000),"** *then click in the white box under Selected text: in the "Mark Citation" window.* The case is automatically copied there.

29. *Click on Mark in the "Mark Citation" window.*

30. *Click on Close in the "Mark Citation" window* to close it.

31. *Point and click on the Show/Hide paragraph icon to remove the paragraph symbols* (see Word 2003 Exhibit 21).

32. Using the cursor keys or the scroll bar, *place the cursor on page 3 of the document two lines under the title "TABLE OF AUTHORITIES."* You are now ready to generate the table.

33. *Click on Insert on the menu bar, point to Reference, then click on Index and Tables…. Click on Cases under Category and then click on OK.*

34. Notice that the table of authorities has been prepared and completed, and that the cases and the page numbers where they appear in the document have been included (see Word 2003 Exhibit 22).

35. To print the document, *click on File on the menu bar, click on Print, then click on OK.* Alternatively, *click on the Printer icon on the toolbar.*

36. To save the document, *click on File from the menu bar and then select Save As…. Under Save in, select the drive or folder where you would like to save the document. Next to "File name"* type **Done—Word 2003 Lesson 11 Document** *and then point and click on Save* to save the document.

37. *Click on File on the menu bar and then on Close* to close the document, or *click on File from the menu bar and then on Exit* to exit Word.

This concludes Lesson 11.

WORD 2003 EXHIBIT 22
Completed table of authorities

Used with permission from Microsoft.

LESSON 12: CREATING A MACRO

In this lesson you will prepare a macro that will automatically type the signature block for a pleading (see Word 2003 Exhibit 23). You will then execute the macro to make sure that it works properly.

WORD 2003 EXHIBIT 23
Creating a pleading
signature block macro

Used with permission from Microsoft.

1. Open Windows. **Double-click on the Microsoft Office Word 2003 icon on the desktop** to open Word 2003 for Windows. Alternatively, **click on the Start button, point the cursor to Programs or All Programs, then click on the Microsoft Word icon** (or **point to Microsoft Office and then click on Microsoft Office Word 2003**). You should be in a new, clean, blank document. If you are not in a clean document, **click on File on the menu bar, click on New, then click on Blank document.**

2. The first thing you need to do to create a new macro is to name the macro and then turn on the record function. **Point and click on Tools on the menu bar, then on Macro, then on Record New Macro.**

3. In the Record Macro task pane, just under "Macro name," type **PleadSignBlock** and then **point and click on OK.** Notice that your cursor now looks like a cassette tape and the "Stop Recording Macro" window has opened. The cassette-tape cursor indicates that Word is now recording all of your keystrokes and commands.

4. **Type the information shown in Word 2003 Exhibit 23.** When you have completed typing the information, **point and click on the Stop Recording button in the "Stop Recording Macro" window.**

5. You will now test your macro to see if it works properly. **Click on File on the menu bar and then on Close to close the document.** At the prompt "Do you want to save the changes to document?" **point and click on No.**

6. **Point and click on the New Blank Document icon on the toolbar** (it looks like a blank sheet of paper and is at the far left on the toolbar).

7. To run the macro, **point and click on Tools on the menu bar, then on Macro, then on Macros.**

8. **In the "Macros" window, point and click on PleadSignBlock and then point and click on Run.** Your pleading signature block should appear in your document.

9. To print the document, *click on File on the menu bar, click on Print, then click on OK.* Alternatively, *click on the Printer icon on the toolbar.*

10. To save the document, *click on File from the menu bar and then select Save As....* Type **Done—Word 2003 Lesson 12 Document** in the "File name" box, *and then point and click on Save to save the document in the default directory.*

11. *Click on File on the menu bar and then on Close* to close the document, or *click on File on the menu bar and then on Exit* to exit Word.

This concludes Lesson 12.

LESSON 13: DRAFTING A WILL

Using the websites at the end of Chapter 2 in the main text, or using a form book from a law library, draft a simple will that would be valid in your state. You will be drafting the will for Thomas Mansell, who is a widower. The will should be dated July 1 of the current year. Mr. Mansell requests the following:

- That his just debts and funeral expenses be paid.
- That his lifelong friend, Dr. Jeff Johnson, receive $20,000 in cash.
- That his local YMCA receives his 100 shares of stock in IBM.
- That all of his remaining property (real or personal) descend to his daughter Sharon Mansell.
- That in the event Mr. Mansell and his daughter die simultaneously, all of his property would descend to Sharon's son Michael Mansell.
- That Dr. Jeff Johnson be appointed the executor of the will; if Dr. Johnson predeceases Mr. Mansell, that Mr. Joe Crawford be appointed executor.

Mr. Mansell has also requested that his will be double-spaced and have one-inch margins. He would like the will to look good and be valid in his state.

- Three witnesses will watch the signing of the will (Shelly Stewart, Dennis Gordon, and Gary Fox).
- John Boesel will notarize the will.

Print out a hard copy of the will and email it to your instructor.

LESSON 14: THE PLEADING WIZARD

Use the Pleading Wizard in Microsoft Word 2003 to create the motion in Exhibit 2–11 of Chapter 2 of the text. To bring up the Pleading Wizard, *click on File on the menu bar, then click on New. Under Templates, click on "On my computer...." Click on the Legal Pleadings tab, and under Create New click on Document. Finally, double-click on the Pleading Wizard icon.* The Pleading Wizard will guide you through creating a pleading form and through the process of completing the form. Use Exhibit 2–11 of the text as a guide, but do not try to copy the format exactly. When the document is completed, print out a hard copy and email the file to your instructor.

ADOBE ACROBAT 9 PRO

I. INTRODUCTION — READ THIS!

Adobe Acrobat lets you view, create, manipulate, and manage files in Adobe's Portable Document Format (PDF). It permits you to present information with a fixed layout similar to paper publication.

II. INSTALLATION INSTRUCTIONS

1. Log in to your CengageBrain.com account.
2. Under "My Courses & Materials," find the Premium Website for Using Computers in the Law Office.
3. *Click "Open" to go to the Premium Website.*
4. *Under "Book Resources," click on the link for "Adobe Acrobat 9 Professional."*
5. *Right-click on the link next to "Download Now" and select "Save Target As" or "Save Link As."*
6. *Choose a folder on your hard drive, such as the Desktop, where you want to save the file, and then click Save.* The files are now being saved to your computer.
7. *In Windows Explorer (Start Button > Computer), open the folder where you saved the file above.*
8. *Double-click the file.*
9. The screen in Installation Exhibit 1 should now be displayed. This process will take a few minutes to complete.
10. Choose the language for the installation and *click OK.*

INSTALLATION EXHIBIT 1

Adobe product screenshots reprinted with permission from Adobe Systems Incorporated.

11. At the next screen, *click Next.*

12. If you have already previously installed Adobe Reader you will see the screen in Installation Exhibit 2. *Click Next.*

Adobe product screenshots reprinted with permission from Adobe Systems Incorporated.

INSTALLATION EXHIBIT 2

13. At the next screen, **type your name** (and organization, if desired) in the text boxes. *Click the button next to "Install the trial version." Click Next.*

14. Choose the "**Typical**" setup type. *Click Next.*

15. At the next screen, choose the default location to install this program by *clicking the Next button.*

16. At the next screen, *click the Install button.*

17. Install is complete. *Click the Finish button.*

Number	Lesson Title	Concepts Covered
BASIC LESSONS		
Lesson 1	Creating a PDF from a Word document	Using PDFMaker, naming and saving a PDF, converting a Word document into a PDF
Lesson 2	Creating a PDF from a Web page	Using PDFMaker, naming and saving a PDF, converting a web page into a PDF
INTERMEDIATE LESSONS		
Lesson 3	Combining Multiple Documents into a Single PDF	Combining files, adding files, moving files into desired order, naming and saving a combined PDF
Lesson 4	Creating a Portfolio	Creating a portfolio, editing a portfolio, naming and saving a PDF
Lesson 5	Adding Security to a PDF	Changing the security settings, adding a password

HANDS-ON EXERCISES

GETTING STARTED

Introduction

Throughout these lessons and exercises, information you need to type into the program will be designated in several different ways:

- Keys to be pressed on the keyboard are designated in brackets, in all caps, and in bold (e.g., press the **[ENTER]** key).
- Movements with the mouse are designated in bold and italics (e.g., ***point to File on the menu bar and click***).
- Words or letters that should be typed are designated in bold (e.g., type **Training Program**).
- Information that is or should be displayed on your computer screen is shown in bold, with quotation marks (e.g., "**Press ENTER to continue.**").

OVERVIEW OF ADOBE ACROBAT

The following tips on using Adobe Acrobat will help you complete these exercises.

Adobe Acrobat Pro 9 is the most commonly used Portable Document Format (PDF) program. A PDF can be used to share files with others who do not have the same software; share files with others regardless of the computer operating system used to view the files; share files that will look the same (layout, fonts) on all computer systems; share files that can be protected from unauthorized viewing, printing, copying, or editing; print files to many different types of printers, and have them all look essentially the same; and create files with hyperlinks and bookmarks that can be electronically shared with others.

When Adobe Acrobat is installed on your computer, it automatically installed PDFMaker, which is used to create PDFs from Microsoft Office applications (Word, Excel, PowerPoint, etc.). If you are using the Office 2007 suite, you can create a PDF by clicking on the Acrobat ribbon. If you are using the Office 2003 suite, you can create a PDF by clicking on the Convert to Adobe PDF button or the Adobe PDF menu on the toolbar and menu bars.

▶ BASIC LESSONS

LESSON 1: CREATING A PDF FROM A WORD DOCUMENT

This lesson shows you how to convert the letter you created in Lesson 1 of the Word-Processing Hands-On Exercises. It explains how to use the PDFMaker application.

1. Open Windows. After it has loaded, ***double-click on the Microsoft Office Word icon on the desktop*** to open Word for Windows. Alternatively, ***click on the Start button, point with the mouse to Programs or All Programs, then click on the Microsoft Word icon*** (or ***point to Microsoft Office, then click on Microsoft Office Word***). You should be in a new, clean, blank document. If you are not in a clean, blank document, ***click on File on the menu bar, click on New, then click on Blank Document.***

2. In this lesson, you will begin by retrieving the document you created in Lesson 1 of the Word 2003 or Word 2007 Hands-On Exercises. To open the file, ***click on File from the menu bar and select Open.*** Type **Letter1** and ***click on Open.*** Alternatively, ***scroll until you find the file, using the horizontal scroll bar, and then point and click on Open.***

3. If you are using Word 2003, on the menu bar, you will find the Adobe PDF menu. ***Click on the Adobe PDF menu. Click the first drop-down item, Convert to Adobe PDF.***

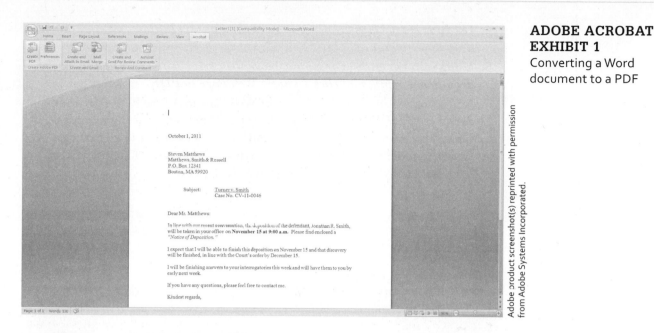

ADOBE ACROBAT
EXHIBIT 1
Converting a Word
document to a PDF

4. *If you are using Word 2007, click the Acrobat Ribbon tab, then click Create PDF* (see Adobe Acrobat Exhibit 1).

5. A new dialog box will open, entitled Save Adobe PDF File As. The "File name" box should display the default file name of "Letter1". The Save as type area should display the default file type of "PDF files."

6. The default settings are fine. *Click on Save.* The software will then create, display, and save your new PDF file.

LESSON 2: CREATING A PDF FROM A WEB PAGE

This lesson shows you how to create a PDF from a web page. It explains how to select part or all of the web page, and how to create, name, and save the new PDF file.

1. Start Windows.

2. Start your Internet browser. Type **http://www.paralegal.delmar.cengage.com/** in the browser and press the [**ENTER**] key.

3. Your screen should now look similar to Adobe Acrobat Exhibit 2.

ADOBE ACROBAT
EXHIBIT 2
Converting a web page to
a PDF

HANDS-ON EXERCISES

4. *Use your cursor keys or mouse to go to the Convert button and click on the drop down menu.*

5. *Using your cursor keys or mouse, move the cursor to the first option on the drop-down menu, and click Convert Web Page to PDF.*

6. A new box will appear, called Convert Web Page to Adobe PDF. *Move your cursor to the line marked File name:.* The default setting is the web page's URL. This is probably not the best name for a file, so let's call it "Paralegal Books." The default setting for Save as type: is Adobe PDF (*.pdf). That is fine, so do not change it. See Adobe Acrobat Exhibit 3.

ADOBE ACROBAT EXHIBIT 3
Saving a PDF

From www.paralegal.delmar.cengage.com. © Delmar, Cengage Learning, Inc. Reproduced by permission. www.cengage.com/permissions.

7. *Click Save* to create and save your new PDF.

8. You can also choose to save just a portion (or portions) of a web page. We will now discuss how to convert only part of a web page to a PDF.

9. Again, open your Internet browser and type **http://www.paralegal.delmar .cengage.com/** in the browser and press the **[ENTER]** key.

10. Again, your screen should now look similar to Adobe Acrobat Exhibit 2.

11. This time, *move the cursor to the Select button and click on it.* After you do so, *move your cursor around the web page.* As you do, notice that the section of the web page you are pointing to now has a red rectangle (consisting of broken red lines) surrounding it. This shows you the section of the web page selected for conversion to PDF.

12. *Move your cursor to the top of the web page over the Cengage logo.* You will see that portion surrounded by red broken lines (see Adobe Acrobat Exhibit 4). Press the **[ENTER]** key. You will notice that the red broken lines have been replaced by blue lines.

13. To convert the selected portion of the web page, you will follow the same procedure used to create the other PDFs. *Using your cursor keys or mouse, move the cursor to the first option on the drop-down menu, and click on "Convert Web Page to PDF."*

14. A new box will appear, called Convert Web Page to Adobe PDF. *Move your cursor to the line marked File name:.* The default setting is the web page's

**ADOBE ACROBAT
EXHIBIT 4**

Selecting a portion of a web page for conversion to a PDF

URL. This is probably not the best name for a file, so let's call it "Paralegal Books-Select." The default setting for Save as type: is Adobe PDF (*.pdf). That is fine, so do not change it. See Adobe Acrobat Exhibit 5.

15. *Click Save* to create and save your new PDF.

This concludes Lesson 2.

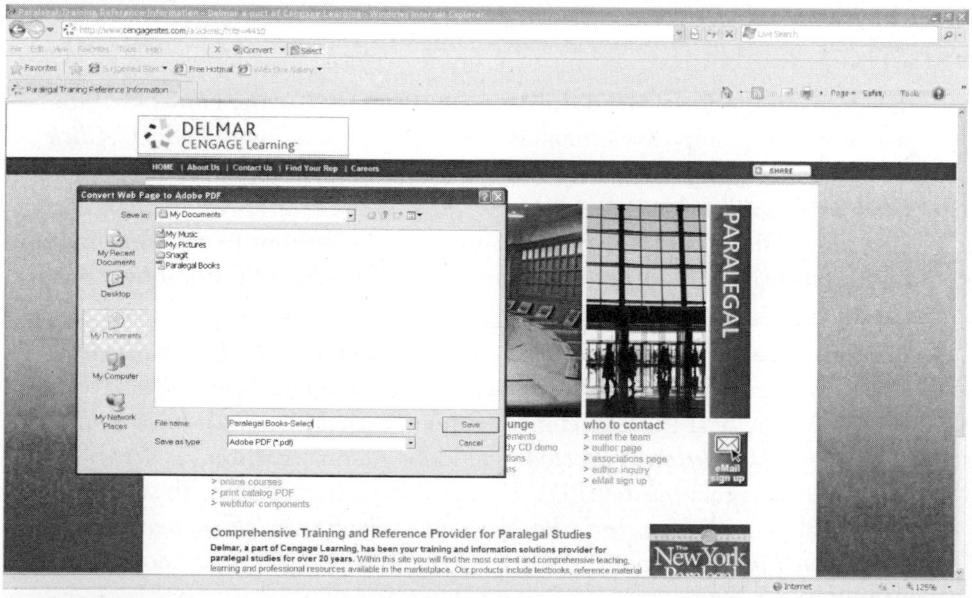

**ADOBE ACROBAT
EXHIBIT 5**

Saving a PDF

▶ INTERMEDIATE LESSONS

LESSON 3: COMBINING MULTIPLE DOCUMENTS INTO A SINGLE PDF

This lesson shows you how to combine separate documents into a single PDF. This lesson assumes that you have completed Lessons 1 and 2 and that you are generally familiar with Adobe Acrobat.

HANDS-ON EXERCISES

1. *Double-click on the Adobe Acrobat Pro 9 icon on the desktop* to open Adobe Acrobat Pro 9. Alternatively, *click on the Start button, point the pointer to Programs or All Programs, then click on Adobe Acrobat Pro 9.* You should be in a new, clean, empty (blank) document.

2. When you want to combine two or more individual PDFs into a single PDF, you will do so within the Adobe Acrobat Pro 9 program. Look at Adobe Acrobat Exhibit 6, and you will notice the Adobe toolbar. The first icon from

ADOBE ACROBAT EXHIBIT 6
Combining PDFs

Adobe product screenshot(s) reprinted with permission from Adobe Systems Incorporated.

the left is a drop-down menu titled Create. *Click on Create.* Notice that the last item on the drop-down menu is Merge Files into a Single PDF …. *Click on the second icon from the left*, which is a drop-down menu called Combine. *Click on Combine.* Notice that the last item on the drop-down menu is Merge Files into a Single PDF. You can use either of these options to combine multiple PDFs into a single PDF. For this lesson, we will use the first drop-down menu, Create.

3. *Click on Create from the menu bar and select Merge Files into a Single PDF….* A new window will open, called "Combine Files." You now have to select the individual PDFs to combine into a single PDF. *First, be sure that the Single PDF button is selected* (see Adobe Acrobat Exhibit 7). We will work with the other button (PDF Portfolio) in the next lesson. To select the individual files, *click on Add Files, located at the upper left corner of the "Combine Files" window.* A drop-down menu will appear (see Adobe Acrobat Exhibit 7).

4. From this drop-down menu, *click on the first option, Add Files….* Another window will appear, called "Add Files." Notice that the Files of type: (at the bottom of this window) defaults to **"Adobe PDF Files (*.pdf)"**. Because you want to combine PDFs, the default is fine.

5. You will first select the "Letter1" PDF file you created in Lesson 1 of the Adobe Acrobat Hands-On Exercises. To select the file, *scroll through the list of your PDFs until you find Letter1. Then, click on Letter1 and select Add Files.*

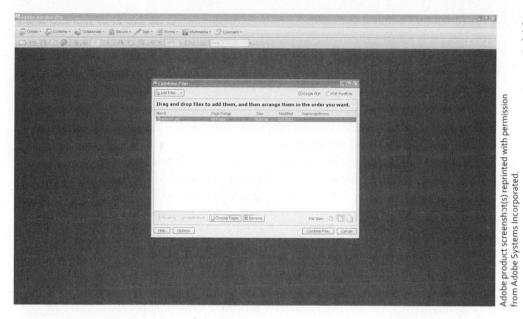

**ADOBE ACROBAT
EXHIBIT 7**
Combining PDFs

HANDS-ON EXERCISES

6. You will notice that "Letter1.pdf" is now listed in the "Combine Files" window (see Adobe Acrobat Exhibit 7). Obviously, you will need more than one file if you are to combine them, so you will now add the PDF you created in Lesson 2, "Paralegal Books." To do so, follow the same procedure listed in Steps 3 and 4 of this exercise.

7. Now "Paralegal Books.pdf" is listed in the "Combine Files" window, under Letter1. If you wanted to change the order of the PDFs, you could change it by first *clicking on one of the files to highlight it and then by clicking on either the Move Up or the Move Down button.* Similarly, you could choose to remove a file (by *clicking Remove*). See Adobe Acrobat Exhibit 7.

8. To create the single PDF, *click on the Combine Files button*. A new, single PDF will be created and a new window, called "Save As," will open. Call this file **Combined PDF 1** and *click Save* (see Adobe Acrobat Exhibit 8).

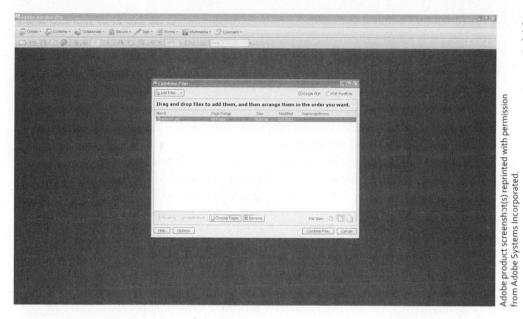

**ADOBE ACROBAT
EXHIBIT 8**
Combining PDFs

9. Your new PDF has been saved.

10. ***Click on File on the menu bar, then on Exit*** to exit Adobe Acrobat Pro 9.

This concludes Lesson 3.

LESSON 4: CREATING A PORTFOLIO

This lesson shows you how to combine separate documents into a PDF Portfolio. This lesson assumes that you have completed Lessons 1 through 3 and that you are generally familiar with Adobe Acrobat.

A PDF Portfolio contains multiple files assembled into a single PDF. The files in a PDF Portfolio can be in different formats and created in different applications. For example, you could have a portfolio that includes text documents, email messages, spreadsheets, digital photographs, and PowerPoint presentations.

In this exercise, you will prepare a Portfolio for a negligence case; it will contain a demand letter (Word), a spreadsheet detailing the injured person's damages (Excel), and a photograph of the damaged vehicle (JPEG).

1. ***Double-click on the Adobe Acrobat Pro 9 icon on the desktop*** to open Adobe Acrobat Pro 9. Alternatively, ***click on the Start button, point the pointer to Programs or All Programs, then click on Adobe Acrobat Pro 9.*** You should be in a new, clean, empty (blank) document.

2. ***On the Adobe Acrobat toolbar, click Combine, the second icon from the left.*** A drop-down menu will appear. ***Click the first menu item, Assemble PDF Portfolio.*** You will notice that the current screen disappears and is replaced by a new screen with the message **"Drag files and folders here to add them"** (see Adobe Acrobat Exhibit 9). (*Note:* You could also do this by first ***clicking on the Create icon and then on the next-to-last item on the drop-down menu, Assemble PDF Portfolio.***)

ADOBE ACROBAT EXHIBIT 9
Creating a PDF portfolio

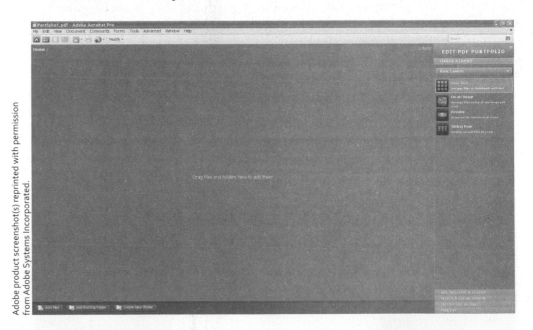

3. You now must open the "Lesson 4" file from the disk supplied with this text. Ensure that the disk is inserted in the disk drive, ***point and click on File on the menu bar, then point and click on Open.*** The "Open" window should now be displayed. ***Point and click on the down arrow to the right of the white box next to "Look in:" and select the drive where the disk is located. Double-click on the Adobe Acrobat folder. Point and double-click on the "Lesson 4" file.***

4. You will now see a list of various documents from different programs, including Word and Excel, as well as a photograph (JPEG).

5. ***Point, click, and drag the Word file from the Lesson 4 file to the Adobe Acrobat screen.*** You will notice that the document is automatically added to the Portfolio. You should also note that the documents have not been converted to the PDF format; rather, they remain Word documents.

6. ***Point, click, and drag the Excel file from the Lesson 4 file to the Adobe Acrobat screen.*** You will notice that the document is automatically added to the Portfolio. You should also note that the documents have not been converted to the PDF format; rather, they remain Excel documents (see Adobe Acrobat Exhibit 10).

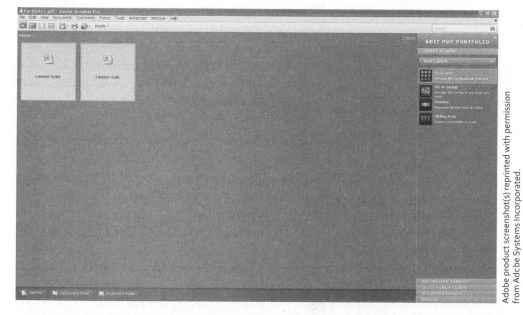

ADOBE ACROBAT EXHIBIT 10
Creating a PDF portfolio

Adobe product screenshot(s) reprinted with permission from Adobe Systems Incorporated.

7. ***Point, click, and drag the car JPEG file from the Lesson 4 file to the Adobe Acrobat screen.*** You will notice that the document is automatically added to the Portfolio. You should also note that the documents have not been converted to the PDF format; rather, they remain JPEGs.

8. You should now have three items in your Portfolio.

9. Alternately, you could also have added these files to the Portfolio by ***clicking Add Files***, which is the first icon on the bottom row of the PDF screen.

10. If you wanted to see a list of the files contained in a Portfolio, you could ***click the second icon on the top toolbar. Click that icon now*** to see a list of the files that have been added to this Portfolio.

11. To return to the original view of the files, ***click the first icon on the top toolbar*** (it looks like a house).

12. To save the portfolio, ***click File, then Save Portfolio As.*** A new window will open called "Save As."

13. In the "File name" box, call this file **Portfolio1**; then ***click OK.***

14. You have successfully created, named, and saved a portfolio.

15. ***Click on File in the menu bar, and then Exit*** to exit Adobe Acrobat Pro 9.

This concludes Lesson 4.

▶ ADVANCED LESSONS

LESSON 5: ADDING SECURITY TO A PDF

This lesson shows you how to use the security features of Adobe Acrobat Pro 9 to enhance the security of a PDF. It is essential that PDFs containing confidential or sensitive information have some degree of security, as they are often created and received by individuals who have not met in person and need to know that their information will be viewed only by persons authorized to do so.

1. ***Double-click on the Adobe Acrobat Pro 9 icon on the desktop*** to open Adobe Acrobat Pro 9. Alternatively, ***click on the Start button, point the pointer to Programs or All Programs, then click on Adobe Acrobat Pro 9.*** You should be in a new, clean, empty (blank) document.

2. Now you need to open the "Lesson 5" file from the disk supplied with this text. Ensure that the disk is inserted in the disk drive, ***point and click on File on the menu bar, then point and click on Open.*** The "Open" window should now be displayed. ***Point and click on the down arrow to the right of the white box next to "Look in:" and select the drive where the disk is located. Double-click on the Adobe Acrobat folder. Point and double-click on the "Lesson 5" file.***

3. You should now have a copy of a demand letter in PDF format.

4. You want to be sure that only authorized persons see this demand letter, so you will enable some of the security features of Adobe Acrobat Pro 9.

5. To do this, ***first point and click on the Secure icon*** (it looks like a padlock). A drop-down menu will appear. ***Click on the fourth menu item, Show Security Properties.***

6. A new window will open, called "Document Properties." Notice that at the top of the window, next to Security Method:, the No Security option appears. Also, notice that at the bottom of the window, under the heading Document Restrictions Summary, all of the options are Allowed (see Adobe Acrobat Exhibit 11).

ADOBE ACROBAT EXHIBIT 11

Adding security to a PDF

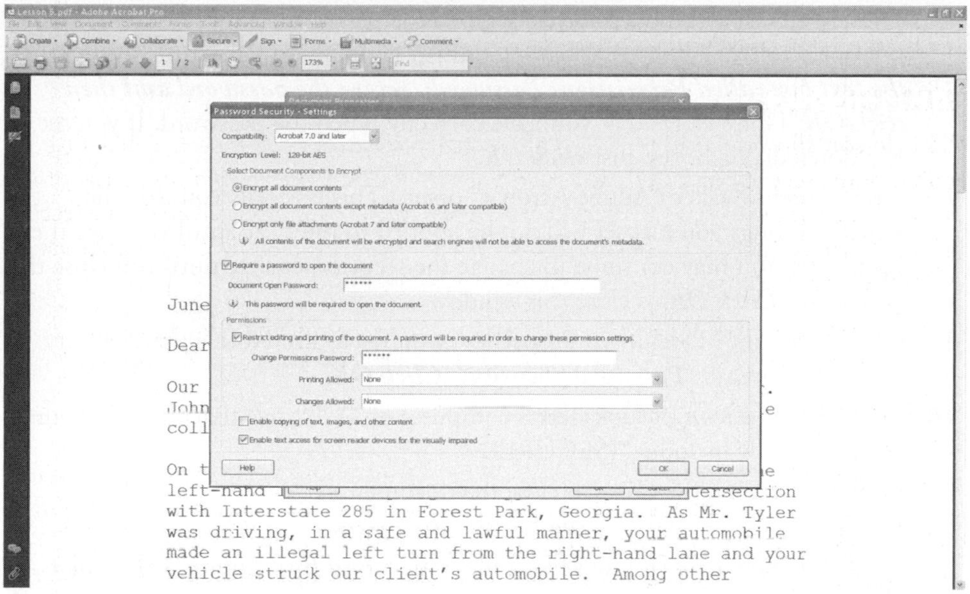

**ADOBE ACROBAT
EXHIBIT 12**
Adding security to a PDF

HANDS-ON EXERCISES

7. ***Click on the drop-down menu next to Security Method: and choose Password Security.*** A new window, called "Password Security – Settings," will open (see Adobe Acrobat Exhibit 12).

8. First, the compatibility setting must be adjusted. This determines what version of Adobe Acrobat a user must have in order to open this PDF. Later versions provide more security than older versions; however, you cannot assume that the user will have the most recent version of Adobe Acrobat. The default setting of Acrobat 7.0 or higher is appropriate, so leave it as is.

9. ***Point and click the box next to "Require a password to open the document."*** Notice that when you do, the text box next to Document Open Password: is no longer shaded (see Adobe Acrobat Exhibit 12).

10. In the text box, type the password **Demand1**. Notice that the password will appear as a series of asterisks. Passwords are case sensitive. Be sure to write down the password so you will be able to find it. If you forget the password, you cannot recover it from the PDF.

11. In addition to restricting access to the document, you can restrict a user's ability to edit and/or print the document. To do so, ***point and click the box next to "Restrict editing and printing of the document. A password will be required in order to change these permission settings."*** Notice that when you do, the text box next to Change Permissions Password: is no longer shaded (see Adobe Acrobat Exhibit 12). Make sure that next to Printing Allowed: and Changes Allowed:, the choice None has been selected.

12. In the text box, type the password **Demand2**. (You cannot use the same password for both restricting access and restricting editing/printing.) Notice that the password appears as a series of asterisks. Passwords are case sensitive. Be sure to write down the password so you will be able to find it. If you forget the password, you cannot recover it from the PDF.

13. After typing the password, ***click OK***. Another window will then open, called "Adobe Acrobat – Confirm Document Open Password." ***Next to the text box called Document Open Password:, retype the password and then click OK.***

This ensures that you have correctly typed the password. Now another window will open, called "Adobe Acrobat – Confirm Permissions Password." ***Next to the text box called Permissions Password:, retype the password and then click OK***. This ensures that you have correctly typed the password. If you see additional dialog boxes, just ***click OK.***

14. A new window called "Adobe Acrobat" opens. This box tells you that the security settings you just set will not be applied to the PDF until you save the document. You may continue to change the security settings until you close the document. ***Click OK*** to close this window.

15. You now see the "Document Properties" window again. Notice that Security Method: now says "**Password Security.**" ***Click OK.***

16. ***Click the Save icon*** (it looks like a computer disk). Notice that the title of the document now includes "(SECURED)."

17. ***Click File, then click Close*** to close the document.

18. Now you will open the same PDF using the security tools you just enabled. ***Click the Open icon*** (it looks like a file folder) ***and find Lesson 5 file, then click OK*** to open it.

19. Notice that when you do so, a new window called "Password" opens. You are required to enter your password to open the PDF. Type your password, **Demand1,** then ***click OK.***

20. Your PDF now appears.

21. ***Click on File in the menu bar, and then on Exit*** to exit Adobe Acrobat Pro 9.

This concludes Lesson 5.

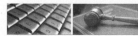

HANDS-ON EXERCISES

HOTDOCS 10

I. INTRODUCTION — READ THIS!

HotDocs lets you transform any PDF or word processor file into an interactive template by marking changeable text with "HotDocs variables." Then the next time you want to generate a completed form or text document, you assemble it from the template you've created.

II. INSTALLATION INSTRUCTIONS

Below are step-by-step instructions for installing HotDocs on your computer. Note that installing this software requires you to restart your system when it is completed.

1. Log in to your CengageBrain.com account.

2. Under "My Courses & Materials," find the Premium Website for Using Computers in the Law Office.

3. *Click "Open" to go to the Premium Website.*

4. *Locate "Book Resources" in the left navigation menu.*

5. *Click on the link for "HotDocs 10."*

6. A screen requesting your contact information and a "Download Code" should now be displayed. You will need to supply the following download code: **k3gh87ht**

7. *Enter the information necessary to complete the form, including the "Download Code", and click "Submit."*

8. You will receive an email response from HotDocs Corporation that will include a link for downloading the HotDocs 10 software. ***Click on the "HotDocs 10 Educational Download" link in the email.*** A web page will open that includes links for both the 32-bit and 64-bit versions of HotDocs.

9. ***Double-click the appropriate file to install HotDocs.*** If you are unsure which version of Windows you have, you can check by ***right-clicking "My Computer", then selecting "Properties."*** Under **System**, you can view the system type. In Windows 7 and Windows Vista, either "32-bit operating system" or "64-bit operating system" will be displayed. In Windows XP, if you don't see "x64 Edition" listed, you're running the 32-bit version of Windows XP. If "x64 Edition" is listed, you're running the 64-bit version of Windows XP. If you are still not sure which version to install, choose the 32-bit version as that is the more common version. If you choose the incorrect version and the program does not load, you can always try the other version.

10. A screen similar to HotDocs Installation Exhibit 1 should now be displayed. ***Click "Run."***

HANDS-ON EXERCISES

**HOTDOCS
INSTALLATION
EXHIBIT 1**

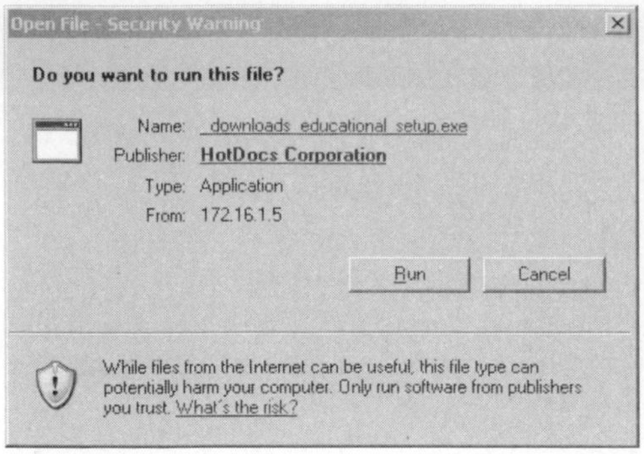

Open File - Security Warning

Do you want to run this file?

Name: _downloads_educational_setup.exe
Publisher: **HotDocs Corporation**
Type: Application
From: 172.16.1.5

[Run]   [Cancel]

⚠ While files from the Internet can be useful, this file type can potentially harm your computer. Only run software from publishers you trust. What's the risk?

11. Another Security Warning window will open, *click "Run."*

12. In the HotDocs Developer 10 Setup window, *click "Next."*

13. In the Software License Agreement window, ***click the button next to "I accept the terms in the license agreement" and click "Next."***

14. The screen in HotDocs Installation Exhibit 2 should now be displayed. ***Click "Next"*** to install the software in the default directory.

15. Choose the word processing programs you would like to use with HotDocs and *click "Next."*

**HOTDOCS
INSTALLATION
EXHIBIT 2**

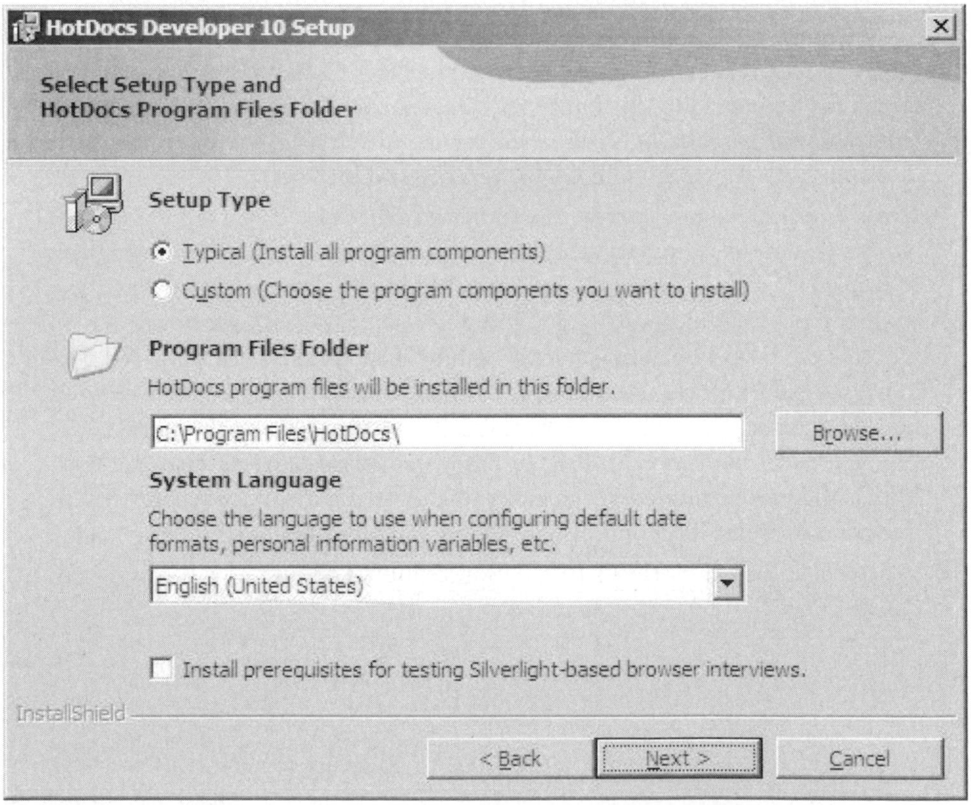

🗗 **HotDocs Developer 10 Setup**

**Select Setup Type and
HotDocs Program Files Folder**

🖥 **Setup Type**

⦿ Typical (Install all program components)

○ Custom (Choose the program components you want to install)

📁 **Program Files Folder**

HotDocs program files will be installed in this folder.

| C:\Program Files\HotDocs\ | [Browse...]

System Language

Choose the language to use when configuring default date formats, personal information variables, etc.

| English (United States) ▾ |

☐ Install prerequisites for testing Silverlight-based browser interviews.

InstallShield

[< Back] [Next >] [Cancel]

16. The screen in HotDocs Installation Exhibit 3 should now be displayed. Confirm the settings listed and *click "Install."*

**HOTDOCS
INSTALLATION
EXHIBIT 3**

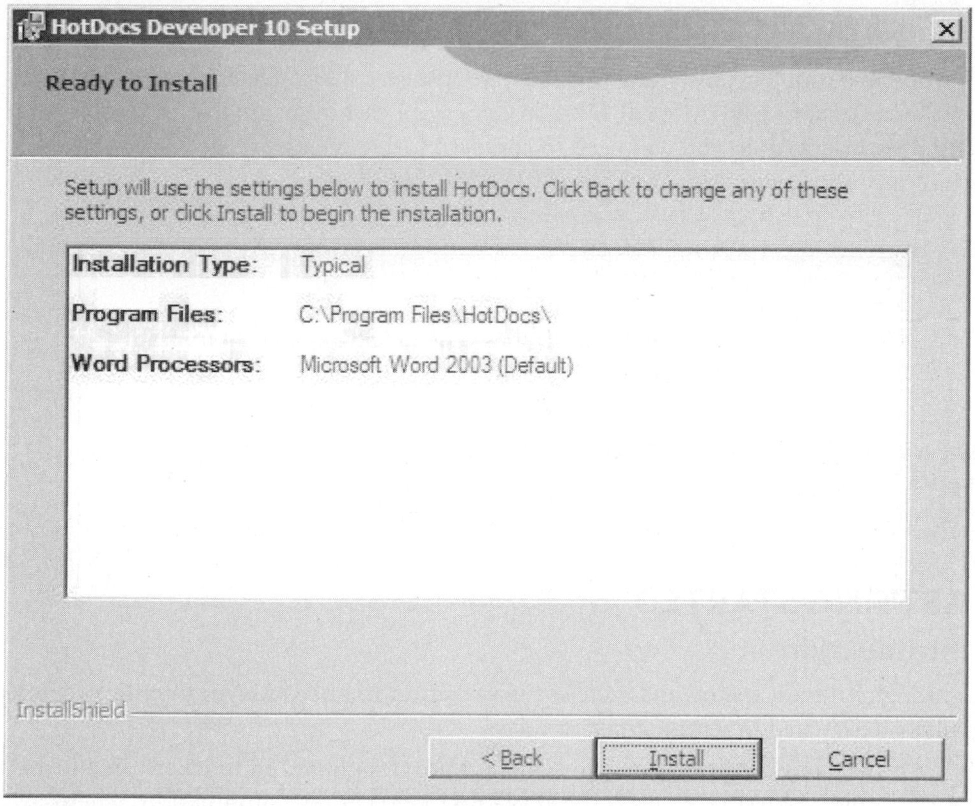

17. The screen in HotDocs Installation Exhibit 4 should now be displayed. *Click "Finish"* to complete the installation.

**HOTDOCS
INSTALLATION
EXHIBIT 4**

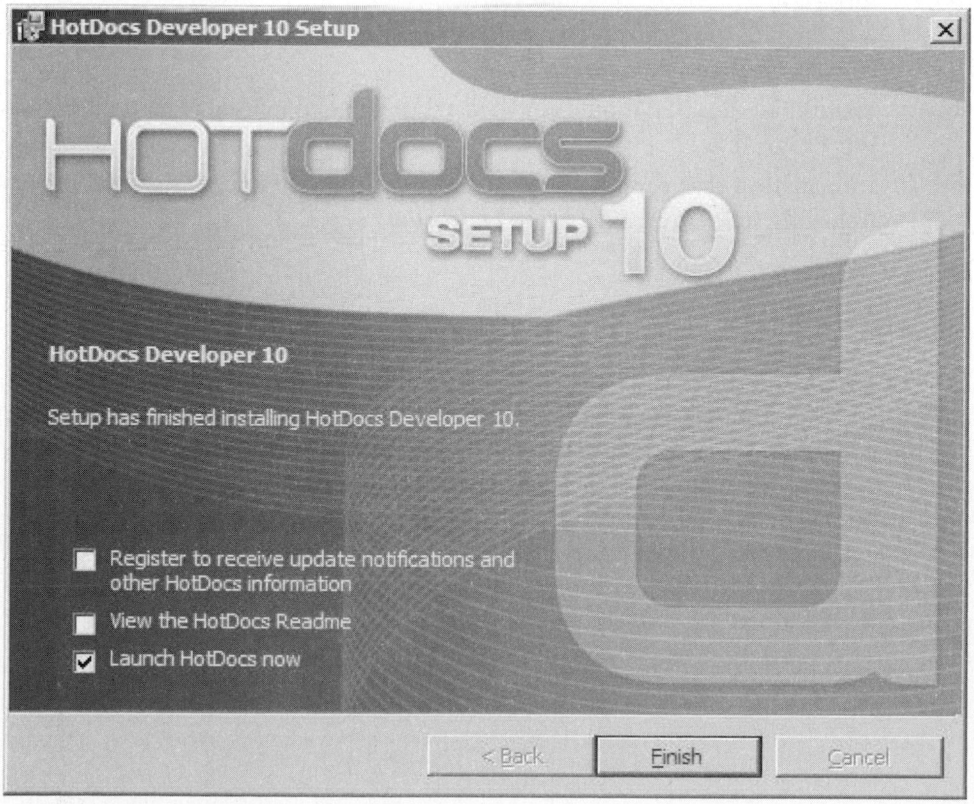

HANDS-ON EXERCISES

18. HotDocs has now been installed. You can open the appropriate module via the *Start Button > All Programs > HotDocs10 > HotDocs Developer* folder.

III. INSTALLATION TECHNICAL SUPPORT

If you have problems installing this software, please contact Delmar Cengage Learning first at (800) 648-7450. If Delmar Cengage Learning is unable to resolve your installation question, you will need to contact HotDocs Ltd. at http://www.hotdocs. com/Support-Home.aspx or phone (801) 615-2200.

Number	Lesson Title	Concepts Covered
BASIC LESSON		
Lesson 1	Creating a Document from a Text Template	Template libraries; assembling a document from an existing template, editing a document, saving and printing
INTERMEDIATE LESSON		
Lesson 2	Creating a New Text Template	Creating a new template library, adding templates to a library, finding a document to convert to a template, creating interview questions

GETTING STARTED
Introduction

Throughout these lessons and exercises, information you need to type into the program will be designated in several different ways:

- Keys to be pressed on the keyboard are designated in brackets, in all caps, and in bold (e.g., press the **[ENTER]** key). A key combination, where two or more keys are pressed at once, is designated with a plus sign between the key names (e.g., **[CTRL]+[BACKSPACE]**). You should not type the plus sign.
- Movements with the mouse are designated in bold and italics (e.g., *point to File on the menu bar and click*).
- Words or letters that should be typed are designated in bold (e.g., type **Training Program**).
- Information that should display on your computer screen is shown in the following style: *Press ENTER to continue.*

OVERVIEW OF HOTDOCS 10

Below are some tips on using HotDocs 10 that will help you complete these exercises.

HotDocs can transform any document into an interactive template that can be changed and adapted to suit the requirements of different cases. This allows you to create a single template for a particular use (e.g., a divorce pleading, articles of incorporation) instead of creating new documents from scratch for each client. This is accomplished by answering a series of questions. In these exercises, you will first complete a prepared text template to assemble a new document. You will then create a new template and assemble a new document from that newly formed text template.

▶ BASIC LESSON

LESSON 1: CREATING A DOCUMENT FROM A TEXT TEMPLATE

This lesson shows you how to assemble a document from a text template. It assumes that you already have a viable text template designed for use with the HotDocs software. (In Lesson 2, you will see how to create a text template from scratch and then assemble a new document using that text template.)

1. Open Windows. *Click on the Start button, point the cursor to Programs or All Programs, then click HotDocs 10, then click HotDocs Developer.* The Demonstration Templates library will appear on your screen (see HotDocs Exhibit 1).

HOTDOCS EXHIBIT 1

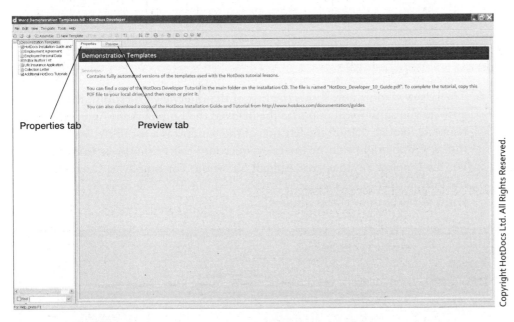

Properties tab   Preview tab

2. In this lesson, you will create an employment agreement using a text template created with HotDocs 10 software. This employment agreement was installed on your computer with the HotDocs 10 software; it is intended as a demonstration template and should not be used for any other purpose.

3. The HotDocs 10 window has two panes. The pane on the left lists the templates contained within the library. Right now, the library contains only the demonstration templates provided with the software. The pane on the right has two tabs; one shows the properties of the selected template and the other shows a preview of the document being assembled.

4. To open the Employment Agreement text template, *click on Employment Agreement File from the list called Demonstration Templates.* A list of Interview topics appears in the left panel. The Employment Agreement template will then appear in the right panel. Click on the Preview tab to see the complete template (see HotDocs Exhibit 2).

5. To begin assembling the employment agreement, *click the Assemble icon on the HotDocs toolbar* (it looks like a green arrow). Two new windows open. The larger of the two is the Interview. The smaller of the two is called Answer File. As this file does not yet contain any information, the Answer File dialog box shows an untitled answer file. *Click OK.*

HOTDOCS EXHIBIT 2

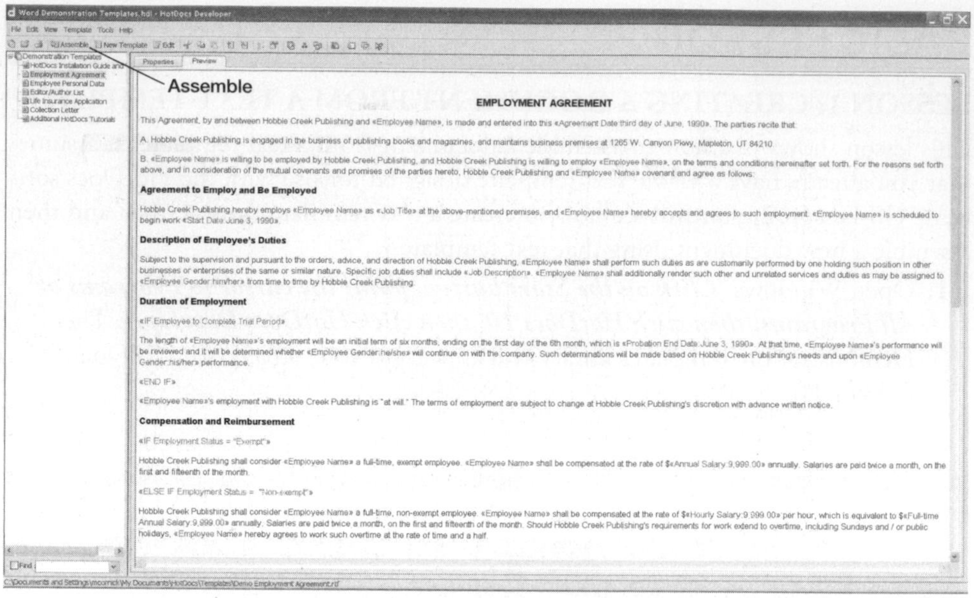

6. The larger window now shows the first of the Interview Questions; the answers you supply will populate the fields of the Employment Agreement text template. Notice that on the left side of the window is a list of the interview topics. On the right side are interview questions called Employee Information. For the Employee Name, type **Abigail Shannon**. For Employee Gender, *click the button next to Female* (see HotDocs Exhibit 3). *Click Next* (one blue arrow at the bottom of the window).

HOTDOCS EXHIBIT 3

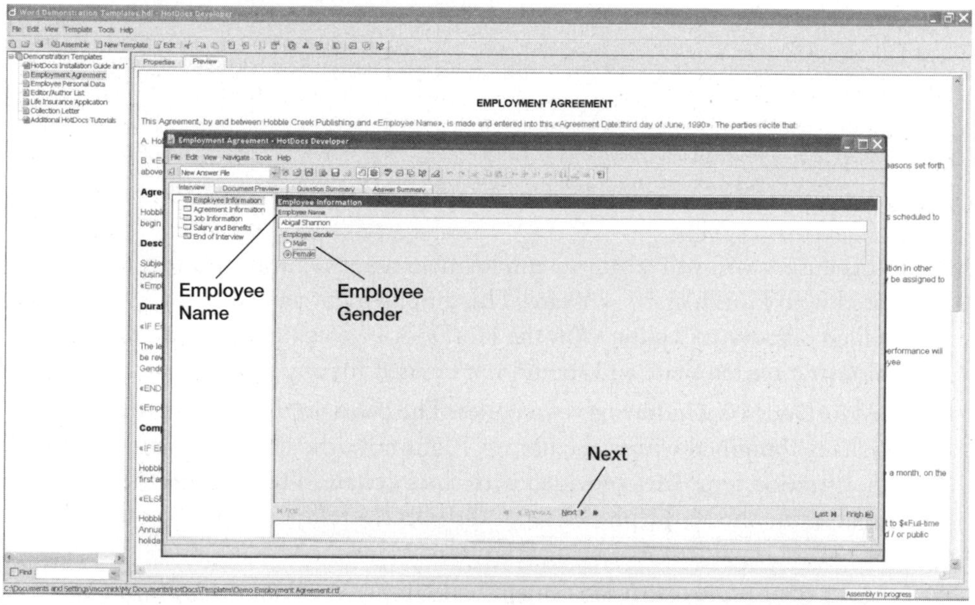

7. The next screen has the interview questions regarding the Agreement Information. Under Agreement Date, type **April 29, 2012**. Under Company Representative, *click the button for Stephanie Hanson*; notice that when you do this, the Agreement Date becomes "29 Apr 2012." Leave the Signature Date blank. *Click Next.*

8. The next screen has the interview questions regarding the Job Information. Under Job Title, type **Creative Director**. Under Complete the following sentence: Job duties shall include, type **Oversee advertising and marketing initiatives; manage staff members; prepare budgets.** Under Start Date,

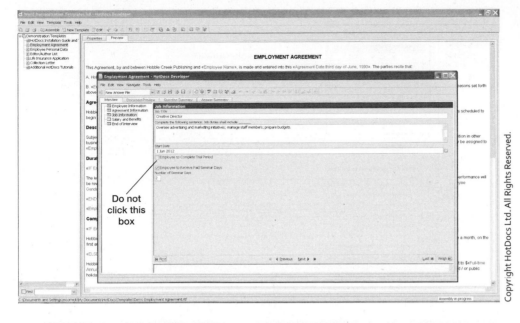

type June 1, 2012. ***Do not click the box next to Employee to Complete Trial Period. Do click the box next to Employee to Receive Paid Seminar Days.*** When you do this, the Number of Seminar Days box is no longer shaded. Type **2** in that box (see HotDocs Exhibit 4). ***Click Next.***

9. The next screen has interview questions regarding Salary and Benefits. ***Under Employment Status, click the button next to Exempt.*** Notice that now a new text box appears called "Annual Salary." (If you had clicked the "Non-exempt" or "Part-time" boxes, the text box would be titled "Hourly Salary.") Under Annual Salary, type **62,500**. Under Number of Vacation Days, type **10**.

10. Notice that there are four tabs: Interview, the window you have been viewing; Document Preview, which provides a preview of the assembled document at any point during the assembly process; Question Summary, which lists the specific questions contained within the interview; and Answer Summary, which lists the answers you provided to the specific questions.

11. You can edit any of the answers by viewing the Document Preview tab. When you edit an answer, HotDocs automatically edits all questions affected by that answer. ***Click the Document Preview tab. Point the cursor to any reference to Abigail Shannon*** (highlighted in blue). ***Right click the mouse and click on Edit Answer.*** This will open a dialog box called Employee Information (see HotDocs Exhibit 5). Type the initial **E.** to make the name "Abigail E. Shannon." ***Click Next at the bottom of the dialog box.*** Notice that every reference to the employee now reads "Abigail E. Shannon."

12. ***Click the Interview tab again. Click Next.*** The next screen is End of Interview. If you failed to answer any questions, you would be prompted to click a button that would take you back to missed question(s). Because we answered all of the questions, we are given the option of sending the assembled document to Microsoft Word. ***Click the first option*** (it looks like a blue arrow), ***then click the box next to Close this window. Click Finish.***

13. Two new windows will open. One is a small dialog box asking if you want to save the answers to this template. It is not necessary to save these answers, so ***click Don't Save.*** You are then asked if you want to save a copy of the assembled document. ***You may click Don't Save.*** The second window is a Word copy of the assembled employment agreement. At this point, the employment agreement document is no longer associated with HotDocs. It is

HOTDOCS EXHIBIT 5

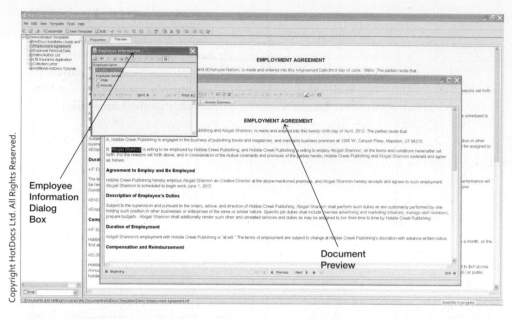

Employee Information Dialog Box

Document Preview

HOTDOCS EXHIBIT 6

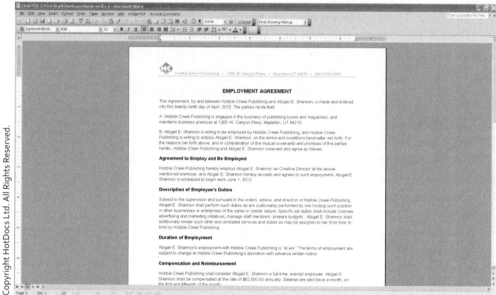

an independent Word document that can be edited, saved, and printed as such (see HotDocs Exhibit 6).

14. On the Employment Agreement Word file, ***click File, then Save As***. Next to File name, type **Shannon Agreement**. ***Click on Save*** to save the document. ***Then click the X at the top right corner of the screen*** to close the file.

This concludes Lesson 1.

▶ INTERMEDIATE LESSON

LESSON 2: CREATING A NEW TEXT TEMPLATE

This lesson will show you how to create a new text template using the HotDocs 10 software. This lesson assumes that you have completed Lesson 1 and that you are familiar with HotDocs 10.

1. Start Windows. ***Click on the Start button, point the cursor to Programs or All Programs, then click HotDocs 10, then click HotDocs Developer.*** The Demonstration Templates library will appear on your screen.

2. ***Click File, then New Library.*** The New Library dialog box will appear. Under File name, type **My Training Templates**, ***then click the [TAB] key twice.*** HotDocs has entered the .hdl suffix to the file name; the program requires this suffix to properly identify the file. Under Title, the program has automatically filled in the title "My Training Templates." This is fine. In the Description box, type **This is the template I created in my Computers in the Law Office class.** Then ***click OK.*** A new library has been created.

3. Your new library is empty; you need to add a template to it.

4. ***Click on the My Training Templates folder.***

5. ***Click the New Template icon*** (it looks like a rectangle with a star in the upper left corner). The New Template dialog box will open. ***Next to Type, select Word RTF Template (.rtf);*** this is the appropriate choice for Word users. Under File name, type **Complaint—Breach of Contract**, then ***click [TAB] key twice.*** Notice that HotDocs has added the suffix .rtf to the file name. ***Click on the text box under Title*** and you will see that HotDocs has suggested the title "Complaint—Breach of Contract." This is fine. Under Description, type **This is the template I created for my Computers in the Law Office class.** (See HotDocs Exhibit 7.)

HOTDOCS EXHIBIT 7

New Template

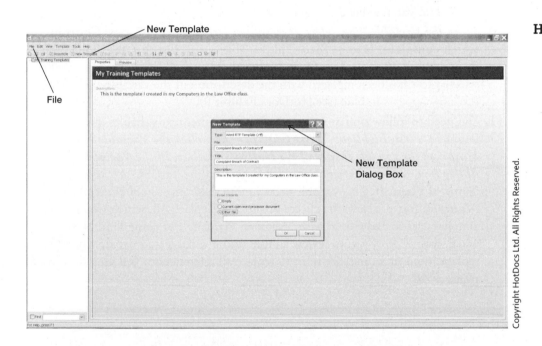

File

New Template
Dialog Box

6. ***Under Initial contents, click the last button, called Other file, then click the Browse button to the right of the text box.***

7. This opens a new window (New Template Initial Contents), which will enable you to choose the text file you will convert to a text template. ***Click "Look in:" and then choose the CD drive for your computer. Click on HotDocs, then click Lesson 2, then click on OK*** to return to the New Template dialog box. The document's folder path and file name now appear in the Other file text box.

8. ***Click OK.*** This creates the new template file and adds it to your library. It also opens the template as a Word document—but notice that a new HotDocs toolbar has been added (see HotDocs Exhibit 8). You will now begin selecting the text fields in this document that are to serve as variables.

9. ***Highlight the text "IN THE SUPERIOR COURT OF FULTON COUNTY" at the top of the page, then click the Variable Field button on the HotDocs***

HOTDOCS EXHIBIT 8

toolbar. It is the first icon on the left side of the toolbar and looks like this: <<>>. The Variable Field dialog box will open.

10. *From the Variable type, select Text.* In the Variable text box, type **Court in which complaint is to be filed**. This variable occurs just this one time in the document, so *click Replace Once.* Notice that the template now shows that the selected text has been replaced with the description of the variable and that the text now appears in blue (see HotDocs Exhibit 9).

11. You need to follow similar steps to replace the other text variables in the template. *First, highlight "TED GOULD" and click the Variable Field button at the top left corner of the HotDocs toolbar. In the Variable Field dialog box, choose Text as the Variable type.* In the Variable text box, type **Name of Plaintiff**. This variable occurs more than once, so *click Replace Multiple.* You also have the choice of clicking Replace All, which would replace all references to Ted Gould with "Name of Plaintiff"; or using Find Next, which would allow you to review all uses of the variable and decide when to replace it one at a time. We want to replace all references to Ted Gould, so *click Replace All*.

HOTDOCS EXHIBIT 9

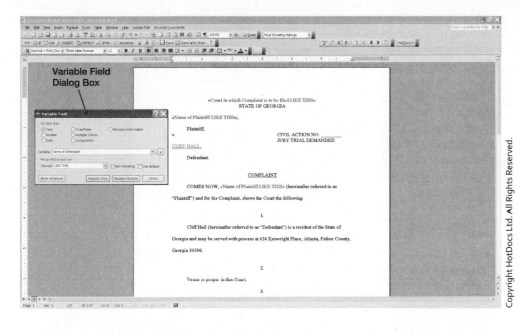

12. Now you will do the same for the defendant. ***Highlight "CLIFF HALL" and click the Variable Field button at the top left corner of the HotDocs toolbar. In the Variable Field dialog box, choose Text as the Variable type.*** In the Variable text box, type **Name of Defendant**. (See HotDocs Exhibit 10.) This variable occurs more than once, so ***click Replace Multiple. Then click Replace All.***

13. Next, ***highlight the Defendant's address and click the Variable Field button at the top left corner of the HotDocs toolbar. In the Variable Field dialog box, choose Text as the Variable type.*** In the Variable text box, type **Defendant's address**. This variable occurs just once, so ***click Replace Once***.

14. Next, ***highlight "January 1, 2012" and click the Variable Field button at the top left corner of the HotDocs toolbar. In the Variable Field dialog box, choose Date as the Variable type.*** In the Variable text box, type **Date contract was created**. This variable occurs just once, so ***click Replace Once***.

15. Now ***highlight "Ten Thousand Dollars" and click the Variable Field button at the top left corner of the HotDocs toolbar. In the Variable Field dialog box, choose Text as the Variable type.*** In the Variable text box, type **Dollar amount of contract**. This variable occurs more than once, so ***click Replace Multiple, then click Replace All.***

16. Next, ***highlight "June 30, 2012" and click the Variable Field button at the top left corner of the HotDocs toolbar. In the Variable Field dialog box, choose Date as the Variable type.*** In the Variable text box, type **Date money was to be repaid**. This variable occurs just once, so ***click Replace Once***.

17. Next, ***highlight the number "10" in paragraph 3 and click the Variable Field button at the top left corner of the HotDocs toolbar. In the Variable Field dialog box, choose Number as the Variable type.*** In the Variable text box, type **Interest rate of loan**. This variable occurs more than once, so ***click Replace Multiple, then click Replace All.*** (See HotDocs Exhibit 11.)

18. The last variables to be replaced are the pronouns used to refer to the parties in the third person. You need to be sure the complaint does not state "he" when you mean "she." To do this, first ***highlight the word "his" in paragraph 5 and click the Variable Field button at the top left corner of the HotDocs toolbar. In the Variable Field dialog box, select Multiple Choice as the Variable type.*** Then type **Party gender in the Variable text box. *Click the Edit Component icon,*** which is located at the far right of the text box where you just typed "Party gender." This opens the Multiple Choice Variable Editor window.

HOTDOCS EXHIBIT 11

19. Type **Male** in the first row of the Option column and **Female** in the second row. ***Click Default Merge Text;*** a drop-down menu of pronouns appears. ***Select "his/her."*** The pronoun "his" appears in the first row and "her" appears in the second row. (See HotDocs Exhibit 12.) ***Then click OK*** to return to the Variable Field dialog box.

HOTDOCS EXHIBIT 12

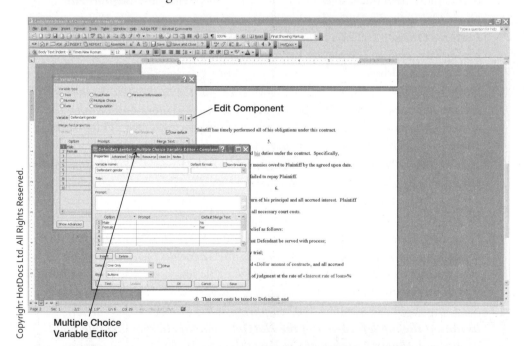

Edit Component

Multiple Choice Variable Editor

20. ***Be sure the Use default box is un-checked***. This will allow you to use the Merge Text column. ***Click Replace Multiple;*** the Find and Replace dialog box appears.

21. ***Select "Find whole words only";*** this will ensure that you only replace the exact word selected (*his*) and not words that contain "his" as part of the word. ***Click Replace All.***

22. ***Click Save and Close on the HotDocs toolbar.***

This concludes Lesson 2.

CHAPTER 3

Spreadsheet Software

FEATURED SOFTWARE

Excel 2007
Excel 2003

SPREADSHEET HANDS-ON EXERCISES

▶ *READ THIS FIRST!*

1. Microsoft Excel 2007
2. Microsoft Excel 2003

I. DETERMINING WHICH TUTORIAL TO COMPLETE

To use the spreadsheet Hands-On Exercises, you must already own or have access to Microsoft Excel 2007 or Excel 2003. If you have one of these programs but do not know which version you are using, it is easy to find out.

1. For Excel 2003, load the program and point to the Help menu, then click About Microsoft Office Excel. It should tell you what version of the program you are using.
2. For Excel 2007, click the Office button, then click Excel Options > Resources; it will tell you what version you are using.

You must know the version of the program you are using and select the correct tutorial version, or the tutorials will not work correctly.

II. USING THE SPREADSHEET HANDS-ON EXERCISES

The spreadsheet Hands-On Exercises in this section are easy to use and contain step-by-step instructions. They start with basic spreadsheet skills and proceed to intermediate and advanced levels. If you already have a good working knowledge of Excel, you may be able to proceed directly to the intermediate and advanced exercises. To be truly ready to use spreadsheets in the legal environment, you must be able to accomplish the tasks and exercises in the advanced lessons.

III. ACCESSING THE DATA FILES ON THE DISK THAT COMES WITH THE TEXT

Some of the intermediate and advanced Excel Hands-On Exercises use documents on the disk that comes with the text.

To access these files in Windows XP, put the disk in your computer, select Start, then My Computer; then select the appropriate drive, double-click on that drive, then double-click on the Excel folder. You should then see a list of the Excel files that are available.

IV. INSTALLATION QUESTIONS

If you have questions regarding installation or loading of the Excel data from the disk included with the text, you may contact Technical Support at 800-648-7450.

Number	Lesson Title	Concepts Covered
BASIC LESSONS		
Lesson 1	Building a Budget Spreadsheet, Part 1	[CTRL]+[HOME] command, moving the pointer, entering text and values, adjusting the width of columns, changing the format of a group of cells to currency, using bold, centering text, entering formulas, using the AutoFill/Copy command to copy formulas, printing and saving a spreadsheet
Lesson 2	Building a Budget Spreadsheet, Part 2	Opening a file, inserting rows, changing the format of cells to percent, building more formulas, creating a bar chart with the Chart Wizard, printing a selection, fitting/compressing data to one printed page
Lesson 3	Building a Damage Projection Spreadsheet	Changing font size, font color, using the AutoSum feature, using the wrap text feature, creating borders, setting decimal points when formatting numbers
INTERMEDIATE LESSONS		
Lesson 4	Child Support Payment Spreadsheet	Creating a white background, creating formulas that multiply cells, creating formulas that use absolute cell references, using the AutoFormat feature
Lesson 5	Loan Amortization Template	Using a template, protecting cells, freezing panes, splitting a screen, hiding columns, using Format Painter
Lesson 6	Statistical Functions	Using functions including average, maximum, minimum, and standard deviation; sorting data; checking for metadata; using the Format Clear command; using conditional formatting; inserting a picture
ADVANCED LESSONS		
Lesson 7	Tools and Techniques 1—Marketing Budget	Creating and manipulating a text box, advanced shading techniques, working with a 3-D style text box, creating vertical and diagonal text, creating a cell comment, using lines and borders
Lesson 8	Tools and Techniques 2—Stock Portfolio	Using the Merge and Center tool, using the Formula Auditing feature, using the oval tool, password-protecting a file

GETTING STARTED

Overview

Microsoft Excel 2007 is a powerful spreadsheet program that allows you to create formulas, "what if" scenarios, graphs, and much more.

Introduction

Throughout these lessons and exercises, information you need to operate the program will be designated in several different ways:

- Keys to be pressed on the keyboard are designated in brackets, in all caps, and in bold (e.g., press the **[ENTER]** key).

- Movements with the mouse pointer are designated in bold and italics (e.g., *point to File and click*).

- Words or letters that should be typed are designated in bold (e.g., type **Training Program**).

- Information that is or should be displayed on your computer screen is shown in bold, with quotation marks (e.g., "**Press ENTER to continue.**").

- Specific menu items and commands are designated with an initial capital letter (e.g., click Open).

OVERVIEW OF EXCEL 2007

I. Worksheet

A. *Entering Commands: The Ribbon*—The primary way of entering commands in Excel 2007 is through the ribbon. The ribbon is a set of commands or tools that change depending on which ribbon is selected (see Excel 2007 Exhibit 1). There are seven ribbon tabs: Home, Insert, Page Layout, Formulas, Data, Review, and View (see Excel 2007 Exhibit 1). Each tab has groups of commands. For example, on the Home tab, the Font group contains a group of commands

EXCEL 2007 EXHIBIT 1
Excel 2007 interface

that relate to font choice, font size, bold, italics, underlining, and other attributes (see Excel 2007 Exhibit 1).

B. *Office Button*—The Office button (see Excel 2007 Exhibit 1) is where a user accesses commands such as New, Open, Save, and Print. The Office button replaces the File menu in previous versions of Excel.

C. *Entering Data*—To enter data, type the text or number in a cell, then press the **[ENTER]** key or one of the arrow (cursor) keys.

D. *Ranges*—A *range* is a group of contiguous cells. Cell ranges can be created by ***clicking and dragging the pointer*** or holding the **[SHIFT]** key down and using the arrow (cursor) keys.

E. *Format*—Cells can be formatted, including changing the font style, font size, shading, border, cell type (currency, percentage, etc.), alignment, and other attributes. To do this, ***click the Home ribbon tab, then clicking one of the Dialog Box Launchers in the Font group, Alignment group, or Number group.*** Each of these dialog box launchers brings up the same "Format Cells" window. You can also enter a number of formatting options directly from the Home tab.

F. *Editing a Cell*—You can edit a cell by ***clicking in the cell and then clicking in the formula bar.*** The formula bar is directly under the ribbon and just to the right of the **fx** sign (see Excel 2007 Exhibit 1). The formula bar shows the current contents of the selected cell, and it allows you to edit the cell contents. You can also edit the contents of a cell by ***clicking in the cell*** and then pressing the **[F2]** key.

G. *Column Width/Row Height*—You can change the width of a column by ***clicking the line to the right of the column heading.*** (This is the line that separates two columns. When you point to a line, the cursor changes to a double-headed vertical arrow.) ***Drag the pointer to the right or left to increase or decrease the column width, respectively.*** Similarly, you can change the height of a row by ***clicking and dragging the horizontal line separating two rows.*** You can also change the width of a column or height of a row by ***clicking somewhere in the column you want to change, clicking the Home tab, then clicking Format in the Cells group.***

H. *Insert*—You can insert one row or column by ***clicking the Home tab, then clicking the down arrow below the Insert icon in the Cells group, and clicking either Insert Sheet Rows or Insert Sheet Columns.*** You can also insert a number of rows or columns by ***dragging the pointer over the number of rows or columns you want to add, clicking the Home tab, clicking the down arrow below the Insert icon in the Cells group, and then clicking either Insert Sheet Rows or Insert Sheet Columns.*** Finally, you can ***right-click and select Insert from the menu.***

I. *Erase/Delete*—You can erase data by ***dragging the pointer over the area*** and then pressing the **[DEL]** key. You can also erase data by ***dragging the pointer over the area, clicking the Home ribbon tab, clicking the down arrow next to the Clear icon in the Editing group, and then clicking Clear All.*** You can delete whole columns or rows by ***pointing and clicking in a column or row, then clicking on the Home ribbon tab, clicking on the down arrow next to Delete in the Cells group, and then clicking either Delete Sheet Rows or Delete Sheet Columns.*** You can also delete whole columns or rows by ***pointing in the column or row and then right-clicking and selecting Delete.***

J. *Quit*—To quit Excel, ***click on the Office button and then click Exit Excel.***

K. *Copy*—To copy data to adjacent columns or rows, ***click in the cell you wish to copy and then select the AutoFill command,*** which is accessed from the small black box at the bottom right corner of the selected cell. ***Drag the pointer to where the data should be placed.*** You can also copy data by ***clicking in the cell, right-clicking, clicking Copy, clicking in the location where the information should be copied,*** and pressing the [**ENTER**] key. Finally, data can be copied by ***clicking and dragging to highlight the information to be copied, clicking the Home tab, then clicking Copy in the Clipboard group.***

L. *Move*—Move data by ***clicking in the cell, right-clicking, selecting Cut, clicking in the location where the information should be inserted,*** and pressing the [**ENTER**] key. Data can also be moved by ***highlighting the information to be copied, clicking the Home tab, then clicking Cut in the Clipboard group.*** Then go to the location where the information should be moved, ***click the Home tab, then click Paste in the Clipboard group.***

M. *Saving and Opening Files*—Save a file by ***clicking the Office button, then clicking Save or Save As,*** and typing the file name. You can also save a file by ***clicking the Save icon*** (it looks like a floppy disk) on the Quick Access toolbar (see Excel 2007 Exhibit 1). Open a file that was previously saved by ***clicking the Office button, clicking Open,*** and typing (or clicking) the name of the file to be opened.

N. *Print*—You can print a file by ***clicking the Office button, then Print, then OK.***

II. Numbers and Formulas

A. *Numbers*—To enter a number in a cell, click in the cell, type the number, and press the [**ENTER**] key or an arrow (cursor) key.

B. *Adding Cells (Addition)*—You can add the contents of two or more cells by three different methods:

1. To add the contents of a range of two or more cells:

    a. Click in the cell where the total should be placed.

    b. ***Click the Home tab, then click the Sum icon in the Editing group*** (see Excel 2007 Exhibit 2). The Sum icon looks like a Greek letter "E." *Note*: To see the name of an icon, point to the icon for a second and the name of the icon will be displayed.

    c. Excel guesses which cells you want to add. Press [**ENTER**] if the correct range has been automatically selected, or select the correct range by highlighting it (i.e., ***click and drag until the range of cells to be added is selected***). Then press [**ENTER**].

2. To add the contents of two cells, which need not comprise a range:

    a. Click in the cell where the total should be placed.

    b. Press = (the equals sign).

    c. Type the address of the first cell to be added (e.g., B4); alternatively, ***click in that cell***.

    d. Press + (the plus sign).

    e. Enter the address of the second cell to be added (or ***click in that cell***).

    f. Press the [**ENTER**] key. (For example, to add the values of cells C4 and C5, you would type **=C4+C5**.)

HANDS-ON EXERCISES

EXCEL 2007 EXHIBIT 2
Budgeting spreadsheet

3. To add the contents of a range of two or more cells:

   a. Click in the cell where the total should be placed.

   b. Type **=SUM(**.

   c. Enter the address of the first cell to be added (or *click in it*).

   d. Type **:** (a colon).

   e. Enter the address of the second cell to be added (or *click in it*).

   f. Type **)** (a closing parenthesis).

   g. Press the **[ENTER]** key. (For example, to add the values of C4 and C5, the formula would read **=SUM(C4:C5)**.)

C. *Subtracting Cells*—To subtract the contents of one or more cells from those of another:

   1. Click in the cell where the result should be placed.

   2. Press **=**.

   3. Enter the first cell address (or *click in it*).

   4. Press **–** (a minus sign).

   5. Enter the second cell address (or *click in it*).

   6. Press the **[ENTER]** key. (For example, to subtract the value of C4 from the value of C5, you would type **=C5–C4**.)

D. *Multiplying Cells*—To multiply the contents of two (or more) cells:

   1. Click in the cell where the result should be placed.

   2. Press **=**.

   3. Enter the first cell address (or *click in it*).

   4. Press ***** (**[SHIFT]+[8]**).

   5. Enter the second cell address (or *click in it*).

   6. Press the **[ENTER]** key. (For example, to multiply the value in C4 times the value in C5, you would type **=C5*C4**.)

E. *Dividing Cells*—To divide the contents of two (or more) cells:

1. Click in the cell where the result should be placed.

2. Press =.

3. Enter the first cell address (or *click in it*).

4. Press / (the forward slash).

5. Enter the second cell address (or *click in it*).

6. Press the **[ENTER]** key. (For example, to divide the value in C4 by the value in C5, you would type =**C4/C5**.)

▶ BASIC LESSONS

LESSON 1: BUILDING A BUDGET SPREADSHEET, PART 1

This lesson shows you how to build the spreadsheet in Excel 2007 Exhibit 2. It explains how to use the [CTRL]+[HOME] command; move the cell pointer; enter text, values, and formulas; adjust the width of columns; change the format of cells to currency; use the bold feature, use the AutoFill and Copy features to copy formulas; and print and save a spreadsheet. Keep in mind that if you make a mistake at any time in this lesson, you may press **[CTRL]+[Z]** to undo what you have done.

1. Open Windows. After it has loaded, *double-click the Microsoft Office Excel 2007 icon on the desktop* to open the program. Alternatively, *click the Start button, point to Programs or All Programs, point to Microsoft Office, then click Microsoft Office Excel 2007.* You should be in a new, clean, blank workbook. If you are not in a blank workbook, *click the Office button* (see Excel 2007 Exhibit 1), *click on New, then double-click Blank Workbook.*

2. Notice that the pointer is at cell A1, and the indicator that displays the address of the current cell (called the "name" box in Excel) says A1. The "name" box is just under the ribbon and all the way to the left (see Excel 2007 Exhibit 2). Also, notice that you can move the pointer around the spreadsheet using the cursor keys. Go back to cell A1 by pressing the **[CTRL]+[HOME]** keys.

3. Go to cell C3 by *clicking in cell C3* or by pressing the **[RIGHT ARROW]** key twice, then pressing the **[DOWN ARROW]** key twice.

4. You will now enter the title of the spreadsheet in cell C3. Type **BUDGET** and then press the **[ENTER]** key.

5. Notice that the pointer is now at cell C4.

6. Press the **[UP ARROW]** key to go back to cell C3. Notice that BUDGET is left aligned. To center **BUDGET** in the cell, *from the Home tab, click the Center icon in the Alignment group.* It is the icon with several lines on it that appear centered (see Excel 2007 Exhibit 3). *Note*: If you hover the mouse over icons on the ribbon for a second, the name of the icon will be displayed. Alternatively, *from the Home tab, click the Alignment Group dialog box launcher. On the Alignment tab, under the Horizontal field, click the down arrow and select Center. Click OK.*

7. You should now be ready to enter the budget information. First, move the cell pointer to where the data should go, then type the data, and finally enter the

EXCEL 2007 EXHIBIT 3
Expanded budget
spreadsheet

data by pressing the **[ENTER]** key or one of the arrow (cursor) keys. Type the remaining row labels as follows:

Item in B4.

EXPENSES in B6.

Utilities in B7.

Equipment Rental in B8.

Rent in B9.

Marketing in B10.

Salaries in B11.

Office Supplies in B12.

TOTAL EXPENSES in B13.

INCOME in B15.

Fees in B16.

Retainers in B17.

TOTAL INCOME in B18.

PROFIT/LOSS in B20.

8. Notice in column B that some of the data entries (such as "EXPENSES" and "Equipment Rental") actually extend into column C. To correct this, you must increase the width of column B. *Put the mouse pointer in the cell lettered B at the top of the screen. Move the pointer to the right edge of the cell.* The pointer should then change to a double-headed vertical arrow and the column width will be displayed in a small box. *Drag the pointer to the right until the column width is 18.00.* Alternatively, you can change the cell width by *placing the cell pointer anywhere in column B. Then, from the Home tab, click Format in the Cells group, then click Column Width. . .,* type **18**, and *click OK.*

9. Notice that all of the data entries now fit in the columns. Enter the following:
Jan in C4.

Budget in C5.
Jan in D4.
Actual in D5.

10. *Click in cell C4 and drag the pointer over to cell D5* (so that the whole cell range is highlighted); *then, from the Home tab, click the Center icon in the Alignment group.*

11. You are now ready to enter values into your spreadsheet.

12. *Move the pointer to cell C7.* Type **1000.** Do not type a dollar sign or comma; these will be added later. Press the **[ENTER]** key to enter the value.

13. Enter the following:
    500 in C8.
    1500 in C9.
    200 in C10.
    10000 in C11.
    750 in C12.
    18000 in C16.
    5000 in C17.
    900 in D7.
    600 in D8.
    1500 in D9.
    200 in D10.
    9750 in D11.
    875 in D12.
    19500 in D16.
    4000 in D17.

14. The values you entered do not have dollar signs or the commas appropriate to a currency format. You will now learn how to format a range of cells for a particular format (such as the Currency format).

15. *Click in cell C7 and drag the pointer over to cell D20. From the Home tab, click the down arrow next to the "Number Format" box, which should say "General." Click Currency. Then click OK.* Notice that dollar signs have been added to all of the values. *Click in any cell to deselect the cell range.*

16. *Click in cell B13 and drag the pointer over to cell D13. Then, from the Home tab, click the Bold icon in the Font group.* This will make the TOTAL EXPENSES row appear in bold.

17. *Click in cell B18 and drag the pointer over to cell D18. Then, from the Home tab, click the Bold icon in the Font group.* This will make the TOTAL INCOME row appear in bold.

18. *Click in cell B20 and drag the pointer over to cell D20. Then, from the Home tab, click on the Bold icon in the Font group.* This will make the PROFIT/LOSS row appear in bold.

19. Your spreadsheet is nearly complete; all you need to add are the six formulas.

20. *Click in cell C13.*

21. Type **=SUM(** and press the **[UP ARROW]** key six times until the cell pointer is at cell C7. Press **.** (a period) to anchor the range.

22. Press the **[DOWN ARROW]** key five times, then press **)** (a closing parenthesis). Press the **[ENTER]** key.

23. Go back to cell C13 and look at the formula in the formula bar. The formula should read "**=SUM(C7:C12)**". The total displayed in the cell

should read $13,950.00. Note that you also could have typed the formula **=C7+C8+C9+C10+C11+C12.**

24. Enter the following formulas:
    =SUM(D7:D12) in D13.
    =SUM(C16:C17) in C18.
    =SUM(D16:D17) in D18.

25. You now need to enter formulas for the PROFIT/LOSS columns. In C20, enter **=C18–C13** (the total should read $9,050.00).

26. *Go to cell C20 and click the AutoFill command* (it is the small black square at the bottom right of the cell). *Drag it one column to the right and release the mouse button.* Notice that the formula has been copied. The total should be $9,675.00. Alternatively, *go to cell C20, right-click, click Copy, move the pointer to cell D20,* and press the **[ENTER]** key.

27. The spreadsheet is now complete. To print the spreadsheet, *click the Office button, then click Print, then click OK.*

28. You will need to save the spreadsheet, because you will use it in Lesson 2. To save the spreadsheet, *click the Office button and then click Save. Under Save in:, select the drive or folder in which you would like to save the document.* Next to File name:, type **Budget1** and *click Save.*

29. To exit Excel, *click the Office button and then click on Exit Excel.*

This concludes Lesson 1.

LESSON 2: BUILDING A BUDGET SPREADSHEET, PART 2

This lesson assumes that you have completed Lesson 1, have saved the spreadsheet from that lesson, and are generally familiar with the concepts covered in that lesson. Lesson 2 gives you experience in opening a file, inserting a row, formatting numbers as percentages, building additional formulas, creating a bar chart, printing selections, and fitting and compressing data onto one printed page. If you did not exit Excel after Lesson 1, skip Steps 1 and 2 in this lesson and go directly to Step 3.

1. Open Windows. *Double-click on the Microsoft Office Excel 2007 icon on the desktop* to open the program. Alternatively, *click the Start button, point to Programs or All Programs, point to Microsoft Office, then click Microsoft Office Excel 2007.* You should now be in a new, clean, blank workbook.

2. To retrieve the spreadsheet from Lesson 1, *click on the Office button and then click Open. Next, click the name of your file* (e.g., **Budget 1**). If you do not see it, *click through the options under "Look in:" to find the file.* When you have found it, *click on Open.*

3. You will be entering the information shown in Excel 2007 Exhibit 3. Notice in Excel 2007 Exhibit 3 that a line for travel appears in row 9. You will insert this row first.

4. *Click in cell B9. From the Home tab, click the down arrow below Insert in the Cells group. On the Insert menu, click Insert Sheet Rows.* A new row is added. You could also *right-click and select Insert* to open a dialog box with the option to insert another row.

5. Enter the following:
    Travel in B9.
    750 in C9.
    650 in D9.

6. Notice that when the new values for travel were entered, all of the formulas were updated. Because you inserted the additional row in the middle of the column, the formulas recognized the new numbers and automatically recalculated to reflect them. Be extremely careful when inserting new rows and columns into spreadsheets that have existing formulas. In some cases, the new number will not be reflected in the totals, such as when rows or columns are inserted at the beginning or end of the range that a formula calculates. It is always prudent to go back to each existing formula, examine the formula range, and make sure the new values are included in the formula range.

7. Change the column width of column E to 12 by **clicking the column heading** (the letter E) at the top of the screen. **Move the pointer to the right edge of the column.** The pointer should change to a double-headed vertical arrow. **Drag the pointer to the right until the column width is 12.** Alternatively, you can change the cell width by **placing the cell pointer anywhere in column E and, from the Home tab, clicking Format in the Cells Group and selecting Column Width. . . ;** then type **12** and **click OK.**

8. Enter the following:
   May in E4.
   Difference in E5.
   Percent in F4.
   Of Budget in F5.

9. **Click in cell E4 and drag the pointer over to cell F5** so that the additional column headings are highlighted. **Right-click. Notice that in addition to a menu, the Mini toolbar appears.** It has a number of formatting options on it, including Font, Font size, Bold, and others. **Click the Bold icon on the Mini toolbar. Point and click the Center icon on the Mini toolbar.**

10. **Click in cell E14 and drag the pointer over to cell F14. Right-click and then click on the Bold icon on the Mini toolbar.**

11. **Click in cell E19 and drag the pointer over to cell F19. Right-click and then select the Bold icon on the Mini toolbar.**

12. **Click in cell E21 and drag the pointer over to cell F21. Right-click and then select the Bold icon on the Mini toolbar.**

13. You are now ready to change the cell formatting for column E to Currency and column F to Percent. **Click in cell E7 and drag the pointer down to cell E21. Right-click and select Format Cells. From the Number tab in the "Format Cells" window, click Currency and then OK. Click in any cell to get rid of the cell range.**

14. **Click in cell F7 and drag the pointer down to cell F21. From the Home tab, click the Percent Style (%) icon in the Number group** (see Excel 2007 Exhibit 3). **Then, from the Home tab, click the Increase Decimal icon twice in the Number group.**

15. **Click in any cell to get rid of the cell range.**

16. All that is left to do is enter the formulas for the two new columns. The entries in the May Difference column subtract the actual amount from the budgeted amount for each expense item. A positive amount in this column means that the office was under budget on that line item. A negative balance means that the office was over budget on that line item. The Percent Of Budget column divides that actual amount by the budgeted amount. This shows the percentage of the budgeted money that was actually spent for each item.

17. You will first build one formula in the May Difference column, and then copy it. **Click in cell E7,** type **=C7–D7,** and press the **[ENTER]** key.

EXCEL 2007 EXHIBIT 4
Completed column grid

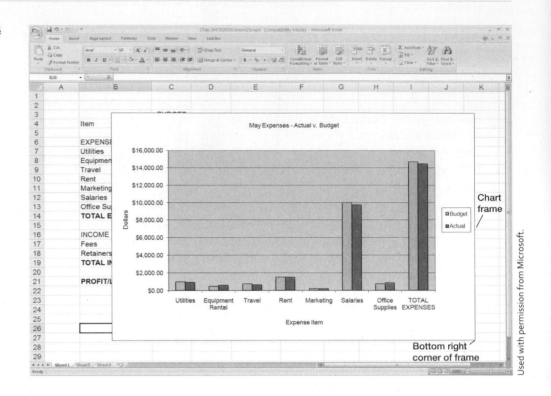

18. Using the AutoFill command or the Copy command, copy this formula down through cell E14. (To copy, *right-click and then click Copy; highlight the area where the information should go; then right-click and select Paste.* Alternatively, you can use the Copy and Paste icons in the Clipboard group on the Home tab.)

19. *Click in cell E17,* type **=C17–D17**, and press the **[ENTER]** key.

20. Using the AutoFill command, copy this formula down through cell E21. Delete the formula in cell E20 by *clicking in cell E20* and pressing the **[DEL]** key.

21. You will now build on the formula in the Percent Of Budget column and copy it. *Click in cell F7,* type **=D7/C7**, and press the **[ENTER]** key.

22. Using the AutoFill command, copy this formula down through cell F21. Delete the formula in cells F15, F16, and F20 by *clicking in the cell* and then pressing the **[DEL]** key.

23. The spreadsheet has now been built. You will now build a column chart that shows budgeted expenses compared to actual expenses (see Excel 2007 Exhibit 4).

24. *Click in cell B7, then drag the pointer down and over to cell D14.*

25. *From the Insert tab, click Column from the Charts group. Under 3-D Column, click the first option, 3-D Clustered Column* (see Excel 2007 Exhibit 5).

26. Notice that a draft column chart has been created. *Click anywhere in the chart frame* (see Excel 2007 Exhibit 4). Your pointer will turn to a four-headed arrow. *Drag the chart across the spreadsheet so the upper left corner of the chart is near cell B4.*

27. *Using the horizontal scroll bar* (see Excel 2007 Exhibit 4), *scroll to the right* so the chart is completely in your screen.

28. *Click the bottom right corner of the chart frame.* Your cursor should change to a two-headed arrow that is diagonal. *Drag the chart so that the bottom right corner ends near cell H22* (see Excel 2007 Exhibit 4).

EXCEL 2007 EXHIBIT 5
Creating a column chart

HANDS-ON EXERCISES

29. Notice that new options have been added to the ribbon (e.g., Chart Tools Design, Layout, and Format). ***Click the Layout ribbon tab under Chart Tools.***

30. ***Click Chart Title in the Labels group, then select Above Chart.*** Notice that a title has been added, "Chart Title."

31. ***Point and click on the "Chart Title" text in the bar chart*** and press the **[DEL]** key until the text is gone. Type **May Expenses—Actual v. Budget**. If you would like to move the title—for example, if it is off-center—just click the title frame and drag it where you would like.

32. ***From the Layout tab (under Chart Tools), click Axis Titles in the Labels group. Click Primary Horizontal Axis Title and then select Title Below Axis.*** Notice that a horizontal axis title of "Axis Title" has been added. ***Click Axis Title*** and use the **[DEL]** key until the text is gone. Type **Expenses**.

33. To change the legend from Series1 and Series2 to Actual and Budget, ***right-click on Series1, then click Select Data.*** The "Select Data Source" window will open. ***Click on Series1 (under Legend Entries (Series)) to highlight it, then click on Edit under the same heading.*** The "Edit Series" window will open. Type **Actual** in the text box under Series name:, ***then click OK. Click on Series2 (under Legend Entries (Series)) to highlight it, then click on Edit under the same heading.*** The "Edit Series" window will open. Type **Budget** in the text box under Series name:, ***then click OK. Click OK in the "Select Data Source" window.***

34. To print the chart, ***drag the pointer from cell G3 to cell Q27. Click the Office button and click Print; then, under Print what, click Selection and then click OK.***

35. You will next print the spreadsheet and the chart on one page. ***Click in cell B3 and drag the pointer until both the spreadsheet and the chart are highlighted*** (roughly cell B3 to cell Q27).

36. ***Click the Page Layout tab, then click the Page Setup dialog box launcher.*** (It is a little box directly under the Print Titles icon in the Page Setup group). The "Page Setup" window should now be displayed. There is another way to bring

up this window: *from the Page Setup group of the Page Layout tab, click Margins, and then click Custom Margins.*

37. *From the Page tab of the "Page Setup" window, click in the circle next to Fit To: and make sure it says "1 page(s) wide by 1 tall"* (it should default to one page). *Then, under Orientation, click on Landscape.*

38. *Click Print and then click OK.* This will compress everything in the print area to one page.

39. To save the spreadsheet, *click the Office button and then click Save As. Under Save in:, select the drive or folder in which you would like to save the document.* Next to File name:, type **Budget2** and *click Save.*

40. To exit Excel, *click the Office button and then click Exit Excel.*

This concludes Lesson 2.

LESSON 3: BUILDING A DAMAGE PROJECTION SPREADSHEET

This lesson shows you how to build the damage projection spreadsheet shown in Excel 2007 Exhibit 6. It explains how to increase the size of type, how to wrap text in a cell, how to use the border features, how to use the font and fill color features, how to use the AutoSum feature, and how to change the decimal places for a number. This lesson assumes that you have successfully completed Lessons 1 and 2. Keep in mind that if you make a mistake at any time in this lesson, you may press **[CTRL]+[Z]** to undo what you have done.

EXCEL 2007 EXHIBIT 6
Damages projection

1. Open Windows. *Double-click the Microsoft Office Excel 2007 icon on the desktop* to open the program. Alternatively, *click on the Start button, point to Programs or All Programs, point to Microsoft Office, then click Microsoft Office Excel 2007.* You should now be in a new, clean, blank workbook. If you are not in a blank workbook, *click the Office button* (see Excel 2007 Exhibit 1), *then click New and double-click Blank Workbook.*

2. To start building the spreadsheet in Excel 2007 Exhibit 6, begin by increasing the size of column C to a width of 37 *(Home tab > Cells group > Format > Column Width).*

3. In cell C3, type **Damage Projection.** With the pointer on C3, *click the Bold icon from the Font group on the Home tab.* Change the size to 14 point by *clicking the Font Size box in the Font group on the Home tab* and typing **14.**

4. Type the text shown in cell C5 (see Excel 2007 Exhibit 6). *Click the Font Size box in the Font group on the Home tab and change the type to 14 point.* Notice that the text goes into the next cell. To wrap part of the text down to the next line within the current cell (see Excel Exhibit 6), *from the Home tab, click the Wrap Text icon in the Alignment group* (see Excel 2007 Exhibit 6). The text now wraps down to the next line within cell C5.

5. Type the text shown in cell C6, make the text 14 point, and wrap the text down so it does not go into cell D6.

6. Type the text shown in cell C8 and make the text 14 point.

7. Type the text and values shown in cells C9 to D13.

8. Type the text shown in cell C14.

9. To enter the formula in cell D14, *click cell D14.* Then, *from the Editing group on the Home tab, click the Sum icon* (see Excel 2007 Exhibit 6). Notice that when you clicked Sum, Excel assumed that you wanted to add the values in D10 to D13. You could adjust the range by pressing the **[SHIFT]+[ARROW]** keys, but the range should be fine as is (i.e., D10 to D13). Press the **[ENTER]** key to enter the formula.

10. *Click in cell C9, drag the mouse pointer to cell D14,* and change the font size to 14 point.

11. *Click in cell C9 and drag the mouse pointer to cell D9. Right-click. On the Mini toolbar, click the down arrow next to the Fill Color icon (the paint bucket) and select the black square.* (You could also click the Fill Color icon in the Font group on the Home tab.) The cells are all black; now you just need to change the font color to white to see the text.

12. With cells C9 and D9 still highlighted, *on the Home tab, click the down arrow next to the Font Color icon in the Font group, and click on the white square.*

13. *Click in cell C10 and drag the mouse pointer to cell D14. From the Font group on the Home tab, click on the down arrow next to the Border icon.* (It is typically just to the left of the Fill Color icon—see Excel 2007 Exhibit 6). Then, *click All Borders* (it looks like a windowpane). Notice that there is now a border around every square that was highlighted.

14. *Click in cell C14 and drag the mouse pointer to cell D14. From the Font group on the Home tab, click the down arrow next to the Border icon again.* Then *click on the Thick Box Border* (it looks like a heavy black window frame). Move the pointer and notice that there is now a heavy black border around cells C14 and D14. *From the Font group on the Home tab, click on the Bold icon again.*

15. *Click in cell D10 and drag the pointer to cell D14. From the Number group on the Home tab, click the dollar sign ($).* Notice that two decimal places are shown (e.g., 25,000.00). It is not necessary to show two decimal places in this projection, so you will now change it to zero decimal places. *From the Number group on the Home tab, click the Decrease Decimal icon twice.* Notice that whole dollars are now shown.

16. To print the spreadsheet, *click the Office button, click Print and then click OK.*

17. To save the spreadsheet, *click on the Office button and then click Save. Under Save in:, select the drive or folder in which you would like to save the document.* Next to File name:, type **Damage Projection** and *click Save.*

18. To exit Excel, *click the Office button and then click Exit Excel.*

This concludes Lesson 3.

▶ INTERMEDIATE LESSONS

LESSON 4: CHILD SUPPORT PAYMENT SPREADSHEET

This lesson shows you how to build the child support payment spreadsheet in Excel 2007 Exhibit 7. It explains how to create a white background, how to create formulas to multiply cells and formulas that use an absolute cell reference, and how to use the AutoFormat feature. This lesson assumes that you have successfully completed Lessons 1 through 3. Keep in mind that if you make a mistake at any time in this lesson, you may press [CTRL]+[Z] to undo what you have done.

EXCEL 2007 EXHIBIT 7
Child support payment spreadsheet

Used with permission from Microsoft.

1. Open Windows. *Double-click the Microsoft Office Excel 2007 icon on the desktop* to open the program. Alternatively, *click the Start button, point to Programs or All Programs, point to Microsoft Office, and then click Microsoft Office Excel 2007.* You should now be in a new, clean, blank workbook. If you are not in a blank workbook, *point and click the Office button* (see Excel 2007 Exhibit 1), *then click New, then double-click on Blank Workbook.*

2. When you start to build the spreadsheet in Excel 2007 Exhibit 7, notice that the background is completely white. A completely white background gives you a crisp, clean canvas on which to work and to which you can add colors and graphics.

3. Press [CTRL]+[A]. The whole spreadsheet is now selected. *From the Font group on the Home tab, click the down arrow next to the Fill Color icon, then click the white square* (it is all the way in the upper right corner). *Click*

in any cell to make the highlighting disappear. Notice that the background of the spreadsheet is completely white.

4. Enter the text shown in cell C1, then change the font to Bold and the font size to 14 point.

5. Increase the width of column C to 20.

6. Enter the text shown in cells C3 to C6.

7. In cell E5, type **.01** and press **[ENTER].** Change the number format to Percent (zero decimal places).

8. Enter the text shown in cells C7 and in the cell range from D7 to G8. *Click on C7 and click on the bold icon from the Font group in the Home tab. Click on D7 and drag the pointer to G8, click on the Italic icon from the Font group in the Home tab.*

9. Enter the text shown in the cell range from C10 to C16.

10. Enter the numbers (values) shown in cells in D11 to E16.

11. In cell F10, type **2500.**

12. In cell G10, type = (an equals sign), *click in cell F10,* then press **[SHIFT]+[8]** (an asterisk will appear). *Click in cell E5* and press the **[F4]** key once. The formula **=F10*E5** should be on the screen; press the **[ENTER]** key. This formula multiplies the accrued arrearage (how much the individual is behind on payments) times the interest rate (which is 1 percent). The reason you pressed **[F4]** is that the formula had to be an absolute cell reference; pressing **[F4]** simply put the dollar signs ($) into the formula for you. The dollar signs tell Excel that this is an absolute cell reference rather than a relative cell reference. Hence, when you copy the formula to other cells (see following steps), the accrued arrearage will always be multiplied by the value in E5. Said another way, the second half of this formula (E5) will not change when the formula is copied to other cells.

13. If you want to find out for yourself why the formula **=F10*E5** will not work once it is copied from cell G10 (where it will work fine), type **=F10*E5** in cell G10 and then copy the formula to cells G11 to G16. Once you have seen the effect of this, delete the changes you made and change the formula in cell G10 to **=F10*E5.**

14. To copy the formula from G10 to cells G11 to G16, *click in cell G10, click the AutoFill handle* (the little black box at the lower right corner of the cell) *and drag the mouse pointer down to cell G16.*

15. In cell F11, type **=F10+G10+D11−E11**. Press the **[ENTER]** key. This formula adds the accrued amount in the previous month with the previous month's interest and the current support due, and then subtracts the current amount paid.

16. To copy the formula from F11 to cells F12 to F16, *click in cell F11, click the AutoFill handle, and drag the mouse pointer down to cell F16.*

17. *Click in cell D10 and drag the mouse pointer to cell G16. Right-click, then click Format Cells. Click the Number tab, click Currency, then click OK.*

18. Notice that the spreadsheet is very plain. We will use the Cell Styles feature to give the spreadsheet some color. *Click in cell C7 and drag the mouse pointer to cell G8. From the Styles Group on the Home tab, click the down arrow next to Cell Styles. Click Accent4* (it is solid purple with white letters).

19. *Click in cell C9 and drag the mouse pointer to cell G16. From the Styles group on the Home tab, click the down arrow next to Cell Styles. Click 20%—Accent1. (It is light blue with black letters.) Click in any cell to make the highlighting disappear.*

20. To add borders to the spreadsheet, *click in cell C9 and drag the mouse pointer to cell G16. From the Font group on the Home tab, click the down arrow*

next to the Border icon. Next, click the All Borders icon (it looks like a windowpane).

21. *Click in cell E5. From the Font group on the Home tab, click the down arrow next to Borders. Click Thick Box Border.* Press the [ENTER] key. The spreadsheet is now complete and should look like Excel 2007 Exhibit 7.

22. To print the spreadsheet, *click the Office button, click Print, then click OK.*

23. To save the spreadsheet, *click the Office button and then click Save. Under Save in:, select the drive or folder in which you would like to save the document.* Next to File name:, type **Child Support Payments** and *click Save.*

24. To exit Excel, *click on the Office button and then click Exit Excel.*

This concludes Lesson 4.

LESSON 5: LOAN AMORTIZATION TEMPLATE

This lesson shows you how to open a loan amortization template and fill it in (see Excel 2007 Exhibit 8). Templates are a great way to simplify complicated spreadsheets. You will also learn how to protect cells, freeze panes, split a screen, hide a column, and use the Format Painter tool. This lesson assumes that you have successfully completed Lessons 1 through 4. Keep in mind that if you make a mistake at any time in this lesson, you may press [CTRL]+[Z] to undo what you have done.

EXCEL 2007 EXHIBIT 8
Loan amortization template

1. Open Windows. *Double-click the Microsoft Office Excel 2007 icon on the desktop* to open the program. Alternatively, *click the Start button, point to Programs or All Programs, point to Microsoft Office, then click Microsoft Office Excel 2007.* You should now be in a new, clean, blank workbook.

2. The first thing you will do to complete the template in Excel 2007 Exhibit 8 is open the "Lesson 5" file from the disk supplied with this text. Ensure that the disk is inserted in the disk drive, *point and click on File on the Office button, then point and click on Open.* The "Open" window should now be displayed. *Point and click on the down arrow to the right of the white box next to "Look in:" and select the drive where the disk is located. Point and*

double-click on the Excel Files folder. Double-click on the Excel 2007 folder. Double-click on the "Lesson 5" file.

3. You should now have the loan amortization spreadsheet shown in Excel 2007 Exhibit 8 open. However, your spreadsheet has no data yet.

4. Enter the following information:
Cell D6: **300000**
Cell D7: **5.75**
Cell D8: **30**
Cell D9: **12**
Cell D10: **1/1/2012**
Cell D11: **0**

(When you click in Cell D11, a note will appear regarding extra payments; just type a zero and press [**ENTER**] and the note will disappear.)

Cell C13: **National Bank**
Cell G13: **Jennifer John**

5. Notice that your spreadsheet now appears nearly identical to Excel 2007 Exhibit 8.

6. Notice in your spreadsheet that just about everything below row 16 is a formula. If a user accidentally deletes one of these formulas, the whole spreadsheet could be affected. You will now turn on the Protection feature and lock some of the cells so they cannot be accidentally deleted.

7. ***Right-click in cell D6. Then click Format Cells . . . . Click the Protection tab in the "Format Cells" window.*** Notice that there is no green check mark next to Locked. Cells D6 to D13 and cell G13 are unlocked even when the Protection feature is turned on. When the Protection feature is off, you can change the lock/unlock format of cells by using the ***right-click, Format Cells > Protection*** command sequence. Interestingly, when a new blank spreadsheet is open in Excel, all cells default to "Locked," but this has no effect because the Protection feature is always turned off in a blank workbook.

8. ***Click Cancel in the "Format Cells" window to close the window.***

9. Let's open a new spreadsheet so you can see that all cells in Excel start out with the format locked. ***Click the Office button, then click New, then double-click Blank Workbook.***

10. You should now have a new, blank spreadsheet displayed. ***Right-click in any cell and then click Format Cells. . . . Click the Protection tab.*** Notice that the cell is locked. However, the cell is not truly locked until you turn on the Protection feature.

11. ***Click Cancel in the "Format Cells" window in the new spreadsheet. Click the Office button and then click Close*** to close the file. You should now be back at your loan amortization spreadsheet.

12. To turn on the Protection feature, ***on the Review tab, click Protect Sheet in the Changes group.***

13. The "Protect Sheet" window should now be displayed (see Excel 2007 Exhibit 9). Make sure that the first two selections under Allow all users of this worksheet to: are selected (e.g., Select locked cells and Select unlocked cells). Notice that you could enter a password in the white box under Password to unprotect sheet. This would completely lock the spreadsheet (so that only unlocked cells could be modified) to users who did not know the password. In this instance, this is not necessary; it is fine for someone to intentionally change the values at the top of the spreadsheet. We are

EXCEL 2007 EXHIBIT 9
Protecting cells

just using this feature to prevent someone from accidentally changing the formulas below row 16.

14. After the first two items are check-marked under Allow all users of this worksheet to:, *click OK.*

15. *Now click in any cell other than D6 to D13 or cell G13 and try to type something in the cell.* You should get an error message that says "**The cell or chart that you are trying to change is protected and therefore read-only.**" *Click OK* to close the error window.

16. The whole spreadsheet is now locked, except for cells D6 to D13 and cell G13, because these were not formatted as locked in the template.

17. Now you will turn off the Protection feature because you are still building the spreadsheet. *On the Review tab, click Unprotect Sheet in the Changes group.*

18. You will now use the Format Painter tool to copy the formatting from one set of cells to another set of cells. Notice that cells F13 and G13 do not look like cells B13 and C13. You will copy the format from cells B13 and C13 to cells F13 and G13.

19. *Point in cell B13 and drag the mouse pointer to cell C13. On the Home tab, click the Format Painter icon in the Clipboard group.* (It looks like a paintbrush). Your pointer now should have a paintbrush icon on it.

20. *Click in cell F13, drag the mouse to cell H13, and then let go of the mouse button. Click anywhere to see the cell.* Notice that the formatting has now been copied.

21. Column E in the amortization schedule of the spreadsheet is the "Extra Payment" column. Assume for the purposes of this exercise that you will not have any extra payments and that you do not need this column, but you want to leave the column there in case you need it at a later date. For now, you can hide column E (and unhide it if you need it later).

22. *Point and right-click on the "E" in the E column heading. From the drop-down menu, click Hide.*

23. *Click in any cell.* The vertical line will disappear. Notice that column E is no longer displayed. The column headings go from D to F.

24. We will now unhide column E. *Point on the D column heading and drag the mouse to the F column heading so that both columns are highlighted. Right-click, then click Unhide on the drop-down menu.* Notice that column E reappears.

25. *Click in any cell to make the highlighting disappear.*

26. *Click in cell D18.* Use the [**DOWN ARROW**] key to go to cell D50. Notice that some column titles, such as "Pmt No.," and "Payment Date," are no longer visible, so it is difficult to know what the numbers mean.

27. Press [**CTRL**]+[**HOME**] to go to the top of the spreadsheet.

28. *Click cell A18.* You will now use the Split Screen command to see the column titles.

29. *On the View tab, click Split in the Window group.*

30. Use the [**DOWN ARROW**] cursor key on the keyboard to go to cell A50. Notice that because you split the screen at row 18, you can still see column titles. Next, use the [**UP ARROW**] cursor key on the keyboard to go to cell A1. You should now see the top portion of your spreadsheet in both the top and bottom screens.

31. *On the View tab, click Split again in the Window group.* The bottom screen is now gone.

32. The Freeze Panes feature is another way to show the column headings when you scroll down a document. The Freeze Panes feature is a convenient way to see both column and row titles at the same time. *Click in cell B18.*

33. *On the View tab, click Freeze Panes in the Window group and then click the first option, Freeze Panes.*

34. Use the [**DOWN ARROW**] key to go to cell B50. Notice that because you froze the screen at cell B18, you can still see column titles. Next, use the [**RIGHT ARROW**] key to go to cell R50. You should still see the "Pmt No." column, including the payment numbers.

35. Press [**CTRL**]+[**HOME**] to go to the beginning of the spreadsheet.

36. *On the View tab, click Freeze Panes in the Window group and then click the first option, Unfreeze Panes.*

37. To print the spreadsheet, *click the Office button, click Print, then click OK.*

38. To save the spreadsheet, *click the Office button and then click Save As. Under Save in: select the drive or folder in which you would like to save the document.* Next to File name:, type **Excel Lesson 5 Spreadsheet DONE** and *click Save.*

39. Templates are a great way to utilize the power of Excel. Many free templates are available on the Internet. Microsoft alone offers more than 100 Excel templates on its website. To access them, *click the Office button, then New.* They are listed to the left under Microsoft Office Online.

40. To exit Excel, *click on the Office button and then click Exit Excel.*

This concludes Lesson 5.

LESSON 6: STATISTICAL FUNCTIONS

This lesson demonstrates how to use and enter statistical formulas such as average, maximum, minimum, and standard deviation. It also shows how to sort data, check

EXCEL 2007 EXHIBIT 10
Statistical spreadsheet

Used with permission from Microsoft.

for metadata in spreadsheets, how to use the Format Clear command, how to use conditional formatting, and how to insert a clip-art file. When the spreadsheet is complete, it will look like Excel 2007 Exhibit 10. Keep in mind that if you make a mistake at any time in this lesson, you may press **[CTRL]+[Z]** to undo what you have done.

1. Open Windows. **Double-click the Microsoft Office Excel 2007 icon on the desktop** to open the program. Alternatively, **click the Start button, point to Programs or All Programs, point to Microsoft Office, then click Microsoft Office Excel 2007.** You should now be in a new, clean, blank workbook. If you are not in a blank workbook, **click the Office button** (see Excel 2007 Exhibit 1), **then click New, then double-click on Blank Workbook.**

2. The first thing you will do to complete the template shown in Excel 2007 Exhibit 10 is open the "Lesson 6" file from the disk supplied with this text. Ensure that the disk is inserted in the disk drive, **point and click on File on the Office button, then point and click on Open.** The "Open" window should now be displayed. **Point and click on the down arrow to the right of the white box next to "Look in:" and select the drive where the disk is located. Point and double-click on the Excel Files folder. Double-click on the Excel 2007 folder. Double-click on the "Lesson 6" file.**

3. You should now see the age discrimination statistical analysis spreadsheet shown in Excel 2007 Exhibit 10; however, your spreadsheet has no formulas in the statistical summary section, the data have not yet been sorted, and there is no clip art yet.

4. You will now enter the formulas in the statistical summary section of the spreadsheet. The first formula will calculate the average age of employees of the company. **Click in cell J11.** Type the following formula: **=AVERAGE(D11:D23)** and then press the **[ENTER]** key. The result

should be 30. *Note*: Here is another way to enter the average function: ***on the Formulas tab, click Insert Function in the Function Library group; next to Or select a category, click the down arrow, then click Statistical > AVERAGE > OK.***

5. The next formula calculates the most units sold. ***Click in cell J12.*** Type the following formula: **=MAX(F11:F23)** and then press the **[ENTER]** key. The result should be 700.

6. The next formula calculates the least units sold. ***Click in cell J13.*** Type the following formula: **=MIN(F11:F23)** and then press the **[ENTER]** key. The result should be 150.

7. The next formula calculates the average units sold. ***Click in cell J14.*** Type the following formula: **=AVERAGE(F11:F23)** and then press the **[ENTER]** key. The result should be 457.

8. The next formula calculates the total units sold. ***Click in cell J15.*** Type the following formula: **=SUM(F11:F23)** and then press the **[ENTER]** key. The result should be 5937.

9. The last formula calculates the standard deviation for units sold. *Standard deviation* is a measure of how widely values are dispersed from the average value (the arithmetic mean). Large standard deviations show that the numbers vary widely from the average. ***On the Formulas tab, click Insert Function in the Function Library group. Next to Or select a category, click the down arrow and select Statistical. Scroll down the list and click* STDEVP** (see Excel 2007 Exhibit 11). Notice that there is a definition for this function. ***Click OK in the "Insert Function" window.***

10. The "Function Arguments" window should now be displayed. In the "Function Arguments" window, next to Number 1, press **[DEL]** until the box is blank. Type **F11:F23,** then ***click OK*** (see Excel 2007 Exhibit 12). The result should be 163.

EXCEL 2007 EXHIBIT 11
Entering a standard deviation formula using the insert function command

HANDS-ON EXERCISES

EXCEL 2007 EXHIBIT 12

Entering a standard deviation formula using the functions argument window

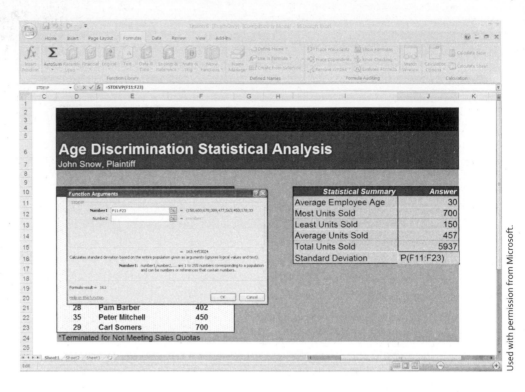

11. You will now sort the data based on the age of the employees. ***Click in D11 and then drag the mouse down to F23. From the Data tab, click Sort in the Sort & Filter group.***

12. The "Sort" window should now be displayed (see Excel 2007 Exhibit 13). *Note*: Even though you just want to sort by age, you must select the full data range that includes all of the information, or the age data will be sorted but the other columns and rows will stay where they are. The data will therefore be mismatched (each age will not be matched with the correct person and number of units sold).

EXCEL 2007 EXHIBIT 13

Sorting data

EXCEL 2007 EXHIBIT 14
Removing metadata

13. *In the "Sort" window, click the down arrow next to Sort by, then click Age* (see Excel 2007 Exhibit 13). Notice that under Order, the default of Smallest to Largest is selected; this is fine, so *click OK in the "Sort" window.* The data should now be sorted according to the age of the individual, with John Snow appearing last in the spreadsheet.

14. You will now ensure that no metadata is included in your document. You must first save the spreadsheet. To save the spreadsheet, *click the Office button and then click Save As. Under Save in:, select the drive or folder in which you would like to save the document.* Next to File name:, type **Excel Lesson 6 Spreadsheet DONE** and *click Save.*

15. Excel 2007 has a special feature called Inspect Document that can extract all metadata from your spreadsheet. *Click the Office button, click Prepare, then click Inspect Document* (see Excel 2007 Exhibit 14). Through the "Document Inspector" window, all of the possible places metadata can hide are checked. *Click Inspect.* Some of the categories may have a Remove All button. If you wanted to remove the metadata, you would just click on Remove All for each category. Because this is just an exercise, we do not need to remove the metadata, so go ahead and *click Close* to close the "Document Inspector" window.

16. Sometimes it is helpful to clear a cell or cells of all formatting information at one time. Notice that cell D6, the one titled "Age Discrimination Statistical Analysis," is elaborately formatted, including 24-point font, white letters, red background, and bold text. You will now quickly remove all of that formatting. *Click in cell D6. Then, on the Home tab, click the down arrow next to the Clear icon in the Editing group* (it looks like an eraser—see Excel 2007 Exhibit 15). *Click Clear Formats.* All of the formatting should disappear. Notice in Excel 2007 Exhibit 15 that one of the options when using the Clear commands is Clear All. Clicking Clear All will not only clear the formatting, but will also clear the contents of the selected cell(s).

17. Press **[CTRL]+[Z]** (the Undo feature) to restore the original formatting to the cell.

EXCEL 2007 EXHIBIT 15
Clear command

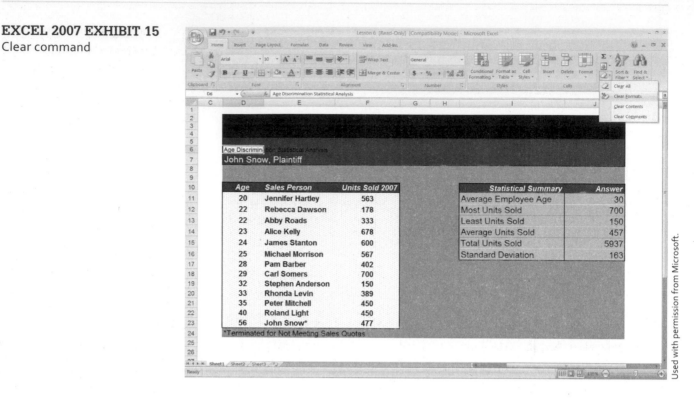

18. Sometimes, particularly in large spreadsheets, it is helpful to have the formatting of a cell change if certain conditions are present. For example, in an actual-versus-budget report, if an item goes over budget by more than 10 percent it might be helpful for that to be bolded so it catches the reader's attention. To accomplish this, you will now learn how to use the Conditional Formatting feature of Excel.

19. Notice that the average sales for the sales team in your spreadsheet is 457. It might be helpful to highlight any salesperson who was over the average. ***Click in F11 and then drag the mouse to F23. Then, from the Home tab, click Conditional Formatting in the Styles group*** (see Excel 2007 Exhibit 16).

EXCEL 2007 EXHIBIT 16
Creating conditional
formatting

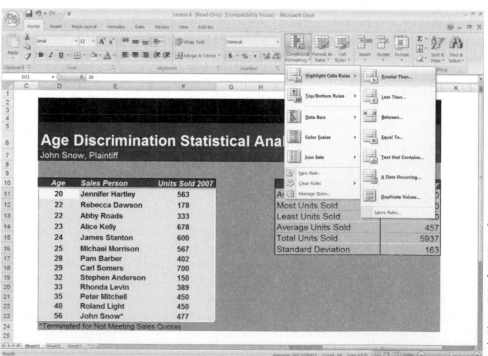

EXCEL 2007 EXHIBIT 17
Creating a "Greater Than" conditional formatting

20. *Point to the first option, Highlight Cells Rules, and then click the first option again, which is Greater Than...* (see Excel 2007 Exhibit 16).

21. The "Greater Than" window should now be displayed (see Excel 2007 Exhibit 17). Press the [**DEL**] key to remove the value under Format cells that are GREATER THAN:.

22. *Click cell J14.* Notice that cell J14 has been entered under Format cells that are GREATER THAN:. Dollar signs have been added to the cell reference because this is an absolute cell reference.

23. *Click the down arrow next to Light Red Fill with Dark Red Text and select Red Text.* Cells over the average will be shown in red text. *Click OK in the "Greater Than" window.*

24. You will now add clip art to your spreadsheet (we are assuming that clip art was included when Excel 2007 was installed). *Click in cell I18. From the Insert tab, click Clip Art in the Illustrations group.*

25. The Clip Art task pane will appear to the right of the screen. Under Search for, type **Money** and then *click Go.* You may get a message that asks if you want to include clip art from Microsoft Office Online; *click No.*

26. *Click on the clip art in Excel 2007 Exhibit 10* (a blue bar chart with people in it and a person climbing a dollar sign). The clip art has now been added to your spreadsheet. *Position the clip art where you want it by clicking and dragging it into position.*

27. *Click the X in the Clip Art task pane* to close the task pane.

28. To print the spreadsheet, *click the Office button, click Print, then click OK.*

29. To save the spreadsheet, *click the Office button and then click Save As.* Choose the directory in which you want to save the file and *click Save.*

30. To exit Excel, *click the Office button and then click Exit Excel.*

This concludes Lesson 6.

▶ ADVANCED LESSONS

LESSON 7: TOOLS AND TECHNIQUES 1—MARKETING BUDGET

In this lesson you will learn how to create visual impact with spreadsheets. You will learn to create and manipulate a text box, use advanced shading techniques, create a 3-D style text box, create vertical text, create diagonal text, use lines and borders, and create a comment. When the spreadsheet is complete, it will look like Excel 2007 Exhibit 18. Keep in mind that if you make a mistake at any time in this lesson, you may press [CTRL]+[Z] to undo what you have done.

1. Open Windows. ***Double-click the Microsoft Office Excel 2007 icon on the desktop*** to open the program. Alternatively, ***click the Start button, point to Programs or All Programs, point to Microsoft Office, then click Microsoft Office Excel 2007.*** You should now be in a new, clean, blank workbook.

2. The first thing you will do to complete the spreadsheet in Excel 2007 Exhibit 18 is open the "Lesson 7" file from the disk supplied with this text. Ensure that the disk is inserted in the disk drive, ***click on the Office button, click on File, then point and click on Open.*** The "Open" window should now be displayed. ***Point and click on the down arrow to the right of the white box next to "Look in:" and select the drive where the disk is located. Point and double-click on the Excel Files folder. Double-click on the Excel 2007 folder. Double-click on the "Lesson 7" file.***

3. You should now have the Marketing Plan spreadsheet in Excel 2007 Exhibit 18 open, except that your spreadsheet is missing some of the formatting that gives it visual impact. You will add the formatting to the spreadsheet to make it more visually compelling.

4. You will first add the text box that holds the title "Marketing Plan," as shown in Excel 2007 Exhibit 18. ***From the Insert tab, click Text Box in the Text group.*** Notice that your mouse pointer just turned into an upside-down letter "T."

EXCEL 2007 EXHIBIT 18
Creating visual impact in spreadsheets

Fog

5. *Point to cell C2 and drag the mouse to about cell F4*. An outline of a box should now be shown from C2 to F4. This is a *text box*.

6. *Click inside the text box. Click the Bold icon and change the font size to 20.*

7. Type **MARKETING PLAN.**

8. *Point and right-click on the outline of the text box you just created. In the drop-down menu, click Format Shape.* The "Format Shape" window should now be displayed (see Excel 2007 Exhibit 19).

9. *In the "Format Shape" window, notice that Fill is currently selected. Click Gradient fill.*

10. *Click the down arrow next to Preset colors:.* This will open a box with many colors; *click Fog.*

11. *Staying in the "Format Shape" window, point to the down arrow next to Direction and click the first option, which is Linear Diagonal.*

12. *Still in the "Format Shape" window, click 3-D Format on the left side of the window.* You will now add a 3-D style to the text box. When the 3-D style choices appear, under Bevel and next to Top, *point to the down arrow and click the first selection under Bevel, which is Circle* (see Excel 2007 Exhibit 20).

13. *Click Close to close the "Format Shape" window. Click in any other cell so you can see the effect.*

14. You will now create the vertical text in Column B that says "Expenses," as shown in Excel 2007 Exhibit 18. Notice that this is actually one long cell. The first thing you will do is merge cells B6 through B53 into one cell; you will then add the text and format it to be vertical.

15. *Click in cell B6, drag the mouse down to cell B53, and then let go of the mouse button.*

16. *From the Home tab, click the Merge & Center icon in the Alignment group.* It looks like a box with an "a" in the middle, with left and right arrows around

EXCEL 2007 EXHIBIT 20
Adding 3-D effect to a text box

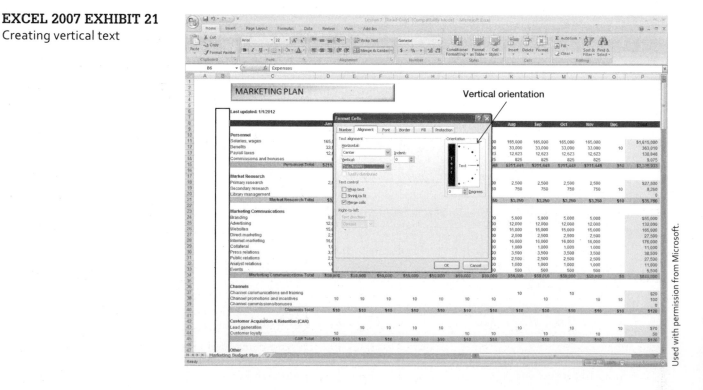

the "a" (see Excel 2007 Exhibit 18). Notice that the selected cells have now been merged into one cell stretching from B6 to B53.

17. With the cursor still in cell B6, ***change the font size to 22 and click the Bold icon.*** Type **Expenses** and press the **[ENTER]** key. The text is shown at the bottom of the cell; you will now correct this.

18. ***Point and right-click anywhere in cell B6, then click Format Cells.*** The "Format Cells" window should now be displayed. ***Click the Alignment tab*** (see Excel 2007 Exhibit 21).

EXCEL 2007 EXHIBIT 21
Creating vertical text

19. *In the "Format Cells" window under Orientation, click the box that shows the word Text displayed vertically* (see Excel 2007 Exhibit 21).

20. *In the "Format Cells" window under Vertical, click the down arrow and select Top (Indent).*

21. *Click OK in the "Format Cells" window.* The word "Expenses" should now be displayed vertically down the cell.

22. *With the pointer still in cell B6, on the Home tab, click the down arrow next to the Fill Color (a paint bucket) icon in the Font group and then select Black.*

23. *On the Home tab, click the down arrow next to the Font Color icon in the Font group and select Yellow.*

24. You will next make the text in cell C6 appear diagonally. *Right-click in cell C6, then click Format Cells.* The "Format Cells" window should now be displayed and the Alignment tab should be selected.

25. *In the "Format Cells" window under Orientation, click the up arrow next to Degrees until it reads 15.*

26. *In the "Format Cells" window, click the Fill tab. Click the yellow square, then click OK.*

27. *Click in any cell to make the highlighting disappear.* The words "Last updated: 1/1/2012" should now be displayed diagonally in black letters on a yellow background.

28. You will now add the comment shown in Excel 2007 Exhibit 18. *Right-click in cell D15. On the drop-down menu, click Insert Comment.* Press **[BACKSPACE]** twice to delete the colon, and then type **This is $40,000 more than last year, but there will be more than enough revenue to cover this.** *Click in any cell to exit the "Comment" box.*

29. *Hover your mouse over cell D15* so you can see the comment.

30. You will now add borders to the spreadsheet. *Point to cell C53 and drag the mouse to cell P53. On the Home tab, click the down arrow next to the Borders icon in the Font group and click All Borders.* The "Totals" row should now have borders around each cell.

31. *Click in cell C8 and drag the mouse to cell P53. On the Home tab, click the down arrow next to the Borders icon in the Font group, then click Thick Box Border.* A thick border now surrounds the data.

32. To print the spreadsheet, *click the Office button, click Print, then click OK.*

33. To save the spreadsheet, *click the Office button and then click Save As. Under Save in: select the drive or folder in which you would like to save the document.* Next to File name:, type **Excel Lesson 7 Spreadsheet DONE** and *click Save.*

34. To exit Excel, *click the Office button and then click Exit Excel.*

This concludes Lesson 7.

LESSON 8: TOOLS AND TECHNIQUES 2—STOCK PORTFOLIO

In this lesson, you will continue to learn and apply helpful tools and techniques using Excel. This includes getting additional practice with using the Merge & Center tool, using the formula auditing feature, using the Oval tool, and password-protecting a file. When your spreadsheet is complete, it will look similar to Excel 2007 Exhibit 22. Some of these tools have been covered in previous lessons, and this lesson will help reinforce your ability to use them effectively. This tutorial assumes that you have completed Lessons 1 through 7, and that you are quite familiar with Excel.

HANDS-ON EXERCISES

EXCEL 2007 EXHIBIT 22
Stock portfolio

1. Open Windows. ***Double-click the Microsoft Office Excel 2007 icon on the desktop*** to open the program. Alternatively, ***click the Start button, point to Programs or All Programs, point on Microsoft Office, then click Microsoft Office Excel 2007.*** You should now be in a new, clean, blank workbook. If you are not in a blank workbook, ***click the Office button*** (see Excel 2007 Exhibit 1), ***then click New, then double-click Blank Workbook.***

2. The first thing you will do to complete the spreadsheet in Excel 2007 Exhibit 22 is open the "Lesson 8" file from the disk supplied with this text. Ensure that the disk is inserted in the disk drive, ***point and click on File on the Office button, then point and click on Open.*** The "Open" window should now be displayed. ***Point and click on the down arrow to the right of the white box next to "Look in:" and select the drive where the disk is located. Point and double-click on the Excel Files folder. Double-click on the Excel 2007 folder. Double-click on the "Lesson 8" file.***

3. You should now have the stock portfolio spreadsheet shown in Excel 2007 Exhibit 22 open, except that your spreadsheet will be missing two rows of data and some of the formatting. You will add the rows and formatting to the spreadsheet.

4. ***On the Home tab, use the Merge & Center icon in the Alignment group to merge cells C5 to I5.***

5. ***Use the Merge & Center icon to merge cells C6 to I6.***

6. ***Use the Merge & Center icon to merge cells C7 to I7.***

7. Make sure the titles are aligned as shown in Excel 2007 Exhibit 22 ***(on the Home tab, use the Left and Center Align icons in the Alignment group).***

8. ***On the Home tab, use the Fill Color icon in the Font group to make the fill color for cell C5 dark blue*** (or any color you choose).

9. ***Use the Fill Color icon to make the fill color for cell C6 purple*** (any light purple is fine).

10. *Use the Fill Color icon to make the fill color for cell C7 gray* (any light gray is fine).

11. The cell range from C8 to I8 is a text graphic box (similar to a text box—it is just more difficult to see). *Right-click the box and select Format Shape. Then, in the Fill section, click Gradient fill. Next to Preset Colors, click on the first one, Early Sunset* (just hover your cursor over a color and the name will be displayed). *Under Direction, click the first option, Linear Diagonal, then click Close to close the "Format Shape" window.*

12. *On the Home tab, use the Borders icon in the Font group to give cells D10 to I21 a border of All Borders.*

13. *From the Insert tab, click Shapes in the Illustrations group. Under Basic Shapes, click the Oval tool* (it should be the second shape). *Start in the upper left corner of cell G21 and drag the mouse to the lower right corner of G21 to make an oval around the total. Note:* You can slightly move the oval by using the cursor keys on the keyboard to nudge it into place so it is centered in the cell.

14. The color of the oval must now be corrected. Notice that the ribbon has changed and that the Drawing Tools Format ribbon is now displayed. *Click the down arrow next to Shape Fill in the Shape Styles group of the Drawing Tools Format tab. Click No Fill.* The oval now surrounds the number, but the line color of the oval must be changed.

15. *Right-click the oval and select Format Shape. On the left side of the "Format Shape" window, click Line Color. Click the down arrow next to Color, click Black, then click Close in the "Format Shape" window. Make an oval in cell H21 identical to that in cell G21, using the same process.*

16. You will now use the Formula Auditing mode to inspect the formulas in the spreadsheet and ensure that they are accurate.

17. *On the Formulas tab, click Show Formulas in the Formula Auditing group.* Scroll over to the right and look at all of the cells in your spreadsheet. Notice that instead of seeing the result of the formulas, you see the formulas themselves. This is a great tool for checking the accuracy of your spreadsheets. Look at your formulas and make sure they are correct. When you are sure your formulas are accurate, *turn off the Formula Auditing mode by clicking on Show Formulas again.*

18. You will now learn how to password-protect your spreadsheet files. *Click the Office button and then click Save As. In the "Save As" window, click Tools* (it is in the lower portion of the window), *then click General Options.* Under File sharing and next to Password to open, type **A. Click OK.** At the "Confirm Password" window, type **A**, then *click OK.* At the "Save As" window, *click Save* to save the file to My Documents (or the folder of your choice—you must remember where you save it). You will then get a prompt that asks whether you want to increase the security of the document by conversion to Office Open XML Format. Because this is just an exercise, *click No.*

19. If you get a compatibility prompt, just *click Continue.*

20. *Click the Office button, then click Close* to close the file.

21. *Now, click the Office button, and under Recent Documents click on the file you just saved.*

22. The "Password" window should now be displayed. Type **A** in the "Password" window. (The password is case-sensitive, so if you typed a capital A when you

created the password, you must type a capital A to open the document.) ***Click OK.*** The file should now be displayed.

23. You can turn off a password in the same way. ***Click the Office button and then Save As. In the "Save As" window, click Tools, then click on General Options.*** Under File sharing and next to Password to open, use the **[DEL]** key to remove the asterisk. ***Click OK and then click Save.*** At the "**Do you want to replace the existing file?**" prompt, ***point and click Yes.***

24. If you get a compatibility prompt, just ***click Continue.***

25. Close the file and then reopen it, and you will see that you no longer need a password to open it.

26. To print the spreadsheet, ***click the Office button, click Print, then click OK.***

27. To exit Excel, ***click the Office button and then click Exit Excel.***

This concludes the Excel 2007 Hands-On Exercises.

HANDS-ON EXERCISES

HANDS-ON EXERCISES

MICROSOFT EXCEL 2003 FOR WINDOWS

Number	Lesson Title	Concepts Covered
BASIC LESSONS		
Lesson 1	Building a Budget Spreadsheet, Part 1	[CTRL]+[HOME] command, moving the pointer, entering text and values, adjusting the width of columns, changing the format of a group of cells to currency, using bold, centering text, entering formulas, using the AutoFill/Copy command to copy formulas, printing and saving a spreadsheet
Lesson 2	Building a Budget Spreadsheet, Part 2	Opening a file, inserting rows, changing the format of cells to percent, building more formulas, creating a bar chart with the Chart Wizard, printing a selection, and fitting/compressing data to one printed page
Lesson 3	Building a Damage Projection Spreadsheet	Changing font size, changing font color, using the AutoSum feature, using the wrap text feature, creating borders, setting decimal points when formatting numbers
INTERMEDIATE LESSONS		
Lesson 4	Child Support Payment Spreadsheet	Creating a white background, creating formulas that multiply cells, creating formulas that use absolute cell references, using the AutoFormat feature
Lesson 5	Loan Amortization Template	Using a template, protecting cells, freezing panes, splitting a screen, hiding columns, using Format Painter
Lesson 6	Statistical Functions	Using functions including average, maximum, minimum, and standard deviation; sorting data; checking for metadata; using the Format Clear command; using conditional formatting; inserting a picture
ADVANCED LESSONS		
Lesson 7	Tools and Techniques 1—Marketing Budget	Creating and manipulating a text box, advanced shading techniques, working with a 3-D style text box, creating vertical and diagonal text, creating a cell comment, using lines and borders
Lesson 8	Tools and Techniques 2—Stock Portfolio	Using the Merge & Center tool, using the fit-to-page feature, printing selections, using the Formula Auditing feature, using the oval tool, password-protecting a file

GETTING STARTED

Overview

Microsoft Excel 2003 is a powerful spreadsheet program that allows you to create formulas, "what if" scenarios, graphs, and much more.

Introduction

Throughout these lessons and exercises, information you need to operate the program will be designated in several different ways:

- Keys to be pressed on the keyboard are designated in brackets, in all caps, and in bold (e.g., press the [**ENTER**] key).
- Movements with the mouse or other pointing device are designated in bold and italics (e.g., ***point to File on the menu bar and click New***).
- Words or letters that should be typed are designated in bold (e.g., type **Training Program**).

- Information that is or should be displayed on your computer screen is shown in boldface within quotation marks: "**Press [ENTER] to continue**."
- Specific menu items and commands are designated with an initial capital letter (e.g., click Open).

OVERVIEW OF EXCEL

I. Worksheet

A. *Menus and Commands*—***Click the toolbar or the menu bar*** to access menus and/or execute commands.

B. *Entering Data*—To enter data, type the text or number, then press the **[ENTER]** key or one of the arrow (cursor) keys.

C. *Ranges*—A *range* is a group of cells. Cell ranges can be created by ***clicking and dragging the mouse pointer*** or holding the **[SHIFT]** key down while using the arrow (cursor) keys.

D. *Format*—Cells can be formatted, including changing the font style, font size, shading, border, cell type (currency, percentage, etc.), alignment, and other attributes. To do so, ***click Format on the menu bar, then click Cells.*** Alternatively, ***right-click on the cell (or within a cell range) and then select Format Cells.***

E. *Editing a Cell*—You can edit a cell by ***clicking the cell and then pointing to the formula bar and editing the displayed content.*** The formula bar is directly under the toolbar and just to the right of the **fx** sign. The formula bar shows the current contents of the selected cell, and it allows you to edit the cell contents. You can also edit the contents of a cell by ***clicking in the cell*** and then pressing the **[F2]** key.

F. *Column Width/Row Height*—You can change the width of a column by ***clicking the line to the right of the column heading.*** (This is the line that separates two columns. When you point to a line, the cursor changes to a double-headed vertical arrow.) ***Drag the pointer to the right or left to increase or decrease the column width, respectively.*** Similarly, you can change the height of a row by ***clicking and dragging the pointer on the horizontal line separating two rows***. You can also change the width of a column by ***clicking somewhere in the column you want to change and clicking Format on the menu bar, then Column, then Width***. You can change the height of a row by going to the row you want to change and ***clicking Format on the menu bar, then Row, then Height***.

G. *Insert*—You can insert one row or column by ***clicking Insert on the menu bar and then clicking either Columns or Rows***. You can also insert a number of rows or columns by ***dragging the pointer over the number of rows or columns you want to add, clicking Insert on the menu bar, then clicking either Columns or Rows***. Finally, you can ***right-click and select Insert from the menu***.

H. *Erase/Delete*—You can erase data by ***dragging the pointer over the area*** and then pressing the **[DEL]** key. You can delete whole columns or rows by ***pointing to a column or row, clicking Edit on the menu bar, then clicking Delete***, and following the menus. You can also delete whole columns or rows by ***pointing to the column or row and then right-clicking and selecting Delete***.

I. *Quit*—To quit Excel, ***click File and then Exit***.

J. *Copy*—To copy data to adjacent columns or rows, ***click in the cell you wish to copy and then select the AutoFill command,*** which is the small black box at the bottom right corner of the selected cell. ***Drag the pointer to where the data should be placed.*** You can also copy data by ***clicking in the cell, right-clicking and selecting Copy, moving the pointer to the location where the information should be copied,*** and pressing the **[ENTER]** key. Data can also be copied by ***clicking and dragging to highlight the information to be copied, clicking Edit on the menu bar, then clicking Copy.*** Then, go to the location where the information should be copied and ***click Edit and then Paste***.

K. *Move*—Move data by ***clicking in the cell, right-clicking, selecting Cut, clicking in the location where the information should be inserted,*** and pressing the **[ENTER]** key. Data can also be moved by ***highlighting the information to be moved, clicking Edit on the menu bar and then Cut, moving the pointer to the location where the information should be copied, and clicking Edit and then Paste.***

L. *Saving and Opening Files*—Save a file by ***clicking File, then clicking Save,*** and typing the file name. You can also save a file by ***clicking the Save icon*** (a floppy disk) on the toolbar. Open a file that was previously saved by ***clicking File and then Open*** and typing (or clicking) the name of the file to be opened.

M. *Print*—You can print a file by ***clicking the Print icon*** on the toolbar or by ***clicking File on the menu bar, then Print, then OK.***

II. Numbers and Formulas

A. *Numbers*—To enter a number in a cell, click in the cell, type the number, and press the **[ENTER]** key or an arrow (cursor) key.

B. *Adding Cells (Addition)*—You can add the contents of two or more cells by three different methods:

1. To add the contents of two or more cells that are in a range (i.e., in adjacent rows and/or columns):

   a. ***Click in the cell location where the total should be placed.***

   b. ***Click the AutoSum icon on the toolbar.*** This icon looks like a Greek "E." *Note:* To see the name of an icon, point to the icon for a second and its name will be displayed.

   c. Excel guesses which values you want to add. Press the **[ENTER]** key if it has automatically selected the correct range, or select the correct range by highlighting the appropriate cells (i.e., ***clicking and dragging until the range of cells to be added is selected***). Press the **[ENTER]** key.

2. To add the contents of any two or more cells:

   a. ***Click in the cell where the total should be placed.***

   b. Press = (the equals sign).

   c. Enter the address of the first value to be added (e.g., B4). Alternatively, ***click in that cell***.

   d. Press + (the plus sign).

   e. Enter the address of the second value to be added (or ***click in that cell***).

   f. Press the **[ENTER]** key. For example, to add the values of cells C4 and C5, you would type **=C4+C5**.

3. To add the contents of a range of two or more cells:

   a. ***Click in the cell where the total should be placed.***

   b. Type **=SUM**.

   c. Enter the address of the cell that defines the beginning of the range (or ***click in that cell***).

d. Press **:** (a colon).

e. Enter the address of the cell that defines the end of the range (or **click in that cell**).

f. Press **)** (a closing parenthesis).

g. Press the **[ENTER]** key. For example, to add the values of all cells between C4 and C6, the formula would read **=SUM(C4:C6)**.

C. *Subtracting Cells*—To subtract the contents of one cell from those of another:

1. **Click on the cell where the result should be placed.**

2. Press **=**.

3. Enter the first cell address (or **click in that cell**).

4. Press **–**.

5. Enter the second cell address (or **click in that cell**).

6. Press the **[ENTER]** key. For example, to subtract the value of C4 from the value of C5, you would type **=C5–C4**.

D. *Multiplying Cells*—To multiply the contents of two or more cells:

1. **Click in the cell where the result should be placed.**

2. Press **=**.

3. Enter the first cell address (or **click in that cell**).

4. Press ***** (**[SHIFT]+[8]**).

5. Enter the second cell address (or **click in that cell**).

6. Press the **[ENTER]** key. For example, to multiply the value in C4 times the value in C5, you would type **=C5*C4**.

E. *Dividing Cells*—To divide the contents of two cells:

1. **Click in the cell where the result should be placed.**

2. Press **=**.

3. Enter the first cell address (or **click in that cell**).

4. Press **/** (the forward slash).

5. Enter the second cell address (or **click in that cell**).

6. Press the **[ENTER]** key. For example, to divide the value in C4 by the value in C5, you would type **=C4/C5**.

BEFORE STARTING LESSON 1—SETTING THE TOOLBAR AND MENU BAR

Before starting Lesson 1, complete the following exercise to adjust the toolbar and menu bar so that they are consistent with the instructions in the lessons.

1. Open Windows. After it has loaded, **double-click the Excel icon on the desktop** to open Excel for Windows. Alternatively, **click the Start button, point to Programs or All Programs, click Microsoft Office, then click on Microsoft Office Excel 2003.** You should be in a new, clean, blank document.

2. **On the View menu, point to Toolbars.**

3. Only the Standard and Formatting toolbars should be checked (see Excel 2003 Exhibit 1). If the Standard and Formatting toolbars are not checked, **click on them to select them** (the check mark indicates that they have been selected). If another toolbar, such as the Chart toolbar, has been selected (marked with a check mark), then **click it to remove the check mark.** Please note that you can only make one change at a time to toolbars, so it may take you a few steps to have only Standard and Formatting selected—or your computer may already be

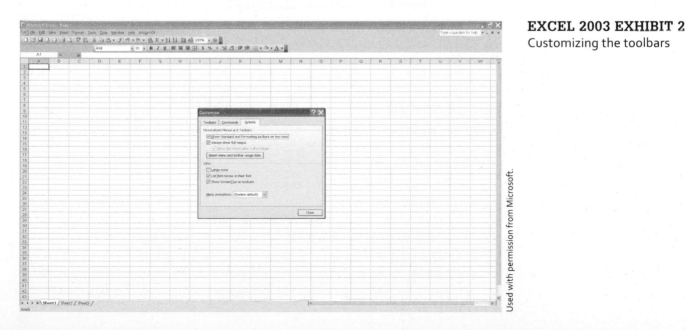

EXCEL 2003 EXHIBIT 1
Selecting toolbars

set for this and you may not have to make any changes. If you do not have to make changes, just press the **[ESC]** key twice to exit out of the View menu.

4. We also want to make sure (a) that the full menus are displayed when you select an item from the menu bar (Excel normally shows only the most recent and/or most commonly used selections), and (b) that the toolbar is shown on two rows so that you can see all the options.

5. *On the View menu bar, point to Toolbars, then click Customize.*

6. *Click on the Options tab.* Then, under "**Personalized Menus and Toolbars**," make sure that there are check marks next to "**Show Standard and Formatting toolbars on two rows**" and "**Always show full menus**" (see Excel 2003 Exhibit 2). *Note:* If there is an option under "**Personalized Menus and Toolbars**" that says "**Standard and Formatting toolbars share one row**," do not check the box, because the toolbars are already on two rows. If there is an option that says "**Menus show recently used commands first**," again, do not check the box (full menus will already be displayed). *Click Close.* You are now ready to begin Lesson 1.

EXCEL 2003 EXHIBIT 2
Customizing the toolbars

▶ BASIC LESSONS

LESSON 1: BUILDING A BUDGET SPREADSHEET, PART 1

This lesson shows you how to build the spreadsheet shown in Excel 2003 Exhibit 3. It explains how to use the [CTRL]+[HOME] command; move the pointer; enter text, values, and formulas; adjust the width of columns; change the format of cells to Currency, use the Bold command, use the AutoFill and Copy commands to copy formulas; and print and save a spreadsheet. Keep in mind that if you make a mistake at any time in this lesson, you may press [CTRL]+[Z] to undo what you have done.

1. Open Windows. After it has loaded, *double-click the Excel icon on the desktop* to open Excel for Windows. Alternatively, *click the Start button, point to Programs or All Programs, point to Microsoft Office, then click Microsoft Office Excel 2003.* You should now be in a new, clean, blank document.

2. Notice that the pointer is at cell A1, and that the indicator displaying the address of the current cell (called the *name box* in Excel) says "**A1.**" The "name" box is just under the toolbar, all the way to the left (see Excel 2003 Exhibit 3). Also, notice that you can move the pointer around the spreadsheet using the cursor keys. Go back to cell A1 by pressing the [CTRL]+[HOME] keys.

3. Go to cell C3 by *clicking in cell C3* or by pressing the [RIGHT ARROW] key twice, then pressing the [DOWN ARROW] key twice.

4. You will now enter the title of the spreadsheet in cell C3. Type **BUDGET** and then press the [ENTER] key.

5. Notice that the pointer is now at cell C4.

6. Press the [UP ARROW] key to go back to cell C3. Notice that "BUDGET" is left-aligned. To center "BUDGET" in the column, *click the Center icon on the toolbar.* It is the icon with several lines on it that appear centered (see Excel 2003 Exhibit 3). *Note:* If you hover the mouse over an icon on the toolbar for a second, the name of the icon will be displayed. Alternatively, you can *click Format, then Cells; click on the Alignment tab, then click Center in the Horizontal field. Click OK.*

7. You should now be ready to enter the budget information. First, move the pointer to where the data should go; then type the data; and finally enter the

EXCEL 2003 EXHIBIT 3
Budgeting spreadsheet

data by pressing the [ENTER] key or one of the arrow (cursor) keys. Type the remaining row labels as follows:

Item in B4.
EXPENSES in B6.
Utilities in B7.
Equipment Rental in B8.
Rent in B9.
Marketing in B10.
Salaries in B11.
Office Supplies in B12.
TOTAL EXPENSES in B13.
INCOME in B15.
Fees in B16.
Retainers in B17.
TOTAL INCOME in B18.
PROFIT/LOSS in B20.

8. Notice in Column B that some of the data entries (such as "EXPENSES" and "Equipment Rental") actually extend into column C. To correct this, you must increase the width of column B. *Point to the shaded cell with a letter B in it at the top of the screen. Move the pointer to the right edge of that cell.* The pointer should change to a double-headed vertical arrow. *Click and drag the pointer to the right until the column width is 18.00.* (A small box should appear displaying the width.) Alternatively, you can change the cell width by *placing the pointer anywhere in column B and clicking Format, then Column, then Width.* Type **18**, then *click OK.*

9. Notice that all of the data entries now fit in the columns. Enter the following:
May in C4.
Budget in C5.
May in D4.
Actual in D5.

10. *Click in C4 and drag the pointer over to cell D5* (so that the whole cell range is highlighted)*, then click the Center icon and the Bold icon on the toolbar.*

11. You are now ready to enter values into your spreadsheet.

12. *Move the cell pointer to cell C7.* Type **1000.** Do not type a dollar sign or commas; these will be added later. Press the [ENTER] key to enter the value.

13. Enter the following:
500 in C8.
1500 in C9.
200 in C10.
10000 in C11.
750 in C12.
18000 in C16.
5000 in C17.
900 in D7.
600 in D8.
1500 in D9.
200 in D10.
9750 in D11.
875 in D12.
19500 in D16.
4000 in D17.

14. The values you entered do not have dollar signs or the commas appropriate for a currency format. You will now learn how to format a range of cells for a particular format (in this exercise, the Currency format).

15. *Click in cell C7 and drag the pointer over to cell D20. On the Format menu, click Cells. On the Number tab, click Currency.* Notice that under "**Decimal Places**" it shows "**2**." If you only wanted to show whole dollars (e.g., $1,000 and not $1,000.00), you could change this to zero. Leave the value as 2 for now. *Click OK to close the "Format Cells" window.* Notice that the cell format has now been changed. *Click in any cell to deselect the cell range.*

16. *Click in cell B13, drag the pointer over to cell D13, and click the Bold icon on the toolbar.* This will make the TOTAL EXPENSES row appear in bold.

17. *Click in cell B18, drag the pointer over to cell D18, and click the Bold icon on the toolbar.* This will make the TOTAL INCOME row appear in bold.

18. *Go to cell B20, drag the mouse over to cell D20, and click the Bold icon on the toolbar.* This will make the PROFIT/LOSS row appear in bold.

19. Your spreadsheet is nearly complete; all you need to insert are the six formulas.

20. *Click in cell C13.*

21. Type =**SUM(** and press the [**UP ARROW**] key six times until the cell pointer is at cell C7. Press **.** (a period) to anchor the range.

22. Press the [**DOWN ARROW**] key five times. Press **)** (a closing parenthesis), then press the [**ENTER**] key.

23. Go back to cell C13 and look at the formula displayed in the formula bar. The formula should read "=**SUM(C7:C12)**." The total displayed in the cell should read $13,950.00. Note that you also could have typed the formula =**C7+C8+C9+C10+C11+12**.

24. Enter the following formulas:
    =**SUM(D7:D12)** in D13.
    =**SUM(C16:C17)** in C18.
    =**SUM(D16:D17)** in D18.

25. We now need to enter formulas for the two PROFIT/LOSS columns. Enter the formula =**C18–C13** in C20. (The total should read $9,050.00.)

26. *Click in cell C20 and click the AutoFill command* (the small black square at the bottom right of the cell). *Drag it one column to the right and release the mouse button.* Notice that the formula has been copied. The total should be $9,675.00. Alternatively, you could *click in cell C20 and, on the Edit menu, click Copy, move the cell pointer to cell D20,* and press the [**ENTER**] key.

27. The spreadsheet is now complete. You will need to save the spreadsheet, as you will use it in Lesson 2.

28. To save the spreadsheet, *on the File menu, click Save* and type **Budget1**. *Click Save again.*

29. If you would like to print the spreadsheet, *click the Print icon on the toolbar* (it looks like a printer).

This concludes Lesson 1.
    To exit Excel, *click on the File menu, then click Exit*.
    To go to Lesson 2, stay at the current screen.

LESSON 2: BUILDING A BUDGET SPREADSHEET, PART 2

This lesson assumes that you have completed Lesson 1, have saved the spreadsheet from that lesson, and are generally familiar with the concepts covered in that lesson.

Lesson 2 gives you experience in opening a file, inserting a row, formatting cells in Percent format, building additional formulas, creating a column chart, printing selections, and fitting and compressing data onto one printed page. If you did not exit Excel after Lesson 1, skip Steps 1 and 2, and go directly to Step 3.

1. Open Windows. **Double-click the Excel icon on the desktop** to open Excel for Windows. Alternatively, **click the Start button, point to Programs or All Programs, point to Microsoft Office, then click Microsoft Office Excel 2003.** You should now be in a clean, blank document.

2. To retrieve the spreadsheet from Lesson 1, **click File on the menu, then click Open. Click on the name of your file** (e.g., Budget 1) **and click Open.**

3. You will be entering the information shown in Excel 2003 Exhibit 4.

4. Notice in Excel 2003 Exhibit 4 that a line for travel appears in row 9. You will insert this row first.

5. **Click in cell B9, right-click, and click Insert. Click Entire Row, then click OK.** A new row has been added. You could also have gone to the **Insert menu and clicked Rows.**

6. Enter the following:
   Travel in B9.
   750 in C9.
   650 in D9.

7. Notice that when the new values for travel were entered, all of the formulas were updated. Because you inserted the additional rows in the middle of the column, the formulas recognized the new numbers and automatically recalculated to reflect them. Be extremely careful when inserting new rows and columns into spreadsheets that have existing formulas. In some cases, the new number will not be reflected in the totals, such as when rows or columns are inserted at the beginning or end of the range that a formula calculates. It is always prudent to go back to each existing formula, examine the formula range, and make sure that the new values are included in the formula range.

HANDS-ON EXERCISES

EXCEL 2003 EXHIBIT 4
Expanded budget spreadsheet

8. Change the column width of Column E to 12 by *pointing and clicking on the shaded cell containing the letter E*, at the top of the screen. *Move your pointer to the right edge of the column.* Your pointer should change to a double-headed vertical arrow. *Drag the mouse pointer to the right until the column width is 12* (the width will appear in a small box). Alternatively, you can change the cell width by *placing the pointer anywhere in column E, clicking Format, then Column, then Width,* and typing **12**. *Click on OK.*

9. Enter the following:
   May in E4.
   Difference in E5.
   Percent in F4.
   Of Budget in F5.

10. *Go to cell E4 and drag the pointer over to cell F5* (so that more column headings are highlighted). *Click the Center icon and then the Bold icon on the toolbar.*

11. *Click in cell E14 and drag the mouse pointer over to cell F14. Then click the Bold icon on the toolbar.*

12. *Click in cell E19 and drag the mouse pointer over to cell F19. Then click the Bold icon on the toolbar.*

13. *Click in cell E21 and drag the mouse pointer over to cell F21. Then click the Bold icon on the toolbar.*

14. You are now ready to change the cell formatting for column E to currency and column F to percent. *Go to cell E7 and drag the mouse pointer down to cell E21. Click Format, then click Cells. On the Number tab, click Currency and then OK. Click in any cell to get rid of the cell range.*

15. *Go to cell F7 and drag the mouse pointer down to cell F21. Click Format, then click Cells. On the Number tab, click Percentage and then click OK. Click in any cell to get rid of the cell range.*

16. All that is left to do is enter the formulas for the two new columns. The entries in the May "Difference" column subtract the actual amount from the budgeted amount for each expense item. A positive amount in this column means that the office was under budget on that line item. A negative balance means that the office was over budget on that line item. The "Percent Of Budget" column divides that actual amount by the budgeted amount. This shows the percentage of the budgeted money that was actually spent for each item.

17. You will first build one formula in the May "Difference" column, and then copy it. *Click in cell E7,* type **=C7–D7**, and press the [**ENTER**] key.

18. Using the AutoFill command or the Copy command, copy this formula down through cell E14.

19. *Click in cell E17,* type **=D17–C17**, and press the [**ENTER**] key.

20. Using the AutoFill command, copy this formula down through cell E21. Delete the formula in cell E20 by *clicking in cell E20* and pressing the [**DEL**] key.

21. You will now build on the formula in the "Percent Of Budget" column and copy it. Go to cell F7, type **=D7/C7**, and press the [**ENTER**] key.

22. Using the AutoFill command, copy this formula down through cell F21. Delete the formula in cells F15, F16, and F20 by *clicking in the cell* and then pressing the [**DEL**] key.

23. The spreadsheet has now been built. We will now build a column chart that shows our budgeted expenses compared to our actual expenses (see Excel 2003 Exhibit 5).

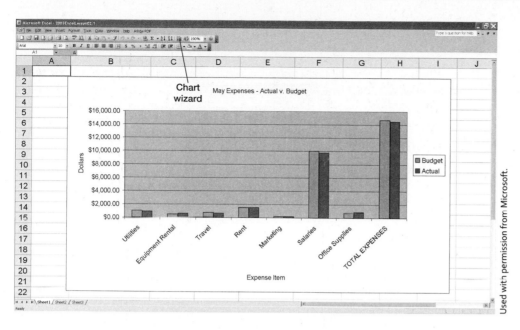

Used with permission from Microsoft.

24. Click in cell B7 and then drag the mouse pointer down and over to cell D14.

25. Click the Chart Wizard icon on the toolbar. It looks like a multicolored column chart/vertical bar chart. Alternatively, you can *select Insert and then click Chart.* The "Chart Wizard – Step 1 of 4 – Chart Type" window is displayed (see Excel 2003 Exhibit 6). This is where you will select the type of chart you want.

Used with permission from Microsoft.

26. Click Column from the Chart type: list. Seven options will be displayed; the first (and default) option, Clustered Column, is fine (see Excel 2003 Exhibit 6). At the bottom of the dialog box is the Press and Hold to View Sample button. Press and hold that button and you will see a preview of the chart you are making. You can use this button to see what your information would look like as a bar chart, pie chart, or any other available graph/chart form.

27. Click Next >. The "Chart Wizard – Step 2 of 4 – Chart Source Data" window is now displayed. This is where you define where the data range will come from for the chart. The data range is correct.

EXCEL 2003 EXHIBIT 7
Chart Wizard: Chart Source
Data

28. *Click the Series tab in the "Chart Wizard – Step 2 of 4 – Chart Source Data" window.*

29. Under S̲eries, Series1 is highlighted in blue. *Click in the white box next to N̲ame:* and type **Budget** (see Excel 2003 Exhibit 7).

30. *Under S̲eries, click Series2. Click in the white box next to N̲ame:* and type **Actual**.

31. *Click N̲ext >.* The "Chart Wizard – Step 3 of 4 – Chart Options" window is now displayed (see Excel 2003 Exhibit 8).

32. The Titles tab should be displayed. In the "Chart title:" box, type **May Expenses – Actual v. Budget**. In the "Category (X) axis:" box, type **Expense Item**. In the "Value (Y) axis:" box, type **Dollars** (see Excel 2003 Exhibit 8). The default values for the other tabs are fine, so *click N̲ext >.*

33. The "Chart Wizard – Step 4 of 4 – Chart Location" window should now be displayed. The "**As object in: Sheet1**" option should be selected. *Click Finish.*

EXCEL 2003 EXHIBIT 8
Chart Wizard: Chart Options

34. The chart is now superimposed over the top of your spreadsheet.

35. *Click in the lower left portion of the chart (in a white space) and then drag the chart over to column H* so the upper left portion of the chart starts at cell H2.

36. *Click the box in the lower right corner of the chart.* The cursor will turn into a double-headed arrow and will say "**Chart Area**". *Drag the box up and to the right* (see Excel 2003 Exhibit 5)—this will expand the chart proportionately and make it larger. Stop expanding the chart when you get to column O and row 21. You may have to use the scroll bars to get to the lower right corner of the chart.

37. The font size is too large, so next you will reduce the size of the font so that all of the information fits in the chart. *Right-click anywhere in the lower left portion of the chart* (in a white space). *Select Format Chart Area. In the Font tab, click 8 under Size. Click OK.*

38. *Click in the chart and then click the Printer icon on the toolbar* to print the chart.

39. To print the spreadsheet, *click out of the chart and click in one of the cells in the spreadsheet.* Press [**CTRL**]+[**HOME**] to go to cell A1.

40. *Click cell B3 and then drag the mouse pointer to cell F21.*

41. *Click File, then click Print. In the "Print" window, under Print What, click Selection. Click OK.* This will print only the portion of the spreadsheet that is highlighted.

42. You will next print the spreadsheet and the chart on one page. *Click on cell B3 and then drag the mouse pointer until both the spreadsheet and the chart are highlighted* (roughly cell B2 to cell O21).

43. *Click File, then click Page Setup. On the Page tab, click Fit to* (it should default to one page). *Click OK.* This will compress everything in the print area to one page.

44. *Click on File, then click Print. In the "Print" window, under Print What, click Selection. Click OK.*

45. To save the document, *click File and then click Save As... .* Type **Budget 2** next to File name:. *Select Save to save the budget to the default directory.*

46. *Click File and then click Close* to close the document, or *click File and then click Exit* to exit Excel.

This concludes Lesson 2.

LESSON 3: BUILDING A DAMAGE PROJECTION SPREADSHEET

This lesson shows you how to build the damage projection spreadsheet shown in Excel 2003 Exhibit 9. It explains how to increase the size of type, how to wrap text in a cell, how to use the border feature, how to use the font and fill color features, how to use the AutoSum feature, and how to change the decimal places for a number. This lesson assumes that you have successfully completed Lessons 1 and 2. Keep in mind that if you make a mistake at any time in this lesson, you may press [**CTRL**]+[**Z**] to undo what you have done.

1. Open Windows. *Double-click the Excel icon on the desktop* to open Excel for Windows. Alternatively, *click the Start button, point to Programs or All Programs, point to Microsoft Office, then click Microsoft Office Excel 2003.* You should now be in a new, clean, blank document.

EXCEL 2003 EXHIBIT 9
Damage projections

Used with permission from Microsoft.

2. To start building the spreadsheet in Excel 2003 Exhibit 9, begin by *increasing the size of column C to a width of 37 (Format > Column > Width).*

3. In cell C3, type **Damage Projection**. With the pointer on C3, *click the Bold icon on the toolbar, then click the Font Size icon on the toolbar and change the size to 14 point.*

4. Type the text in cell C5 (see Excel 2003 Exhibit 9). *Click the Font Size icon on the toolbar and change the type size to 14 point.* Notice that the text goes into the next cell. To wrap part of the text down to the next line within the current cell, *click in cell C5, click Format, then click Cells. Click the Alignment tab. Under Text control, click Wrap text. Click OK.* The text has now been wrapped down to the next line within cell C5.

5. Type the text in cell C6, make the text 14 point, and wrap the text down so it does not go into cell D6. *Note*: You can *right-click in the cell, then click Format Cells* to get to the window to wrap text.

6. Type the text in cell C8 and make the text 14 point.

7. Type the text and values in cells C9 to D13.

8. Type the text in cell C14.

9. To enter the formula in cell D14, *click on cell D14, then click the AutoSum icon on the toolbar* (see Excel 2003 Exhibit 9). Notice that AutoSum assumed that you wanted to add the values in D10 to D13. You could adjust the range by pressing the **[SHIFT]+[ARROW] keys**, but the range should be fine as is (i.e., D10 to D13). Press the **[ENTER]** key to enter the formula.

10. *Click in cell C9 and drag the mouse pointer to cell D14. Click the Font Size icon on the toolbar and change the point size to 14 point.*

11. *Click in cell C9 and drag the mouse pointer to cell D9. Click Format, then click Cells. In the Patterns tab under Color, click the black square, then click OK.* (You could also *click the Fill Color icon on the toolbar* to do this; it looks like a paint bucket.) The cells are all black; now you just need to change the font color to white to see the text.

12. With cells C9 and D9 still highlighted, *click Format, then click Cells. In the Font tab under Color from the drop down menu, click on the white square, then click OK.* (You could also *click the Font Color icon on the toolbar*—it looks like an "A" with a red box beneath it.)

13. ***Click in cell C10 and drag the mouse pointer to cell D14. Click the down arrow next to the Border icon on the toolbar.*** (It is typically just to the left of the Fill Color icon—see Excel 2003 Exhibit 9). ***Click the Borders icon,*** which looks like a windowpane. (Remember, just put the mouse pointer over the icon for a second and the name of the icon will appear.) Notice that a border now appears around every square that was highlighted.

14. ***Click in cell C14 and drag the mouse pointer to cell D14. Click the down arrow next to the Border icon on the toolbar. Click the Thick Box Border icon*** (it looks like a heavy black window frame). Move the pointer and notice that there is now a heavy black border around cells C14 and D14.

15. ***Click in cell D10 and drag the mouse pointer to cell D14. Right-click, then click Format Cells. Click Number, then click Currency. Change decimal places to 0. Click OK.***

16. ***Click the Printer icon on the toolbar*** to print the spreadsheet.

17. To save the spreadsheet, ***click File, then click Save.*** Type **Damage Projection** next to File name:. ***Select Save to save the file to the default directory.***

18. ***Click File and then click Close*** to close the document, or ***click File and then click Exit*** to exit Excel.

This concludes Lesson 3.

▶ INTERMEDIATE LESSONS

LESSON 4: CHILD SUPPORT PAYMENT SPREADSHEET

This lesson shows you how to build the child support payment spreadsheet shown in Excel 2003 Exhibit 10. It explains how to create a white background, how to create formulas to multiply cells and formulas that use an absolute cell reference, and how to use the AutoFormat feature. This lesson assumes that you have successfully completed Lessons 1 through 3. Keep in mind that if you make a mistake at any time in this lesson, you may press [**CTRL**]+[**Z**] to undo what you have done.

1. Open Windows. ***Double-click the Excel icon on the desktop*** to open Excel for Windows. Alternatively, ***click the Start button, point to Programs or All Programs, point to Microsoft Office, then click Microsoft Office Excel 2003.*** You should now be in a new, clean, blank document.

2. As you start to build the spreadsheet in Excel 2003 Exhibit 10, notice that the background is completely white. A completely white background gives you a crisp, clean canvas on which to work and to which you can add colors and graphics.

3. Press [**CTRL**]+[**A**] on the keyboard. The whole spreadsheet is now selected. ***Click the down arrow next to the Fill Color icon on the toolbar.*** (The icon looks like a paint bucket.) ***Click the white square that is all the way in the lower right corner. Click in any cell to make the highlighting disappear.*** Notice that the background of the spreadsheet is now completely white.

4. Enter the text shown in cell C1; change the font style to bold and the font size to 14 point.

5. Increase the width of column C to 20.

6. Enter the text shown in cells C3 to C6.

7. In cell E5, type **.01** and press [**ENTER**]. ***Click again in cell E5, then click the Percent Style icon on the toolbar.*** (The icon looks like a percent sign [%].)

8. Enter the text shown in cell C7 and in the cell range from D7 to G8.

EXCEL 2003 EXHIBIT 10
Child support payment
spreadsheet

Fill color

CHILD SUPPORT PAYMENTS - HALL v. HALL

Beginning Balance $2500
Monthly Payments $500
Interest=Accrued Arrearage   1%
Accrued Arrearage= Previous Arrearage + Previous Interest + Support Due - Support Paid

Month	Support Due	Support Paid	Accrued Arrearage	Monthly Interest
Beginning Bal Jan. 2012			$2,500.00	$25.00
February	$500.00	$100.00	$2,925.00	$29.25
March	$500.00	$500.00	$2,954.25	$29.54
April	$500.00	$0.00	$3,483.79	$34.84
May	$500.00	$250.00	$3,768.63	$37.69
June	$500.00	$750.00	$3,556.32	$35.56
July	$500.00	$0.00	$4,091.88	$40.92

Used with permission from Microsoft.

9. Enter the text shown in the cell range from C10 to C16.

10. Enter the numbers (values) shown in cells in D11 to D16, and E11 to E16.

11. In cell F10, type **2500**.

12. In cell G10, type =, *click in cell F10*, press [**SHIFT**]+[**8**] (an asterisk will appear), then *click in cell E5* and press the [**F4**] key once. The formula "**=F10*E5**" should be on the screen; press the [**ENTER**] key. The formula multiplies the accrued arrearage (how much the individual is behind on payments) times the interest rate (which is 1 percent). The reason you pressed [**F4**] is that the formula had to be an absolute cell reference; pressing [**F4**] simply put the dollar signs ($) into the formula for you. The dollar sign notifies Excel that this is an absolute cell reference, rather than a relative cell reference. Hence, when you copy the formula to other cells (see following material later in this lesson), the accrued arrearage will always be multiplied by the value in E5. Said another way, the second half of this formula (E5) will not change when the formula is copied to other cells.

13. If you want to find out for yourself why the formula **=F10*E5** will not work once it is copied from cell G10 (where it will work fine), type **=F10*E5** into cell G10 and then copy the formula to cells G11 to G16. Once you have seen the effect of this, delete the changes you made and change the formula in cell G10 to **=F10*E5**.

14. To copy the formula from G10 to cells G11 to G16, *click cell G10, click the AutoFill handle* (it looks like a little black box in the lower right corner of the cell), *and drag the mouse pointer down to cell G16.*

15. In cell F11, type **=F10+G10+D11–E11** and press the [**ENTER**] key. The formula adds the accrued amount in the previous month to the previous month's interest and the current support due, and then subtracts the current amount paid.

16. To copy the formula from F11 to cells F12 to F16, *click in cell F11, click the AutoFill handle, and drag the mouse pointer down to cell F16.*

17. *Click cell D10 and drag the mouse pointer to cell G16. Right-click, then click Format Cells. Click the Number tab, click Currency, then click OK.*

18. Notice that the spreadsheet is very plain. You now will use the AutoFormat feature to give the spreadsheet some color. *Click in cell C7 and drag the mouse pointer to cell G16.*

19. *Click Format, then click AutoFormat.* The "AutoFormat" window should now be displayed. *Click on the second spreadsheet format on the right (Classic 3) in the "AutoFormat" window. Click OK. Click in any cell to make the highlighting disappear.* The spreadsheet should now have a blue and gray background.

20. To add borders to the spreadsheet, *click in cell C9 and drag the mouse pointer to cell G16. Click the down arrow next to the Borders icon on the toolbar. Click the All Borders icon* (it looks like a windowpane). The spreadsheet is now complete and should look like Excel 2003 Exhibit 10.

21. *Click the Print icon on the toolbar* to print the spreadsheet.

22. To save the document, *click File and then click Save.* Type **Child Support Payments** next to File name:. *Select Save* to save the file to the default directory.

23. *Click File and then click Close* to close the document, or *click File and then click Exit* to exit Excel.

This concludes Lesson 4.

LESSON 5: LOAN AMORTIZATION TEMPLATE

This lesson shows you how to open a loan amortization template and fill it out (see Excel 2003 Exhibit 11). Templates are a great way to simplify complicated spreadsheets. You will also learn how to protect cells, freeze panes, split a screen, hide a column, and use the Format Painter tool. This lesson assumes that you have successfully completed Lessons 1 through 4. Keep in mind that if you make a mistake at any time in this lesson, you may press [CTRL]+[Z] to undo what you have done.

1. Open Windows. *Double-click the Excel icon on the desktop* to open Excel for Windows. Alternatively, *click the Start button, point to Programs or All Programs, point to Microsoft Office, then click Microsoft Office Excel 2003.* You should now be in a new, clean, blank document.

2. The first thing you will do to complete the template shown in Excel 2003 Exhibit 11 is open the "Lesson 5" file from the disk supplied with this text. Ensure that the disk is fully inserted in the disk drive, *point and click on File on the menu bar, then point and click to Open.* The "Open" window should

EXCEL 2003 EXHIBIT 11
Loan amortization template

Used with permission from Microsoft.

now be displayed. *Point and click on the down arrow to the right of the white box next to "Look in:" and select the drive where the disk is located. Point and double-click on the Excel Files folder. Double-click on the Excel 2003 folder. Double-click on the "Lesson 5" file.*

3. You should now have the loan amortization spreadsheet shown in Excel 2003 Exhibit 11 loaded; however, your spreadsheet contains no data yet.

4. Enter the following information:
   Cell D6: **300000**
   Cell D7: **5.75**
   Cell D8: **30**
   Cell D9: **12**
   Cell D10: **1/1/2012**
   Cell D11: **0** (When you click in Cell D11, a note will appear regarding extra payments; just type a zero and press the [**ENTER**] key and the note will disappear.)
   Cell C13: **National Bank**
   Cell G13: **Jennifer John**

5. Notice that your spreadsheet now appears nearly identical to Excel 2003 Exhibit 11.

6. Notice that just about everything below row 16 in your spreadsheet is a formula. If a user accidentally deleted one of these formulas, the whole spreadsheet could be affected. You will now turn on the Protection feature and lock some of the cells so that they cannot be accidentally deleted.

7. *Right-click in cell D6. Then, click Format Cells... . Click the Protection tab in the "Format Cells" window.* Notice that there is no green check mark next to Locked. Cells D6 to D13 and cell G13 are unlocked even when Protection is turned on. When Protection is off, you can change the locked/unlocked format of cells at will by using the Format > Cells > Protection command sequence. Interestingly, when a new blank spreadsheet is opened in Excel, all cells default to Locked.

8. *Click Cancel in the "Format Cells" window to close the window.*

9. Let's open a new spreadsheet so you can see that all cells in Excel start out with the Locked format. *Click the New File icon on the toolbar;* it is the very first icon on the left. You should now have a new blank spreadsheet displayed. *Right-click in any cell and then click Format Cells. Click the Protection tab.* Notice that the cell seems locked. However, the cell will not be truly locked until you turn on the Protection feature.

10. *Click Cancel in the "Format Cells" window in the new spreadsheet. Click File and then click Close to close the file.* You should now be back at your loan amortization spreadsheet.

11. To turn on the Protection feature, *click Tools, point to Protection, then click Protect Sheet.*

12. The "Protect Sheet" window should now be displayed (see Excel 2003 Exhibit 12). Make sure that the first two selections under "**Allow all users of this worksheet to:**" are selected ("**Select locked cells**" and "**Select unlocked cells**"). Notice that you can enter a password in the white box under "**Password to unprotect sheet:**". This would completely lock the spreadsheet (only unlocked cells could be modified) to users who did not know the password. In this instance, this is not necessary; it is fine for someone to intentionally change the spreadsheet—you are just using this feature to prevent someone from accidentally changing information.

Loan Amortization Spreadsheet

New file — Format painter

13. After ensuring that the first two items are checked under "**Allow all users of this worksheet to:**", *click OK.*

14. *Click in any cell other than D6 to D13 or cell G13 and try to type something in the cell.* Notice that you get an error message saying: "**The cell or chart you are trying to change is protected and therefore read-only.**" *Click OK to close the error window.*

15. The whole spreadsheet is now locked, except for cells D6 to D13 and cell G13, because in the template these were not formatted as locked.

16. You will now turn off the Protection feature, since you are still building the spreadsheet. *Click Tools on the menu bar, point to Protection, then click Unprotect Sheet.*

17. You will now use the Format Painter tool to copy the formatting from one set of cells to another set of cells. Notice that cells F13 and G13 do not look like cells B13 and C13. You will now copy the format from cells B13 and C13 to cells F13 and G13.

18. *Point to cell B13 and drag the mouse pointer to cell C13. Click the Format Painter icon on the toolbar* (the icon that looks like a paintbrush—see Excel 2003 Exhibit 11). Your pointer should now have a paintbrush on it.

19. *Click in cell F13 and drag the mouse pointer to cell H13, then let go of the mouse button.* Notice that the formatting has now been copied.

20. Notice that column E in the amortization schedule of the spreadsheet is the "Extra Payment" column. Assume for the purposes of this exercise that you will not have any extra payments and that you do not need this column; however, you want to leave the column there in case you need it at a later date. For now, you will hide column E until you need it.

21. *Right-click on the cell with an "E" in it* (the E column heading) (see Excel 2003 Exhibit 11). *From the drop-down menu, click Hide.*

22. *Click in any cell to make the vertical line disappear.* Notice that column E is no longer displayed. The next column heading has changed from E to F.

23. You will now unhide column E. *Point on the "D" column heading, drag the mouse pointer to the "F" column heading, then right-click the mouse. Click Unhide on the drop-down menu.* Notice that column E reappears.

24. *Click in any cell to make the highlighting disappear.*

25. *Click in cell D18.* Use the [**DOWN ARROW**] key to go to cell D50. Notice that some column titles, such as "Pmt No." and "Payment Date," are not shown, so it is difficult to know what the numbers mean.

26. Press [**CTRL**]+[**HOME**] to go to the top of the spreadsheet.

27. *Click in cell A18.* You will now use the Split Screen command to see the column titles.

28. *Click Window on the menu bar and then click Split.* Use the [**DOWN ARROW**] key to go to cell A50. Notice that because you split the screen at row 18, you can still see column titles. Next, use the [**UP ARROW**] key to go to cell A1. Notice that you now see the top portion of your spreadsheet in both the top and bottom screens.

29. *Click Window on the menu bar and then click Remove Split.* The bottom screen is now gone.

30. The Freeze Panes feature is another way to show the column headings when you scroll down a document. *Click in cell B18.*

31. *Click Windows on the menu bar and then click Freeze Panes.* Use the [**DOWN ARROW**] key to go to cell B50. Notice that because you froze the screen at cell B18, you can still see column titles. Next, use the [**RIGHT ARROW**] key to go to cell R50. Notice that you can still see the "Pmt No." column, including the payment numbers. The Freeze Panes feature is a convenient way to see both column and row titles at the same time.

32. *Click Window on the menu bar and then click Unfreeze Panes.*

33. *Click the Print icon on the toolbar* to print the spreadsheet.

34. To save the document, *click File on the menu bar and then click Save As... .* Under Save in:, choose the location where you want the file to be saved. Type **Excel Lesson 5 Spreadsheet DONE** next to File name:. *Select Save* to save the file.

35. Templates are a great way to utilize the power of Excel. Many free templates are available on the Internet. Microsoft alone offers more than 100 Excel templates on its website. To access them, *click File on the menu bar and then click New. Under Templates, click Templates on Office Online.*

36. *Click File on the menu bar and then click Close* to close the document, or *click File and then click Exit* to exit Excel.

This concludes Lesson 5.

LESSON 6: STATISTICAL FUNCTIONS

This lesson demonstrates how to use and enter statistical formulas such as average, maximum, minimum, and standard deviation. It also shows how to sort data, check for metadata in spreadsheets, use the Format Clear commands, use conditional formatting, and insert a clip-art file. When the spreadsheet is complete, it will look like Excel 2003 Exhibit 13. Keep in mind that if you make a mistake at any time in this lesson, you may press [**CTRL**]+[**Z**] to undo what you have done.

1. Open Windows. *Double-click the Excel icon on the desktop* to open Excel 2003 for Windows. Alternatively, *click the Start button, point to Programs or All Programs, point to Microsoft Office, then click Microsoft Office Excel 2003.* You should be in a new, clean, blank document.

2. The first thing you will do to complete the spreadsheet in Excel 2003 Exhibit 13 is open the "Lesson 6" file from the disk supplied with this text. Ensure that the disk is inserted in the disk drive, *point and click on File on the menu bar, then point and click on Open.* The "Open" window should now be

EXCEL 2003 EXHIBIT 13
Statistical spreadsheet

displayed. *Point and click on the down arrow to the right of the white box next to "Look in:" and select the drive where the disk is located. Point and double-click on the Excel Files folder. Double-click on the Excel 2003 folder. Double-click on the "Lesson 6" file.*

3. You should now have the age discrimination statistical analysis spreadsheet shown in Excel 2003 Exhibit 13 open; however, your spreadsheet has no formulas in the statistical summary section, the data have not yet been sorted, and there is no clip art yet.

4. You will now enter the formulas in the statistical summary section of the spreadsheet. The first formula calculates the average age of employees of the company. *Click in cell J11.* Type the formula **=AVERAGE(D11:D23)** and then press the [ENTER] key. The result should be 30. *Note*: Another way to enter the average function is to *click Insert on the menu bar and then click Function. Next, under Or select a category:, click the down arrow and select Statistical.* Notice that Average is one of the functions listed.

5. The next formula calculates the most units sold. *Click in cell J12.* Type the formula **=MAX(F11:F23)** and then press the [ENTER] key. The result should be 700.

6. The next formula calculates the least units sold. *Click in cell J13.* Type the formula **=MIN(F11:F23)** and then press the [ENTER] key. The result should be 150.

7. The next formula calculates the average units sold. *Click in cell J14.* Type the formula **=AVERAGE(F11:F23)** and then press the [ENTER] key. The result should be 457.

8. *Point and click on cell J15.* Type the formula **=SUM(F11:F23)** and then press the [ENTER] key. The result should be 5937.

9. The last formula calculates the standard deviation for units sold. The standard deviation is a measure of how widely values are dispersed from the average value (the arithmetic mean). Large standard deviations show that the numbers vary widely from the average. *Click Insert on the menu bar, then click Function.* The "Insert Function" window should now be displayed. *In the "Insert Function" window under Or select a category:, click the down arrow and select Statistical. Scroll down the list and under Select a function, click*

EXCEL 2003 EXHIBIT 14
Entering a standard
deviation formula using the
insert function command

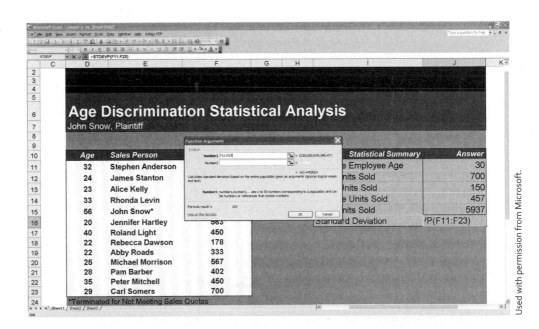

STDEVP (see Excel 2003 Exhibit 14). Notice that there is a definition for this function. ***Click OK in the "Insert Function" window.***

10. The "Function Arguments" window should now be displayed (see Excel 2003 Exhibit 15). In the "Function Arguments" window next to **Number 1,** press the **[DEL]** key until the box is blank. Type **F11:F23** and then ***click OK*** (see Excel 2003 Exhibit 15). The result should be 163.

EXCEL 2003 EXHIBIT 15
Entering a standard
deviation formula using the
insert function arguments
window

Age	Sales Person	Units Sold 2007		Statistical Summary	Answer
32	Stephen Anderson			e Employee Age	30
24	James Stanton			nits Sold	700
23	Alice Kelly			Units Sold	150
33	Rhonda Levin			e Units Sold	457
56	John Snow*			nits Sold	5937
20	Jennifer Hartley	563		Standard Deviation	/P(F11:F23)
40	Roland Light	450			
22	Rebecca Dawson	178			
22	Abby Roads	333			
25	Michael Morrison	567			
28	Pam Barber	402			
35	Peter Mitchell	450			
29	Carl Somers	700			

*Terminated for Not Meeting Sales Quotas

11. You will now sort the data based on the age of the employees. ***Click in cell D11 and then drag the mouse pointer down to F23. Click Data on the menu bar and then click Sort.*** The "Sort" window should now be displayed (see Excel 2003 Exhibit 16). *Note*: Even though you just want to sort by age, you must select the full data range, which includes all of the information, or the "Age" data will be sorted but the other columns and rows will stay where they are. The data will then be mismatched (i.e., the age data will not be matched with the correct persons or number of units sold).

EXCEL 2003 EXHIBIT 16
Sorting data

12. *Click the down arrow under Sort by, then click Age.* Notice that Ascending is selected; this is fine, so *click OK in the "Sort" window.* The data should now be sorted according to the age of the individual, with John Snow appearing last in the spreadsheet.

13. You will now look at the properties of the document to make sure no metadata are included. *Click File on the menu bar, then click Properties.* It would not be good if you were to electronically send this document out of the office, as a number of things show up in the Properties section. It is always a good idea to look at a document's properties before emailing or sending the document out of the office. Use the [DEL] key to delete the information contained in the "Properties" window. When you are done, *click OK* to close the window.

14. Sometimes it is helpful to clear a cell or cells of all formatting information at one time. Notice that cell D6, titled "Age Discrimination Statistical Analysis," is formatted in several different ways, including 24-point type, white letters, red background, and bold. You will now quickly remove all of that formatting. *Click in cell D6, click Edit on the menu bar, point to Clear, then click Formats* (see Excel 2003 Exhibit 17). Notice that all of the formatting is gone.

EXCEL 2003 EXHIBIT 17
Clear formatting/contents of a cell(s)

EXCEL 2003 EXHIBIT 18
Conditional formatting window

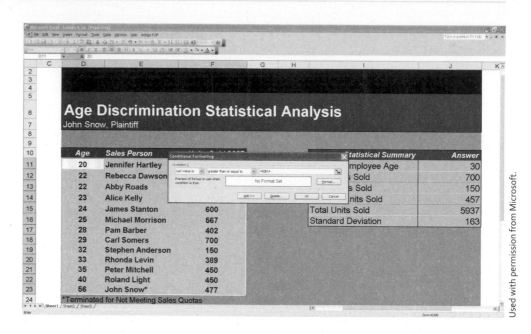

Notice further, in Excel 2003 Exhibit 17, that one of the options when using the Clear command is All. Selecting this will not only clear the format, but will also clear the contents of the selected cell(s).

15. Press **[CTRL]+[Z]** (the Undo feature) to restore the original formatting to the cell.

16. You will now learn how to use the Conditional Formatting feature of Excel. Sometimes, particularly in large spreadsheets, it is helpful to have the formatting of a cell change if certain conditions are present. For example, in an actual vs. budget report, if an item goes over budget by more than 10 percent, it might be helpful for it to be bolded.

17. Notice that the average sales for the sales team in your spreadsheet is 457. It might be helpful to highlight any salesperson who was over the average. *Click in cell F11 and then drag the mouse pointer to F23. Click Format on the menu bar and then click Conditional Formatting.* The "Conditional Formatting" window should now be displayed (see Excel 2003 Exhibit 18).

18. Change the selections in the "Conditional Formatting" window so that they match those in Excel 2003 Exhibit 18 (e.g., **Cell Value Is greater than or equal to =J14**). This will automatically format any cell greater than or equal to the sales average, no matter what that cell is.

19. *Click Format in the "Conditional Formatting" window. Click the down arrow next to Color. Click the red square and then click OK in the "Format Cells" window.*

20. *Click OK in the "Conditional Formatting" window. Click in any cell to make the highlighting disappear.* Notice that any cell with a value greater than or equal to 457 now appears in red.

21. You will now add clip art to your spreadsheet (assuming that clip art was included when Excel 2003 was installed on your computer). *Click in cell I18. Click Insert on the menu bar, then point to Picture, then click Clip Art.*

22. The Clip Art task pane will appear to the right of the screen. Under Search for, type **Money** and then *click Go. Click the clip art shown in Excel 2003 Exhibit 13* (the image that has a blue bar chart with people in it and a person climbing a dollar sign). The clip art has now been added to your spreadsheet.

23. *Click the "X" in the Clip Art task pane* to close the task pane.

24. *Click the Print icon on the toolbar* to print the spreadsheet.

25. To save the document, *click File on the menu bar and then click Save As... .* Under Save in:, choose the location where you want the file to be saved. Type **Excel Lesson 6 Spreadsheet DONE** next to File name:. *Click Save* to save the file.

26. *Click File on the menu bar and then click Close* to close the document, or *click File and then click Exit* to exit Excel.

This concludes Lesson 6.

▶ ADVANCED LESSONS

LESSON 7: TOOLS AND TECHNIQUES 1—MARKETING BUDGET

In this lesson you will learn how to create visual impact with spreadsheets. You will learn to create and manipulate a text box, use advanced shading techniques, create a 3-D style text box, create vertical text, create diagonal text, use lines and borders, and create a comment. When the spreadsheet is complete, it will look like Excel 2003 Exhibit 19. Keep in mind that if you make a mistake at any time in this lesson, you may press [CTRL]+[Z] to undo what you have done.

1. Open Windows. *Double-click on the Excel icon on the desktop* to open Excel for Windows. Alternatively, *click the Start button, point to Programs or All Programs, point to Microsoft Office, then click Microsoft Office Excel 2003.* You should be in a new, clean, blank document.

2. The first thing you will do to complete the spreadsheet in Excel 2003 Exhibit 19 is open the "Lesson 7" file from the disk supplied with this text. Ensure that the disk is inserted in the disk drive, *point and click on File on the menu bar, then point and click on Open.* The "Open" window should now be displayed. *Point and click on the down arrow to the right of the white box next to "Look in:" and select the drive where the disk is located. Point and double-click on the Excel Files folder. Double-click on the Excel 2003 folder. Double-click on the "Lesson 7" file.*

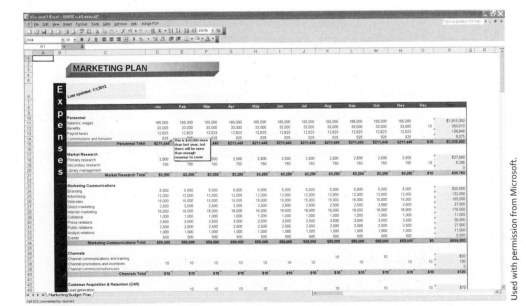

EXCEL 2003 EXHIBIT 19
Creating visual impact in spreadsheets

3. You should now have the marketing plan spreadsheet in Excel 2003 Exhibit 19 open; however, the spreadsheet is missing some of the formatting that gives it visual impact. You will add formatting to the spreadsheet to make it more visually compelling.

4. You will first add the text box that holds the title "Marketing Plan," as shown in Excel 2003 Exhibit 19. To do this, you need access to the Drawing toolbar. *Click View on the menu bar, point to Toolbars, then click Drawing.* The Drawing toolbar should now be displayed at the bottom of the screen.

5. *In the Drawing toolbar at the bottom of the page, click the Text Box icon.* (It looks like a rectangle with an "A" in it. It is *not* the icon with a large blue graphic "A." (Remember that you can hover your mouse over any icon to see its name.) Notice that your mouse pointer has turned into an upside-down letter "T."

6. *Point to cell C2 and drag the mouse pointer to about cell F4.* An outline of a box should now be shown from C2 to F4. This is a text box.

7. *Click inside the text box. Click the Bold icon on the toolbar.*

8. *Click the down arrow next to the Font Size icon on the toolbar and select 20.*

9. Type **MARKETING PLAN.**

10. *Right-click on the outline of the text box you just created. In the drop-down menu, click Format Text Box.* The "Format Text Box" window should now be displayed.

11. *Click the Colors and Lines tab* (see Excel 2003 Exhibit 20). *Under Fill and to the right of Color, click the down arrow* (see Excel 2003 Exhibit 20). This will open a box with many colors; *click Fill Effects.* The "Fill Effects" window should now be displayed. The Gradient tab should be selected.

12. *In the Gradient tab under Colors, click Preset. Click the down arrow next to Present colors, then scroll down and click Fog* (see Excel 2003 Exhibit 21).

13. *Now—still in the "Fill Effects" window and in the Gradient tab—click Vertical under Shading styles* (see Excel 2003 Exhibit 21). Notice that four boxes appear under Variants. This gives you four additional styles you can select. *Select one of the four that you like.*

EXCEL 2003 EXHIBIT 20
Formatting text box

Used with permission from Microsoft.

14. *Click OK in the "Fill Effects" window. Click OK in the "Format Text Box" window.*

15. *Click in any cell to make the highlighting disappear.*

16. You will now add a 3-D style to the text box. *Click in the Marketing Plan text box. Click the 3-D Style icon on the Drawing toolbar* (it is the very last icon, all the way to the right on the Drawing toolbar).

17. When the 3-D style choices appear, *click the third icon to the right on the first row (3-D Style 3). Click in any cell to make the highlighting disappear.* The text box should now have a 3-D box around it (see Excel 2003 Exhibit 19).

18. You will now create the vertical text in column B that says "Expenses," as shown in Excel 2003 Exhibit 19. Notice that this is actually one long cell. The first thing you will do is merge cells B6 through B53 into one cell; you will then add the text and format the cell to be vertical.

19. *Click in cell B6, drag the mouse pointer down to cell B53 and then let go of the mouse button.*

20. *Click the Merge and Center icon on the toolbar.* (It is just to the right of the Align Right icon. It looks like a box with an "a" in the middle with left and right arrows around the "a.") Notice that the selected cells have been merged into one cell now, extending from B6 to B53.

21. With the pointer still in cell B6, *click the down arrow next to the Font Size icon and click 22. Click the Bold icon.* Type **Expenses** and press the **[ENTER]** key.

22. *Right-click anywhere in cell B6, then click Format Cells.* The "Format Cells" window should now be displayed, and the Alignment tab should be selected (see Excel 2003 Exhibit 22).

23. *In the "Format Cells" window under Orientation, click the box that shows the word "Text" displayed vertically* (i.e., written from top to bottom instead of from left to right—see Excel 2003 Exhibit 22).

24. *In the "Format Cells" window under Vertical:, click the down arrow and select Top (Indent)* (see Excel 2003 Exhibit 22).

25. *Click OK in the "Format Cells" window.* The word "Expenses" should now be displayed vertically down the cell.

HANDS-ON EXERCISES

EXCEL 2003 EXHIBIT 22
Creating vertical text

26. *With the pointer still in cell B6, click the down arrow next to the Fill Color icon* (it looks like a paint bucket with a color under it) *on the toolbar and select black. Click the down arrow next to the Font Color icon* (it looks like an "A" with a color under it) *and select yellow.*

27. You will next make the text in cell C6 appear diagonally. *Right-click on cell C6. Point and click on Format Cells.* The "Format Cells" window should now be displayed and the Alignment tab should be selected (see Excel 2003 Exhibit 22).

28. *In the "Format Cells" window under Orientation, click the up arrow next to Degrees until it says 15.*

29. *In the "Format Cells" window, click the Patterns tab. Click the yellow square, then click OK.*

30. *Click in any cell to make the highlighting disappear.* The words "Last updated: 1/1/2012" should now be displayed diagonally in black letters with a yellow background.

31. You will now add the Comment shown in Excel 2003 Exhibit 19. *Right-click in cell D15. On the drop-down menu, click Insert Comment.* Press the **[BACKSPACE]** key twice to delete the colon, and then type **This is $40,000 more than last year, but there will be more than enough revenue to cover this.** *Click in any cell to exit the "Comment" box.*

32. *Hover your mouse pointer over cell D15 to see the comment.*

33. You will now add borders to the spreadsheet. *Point to cell C53 and drag the mouse pointer to cell P53. Click the down arrow next to the Borders icon on the toolbar* (just to the left of the Fill Color icon). A number of borders are displayed; *point and click on the All Borders icon* (it looks like a windowpane). The "Totals" row should now have borders around each cell.

34. *Click in cell C8 and drag the mouse pointer to cell P53. Click the down arrow next to the Borders icon on the toolbar, and click the border that looks like a single box with a thick border around it (the Thick Box Border icon).* A thick border now surrounds the data.

35. *Click on the Printer icon on the toolbar* to print the spreadsheet.

36. To save the document, *click File on the menu bar and then click Save As... .* Under Save in:, choose the location where you want the file to be saved. Type **Excel Lesson 7 Spreadsheet DONE** next to File name:. *Select Save* to save the file.

37. *Click File on the menu bar and then click Close* to close the document, or *click File and then click Exit* to exit Excel.

This concludes Lesson 7.

LESSON 8: TOOLS AND TECHNIQUES 2—STOCK PORTFOLIO

In this lesson, you will continue to learn and apply helpful tools and techniques using Excel. This includes getting additional practice using the Merge and Center tool, using the Fit to Page feature, printing selections, using the Formula Auditing feature, using the oval tool, and password-protecting a file. When your spreadsheet is complete, it will look similar to Excel 2003 Exhibit 23.

Some of these tools have been covered in previous lessons, but this lesson will reinforce your ability to use them effectively. This tutorial assumes that you have completed Lessons 1 through 7, and that you are quite familiar with Excel.

1. Open Windows. *Double-click on the Excel icon on the desktop* to open Excel for Windows. Alternatively, *click the Start button, point to Programs or All Programs, point to Microsoft Office, then click Microsoft Office Excel 2003.* You should now be in a new, clean, blank document.

2. The first thing you will do to complete the spreadsheet shown in Excel 2003 Exhibit 23 is open the "Lesson 8" file from the disk supplied with this text. Ensure that the disk is inserted in the disk drive, *point and click on File on the menu bar, then point and click on Open.* The "Open" window should now be displayed. *Point and click on the down arrow to the right of the white box next to "Look in:" and select the drive where the disk is located. Point and double-click on the Excel Files folder. Double-click on the Excel 2003 folder. Double-click on the "Lesson 8" file.*

3. You should now have the stock portfolio spreadsheet shown in Excel 2003 Exhibit 23 open; however, your spreadsheet will be missing two rows of data and some of the formatting. You will add the rows and formatting to the spreadsheet.

HANDS-ON EXERCISES

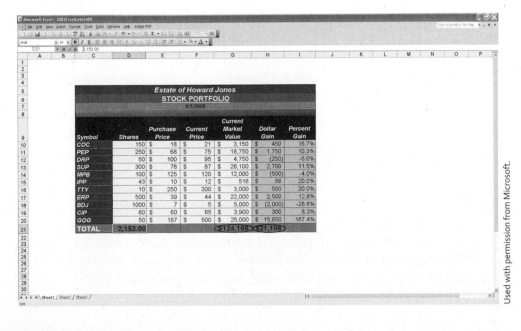

EXCEL 2003 EXHIBIT 23
Stock portfolio

Used with permission from Microsoft.

4. *Use the Merge and Center icon on the toolbar to merge cells C5 to I5.*

5. *Use the Merge and Center icon on the toolbar to merge cells C6 to I6.*

6. *Use the Merge and Center icon on the toolbar to merge cells C7 to I7.*

7. Make sure the titles are aligned as shown in Excel 2003 Exhibit 23 (use the Left Align and Center Align icons on the toolbar).

8. *Use the Fill Color icon on the toolbar to make the fill color for cell C5 Dark Blue.*

9. *Use the Fill Color icon on the toolbar to make the fill color for cell C6 Indigo.*

10. *Use the Fill Color icon on the toolbar to make the fill color for cell C7 Light Blue.*

11. The cell range from C8 to I8 is a text graphic box (similar to a text box). *Right-click the box, select Format AutoShape, and change the fill color to a fill effect of Preset, Early Sunset, with a shading style of Diagonal Up.*

12. *Use the Borders icon on the toolbar to give cells D10 to I21 a border of All Borders.*

13. *On the Drawing toolbar, click the Oval tool, which looks like a circle.* (If the Drawing toolbar does not appear, *click View > Toolbars > Drawing). Start in the upper left corner of cell G21 and drag the mouse pointer to the lower right corner of G21 to make an oval around the total.* Note: You can slightly move the ovals by using the cursor keys on the keyboard to nudge them into place so that they are centered in the cell.

14. *Right-click the oval and select Format AutoShape. Change the fill color to No Fill, and change the line weight to 1.75. Click OK.*

15. *Repeat the same process in cell H21.*

16. You will now use the Formula Auditing mode to inspect the formulas that are in the spreadsheet and ensure that they are accurate.

17. *Click Tools on the menu bar, point to Formula Auditing, then click Formula Auditing Mode.* Scroll over to the right and look at all of the cells in your spreadsheet. Notice that instead of seeing the results of the formulas, you see the formulas themselves. This is a great tool for checking the accuracy of your spreadsheets. Look at your formulas and make sure they are correct. When you are certain that your formulas are accurate, *turn off Formula Auditing mode by clicking Tools on the menu bar, pointing to Formula Auditing, then clicking Formula Auditing Mode again.* This will turn formula auditing off.

18. You will now learn how to password-protect your spreadsheet files. *Click File from the menu bar, then click Save As.... In the "Save As" window, click Tools and then click General Options.* Under File sharing and next to Password to open, type **A**, and *click OK.* At the "Confirm Password" window, type **A** and then *click OK.* At the "Save As" window, *save the file to My Documents* (or the folder of your choice—you must remember where you saved it).

19. *Click File on the menu bar and then click Close* to close the file.

20. *Click File again; then, at the bottom of the drop-down menu, click the name of the file you just saved.*

21. The "Password" window should now be displayed. Type **A** in the "Password" window and then *click OK.* The file should now be displayed.

22. You can turn off a password in the same way. *Click File, then click Save As.... In the "Save As" window, click Tools and then click General Options.* Under

File sharing, next to Password to open, use the **[DEL]** key to remove the asterisk. ***Click OK. Click Save in the "Save As" window.*** At the "**Do you want to replace the existing file?**" prompt, ***click Yes.***

23. Close the file and then reopen it and you will see that you no longer need a password to open it.

24. ***Click the Print icon on the toolbar;*** the spreadsheet will most likely print on two pages.

25. You will now learn how to use the Fit to command to force Excel to print a spreadsheet on one page.

26. ***Click in cell C5 and drag the mouse pointer down to cell I21. Click File on the menu bar, then click Page Setup. In Page tab under Scaling, click Fit to, select one page, then click OK.***

27. ***With the cell range from C5 to I21 still highlighted, click File and then click Print. Under Print What, click Selection, then click Preview.*** Notice that the spreadsheet will print on one page. If you want to actually print the spreadsheet, ***click Print.*** To close the Print Preview screen, ***click Close.***

28. ***Click in any cell to make the highlighting disappear.***

29. To save the document, ***click on File on the menu bar and then click Save As… .*** Under Save in:, choose the location where you want the file to be saved. Type **Excel Lesson 8 Spreadsheet DONE** next to File name:. ***Select Save*** to save the file.

30. ***Click File and then click Close*** to close the document, or ***click File and then click Exit*** to exit Excel.

This concludes the Excel 2003 Hands-On Exercises.

CHAPTER 4

Legal Timekeeping and Billing Software

FEATURED SOFTWARE
Tabs3 Billing Software

TABS3 BILLING SOFTWARE

▶ *READ THIS FIRST!*

I. INTRODUCTION–READ THIS!

The Tabs3 timekeeping and billing program demonstration version is a full working version of the program with a few limitations. The main limitation is that only a limited number of clients can be entered into the program. The demonstration version does *not* time out (quit working after a set number of days).

II. USING THE TABS3 HANDS-ON EXERCISES

The Tabs3 Hands-On Exercises are easy to use and contain step-by-step instructions. Each lesson builds on the previous exercise, so please complete the Hands-On Exercises in order. Tabs3 is a user-friendly program, so using the program should be intuitive. Tabs3 also comes with sample data, so you should be able to try many features of the program.

III. INSTALLATION INSTRUCTIONS

Below are step-by-step instructions for loading the Tabs3 timekeeping and billing demonstration version on your computer.

1. *Insert the disk supplied with this text into your computer.*
2. When prompted with "What do you want Windows to do?" *select "Open folder to view files using Windows Explorer," then click OK.* If your computer does not automatically recognize that you have inserted a disk, double-click the My Computer icon, then double-click the drive where the disk is.
3. *Double-click the Tabs3 folder. Then double-click the launch.exe file.* This will start the Tabs3 installation wizard.

4. The screen in Tabs3 Installation Exhibit 1 should now be displayed. ***Click "Next."***

TABS3 INSTALLATION EXHIBIT 1

5. Your screen will look like Tabs3 Installation Exhibit 2. ***Click "Install Tabs3 Trial Software."***

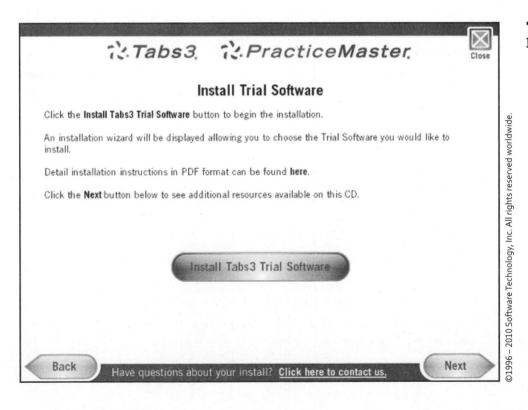

TABS3 INSTALLATION EXHIBIT 2

HANDS-ON EXERCISES

6. The Tabs3 Trial Software Setup window should now be displayed. (See Installation Exhibit 3.) ***Click "Next."***

TABS3 INSTALLATION EXHIBIT 3

7. Your screen will look like Tabs3 Installation Exhibit 4. Review the license agreement, then ***click "Yes."***

TABS3 INSTALLATION EXHIBIT 4

8. Your screen will look like Tabs3 Installation Exhibit 5. ***Click "Next."***

**TABS3 INSTALLATION
EXHIBIT 5**

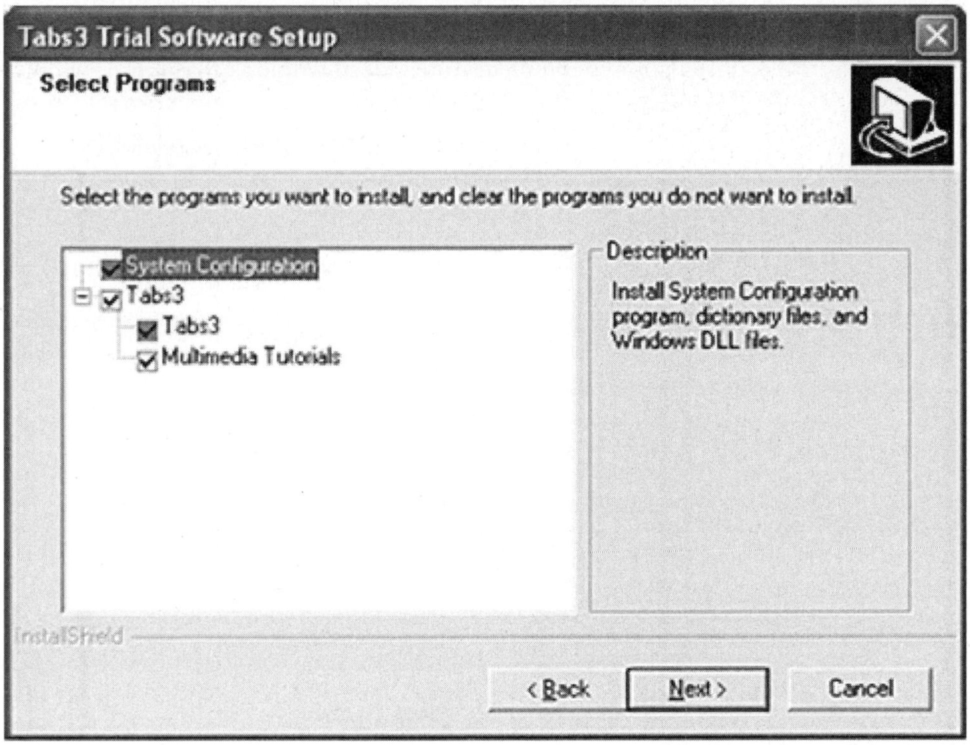

9. Your screen will look like Tabs3 Installation Exhibit 6. ***Click "Next."***

**TABS3 INSTALLATION
EXHIBIT 6**

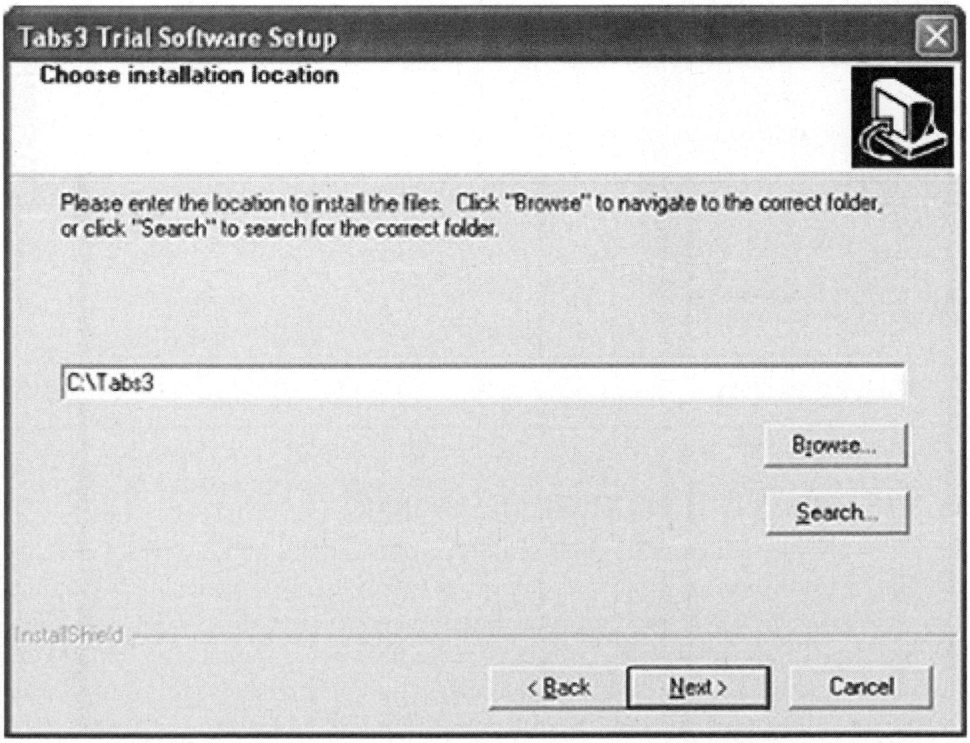

HANDS-ON EXERCISES

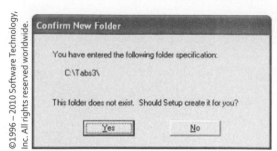

Confirm New Folder

You have entered the following folder specification:

C:\Tabs3\

This folder does not exist. Should Setup create it for you?

[Yes]   [No]

**TABS3 INSTALLATION
EXHIBIT 7**

10. You may be asked to confirm the creation of a new folder (see Tabs3 Installation Exhibit 7). ***Click "Yes."***

11. You may be asked if you wish to install starter data. ***Click "Yes"*** (see Tabs3 Installation Exhibit 8).

12. Installation is complete. Your screen will look like Tabs3 Installation Exhibit 9. ***Click "Finish."***

**TABS3 INSTALLATION
EXHIBIT 8**

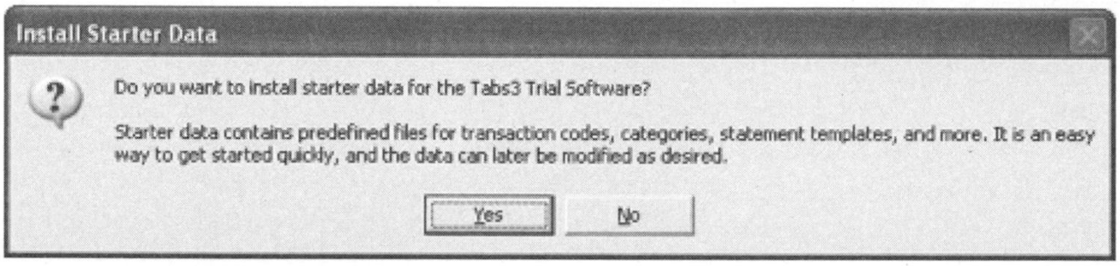

Install Starter Data

? Do you want to install starter data for the Tabs3 Trial Software?

Starter data contains predefined files for transaction codes, categories, statement templates, and more. It is an easy way to get started quickly, and the data can later be modified as desired.

[Yes]   [No]

**TABS3 INSTALLATION
EXHIBIT 9**

Tabs3 Trial Software Setup

InstallShield Wizard Complete

The InstallShield Wizard has successfully installed Tabs3 Trial Software. Click Finish to exit the wizard.

[< Back]   [Finish]   [Cancel]

IV. INSTALLATION TECHNICAL SUPPORT

If you have problems installing the demonstration version of Tabs3 from the disk included with this text, please contact Delmar Cengage Learning Technical Support first at (800) 648-7450. Please note that Tabs3 is a licensed product of Software Technology, Inc. If Delmar Cengage Learning Technical Support is unable to resolve your installation question, or if you have a non-installation–related question, you will need to contact Software Technology, Inc. directly at (402) 423-1440.

HANDS-ON EXERCISES

TABS3 BILLING SOFTWARE

Number	Lesson Title	Concepts Covered
BASIC LESSONS		
Lesson 1	Introduction to Tabs3	An introduction to the Tabs3 interface
Lesson 2	Entering a New Client	Entering a new client into Tabs3, including entering contact data, setup, rates, billing, and statement information
INTERMEDIATE LESSONS		
Lesson 3	Entering Fee/Time Records	Entering several different types of fee/time record entries
Lesson 4	Entering Cost/Expense Records and Using the Fee Timer Feature	Entering several different types of cost/expense records and learning how to use the Fee Timer feature
Lesson 5	Generating and Printing Draft and Final Statements	Generate and print draft statements and final statements; update statements
Lesson 6	Entering a Payment	Enter and apply a payment
ADVANCED LESSON		
Lesson 7	Processing and Printing Reports	Process and print a number of management, productivity, and client reports

GETTING STARTED

Introduction

Throughout these lessons and exercises, information you need to type into the software will be designated in several different ways:

- Keys to be pressed on the keyboard are designated in brackets, in all caps, and in bold (e.g., press the **[ENTER]** key).
- Movements with the cursor are designated in bold and italics (e.g., ***point to File on the menu bar and click***).
- Words or letters that should be typed are designated in bold (e.g., type **Training Program**).
- Information that is or should be displayed on your computer screen is shown in bold, with quotation marks (e.g., **"Press ENTER to continue."**).
- Specific menu items and commands are designated with an initial capital letter (e.g., click Open).

OVERVIEW OF TABS3

Tabs3 is a full featured time, accounting, and billing system. Software Technology, Inc., also produces additional modules that integrate with the billing software, including general ledger software, accounts payable software, trust accounting software, Tabs3 and GLS Report Writers, and PracticeManager case management software. This tutorial covers only the billing software. Tabs3 Exhibit 1 shows the main Tabs3 window with task folders displayed. With Tabs3, you can enter new clients, fee/time records, expense entries, and payments; run billing/management

TABS3 EXHIBIT 1
Tabs3 window with task
folders

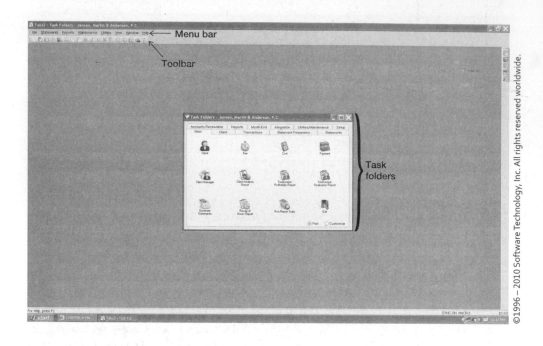

Menu bar

Toolbar

Task
folders

reports; and control a firm's overall billing system. Tabs3 is robust and offers many advanced billing features, and it is also easy to use. By the end of the exercises, you should have a good understanding of the basics of legal time entry and billing with Tabs3.

▶ BASIC LESSONS

LESSON 1: INTRODUCTION TO TABS3

This lesson introduces you to Tabs3. It explains basic information about the Tabs3 interface, including an overview of clients, fees, costs, payments, generating bills and statements, and running reports.

Before you start, install the Tabs3 trial version on your computer by following the instructions entitled "Tabs3 Hands-On Exercises—Read This First!" *Note:* The Tabs3 Billing Software trial version does *not* time out (quit working after a set number of days). The main limitation of the trial version is that only 30 clients can be entered into the software.

1. Open Windows. After it has loaded, ***double-click Tabs3 with Sample Data on the desktop,*** or ***click the Start button on the Windows desktop, point to Programs or All Programs, point to the Tabs3 & PracticeMaster group, point to Trial Software with Sample Data, then click Tabs3 with Sample Data.*** Tabs3 will then open with sample data already present in the software. *Note:* If a message about the integration between Tabs3 and PracticeMaster is displayed, you have opened the trial software without sample data. ***Click OK, then click Close in the "Tip of the Day" window***. Press **[CTRL]+[S]** to save customization settings, ***click the Close icon*** (the red square with a white "X") to exit the software, and then try again to open the program.

2. The "Tip of the Day" window should now be displayed. ***Click Close in the "Tip of the Day" window.*** *Note:* If you do not want to see the Tip of the Day, ***select the* "Do not show tips at startup" *box before clicking Close.***

3. The screen in Tabs3 Exhibit 2 should now be displayed. The Tabs3 window states that sample data is being used and that the system date in use with the

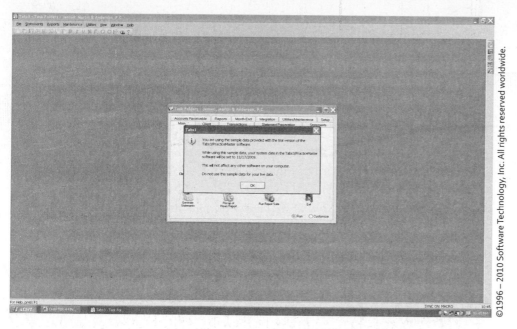

TABS3 EXHIBIT 2
Sample data/date notice

sample data is set to 11/17/2009. This date will not affect any other software on your computer.

4. **Click OK in the "Tabs3" window.** The screen in Tabs3 Exhibit 1 should now be displayed. Notice the "Task Folders—Jensen, Martin & Anderson, P.C." window (hereinafter referred to as the "Task Folders" window) in the middle of the screen in Tabs3 Exhibit 1. *Note:* Sample data for the fictitious law firm of Jensen, Martin & Anderson, P.C. are used throughout this tutorial.

5. Notice in Tabs3 Exhibit 1 that the Main tab in the "Task Folders" window is currently displayed (other tabs include Client, Transactions, Statements, Reports, etc.). The icons change depending on which tab is selected.

6. **Click the Client icon in the "Task Folders" window.**

7. A blank "Client Information" window should now be displayed. This is where you enter information about a client, such as name, contact information, billing options, setup options, statement options, and so on. In Lesson 2 you will set up a new client using this window.

8. **Click the Close icon** (the red square with a white "X") **at the upper right of the "Client Information" window.** *Note:* To have the computer display the name of an icon, just hover the cursor over the icon for a second; the name will be displayed.

9. **Click Fee in the "Task Folders" window.**

10. The "Fee Entry" window should now be displayed. This is where client time/fee entries (time records) are entered into Tabs3. In this window, the user designates the client to be billed, timekeeper, date of the record, transaction code (the activity), number of hours worked, a description of the activity, and other data. In Lesson 3, you will enter a number of fee records into Tabs3.

11. **Click the Close icon in the upper right of the "Fee Entry" window.**

12. **Click Cost in the "Task Folders" window.**

13. The "Rapid Cost Entry" window should now be displayed. This is where client cost entries (cost records or expenses) are entered into Tabs3. These include costs such as photocopying, courier fees, transcription fees, and travel expenses.

In this window the user designates the client to be billed, the date the cost was incurred, a description of the cost, and related information. In Lesson 4, you will enter a number of cost records into Tabs3.

14. *Click the Close icon in the upper right of the "Rapid Cost Entry" window.*

15. *Click Generate Statements in the "Task Folders" window.*

16. The "Generate Statements" window should now be displayed. This is where users designate which clients to bill.

17. *Click the Transactions tab in the "Generate Statements" window.* This is where users control what type of fees, expenses, advances, and payments are billed/credited to a client.

18. *Click the Options tab in the "Generate Statements" window.* This is where users select whether to produce draft (pre-billing) statements or final statements, and assign beginning statement numbers, individual billing thresholds (e.g., only producing statements that are more than $100), and related options.

19. *Click the Close icon at the upper right of the "Generate Statements" window.*

20. *Click Payment in the "Task Folders" window.*

21. The "Rapid Payment Entry" window should now be displayed. This is where users can enter and apply payments to client invoices and accounts.

22. *Click the Close icon at the upper right of the "Rapid Payment Entry" window.*

23. *Click the Client tab in the "Task Folders" window.* Notice that the icons have now changed.

24. *Click each of the tabs in the "Task Folders" window to see all of the icons listed.*

25. *Click back to the Main tab in the "Task Folders" window.*

26. *Click File on the menu bar and then click Exit.*

This concludes Lesson 1.

LESSON 2: ENTERING A NEW CLIENT

In this lesson you will learn how to enter a new client into Tabs3. In doing so, you will explore the many options users have to set up a client with respect to billing and payments.

1. Open Windows. *Double-click Tabs3 with Sample Data on the desktop, or click the Start button on the Windows desktop, point to Programs or All Programs, point to the Tabs3 & PracticeMaster group, point to Trial Software with Sample Data, then click Tabs3 with Sample Data.* Tabs3 will then open with sample data already present in the software.

2. The "Tip of the Day" window may now be displayed. *Click Close in the "Tip of the Day" window.*

3. *Click OK in the "Tabs3" window* to acknowledge the 11/17/2009 date.

4. *Click Client in the "Task Folders" window.* The "Client Information" window should now be displayed (see Tabs3 Exhibit 3). Notice that the Address tab is selected.

5. Your cursor should be in the Client ID field. *Click the New icon on the toolbar* (see Tabs3 Exhibit 3). Tabs3 automatically generates the next Client ID number, which is 851.00.

TABS3 EXHIBIT 3
Entering a new client in the Address tab of the "Client Information" window

6. Enter the following information in the Address tab of the "Client Information" window (see Tabs3 Exhibit 3). *Note:* You can press the [**TAB**] key to move forward through the fields, or press [**SHIFT**]+[**TAB**] to move backward through the fields. If a field is left blank in the following list, just skip it.

FIELD	INFORMATION TO BE ENTERED
Name (Last/First):	**Richards/Sherry**
Work Description:	**Richards v. EZ Pest Control**
Name Search:	**Richards/Sherry**
Address Line 1:	**2000 Clayton Boulevard**
Address Line 2:	
Address Line 3:	
City:	**Atlanta**
State:	**GA**
Zip:	**30303**
Country:	
Location:	
Date Opened:	**11/17/2009**
Date Closed:	**mm/dd/yyyy**
Contact:	
Office:	**888-555-5429**
Home:	**888-555-3999**
Fax:	
Cellular:	**888-555-5567**
E-mail:	**srichards@aom.com**

7. *Click the Setup tab in the "Client Information" window* (see Tabs3 Exhibit 4).

TABS3 EXHIBIT 4
Entering a new client—
Setup options

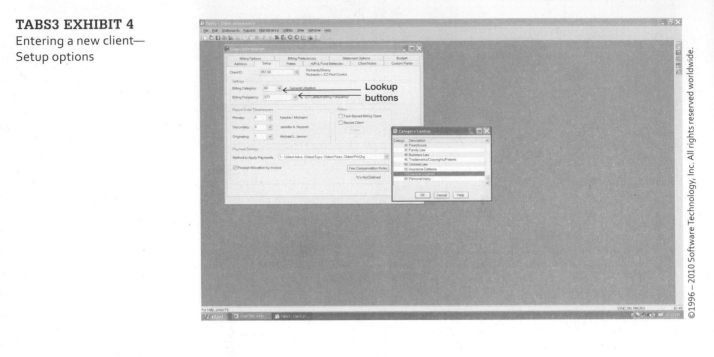

8. *Click the Lookup button.* (It is the down arrow to the right of the Billing Category field.) The "Category Lookup" window should now be displayed (see Tabs3 Exhibit 4). *Scroll down, click 60 General Litigation, then click OK in the "Category Lookup" window.*

9. *Click the Lookup button* (down arrow) *to the right of Billing Frequency:.* The "Billing Frequency Lookup" window should now be displayed. Notice that you can select Bill on Demand, Monthly, Quarterly, etc. We will use the default setting of STI, so just *click Cancel in the "Billing Frequency Lookup" window.*

10. *Under Report Order Timekeepers, click the Lookup button* (down arrow) *next to Primary:.* The "Timekeeper Lookup" window should now be displayed.

11. *Double-click Kendra I. Michaels.* The primary timekeeper is the attorney who is responsible for the case; in this example the primary timekeeper is an associate.

12. *Under Report Order Timekeepers, click the Lookup button* (down arrow) *next to Secondary:.* The "Timekeeper Lookup" window should again be displayed.

13. *Double-click on Jennifer A. Noonan.* The secondary timekeeper is the support staff person who is responsible for the case; in this example, the secondary timekeeper is a paralegal. (*Note:* The *originating timekeeper* is the person who brought the client to the firm. We will leave the originating timekeeper as Michael L. Jensen.)

14. *Click the Rates tab in the "Client Information" window* (see Tabs3 Exhibit 5). Notice that the screen has a number of options for customizing the billing rate for a client. In this example, the Billing Rate Code that will be used is "1 - Timekeeper Rate 1" (see Tabs3 Exhibit 5). This indicates that each timekeeper's Hourly Rate 1 will be used as the default billing rate.

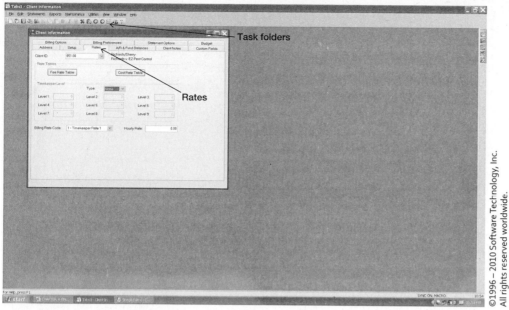

TABS3 EXHIBIT 5
Entering a new client—
Rates options

15. You will now look at what the Timekeeper Rate 1 amount is for Kendra I. Michaels and Jennifer A. Noonan. ***Click the Task Folders icon on the toolbar*** (see Tabs3 Exhibit 5). The "Task Folders" window should now be displayed.

16. ***Click the Setup tab in the "Task Folders" window.***

17. ***Click Timekeeper on the Setup tab.***

18. ***In the "Miscellaneous" window, click the Lookup button next to Timekeeper:*** (see Tabs3 Exhibit 6).

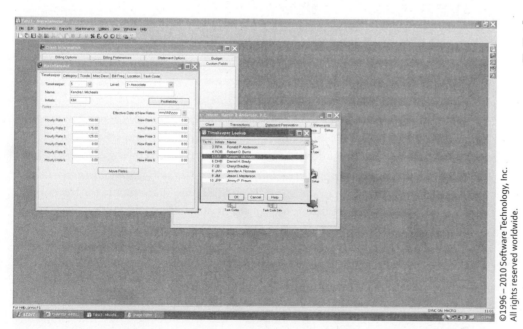

TABS3 EXHIBIT 6
Hourly rates for Kendra I. Michaels

19. ***Double-click Kendra I. Michaels.*** Notice that the amount in her Hourly Rate 1: field is $150.00.

20. ***In the "Miscellaneous" window, click the Lookup button next to Timekeeper.***

21. ***Double-click Jennifer A. Noonan.*** Notice that the amount in her Hourly Rate 1: field as a paralegal is $100.00.

22. ***Click the Close icon at the upper right of the "Miscellaneous" window.***

23. ***Click anywhere in the "Client Information" window.*** *(Note:* To move a window, just ***click and drag the title bar at the top of the window***).

24. ***Click the A/R & Fund Balances tab in the "Client Information" window.*** Once fees, expenses, and billings have been entered, this tab will contain current balances for the client.

25. ***Click the Client Notes tab in the "Client Information" window.***

26. ***Put your cursor in the Client Notes field.*** Type **Client says she wants to be billed monthly, but will generally pay the balance owed every 60 days.** (see Tabs3 Exhibit 7).

TABS3 EXHIBIT 7
Entering a new client—
Client Notes

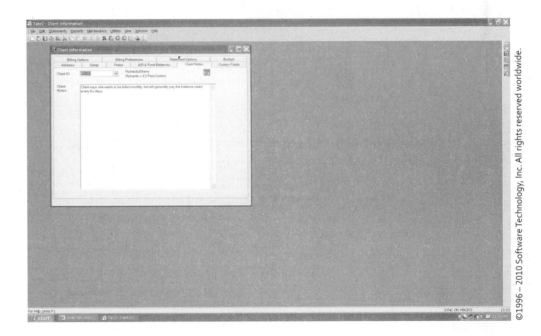

27. ***Click the Billing Options tab in the "Client Information" window.*** This window is where users can set up a billing threshold, a courtesy discount, sales tax, or a finance charge. This client does not have or need any special billing options.

28. ***Click the Billing Preferences tab in the "Client Information" window.*** This window is where users can set up additional billing requirements for the client, such as special billing instructions or a secondary billing address. Again, this client has no special needs.

29. ***Click the Statement Options tab in the "Client Information" window.*** This window allows users to set up and customize the billing templates for the client. The default options are fine for this client.

30. ***Click the Budget and Custom Fields tabs in the "Client Information" window*** to see what these tabs look like. You will not enter any information in these tabs.

31. ***Click the Save icon on the toolbar*** (it looks like a floppy disk).

32. ***Click the Close icon at the upper right of the "Client Information" window.***

33. To make sure the client has been entered into Tabs3, ***click the Main tab in the "Task Folders" window, then click the Client icon.***

34. *In the "Client Information" window, click the down arrow next to the Client ID: field.* The "Client Lookup" screen should now be displayed.

35. *Double-click on 851.00 richards/sherry.* The information for *Sherry Richards* and *Richards v. EZ Pest Control* should now be displayed.

36. *Click the Close icon at the upper right of the "Client Information" window.*

37. *Click File on the menu bar and then click Exit.*

This concludes Lesson 2.

▶ INTERMEDIATE LESSONS

LESSON 3: ENTERING FEE/TIME RECORDS

In this lesson, you will learn how to enter time records into Tabs3.

1. Open Windows. *Double-click Tabs3 with Sample Data on the desktop, or click the Start button on the Windows desktop, point to Programs or All Programs, point to the Tabs3 & PracticeMaster group, point to Trial Software with Sample Data, then click Tabs3 with Sample Data.* Tabs3 will then open with sample data already entered into the program.

2. The "Tip of the Day" window may now be displayed. *Click Close in the "Tip of the Day" window.*

3. *Click OK in the "Tabs3" window* to acknowledge the 11/17/2009 date.

4. *Click Fee in the "Task Folders" window.*

5. *Click the Detail/Rapid icon on the toolbar in the "Fee Entry" window* (*not* the main toolbar—see Tabs3 Exhibit 8). Notice that fewer fields are now displayed. The Detail/Rapid icon toggles between a detail fee entry window that has several fields, and a rapid data entry window that has fewer fields.

6. Your cursor should already be in the Client ID: field, with the last Client ID number, 851.00, listed. Press the **[TAB]** key to go to the Reference: field.

7. Press the **[TAB]** key to go to the Timekeeper: field.

8. *Click the Lookup button next to the Timekeeper: field. Double-click on Jennifer A. Noonan.*

Detail/Rapid Toggle

TABS3 EXHIBIT 8
Entering a fee/time record

9. At the Date: field, press the [TAB] key to accept the default date of 11/17/2009.

10. ***Click the Lookup button next to the Tcode: (transaction code) field.*** The "Tcode Lookup" window should now be displayed. ***Double-click on 3 TC Telephone conference with.***

11. In the Hours Worked: field, type **.50** and then press the [TAB] key.

12. The cursor should now be in the Amount: field with 50.00 highlighted. Press the [TAB] key.

13. The cursor should now be in the Description: field. At the end of **"Telephone conference with"** type **client.** and then press the [TAB] key.

14. ***Click the Save icon on the main toolbar.*** A blank fee/time record is now displayed.

15. Enter and save each of the following fee/time records:

FIELD	INFORMATION TO BE ENTERED
Client ID:	851.00
Reference:	
Timekeeper:	5
Date:	11/17/2009
Tcode:	8
Hours Worked:	6.00
Hours to Bill:	6.00
Rate:	150.00
Amount:	900.00
Description:	Draft and revise Response to Motion for Summary Judgment.
Category:	60
Bill Code:	0 – Billable / Printable

FIELD	INFORMATION TO BE ENTERED
Client ID:	851.00
Reference:	
Timekeeper:	8
Date:	11/17/2009
Tcode:	10
Hours Worked:	3.00
Hours to Bill:	3.00
Rate:	100.00
Amount:	300.00
Description:	Legal research—relevant case law in support of Response to Motion for Summary Judgment.
Category:	60
Bill Code:	0 – Billable / Printable

FIELD	INFORMATION TO BE ENTERED
Client ID:	851.00
Reference:	
Timekeeper:	2
Date:	11/18/2009
Tcode:	3
Hours Worked:	1.00
Hours to Bill:	1.00
Rate:	225.00
Amount:	225.00
Description:	**Telephone conference with expert witness**
Category:	60
Bill Code:	0 – Billable / Printable

FIELD	INFORMATION TO BE ENTERED
Client ID:	851.00
Reference:	
Timekeeper:	8
Date:	11/18/2009
Tcode:	3
Hours Worked:	1.00
Hours to Bill:	1.00
Rate:	100.00
Amount:	100.00
Description:	**Telephone conference with client regarding Response to Motion for Summary Judgment**
Category:	60
Bill Code:	0 – Billable / Printable

16. *Click the Save icon on the main toolbar.*

17. Notice in the bottom of the "Fee" window that you can see the prior fee/time records you have entered. *Click the Close icon at the upper right of the "Fee – Richards/Sherry" window.*

18. The "Fee Verification List" window should now be displayed. This feature can print a report summarizing all of the entries you just made. This is not necessary for the small number of time records you just entered, so *click the Close icon in the "Fee Verification List" window.*

19. *Click File on the menu bar and then click Exit.*

This concludes Lesson 3.

HANDS-ON EXERCISES

LESSON 4: ENTERING COST/EXPENSE RECORDS AND USING THE FEE TIMER FEATURE

In this lesson, you will learn how to enter cost/expense records into Tabs3 and how to use the Fee Timer feature.

1. Open Windows. *Double-click Tabs3 with Sample Data on the desktop,* or *click the Start button on the Windows desktop, point to Programs or All Programs, point to Tabs3 & PracticeMaster group, point to Trial Software with Sample Data, then click Tabs3 with Sample Data.* Tabs3 will then open with sample data already present in the software.

2. The "Tip of the Day" window may now be displayed. *Click Close in the "Tip of the Day" window.*

3. *Click OK in the "Tabs3" window* to acknowledge the 11/17/2009 date.

4. *Click Cost in the "Task Folders" window.*

5. *The "Rapid Cost Entry" window should now be displayed* (see Tabs3 Exhibit 9).

TABS3 EXHIBIT 9
Entering a cost/expense record

6. Your cursor should be in the Client ID: field with **851.00** filled in. Press the **[TAB]** key to accept the entry.

7. Press the **[TAB]** key again to go to the Date: field.

8. Press the **[TAB]** key to accept the default date of 11/17/2009.

9. *Click the Lookup button next to the Tcode: field. Scroll and double-click on "251 COP Photocopy charges."*

10. In the Units: field, type **151** (151 copies at the firm default rate of 20 cents a copy). Press the **[TAB]** key.

11. The calculation in the Amount: field is $30.20. Press the **[TAB]** key.

12. In the Description: field, enter **Photocopy charges—Response to Motion for Summary Judgment.**

13. *Click the Save icon on the main toolbar.*

14. Enter and save each of the following cost/expense records:

FIELD	INFORMATION TO BE ENTERED
Client ID:	851.00
Reference:	
Date:	11/17/2009
Tcode:	102
Units:	1.00
Rate:	
Amount:	20.00
Description:	Courier fee—info re: Response to Motion for Summary Judgment

FIELD	INFORMATION TO BE ENTERED
Client ID:	851.00
Reference:	
Date:	11/17/2009
Tcode:	106
Units:	1.00
Rate:	
Amount:	50
Description:	Online legal research—Response to Motion for Summary Judgment

FIELD	INFORMATION TO BE ENTERED
Client ID:	851.00
Reference:	
Date:	11/17/2009
Tcode:	107
Units:	1.00
Rate:	
Amount:	375.00
Description:	Transcription fees—defendant's deposition

15. *Click the Save icon on the main toolbar.*

16. *Click the Close icon* (the red square with a white "X") *at the upper right of the "Rapid Cost Entry" window.*

17. *Click on the Close icon at the upper right of the "Cost Verification List" window.*

18. You will now learn how to use the Fee Timer feature in Tabs3. *Click Fee in the "Task Folder" window.* The "Fee Entry" window should now be displayed.

19. *Click the green triangle just to the right of the word "Timer" in the "Fee Entry" window.* This is the Start Timer icon. Notice that the timer begins to count. The timer is now timing how long it takes you to complete a task such as making a phone call or drafting a letter.

20. Fill in the rest of the following information in the "Fee Entry" window:

FIELD	INFORMATION TO BE ENTERED
Client ID:	851.00
Reference:	
Timekeeper:	5
Date:	11/15/2009
Tcode:	3
Hours Worked:	0.00
Hours to Bill:	0.00
Rate:	150
Amount:	0.00
Description:	Telephone conference with counsel
Category:	60
Bill Code:	0 – Billable / Printable

21. *Click the red square next to Timer: on the Fee Entry toolbar to stop the timer.* (Assuming it took you less than a few minutes to enter the fee information, the value should be $15.00).

22. *Click the Save icon on the main toolbar.*

23. A window should now be displayed asking you if you want to **"Add timer to Hours?"** *Click Yes.*

24. *At the window that displays* **"Add to Amount?"**, *click Yes.* Notice at the bottom of the screen that the entry has been added and a cost of $15.00 has been recorded.

25. *Click the Close icon at the upper right of the "Fee-Richards/Sherry" window.*

26. *Click the Close icon at the upper right of the "Fee Verification List" window.*

27. *Click File on the menu bar and then click Exit.*

This concludes Lesson 4.

LESSON 5: GENERATING AND PRINTING DRAFT AND FINAL STATEMENTS

In this lesson, you will learn how to generate and print draft and final statements in Tabs3.

1. Open Windows. *Double-click Tabs3 with Sample Data on the desktop, or click the Start button on the Windows desktop, point to Programs or All Programs, point to the Tabs3 & PracticeMaster group, point to Trial Software with Sample Data, then click Tabs3 with Sample Data.* Tabs3 will then open with sample data already present in the software.

2. The "Tip of the Day" window may now be displayed. *Click Close in the "Tip of the Day" window.*

3. *Click OK in the "Tabs3" window* to acknowledge the 11/17/2009 date.

4. *Click Generate Statements in the "Task Folders" window.*

5. In the Client ID: field, type **851** and then press the **[TAB]** key. At the Thru: field, press the **[TAB]** key again.

6. *Click the Options tab in the "Generate Statements" window.* Notice that the default entry for Statement Type: is "Draft." Because you want to print a draft statement for Sherry Richards, leave it as is.

7. ***Click the Lookup button next to Statement Date: and select* November 18, 2009.** *(Note:* Statements are usually done at the end of the month, but this client has asked for a special mid-month bill.)

8. ***Click OK in the "Generate Statements" window.***

9. ***In the "Generate Statements" window, click the Lookup button under Selected Printer: to select a printer and then click Printer:.***

10. ***Click OK in the "Generate Statements" window.*** *(Note:* You can also save the statement as a PDF or text file, or print it to the DropBox for easy attachment to an email).

11. The draft statement should look similar to Tabs3 Exhibit 10. Normally, the timekeeper responsible for the case reviews and approves the draft statement. The next steps instruct you how to mark a statement as having been reviewed, how to run the statement as final, and how to update a statement.

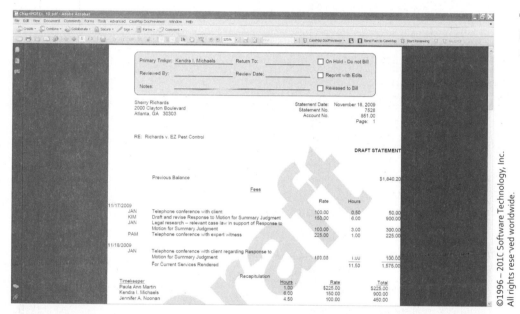

TABS3 EXHIBIT 10
Draft statement for
Richards v. EZ Pest Control

12. ***Click the Close icon at the upper right of the "Generate Statements" window.***

13. ***Click Statements on the menu bar*** (see Tabs3 Exhibit 11).

TABS3 EXHIBIT 11
Pre-billing tracking

HANDS-ON EXERCISES

14. *Click Pre-Bill Tracking.* The "Pre-Bill Tracking" window should now be displayed (see Tabs3 Exhibit 11).

15. *Double-click "851.00, Richards/Sherry, Richards v. EZ Pest Control."* Notice that a check mark appears in the "R" column. This means that the statement has been reviewed and is ready for a final statement.

16. *Click Final Statements in the "Pre-Bill Tracking" window.*

17. The "Generate Statements" window is now displayed. *Click the Options tab in the "Generate Statements" window.* Change the statement date to **11/18/2009**.

18. *Click OK in the "Generate Statements" window.*

19. *In the "Generate Statements" window, click the Lookup button under Selected Printer: to select a printer. Then click Printer.*

20. *Click OK in the "Generate Statements" window.* (*Note:* You can also save the statement as a PDF or text file, or print it to the DropBox for easy attachment to an email. Also, note that the DropBox is cleared each time the software is closed. Therefore, if you are waiting to print statements or other documents for class and are using the DropBox as a temporary holding area, the files must be printed or saved to another location before you close the software.)

21. The final statement produced should be similar to Tabs3 Exhibit 12.

TABS3 EXHIBIT 12
Final statement—Sherry Richards

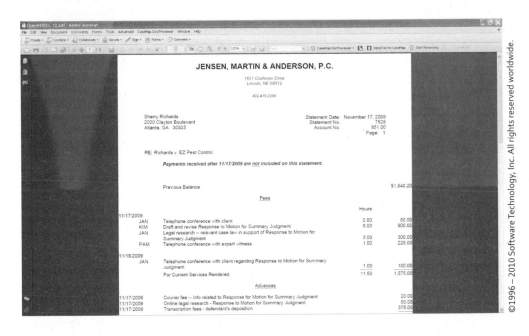

22. *Click the Close icon at the upper right of the "Generate Statements" window.*

23. *Click the Close icon at the upper right of the "Pre-Bill Tracking" window.*

24. The final stage in the billing process in Tabs3 is to run the Update Statements program. In Tabs3, changes can be made to the final statements until the Update Statements program is run. The Update Statements program updates accounts receivable and billed productivity information, and moves work-in-process transactions into the archive.

25. *Click the Statements tab (not the Statement Preparation tab) in the "Task Folders" window. Click Update Statements.*

26. A warning window will be displayed asking if you would like to back up your data first. *Click No. Note:* When using the full version of the software and running bills in an office setting, you will want to click Yes to create a backup.

27. In the "Update Statements" window, in the Client ID: field, type **851** in the first box, and press the [**TAB**] key. *Click OK.*

28. When the "Update Statements Status" window indicates that **"Statements are now updated,"** *click OK in the "Update Statements Status" window.*

29. *Click the Close icon at the upper right of the "Update Statements" window.*

30. *In the "Update Statements Verification List" window, click Cancel.*

31. *In the "Task Folders" window, click the Main tab, then click Client.*

32. *In the "Client Information" window, click the A/R & Fund Balances tab.* Notice that you can see the total balance due and the amount due for fees, expenses, and advances. The billing process has been successful.

33. *Click the Close icon at the upper right of the "Client Information" window.*

34. *Click File on the menu bar and then click Exit.*

This concludes Lesson 5.

LESSON 6: ENTERING A PAYMENT

In this lesson, you will learn how to enter a payment and apply it to a client's accounts receivable balance.

1. Open Windows. ***Double-click Tabs3 with Sample Data on the desktop,*** or ***click the Start button on the Windows desktop, point to Programs or All Programs, point to the Tabs3 & PracticeMaster Technology group, point to Trial Software with Sample Data, then click Tabs3 with Sample Data.*** Tabs3 will then open with sample data already present in the software.

2. The "Tip of the Day" window may now be displayed. ***Click Close in the "Tip of the Day" window.***

3. ***Click OK in the "Tabs3" window*** to acknowledge the 11/17/2009 date.

4. ***Click Payment in the "Task Folders" window.*** The "Rapid Payment Entry" window should now be displayed (see Tabs3 Exhibit 13).

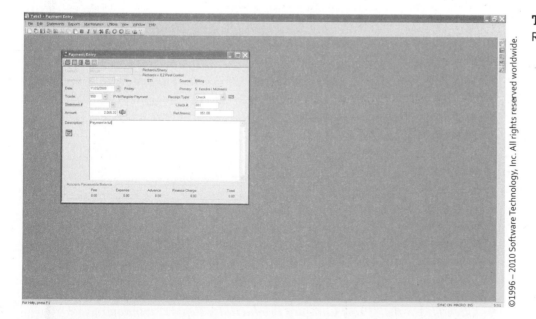

TABS3 EXHIBIT 13
Recording a payment

5. The cursor should be in the Client ID: field with **851.00** already entered. Press the [**TAB**] key to go to the Reference: field.

6. Press the [**TAB**] key to go to the Date: field.

7. Enter **11/20/2009** in the Date: field.

8. Press the **[TAB]** key to go to the Tcode: field. A Tcode of **900** should be entered in the field.

9. Press the **[TAB]** key to go to the Statement: field.

10. Press the **[TAB]** key to go to the Amount: field. In the Amount: field, type **2065.20**

11. Press the **[TAB]** key to go to the Description: field. In the Description: field, type **Payment in full.**

12. Press the **[TAB]** key to go to the Receipt Type: field.

13. Press the **[TAB]** key to accept the default value of Check.

14. In the Check #: field, **enter 881** as the check number.

15. *Click the Save icon on the main toolbar.* The "Unapplied Payment Options - Client 851.00" window is now displayed. *Click OK.*

16. *Click the Close icon* (the red square with a white "X") *at the upper right of the "Rapid Payment Entry" window.*

17. *Click the Close icon at the upper right of the "Payment Verification List" window.*

18. *In the "Task Folders" window, click Client.*

19. The number **851** should be displayed in the Client ID: field. *Click the A/R & Fund Balances tab in the "Client Information" window.* Notice that the Amount Due: is $0.00 and the Last Payment Amount: is $2,065.20.

20. *Click the Close icon at the upper right of the "Client Information" window.*

21. *Click File on the menu bar and then click Exit.*

This concludes Lesson 6.

▶ ADVANCED LESSON

LESSON 7: PROCESSING AND PRINTING REPORTS

In this lesson, you will learn how to process and print several reports using Tabs3.

1. Open Windows. *Double-click Tabs3 with Sample Data on the desktop, or click the Start button on the Windows desktop, point to Programs or All Programs, point to the Tabs3 & PracticeMaster group, point to Trial Software with Sample Data, then click Tabs3 with Sample Data.* Tabs3 will then open with sample data already entered into the program.

2. The "Tip of the Day" window may now be displayed. *Click Close in the "Tip of the Day" window.*

3. *Click OK in the "Tabs3" window* to acknowledge the 11/17/2009 date.

4. *Click the Reports tab in the "Task Folders" window.*

5. *Click Productivity Reports.*

6. *Click Category Productivity.*

7. The default values for the report are all fine, so *click OK in the "Category Productivity Report" window.*

8. *In the "Print Category Productivity Report" window, click the Lookup button under Selected Printer: to select a printer; then select Printer:.*

9. *Click OK in the "Print Category Productivity Report" window.* (*Note:* You can also save the statement as a PDF or text file, or print it to the DropBox for easy attachment to an email.)

10. The report breaks out hours worked, billed hours, and other information by category (case type) for the reporting period of August to November 2009.

11. ***Click the Close icon*** (the red square with a white "X") ***at the upper right of the "Category Productivity Report" window.***

12. ***Click Productivity Reports in the Reports tab of the "Task Folders" window.***

13. Print the Timekeeper Productivity report.

14. Print the Timekeeper Analysis Report.

15. Print the Client Analysis Report.

16. ***At the Reports tab of the "Task Folders" window, click Management Reports.***

17. Print the Client Realization Report.

18. Print the Timekeeper Realization Report.

19. Print the Timekeeper Profitability Report.

20. ***At the Reports tab of the "Task Folders" window, click A/R Reports.***

21. ***Print the Collections Report.***

22. ***Print the A/R by Invoice Report.***

23. ***Close all of the open windows.***

24. ***Click File on the menu bar and then click Exit.***

This concludes the Tabs3 Hands-On Exercises.

HANDS-ON EXERCISES

CHAPTER 5

Databases, Case Management, and Docket Control Software

FEATURED SOFTWARE
AbacusLaw

ABACUSLAW CASE MANAGEMENT PROGRAM

I. INTRODUCTION

AbacusLaw is an integrated practice management database that manages all calendar, case, and client information. It integrates document management, document assembly, conflict of interest checks, reporting, form generation, and time, billing, and accounting. The AbacusLaw demonstration version is a full, working version of the program (with a few limitations). **The program demonstration version times out 30 days after installation. This means that the program will only work for 30 days from when you install it. So, it is highly recommended that you do not install the program on your computer until you are actually ready to go through the Hands-On Exercises and learn the program.** When you are ready to install the program, follow the instructions below.

II. USING THE ABACUSLAW HANDS-ON EXERCISES

The AbacusLaw Hands-On Exercises are easy to use and contain step-by-step instructions. Each lesson builds on the previous exercise so please complete the Hands-On Exercises in order. AbacusLaw comes with sample data so you should be able to utilize many features of the program.

III. INSTALLATION INSTRUCTIONS

1. Log in to your CengageBrain.com account.
2. Under "My Courses & Materials", find the Premium Web site for Using Computers in the Law Office.
3. *Click "Open" to go to the Premium Web site.*
4. Locate "Book Resources" in the left navigation menu.
5. *Click on the link for "AbacusLaw Gold".*
6. *Click on "Download 30 day trial of AbacusLaw Gold."*
7. Your screen will show a File Download—Security Warning asking you if you want to run or save this file, as shown in AbacusLaw Installation Exhibit 1. *Click Run. In the "Internet Explorer—Security Warning" window click Run.*

File Download - Security Warning

Do you want to run or save this file?

Name: abacusgold2010ALL.exe
Type: Application, 94.7MB
From: **downloads.abacuslaw.com**

[Run]   [Save]   [Cancel]

While files from the Internet can be useful, this file type can potentially harm your computer. If you do not trust the source, do not run or save this software. What's the risk?

Courtesy Abacus Data Systems

ABACUSLAW INSTALLATION EXHIBIT 1

8. **Enter a Customer ID** in the "AbacusLaw Installation" screen, as shown in AbacusLaw Installation Exhibit 2. If it is not one you received from Abacus, enter your name and school. ***Click Next***. You will still be able to proceed with installation after ***Clicking OK*** to the screen shown in AbacusLaw Installation Exhibit 3.

AbacusLaw Installation

Welcome to AbacusLaw!

For networks, be sure to install at the SERVER itself, not from a workstation. Enter your Customer ID and Firmname, then press the Next button to begin. Or press Cancel if you do not want to install at this time.

Please exit all Abacus software, including MessageSlips and AbacusLaw, before continuing this installation.

Enter your Customer ID   [   ]

Enter your Firm Name   [   ]

[< Back]   [Next >]   [Cancel]

Courtesy Abacus Data Systems

ABACUSLAW INSTALLATION EXHIBIT 2

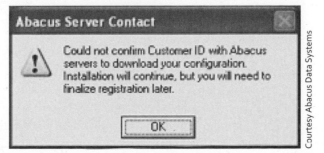

Abacus Server Contact

Could not confirm Customer ID with Abacus servers to download your configuration. Installation will continue, but you will need to finalize registration later.

[OK]

Courtesy Abacus Data Systems

ABACUSLAW INSTALLATION EXHIBIT 3

HANDS-ON EXERCISES

9. The Abacus License agreement window should now be displayed. (See AbacusLaw Installation Exhibit 4). ***Click Accept.***

ABACUSLAW INSTALLATION EXHIBIT 4

Courtesy Abacus Data Systems

10. The Select Components window should now be displayed (see AbacusLaw Installation Exhibit 5). ***Make sure all options other than "AbacusLaw"*** are deselected (see AbacusLaw Installation Exhibit 5). When you are done only "AbacusLaw" should have a check mark next to it. ***Click Next.***

ABACUSLAW INSTALLATION EXHIBIT 5

Courtesy Abacus Data Systems

11. The Select Destination Directory window should now be displayed (see AbacusLaw Installation Exhibit 6). While you could click Browse to change where AbacusLaw will be saved on your computer, it is not recommended that you change this setting. ***Click Next.***

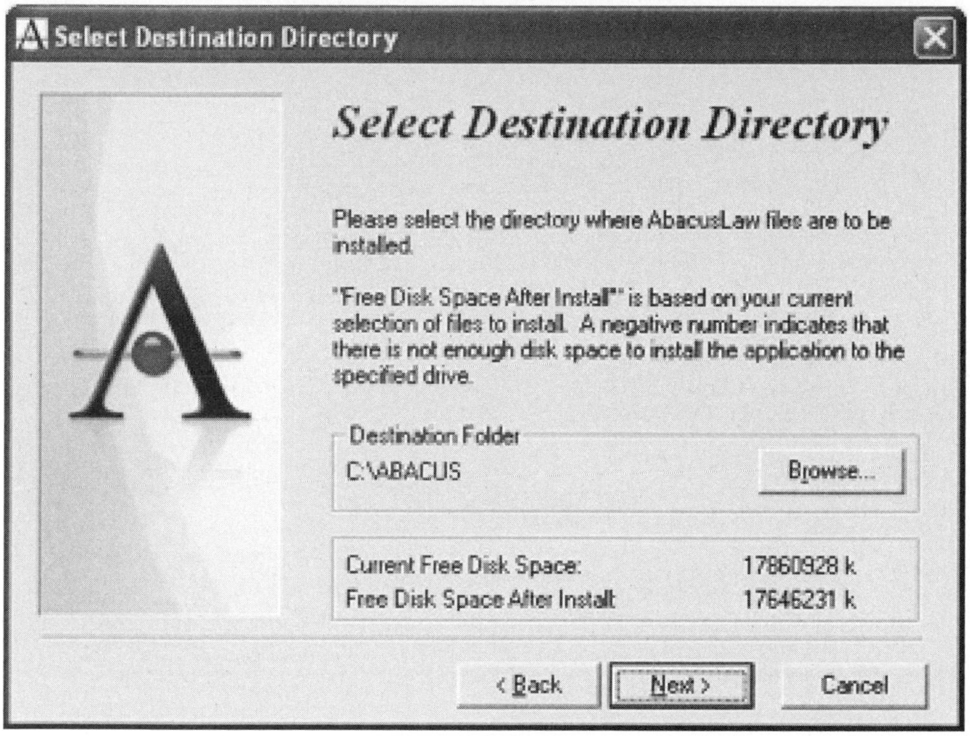

Courtesy Abacus Data Systems

ABACUSLAW INSTALLATION EXHIBIT 6

12. The Start Installation window (see AbacusLaw Installation Exhibit 7) should now be displayed and the screen should say Ready to Install. ***Click Next.***

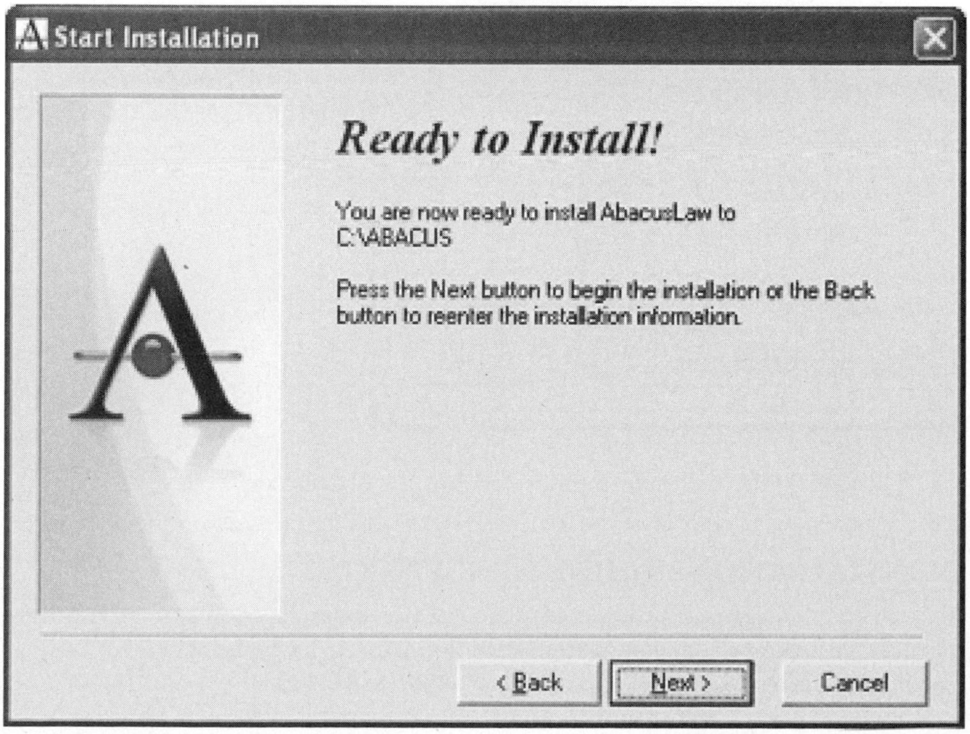

Courtesy Abacus Data Systems

ABACUSLAW INSTALLATION EXHIBIT 7

HANDS-ON EXERCISES

13. The Installing window should now be displayed and the program should start installing (see AbacusLaw Installation Exhibit 8).

**ABACUSLAW
INSTALLATION
EXHIBIT 8**

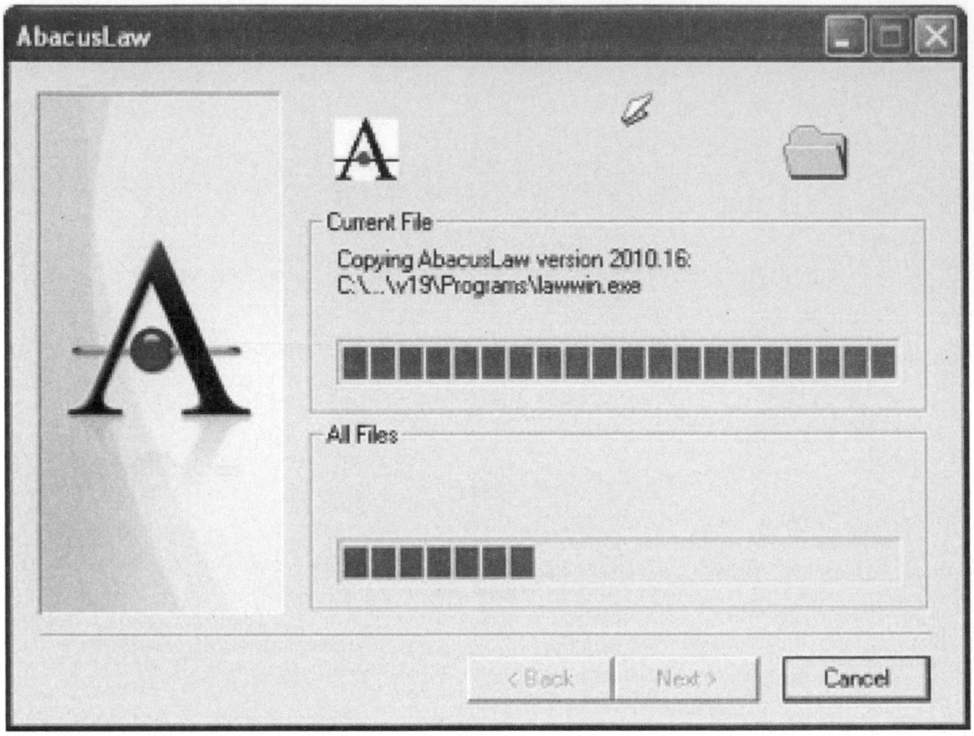

Courtesy Abacus Data Systems

14. AbacusLaw will launch and initialize itself. If you are asked to enter your initials as the User ID in the User Log on window, you should do so and then **Click OK.** (Be sure to do this carefully as you will be asked to enter the same User ID every time you open this program.) See AbacusLaw Installation Exhibit 9. **In the "AbacusLaw Installation Complete" window, click Finish.**

**ABACUSLAW
INSTALLATION
EXHIBIT 9**

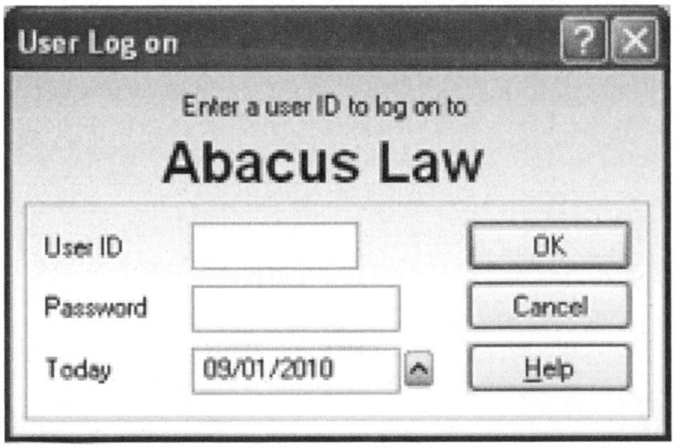

Courtesy Abacus Data Systems

15. This concludes the installation instructions for AbacusLaw.

16. You are now ready to start the AbacusLaw Hands-On Exercises on the next page.

IV. INSTALLATION TECHNICAL SUPPORT

AbacusLaw is a licensed product of Abacus Data Systems: However, if you have problems installing the demonstration version of AbacusLaw, please contact Delmar Cengage Learning Technical Support first at (800) 648-7450.

Number	Lesson Title	Concepts Covered
BASIC LESSONS		
Lesson 1	Introduction to AbacusLaw	Viewing and learning about the AbacusLaw interface, including an overview of calendars, events, contacts, and matters
Lesson 2	Entering New Contacts	Entering new contacts and printing a list of contacts to the screen
INTERMEDIATE LESSONS		
Lesson 3	Entering New Matters/Cases	Entering new matters/cases and associating them with clients
Lesson 4	Creating Events, Part 1	Adding a staff person who can perform events; creating events, including appointments, reminders, things to do, and calls to be made
Lesson 5	Creating Events, Part 2	Entering a recurring event; making a rule-based entry; working with the Date Calculator
Lesson 6	Creating Linked Names and Linked Notes, and Checking for Conflicts	Associating a non-client–linked name with a case; creating notes that are linked to contacts and matters; checking for conflicts of interest
ADVANCED LESSONS		
Lesson 7	Linking Documents; Using the Call Manager and the Form Generation Feature	Using the Call Manager feature; using the Form Generation feature
Lesson 8	Reports	Running a number of event and matter reports

GETTING STARTED

Introduction

Throughout these lessons and exercises, information you need to type into the software will be designated in several different ways:

- Keys to be pressed on the keyboard are designated in brackets, in all caps, and in bold (e.g., press the **[ENTER]** key).
- Movements with the mouse pointer are designated in bold and italics (e.g., *point to File on the menu bar and click*).
- Words or letters that should be typed are designated in bold (e.g., type **Training Program**).
- Information that is or should be displayed on your computer screen is shown in bold, with quotation marks (e.g., **"Press ENTER to continue."**).
- Specific menu items and commands are designated with an initial capital letter (e.g., click Open).

OVERVIEW OF ABACUSLAW

AbacusLaw is a full-featured legal case management program. AbacusLaw Exhibit 1 shows the daily organizer calendar and the program's menu bar and toolbar. With AbacusLaw, you can track case information; create and manage contract information for clients and others; make case notes and diaries; create calendar events that are tied (linked) to a case; and create a myriad of reminders, things-to-do, and calls-to-make entries. You can also link electronic documents to cases, create forms and routine letters using its document assembly capabilities, make recurring calendar entries, create rule-based entries, search and query the database for information, and print reports. Additional information about AbacusLaw will be provided as you complete these exercises. By the time you have finished these exercises, you should have a good understanding of the basics of legal case management and the AbacusLaw program.

ABACUSLAW EXHIBIT 1

AbacusLaw Daily Organizer, menu bar, and toolbar

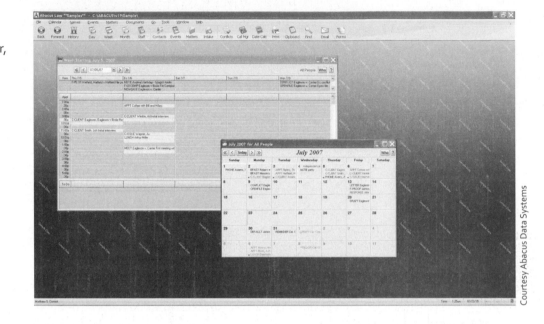

Courtesy Abacus Data Systems

▶ BASIC LESSONS

LESSON 1: INTRODUCTION TO ABACUSLAW

This lesson introduces you to AbacusLaw. It explains basic information about the AbacusLaw interface, including an overview of Calendars, Contacts, Matters, and Events.

Install the AbacusLaw demonstration version on your computer, following the instructions at the beginning of these exercises. Note that the AbacusLaw demonstration version will time out (cease to work) 30 days after installation. Therefore, do not install the program on your computer until you are ready to complete these Hands-On Exercises.

1. The first thing you will do in this lesson is populate AbacusLaw with sample data. *If you start AbacusLaw from the icon on the desktop, the sample data will not be loaded,* so please follow these directions.

2. Start Windows. ***Click the Start button on the Windows desktop, point to Programs or All Programs, point to the AbacusLaw group, then click Sample Data.*** This will load Abacus with some sample data. The "First User Setup" window should now be displayed. ***Click OK.***

3. The "User Log on" window should now be displayed (see AbacusLaw Exhibit 2). If you get a message requesting you to set yourself up as the first user, ***click OK***; the AbacusLaw desktop (see AbacusLaw Exhibit 2) should say **"Sample Data."**

4. In the User ID field of the "User Log on" window, type your initials (see AbacusLaw Exhibit 2). It is important that you enter the same initials each time you load Abacus. Do not type anything in the Password field. ***Click OK in the***

Abacus
menu bar

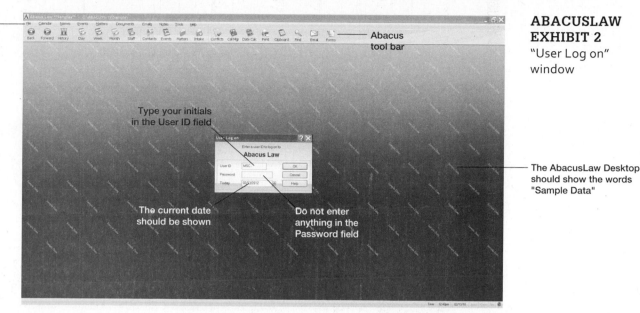

Type your initials
in the User ID field

The current date
should be shown

Do not enter
anything in the
Password field

Abacus
tool bar

**ABACUSLAW
EXHIBIT 2**
"User Log on"
window

The AbacusLaw Desktop
should show the words
"Sample Data"

Courtesy Abacus Data Systems

"User Log on" window. Abacus will notify you that only these initials will be valid to open the demonstration version of Abacus.

5. The "Tip of the Day" window should now be displayed on your screen. ***Click OK in the "Tip of the Day" window.*** You should now be at the Abacus desktop with the name plate that reads **"Your name appears here after registration."**

6. ***Click the icon that says Day on the toolbar.*** AbacusLaw refers to this as the Daily Organizer. (To see the name of any icon, just ***hover the cursor on the icon for a second*** and its name will appear.)

7. The "Daily Organizer" window should now be displayed for the current day. The Daily Organizer is where you manage your daily calendar. The current date should be displayed at the top of the "Daily Organizer" window. ***Click the current date in the Daily Organizer,*** type **070207,** and then press the **[ENTER]** key.

8. Your screen should now look like AbacusLaw Exhibit 3, except that the "Who setting for Calendars" window is not yet open. The entries you see are sample data that was already loaded in the program. ***Click the less-than sign (<), which is the Previous Day icon, next to the date 07/02/07 in the "Daily Organizer" window*** (see AbacusLaw Exhibit 3). The date box should now show 07/01/07. *Note:* If the "Daily Organizer" window is too small, you can adjust its size by ***placing the cursor over the borders of the window, then clicking and dragging the window to the desired size.***

9. ***Click the greater-than sign (>), which is the Next Day icon, next to the date 07/01/07 in the "Daily Organizer" window*** (see AbacusLaw Exhibit 3). The date should once again be 07/02/07.

10. ***Click the up arrow just to the right of the date 07/02/07.*** This is the three-month pop-up calendar. By clicking on the left and right arrows in the three-month calendar, you can go backward or forward three months at a time. ***Click the Close icon*** (a red square with a white X in it) ***in the upper right corner of the three-month calendar window*** to close the window.

11. In the Daily Organizer, notice that the appointments at 7:30a. and 8:00a. are in red. This indicates a scheduling conflict. However, also notice the up arrow

HANDS-ON EXERCISES

ABACUSLAW EXHIBIT 3
Daily Organizer

Courtesy Abacus Data Systems

next to All People in the upper right of the "Daily Organizer" window. **"All People"** means that you are looking at the Daily Organizer for everyone in the office. Because everyone's calendar is being shown at the same time in the Daily Organizer, there may or may not be an actual scheduling conflict; one person could be going to one breakfast, and another person going to the other breakfast.

12. *Point and click on the up arrow next to All People* (see AbacusLaw Exhibit 3). Notice that the "'Who' Setting for Calendars" window is displayed (see AbacusLaw Exhibit 3). Notice that several people as well as several conference rooms are listed.

13. *Click the box to the left of AMS (Arthur M. Simon) in the "'Who' Setting for Calendars" window. Click OK at the bottom of the "'Who' Setting for Calendars" window.* The upper right of the "Daily Organizer" window now shows the name **"Arthur M. Simon,"** so you are just looking at his schedule now. Notice that one of the breakfast entries for the morning is now gone, so there is no actual scheduling conflict.

14. *Double-click* **NOTE Flowers for Sylvia's Birthday** *in the Reminders section of the "Daily Organizer" window.* The "Event" window for this note is now displayed. Notice at the bottom of the "Event" window that the field is blank next to Name and Matter. This means that the event is not related or associated with a contact name or matter. *Note:* If you do not see the Name and Matter fields, click the More button in the "Event" window.

15. Notice also that an **N** is displayed at the bottom of the window next to the Status field. *Click the up arrow to the right of the N on the Status line.* The "Valid STATUS Entries" window is now displayed. This is where you can indicate if the item has been completed or not. *Click the Close icon* (the red square with a white X) *in the "Valid STATUS Entries" window.*

16. *Click the Close icon* (the red square with a white X) *in the "Event" window.*

17. Look again at the "**Flowers for Sylvia's Birthday**" reminder and notice that to the left of it there is a an empty white box (see AbacusLaw Exhibit 3). When a user clicks the box, a check mark appears, indicating that the item has been completed. Notice that all of the event entries have the white box for indicating when an item has been completed.

18. *Point to the 7:00a entry for "BFAST Rotary Monthly breakfast" and keep the cursor over that entry for a few seconds.* Notice that a light yellow drop-down box shows additional information regarding the entry. You can point to any entry on any calendar and see the expanded information without having to open the item.

19. *Double-click the 10:00a entry for "C-CLIENT Eagleson, Eagleson v. Birdie Initial Meeting."* The "Event" window should now be displayed. Notice that, at the bottom of the window next to the Name field, **"Eagleson, George"** is shown (see AbacusLaw Exhibit 4). Also, notice that next to the Matter field the case of **"Eagleson v Birdie"** is shown. This indicates that this event—a client conference—is linked to "Eagleson, George" in the Contacts list, and is also linked to the matter (case) of *Eagleson v. Birdie.*

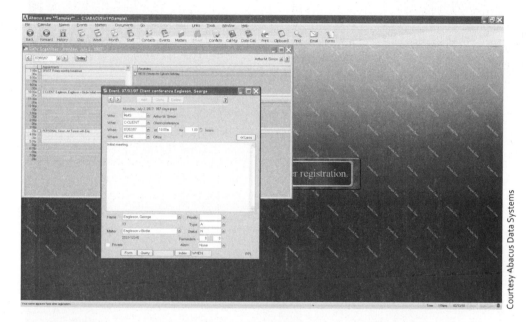

ABACUSLAW EXHIBIT 4
"Event" window for a client conference linked to a name and matter

Courtesy Abacus Data Systems

20. *Click the Close icon* (the red square with a white X) *in the "Event" window to close it.*

21. *Click the Close icon* (the red square with a white X) *in the "Daily Organizer" window to close it.*

22. *Click the Contacts icon on the toolbar.* The "Names Browse" window should now be displayed (see AbacusLaw Exhibit 5). Press the **[HOME]** key if the first entry, **"Adams, Roger,"** is not selected. Notice that in the "Names Browse" window there are three columns: Name, ID, and Class. You can easily see the different types of contacts by looking at the Class field. For each name you can see the class of the entry. For example, "Adams, Roger" has been assigned the class of Client. Notice also that the contact information for each name is displayed on the right side of the "Names Browse" window when a client is selected. Remember, if a window is too small, you can adjust the size by *placing the cursor over the borders of the window, then clicking and dragging the window to the desired size.*

23. *Click the right arrow in the horizontal scroll bar* (see AbacusLaw Exhibit 5) to scroll to the right and see the additional fields in the window.

24. *Click the left arrow in the horizontal scroll bar* to once again display the Name, ID, and Class fields.

25. *Click the Adams, Roger name, then click the column heading Class.* This will sort the name entries by class. Notice all of the client entries.

**ABACUSLAW
EXHIBIT 5**

Contacts—"Names Browse"
window

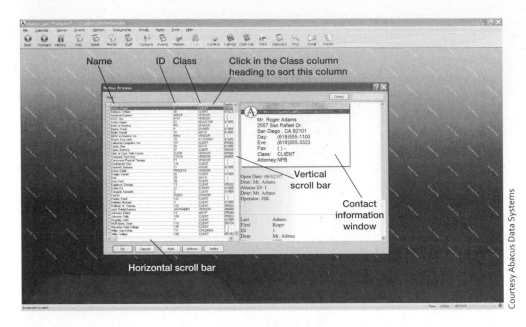

Courtesy Abacus Data Systems

26. *Click the Names column heading* to display the contacts sorted by name.

27. *Double-click on the Adams, Roger entry.*

28. The "Name: Adams, Roger" window should now be displayed (see AbacusLaw Exhibit 6).

**ABACUSLAW
EXHIBIT 6**

"Name" window

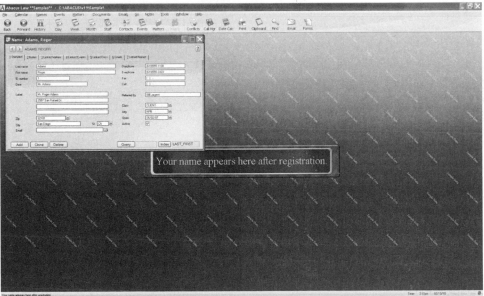

Courtesy Abacus Data Systems

29. *Click the Notes tab in the "Name: Adams, Roger" window.* Notice that the first note is a memo entry; other entries include additional memos as well as phone entries and a background entry.

30. *Click the Linked Matters tab in the "Name: Adams, Roger" window.* Notice that two matters are shown, "Adams, Roger v. City of Jupiter" and "Main Street Center" (a real estate matter).

31. *Click the Linked Events tab in the "Name: Adams, Roger" window.* Notice that you can scroll to the right to see the other fields in the event entries.

32. *Click the Linked Docs tab.* Notice that there are no documents listed.

33. *Click the Emails tab.* Notice that there are no emails listed.

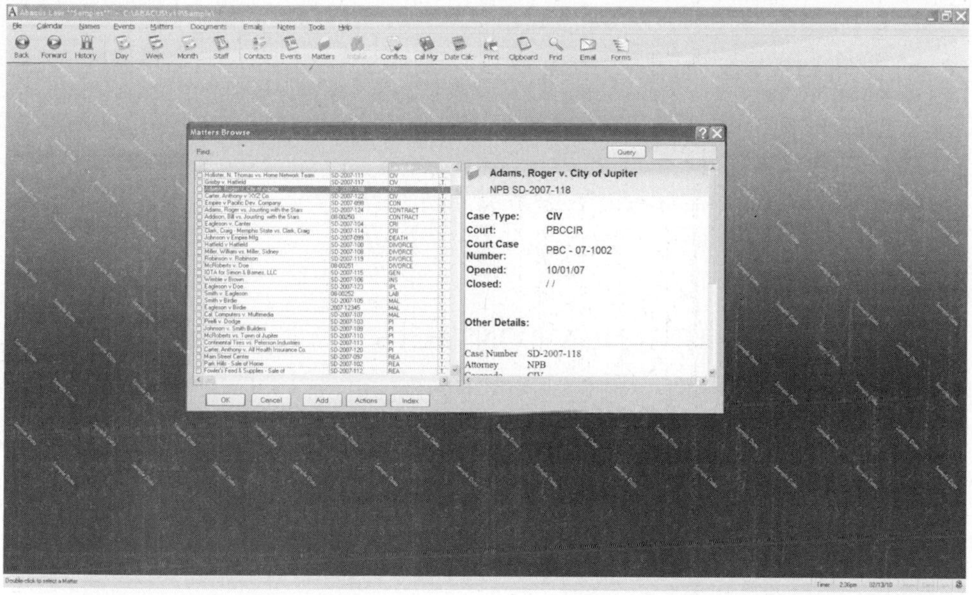

**ABACUSLAW
EXHIBIT 7**
"Matters Browse" window

34. ***Click the Linked Names tab.*** Notice that one name, "Barker, Frank," is listed. Mr. Barker is the owner of the Main Street Center building that Roger Adams is purchasing.

35. ***Click the Standard tab in the "Name: Adams, Roger" window*** to return to the contact information for Roger Adams.

36. ***Click the Close icon in the "Name: Adams, Roger" window to close it.***

37. ***Click Matters on the toolbar.*** The "Matters Browse" window should now be displayed (see AbacusLaw Exhibit 7). ***Select the Adams, Roger v. City of Jupiter case*** and notice that information about the case is shown on the right side of the "Matters Browse" window. Notice also that the third column header is **"Casecode."** This column lists the type of case for each matter.

38. ***Click the column heading Casecode.*** Press the **[HOME]** key to go to the beginning of the list. Notice that several types of cases are listed.

39. ***Double-click on the Adams, Roger v. City of Jupiter matter in the "Matters Browse" window.*** The "Matter: Adams, Roger v. City of Jupiter" window should now be displayed (see AbacusLaw Exhibit 8).

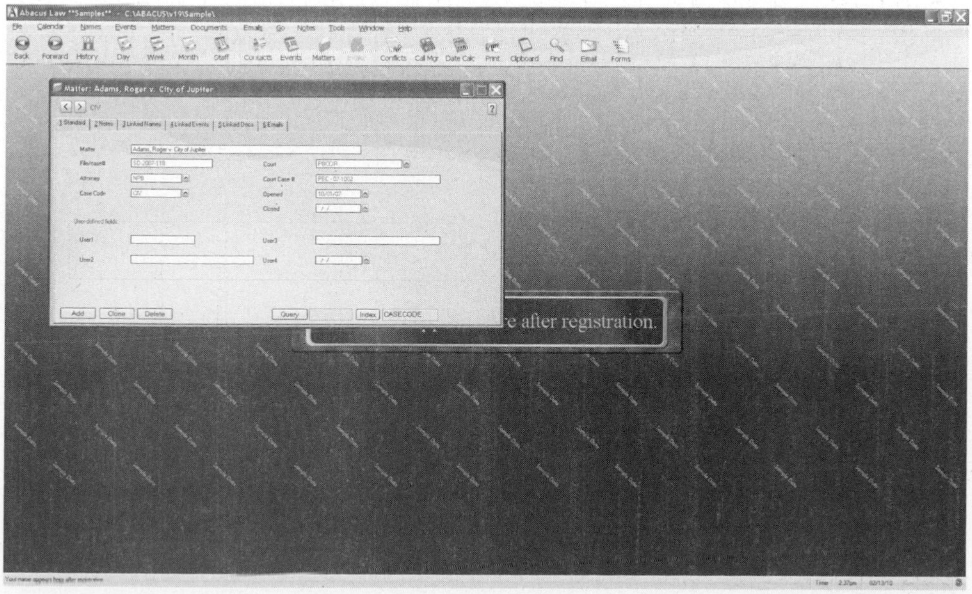

**ABACUSLAW
EXHIBIT 8**
"Matter:" window

40. *Click each of the tabs in the "Matter: Adams, Roger v. City of Jupiter" window.* Notice that they are similar to the tabs you accessed in the "Name" window.

41. *Click the Close icon in the "Matter: Adams, Roger v. City of Jupiter" window* to close the window.

42. *Click File on the menu bar and then click Exit.*

43. At the **"Please register now!"** window, *click OK.*

This concludes Lesson 1.

LESSON 2: ENTERING NEW CONTACTS

In this lesson, you will learn to enter new contacts into AbacusLaw and print a list of contacts to the screen. In subsequent lessons you will link matters, events, and documents to the names you create in this lesson. This lesson assumes that you have completed Lesson 1 and are familiar with the AbacusLaw interface.

1. The first thing you will do in this lesson is populate AbacusLaw with sample data. *If you start AbacusLaw from the icon on the desktop, the sample data will not be loaded,* so please follow these directions.

2. Start Windows. *Click the Start button on the Windows desktop, point to Programs or All Programs, point to the AbacusLaw group, then click Sample Data.* This will populate Abacus with some sample data.

3. The "User Log on" window should now be displayed. Note that the AbacusLaw desktop should say **"Sample Data."**

4. In the User ID field of the "User Log on" window, type the same initials you entered in Lesson 1. It is important that you enter the same initials each time you start Abacus. Do not type anything in the Password field. *Click OK in the "User Log on" window.*

5. The "Tip of the Day" window should now be displayed on your screen. *Click OK in the "Tip of the Day" window.* You should now be at the Abacus desktop with the name plate that reads **"Your name appears here after registration."**

6. *Click Contacts on the toolbar.* The "Names Browse" window will be displayed. *Click Add.*

7. The "Adding a new Name" window should be displayed (see AbacusLaw Exhibit 9). Enter the following contact information into the "Adding a

ABACUSLAW EXHIBIT 9

"Adding a new Name" window

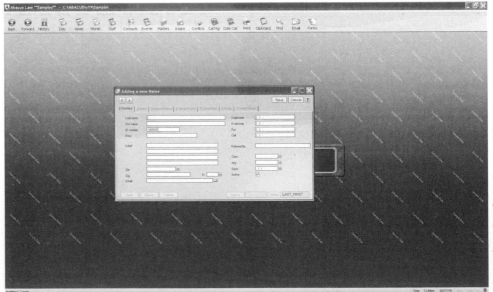

Courtesy Abacus Data Systems

new Name" window. You can use the [**TAB**] key to go the next field, or [**SHIFT**]+[**TAB**] to go to the previous field. You can also use the cursor to point and click in a field. In the following data list, when you come to a field that is blank, just skip over it. *Note:* After you enter the Zip Code, if the "An Invalid Zip Code was Entered" window opens, ***click Add.*** The "Zip Codes" window will open. ***Enter the Zip Code, City, and State, and click OK to close the Zip Codes window,*** and then ***click OK in the "An Invalid Zip Code was Entered" window.***

FIELD NAME	DATA TO ENTER
Last name	**Magrino**
First name	**Cathy**
ID number	**1001**
Dear	**Cathy**
Label	**Cathy Magrino**
	93 Winspear Lane
Zip	**90014**
City	**Los Angeles**
St.	**CA**
Email	**cmagrino@msc.uclo.com**
Dayphone	**323 555 2343**
Evenphone	
Fax	
Cell	
Referred By	
Class	**CLIENT**
Atty	**AMS**
Open	**06/01/12**

8. When you have entered all of the information (your screen should look similar to AbacusLaw Exhibit 10), ***click Save in the "Adding a new Name" window.***

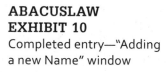

ABACUSLAW EXHIBIT 10
Completed entry—"Adding a new Name" window

9. You will now make three additional contact entries, including one additional client, one attorney, and one vendor.

10. *In the "Name: Magrino, Cathy" window, click Add* to add another name. Enter the data from the following list into AbacusLaw. *Note:* When you have completed an entry, **click Save** to save the record. Then, **click Add** to add the next record. Once the records are entered, you can use the Previous Record (<) and Next Record (>) icons (see AbacusLaw Exhibit 10) to go between records if you need to.

FIELD NAME	DATA TO ENTER
Last name	Gleason
First name	Colleen
ID number	1002
Dear	Colleen
Label	Colleen Gleason
	300 Porter Ave
Zip	92037
City	La Jolla
St.	CA
Email	cgleason@aom.com
Dayphone	858 555 8933
Evenphone	
Fax	
Cell	
Referred By	
Class	CLIENT
Atty	AMS
Open	06/01/12
Last name	McKie
First name	Dianne
ID number	1003
Dear	Ms. McKie
Label	Dianne McKie
	McKie & Baskind
	100 Ellicott Circle
Zip	90014
City	Los Angeles
St.	CA
Email	dmckie@mckiebaskindlaw.com
Dayphone	323 555 8001
Evenphone	
Fax	

FIELD NAME	DATA TO ENTER
Cell	
Referred By	
Class	**ATTORNEY**
Atty	
Open	06/01/12
Last name	**Krakes**
First name	**Margaret**
ID number	**1004**
Dear	**Ms. Krakes**
Label	**Margaret Krakes**
	UB Equipment, Inc.
	18 Blue Bird Ave
Zip	**92101**
City	**San Diego**
St.	**CA**
Email	**mkrakes@ub.equip.com**
Dayphone	**858 555 0003**
Evenphone	
Fax	
Cell	
Referred By	
Class	**VENDOR**
Atty	
Open	06/01/12

11. Once you have saved the last record, *click the Close icon in the "Name: Krakes, Margaret" window to close it.*

12. *Click Contacts on the toolbar.* The **"Names Browse"** window should now be displayed.

13. *Click Query in the upper right of the "Names Browse" window. Click Quick query in the drop-down menu.*

14. *Click in the Last name field* and type **Gleason**, *then click OK.*

15. The entry for **"Gleason, Colleen"** should be displayed in the **"Names Browse"** window.

16. *Click Query. Then, click Clear current query.* The **"Names Browse"** window should now be displayed. Press the **[HOME]** key to go to the beginning of the list.

17. *Click Actions in the "Names Browse" window. Point to Reports and click All (in query).* The **"Names Report Control"** window should now be displayed. Next to **Output to,** notice that "Screen" is selected. (*Note:* If **"Screen"** is not selected, *click Output to, then click Screen, then click OK.)* You will be printing a Names report to the screen. *Point and click on Print.* If a printer

**ABACUSLAW
EXHIBIT 11**
Names List report

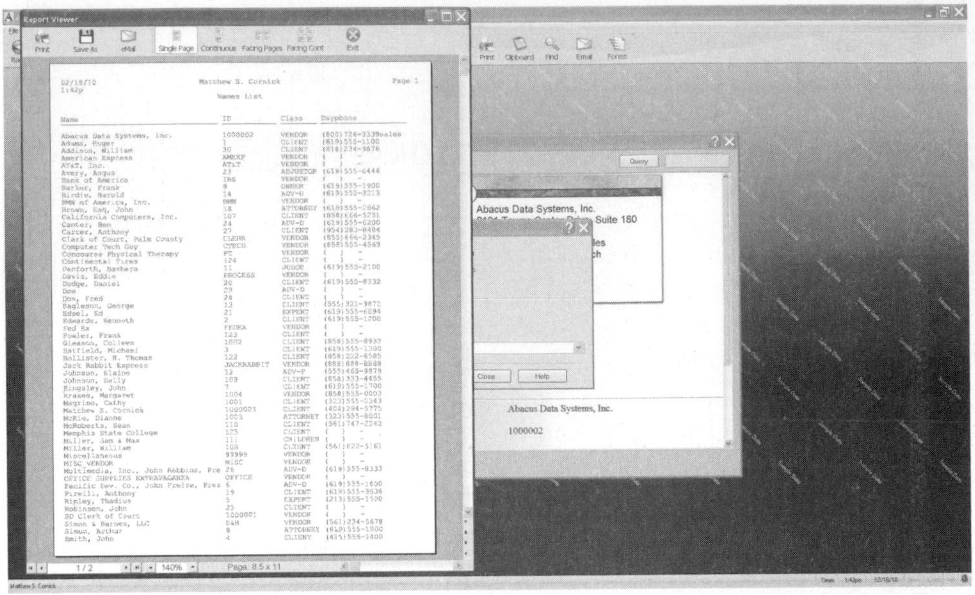

window opens, just *click Print.* (*Note:* The program will not actually print the report to the printer at this time; it will only print to the screen.) The Names List report should now be displayed. See AbacusLaw Exhibit 11.

18. *Click the Exit icon* (a red X) *on the toolbar. At the "Names Report Control" window, click Close.*

19. *Click the Close icon* (the red square with a white X) *in the "Names Browse" window to close it.*

20. *Click File on the menu bar and then click Exit* (the very last entry under the Recent Files Accessed list).

21. At the **"Please register now!"** window, *click OK.*

This concludes Lesson 2.

▶ INTERMEDIATE LESSONS

LESSON 3: ENTERING NEW MATTERS/CASES

In this lesson, you will enter new matters and cases and associate them with existing clients. This lesson assumes that you have completed Lessons 1 and 2 and that you are familiar with the AbacusLaw interface.

1. The first thing you will do in this lesson is populate AbacusLaw with sample data. *If you start AbacusLaw from the icon on the desktop, the sample data will not be loaded,* so please follow these directions.

2. Start Windows. *Click the Start button on the Windows desktop, point to Programs or All Programs, point to the AbacusLaw group, then click Sample Data.* This will populate Abacus with some sample data.

3. The **"User Log on"** window should now be displayed. Note that the AbacusLaw desktop should say **"Sample Data."**

4. In the User ID field of the **"User Log on"** window, type the same initials you entered in Lesson 1. It is important that you enter the same initials each time you start Abacus. Do not type anything in the Password field. *Click OK in the "User Log on" window.*

5. The "Tip of the Day" window should now be displayed on your screen. *Click OK in the "Tip of the Day" window.* You should now be at the Abacus desktop with the name plate that reads **"Your name appears here after registration."**

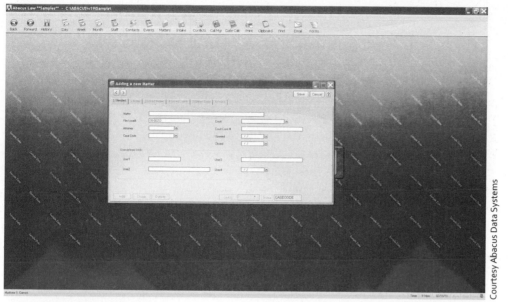

**ABACUSLAW
EXHIBIT 12**
Adding a new matter

Courtesy Abacus Data Systems

6. *Click Matters on the toolbar, then click Add in the "Matters Browse" window.* The "Adding a new Matter" window should be displayed (see AbacusLaw Exhibit 12).

7. Enter the matter information from the following list in the "Adding a new Matter" window. You can use the [**TAB**] key to go the next field, or [**SHIFT**]+[**TAB**] to go to the previous field. You can also use the mouse to click in a field. In the following data list, when you come to a blank field, just skip over it. *Note:* When you get to the Court field, you will not see an existing entry for LASUPER. *Click the up arrow next to Court field. In the "Valid Court Entries" window, click Import.* The "Import old 'Where Codes' to Courts" window is now displayed. *Click OK. In the "Valid WHERE Entries" window select LASUPER and click OK. Click OK in the "Valid Court Entries" window.*

FIELD NAME	DATA TO ENTER
Matter	**Magrino v. American Insurance**
File/case#	**2012–8743**
Attorney	**AMS**
Case Code	**INS**
Court	**LASUPER**
Court Case #	
Opened	**06 01 12**
Closed	
User1	
User2	
User3	
User4	

8. When you have finished entering the information, *click Save in the "Adding a new Matter" window.*

9. You will now create a link (or relationship) between Cathy Magrino in the Contact portion of the program and *Magrino v. American Insurance* in the

Matter portion of the program. *In the "Matter: Magrino v. American Insurance" window, click the Linked Names tab.* (It is the third tab.) *Click Add link.* The "Names Browse" window should now be displayed.

10. *In the "Names Browse" window, scroll down until you see the entry for Magrino, Cathy and then click it. In the "Names Browse" window, click OK.*

11. The "Name-to-Matter Link" window should now be displayed (see AbacusLaw Exhibit 13). *Click the up arrow next to Link Type in the "Name-to-Matter Link" window.* The "Valid ATTACHTYPE Entries" window will now be displayed. *In this window, scroll until you come to CLIENT and click it;* (see AbacusLaw Exhibit 13) *then click OK.*

ABACUSLAW EXHIBIT 13

Linking a name with a matter

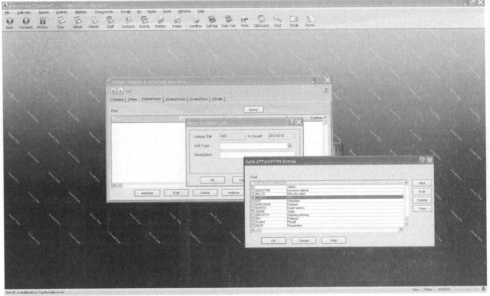

Courtesy Abacus Data Systems

12. In the "Name-to-Matter Link" window, in the text box next to Description: after the word Client, type – **Plaintiff,** then *click OK.* Notice in the "Matter: Magrino v. American Insurance" window that the name "Magrino, Cathy" now shows up in the Linked Names tab.

13. *Click the Close icon* (the red square with a white X) *in the "Matter: Magrino v. American Insurance" window to close the window.*

14. You will now check to see if the "Magrino, Cathy" entry in the Contact section of the program is linked to the matter *Magrino v. American Insurance. **Click Contacts on the toolbar, and scroll until you find "Magrino, Cathy." Click Magrino, Cathy then click OK. In the "Name: Magrino, Cathy" window, click the Linked Matters tab.*** The *Magrino v. American Insurance* matter should be shown (see AbacusLaw Exhibit 14).

15. *Double-click Magrino v. American Insurance in the "Name: Magrino, Cathy" window.* The "Matter: Magrino v. American Insurance" window is now displayed. The name and matter are linked.

16. *Click the Close icon* (the red square with a white X) *in the "Matter: Magrino v. American Insurance" window to close that window.*

17. *Click the Close icon in the "Name: Magrino, Cathy" window to close that window.*

18. You will now create one more matter and link it to another client. *Click Matters on the toolbar, then click Add in the "Matters Browse" window.* The "Adding a new Matter" window should be displayed.

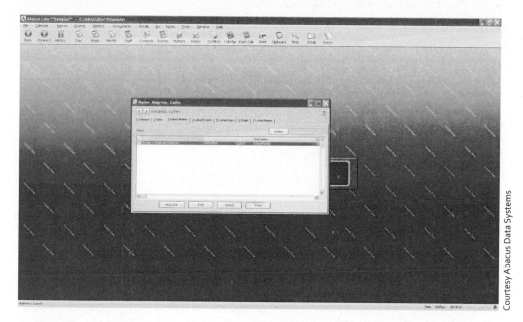

Courtesy Abacus Data Systems

ABACUSLAW EXHIBIT 14
Contact name linked with a matter

19. Enter the matter information from the following list in the "Adding a new Matter" window. *Note:* When you get to Case Code, you will not see an existing entry for Adoption, so you will need to add it. ***In the "Valid CASECODE Entries" window, click Add.*** In the "New 'CASECODE' Code" window, type **Adoption** and then ***click OK.*** In the "CASECODE Code Description" window, type **Adoption in Family Court** and then ***click OK.*** Now, ***click ADOPTION in the "Valid CASECODE Entries" window, then click OK.*** A nice feature in Abacus is that you can create new items on the fly without having to get out of where you are and go to a special screen. You will also have to add the court. To do so, ***click the up arrow to the left of Court. In the "Valid Court Entries" window, click Populate. In the "Tag all Courts to add from the Abacus master list" window, scroll down until you see "SD FAMILY LAW Superior Court of California, County of San Diego," then click the box next to the desired court and click OK.*** See AbacusLaw Exhibit 15. The "Valid Court Entries" window now lists the San Diego Family Court. ***Move your cursor to choose San Diego Family Court and click OK.***

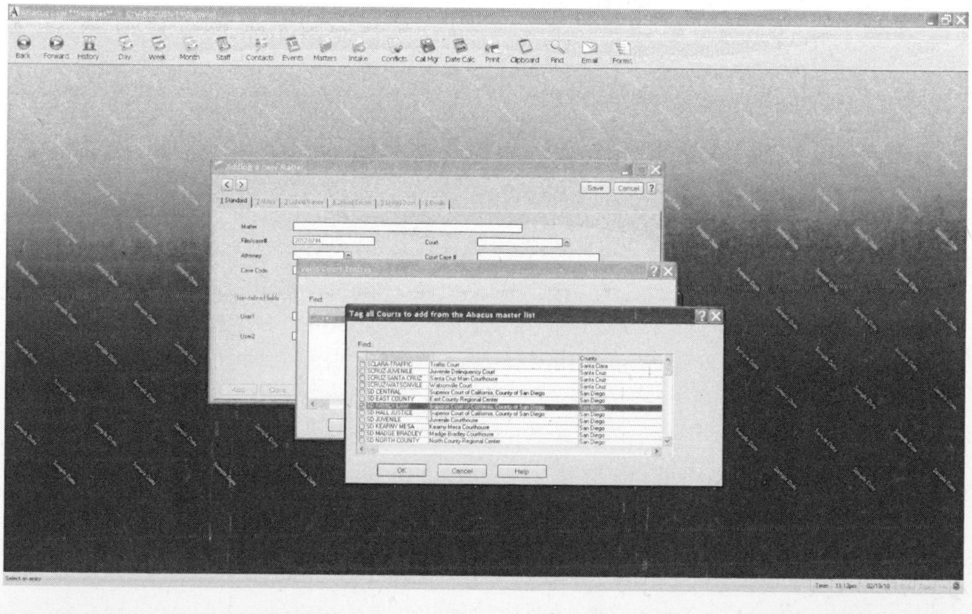

Courtesy Abacus Data Systems

ABACUSLAW EXHIBIT 15
Selecting a jurisdiction

FIELD NAME	DATA TO ENTER
Matter	**Gleason Adoption**
File/case#	**2012-A-203**
Attorney	**AMS**
Case Code	**ADOPTION**
Court	**SD FAMILY LAW**
Court Case #	
Opened	**06 01 12**
Closed	
User1	
User2	
User3	
User4	

20. When you have finished entering the information, *click Save in the "Adding a new Matter" window.*

21. You will now create a link (or relationship) between "Colleen Gleason" in the Contact portion of the program and "Gleason Adoption" in the Matter portion of the program. *In the "Matter: Gleason Adoption" window, click the Linked Names tab. Click Add link.* The "Names Browse" window should now be displayed.

22. *In the "Names Browse" window, scroll down until you see the entry for Gleason, Colleen; click it. Then, in the "Names Browse" window, click OK.*

23. The "Name-to-Matter Link" window should now be displayed. *Click the up arrow next to Link Type in the "Name-to-Matter Link" window.* The "Valid ATTACHTYPE Entries" window will now be displayed. *In that window, scroll until you come to CLIENT and then click OK.*

24. In the "Name-to-Matter Link" window, next to Description, type – **Plaintiff** and then *click OK.* Notice that in the "Matter: Gleason Adoption" window, the name "Gleason, Colleen" now shows up in the Linked Names tab.

25. *Click the Close icon* (the red square with a white X) *in the "Matter: Gleason Adoption" window to close that window.*

26. *Click File on the menu bar and then click Exit* (the very last entry under the Recent Files Accessed list).

27. At the **"Please register now!"** window, *click OK.*

This concludes Lesson 3.

LESSON 4: CREATING EVENTS, PART 1

In this lesson, you will add a staff person to the list of people available to perform work for clients. You will also create events, including appointments, reminders, and things to do, that are either related and unrelated to cases. This lesson assumes that you have completed Lessons 1 through 3, and that you are familiar with the AbacusLaw interface.

1. The first thing you will do in this lesson is populate AbacusLaw with sample data. *If you start AbacusLaw from the icon on the desktop, the sample data will not be loaded,* so please follow these directions.

2. Start Windows. ***Click the Start button on the Windows desktop, point to Programs or All Programs, point to the AbacusLaw group, then click Sample Data.*** This will populate Abacus with some sample data.

3. The "User Log on" window should now be displayed and the AbacusLaw desktop should say **"Sample Data."**

4. In the "User Log on" window, in the User ID field, type the same initials you entered in Lesson 1. It is important that you enter the same initials each time you start Abacus. Do not type anything in the Password field. ***Click OK in the "User Log on" window.***

5. The "Tip of the Day" window should now be displayed on your screen. ***Click OK in the "Tip of the Day" window.*** You should now be at the Abacus desktop with the name plate that reads **"Your name appears here after registration."**

6. The first thing you will do in this lesson is to add a paralegal staff member to AbacusLaw. ***Click File on the menu bar, then point to Setup and click Codes....*** The "Code Types" window should now be displayed (see AbacusLaw Exhibit 16).

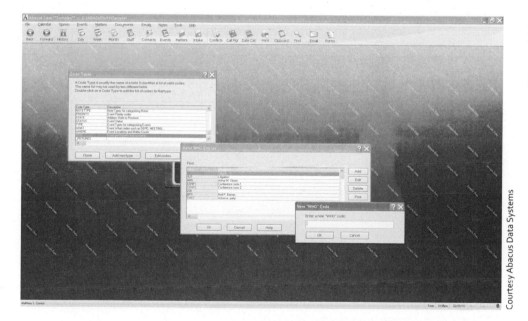

ABACUSLAW EXHIBIT 16
Entering a new staff member in the "New "WHO" Code" window

7. ***In the "Code Types" window, scroll down and click the WHO code type. Then click Edit codes*** (see AbacusLaw Exhibit 16). The "Valid WHO Entries" window should now be displayed.

8. ***Click Add.*** The "New "WHO" Code" window should now be displayed (see AbacusLaw Exhibit 16). Under Enter a new "WHO" code:, type **DIANA** and then ***click OK.***

9. The "WHO Code Description" window should now be displayed. Under Description for DIANA: type **Nita, Paralegal** and then ***click OK.*** The entry should now appear in the "Valid WHO Entries" window. ***Click OK in the "Valid WHO Entries" window.***

10. ***Click Close in the "Code Types" window.***

11. You will now enter a number of appointments, reminders, things to do, and calls to be made into Diana Nita's calendar. ***Click Day on the toolbar to load the Daily Organizer.***

12. *Change the date in the Daily Organizer to 06/11/12* and then press the [ENTER] key.

13. *Click the up arrow next to All People in the upper right corner of the "Daily Organizer—Monday, June 11, 2012" window.* The "'Who' Setting for Calendars" window should now be displayed.

14. *Click Diana—Diana Nita, Paralegal, then click OK.* Notice that the Daily Organizer is now set for Diana Nita, Paralegal.

15. The first event entry you will make will not be linked to a case. *In the "Daily Organizer—Monday, June 11, 2012" window, double-click on 12:00p.*

16. The "Adding a new Event" window should now be displayed (see AbacusLaw Exhibit 17). *Note:* The "Adding a new Event" window can either be expanded (More) or contracted (Less). In AbacusLaw Exhibit 17, the screen is contracted, so to see additional options (such as name and matter), you would just click More. The contracted screen is fine for this entry.

ABACUSLAW EXHIBIT 17

Entering a new event not associated with a matter

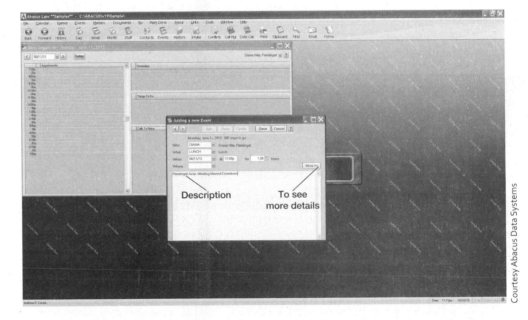

Courtesy Abacus Data Systems

17. **"DIANA"** should already be in the Who field. *In the What field, click the up arrow.* The "Valid WHAT Entries" window should now be displayed. There are many entries in this screen, so type **L** to take you to the WHAT entries that begin with L, *click LUNCH, then click OK.*

18. The date of 06/11/12 at 12:00p should already be entered. *Click 0.50 next to "hours" and change it to 1.00.*

19. In the Description field, type **Paralegal Assn. Lunch, Marriott Downtown**. See AbacusLaw Exhibit 17.

20. *Click Save.* The entry should now be made in your calendar.

21. You will now enter an event linked with a case. *In the "Daily Organizer— Monday, June 11, 2012" window, double-click on 1:30p.* Because you will be linking the event to a contact and a matter, you need the expanded (More) version of the "Adding a new Event" window. If you do not see the Name and Matter fields on your screen, *click More >> in the "Adding a new Event" window* (see AbacusLaw Exhibit 17).

22. Enter the matter information from the following list in the "Adding a new Event" window. You can use the **[TAB]** key to go the next field, or **[SHIFT]+[TAB]** to go to the previous field. You can also use the mouse to click in a field. In the following list, when you come to a blank field, just skip over it. ***When you get to the Name field, just point on the up arrow, scroll to Magrino, Cathy in the "Names Browse" window, and click OK.*** Because the "Magrino, Cathy" entry is linked to *Magrino v. American Insurance,* the case should automatically appear in the Matter field.

FIELD NAME	DATA TO ENTER
Who	**DIANA**
What	**C-CLIENT**
When	**06/08/12 at 1:30p for 3.00 hours**
Where	**HERE**
Description (open light yellow box)	**Discuss electronic discovery production issues with client**
Name	**Magrino, Cathy**
Matter	**Magrino v. American Insurance**
Priority	
Type	**A**
Status	**N**
Reminders -	**3 5**

23. When you have finished entering all of the data, ***click Save in the "Adding a new Event" window.*** The entry should now appear in your Daily Organizer.

24. You entered three-day and five-day reminders for the entry you just made. Let's see if the reminders appear correctly in the calendar. ***Click on the Previous Day icon (<) just to the left of the date in the Daily Organizer*** (see AbacusLaw Exhibit 17) ***three times so that the date 06/08/12 is shown in the Daily Organizer.*** The reminder for the client conference on 6/11/12 regarding electronic discovery should be shown in the Appointments section of the Daily Organizer.

25. ***Click the Next Day icon (>) just to the right of the date in the Daily Organizer*** (see AbacusLaw Exhibit 17) ***four times so that the date 06/12/12 is displayed in the Daily Organizer.***

26. You will now make a Things To Do entry. ***In the "Daily Organizer—Tuesday, June 12, 2012" window, double-click just below Things to Do.*** The "Adding a new Event" window should now be displayed. Notice that AbacusLaw entered **"NOTE"** in the What field. Also, in the When field next to the date of 06/12/12, it says **"TO-DO"** for this entry.

27. Enter the matter information from the following list in the "Adding a new Event" window.

FIELD NAME	DATA TO ENTER
Who	DIANA
What	NOTE
When	06/12/12 TO-DO
Where	HERE
Description (open light yellow box)	Send Digital Media Equipment, Inc. an electronic discovery request in Magrino case.
Name	Magrino, Cathy
Matter	Magrino v. American Insurance
Priority	
Type	T
Status	N
Reminders -	0 0

28. When you have finished entering all of the data, **click Save in the "Adding a new Event" window.** The entry should now appear in your Daily Organizer under Things To Do. *Note:* Items entered in Things to Do will perpetually stay in the Daily Organizer section of Things To Do (once the item is overdue) until the user marks it Done. Notice that in the Things To Do section of the Daily Organizer, there is a white box next to the entry you just made. You would click the box to indicate that the item had been completed. Once that box is checked, the item no longer shows up in the Things To Do section of the Daily Organizer.

29. You will now make a Calls to Make entry. ***In the "Daily Organizer—Tuesday, June 12, 2008" window, double-click just below Calls to Make.*** The "Adding a new Event" window should now be displayed. Notice that AbacusLaw entered **"PHONE"** in the What field. Also, in the When field next to the date of 06/12/12, it says **"TO-DO"** for this entry.

30. Enter the matter information from the following list in the "Adding a new Event" window.

FIELD NAME	DATA TO ENTER
Who	DIANA
What	PHONE
When	06/12/12 TO-DO
Where	HERE
Description (open light yellow box)	Call Colleen Gleason to see if she returned from Russia with child.
Name	Gleason, Colleen
Matter	Gleason Adoption
Priority	
Type	P
Status	N
Reminders -	0 0

31. When you have finished entering all of the data, **_click Save in the "Adding a new Event" window._** The entry should now appear in your Daily Organizer under Calls to Make. Notice that Abacus automatically entered the client's phone number in the entry. *Note:* You can also make entries in the Reminders section of the Daily Organizer by **double-clicking just below Reminders.** Reminders just show up on the day they are scheduled for and do not carry forward from day to day, even if they are not marked as completed.

32. Create the following events:

Date:	6/12/2012 Appointment
Who	DIANA
What	DRAFT
When	06/12/12 at 9:00a for 8.00 hours
Where	HERE
Description (open light yellow box)	Draft discovery documents
Name	Magrino, Cathy
Matter	Magrino v. American Insurance
Priority	1
Type	A
Status	N
Reminders -	1 0
Date:	6/13/2012 Things to Do
Who	DIANA
What	NOTE
When	06/13/12 TO-DO for 0.00 hours
Where	HERE
Description (open light yellow box)	Work on Depo Summary of Plaintiff
Name	Magrino, Cathy
Matter	Magrino v. American Insurance
Priority	
Type	T
Status	N
Reminders -	0 0
Date:	6/14/2012 Appointment
Who	DIANA
What	APPT
When	06/14/12 at 9:30a for 2.00 hours
Where	HERE
Description (open light yellow box)	Call immigration agency as scheduled re: adoption papers

Name	Gleason, Colleen
Matter	Gleason Adoption
Priority	1
Type	A
Status	N
Reminders -	1 3
Date:	6/13/2012 Appointment
Who	DIANA
What	APPT
When	06/13/12 at 9:00a for 3.00 hours
Where	HERE
Description (open light yellow box)	Draft responses to Defendant's discovery requests
Name	Magrino, Cathy
Matter	Magrino v. American Insurance
Priority	1
Type	T
Status	N
Reminders -	1 3
Date:	6/11/2012 Appointment
Who	DIANA
What	APPT
When	06/11/12 at 9:00a for 2.50 hours
Where	HERE
Description (open light yellow box)	Draft amended Adoption papers
Name	Gleason, Colleen
Matter	Gleason Adoption
Priority	
Type	T
Status	N
Reminders -	0 0
Date:	6/13/2012 Appointment
Who	DIANA
What	APPT
When	06/13/12 at 2:00p for 2.00 hours
Where	HERE
Description (open light yellow box)	Meet with Arthur to discuss electronic discovery issues and discovery responses

Name	**Magrino, Cathy**
Matter	**Magrino v. American Insurance**
Priority	
Type	**T**
Status	**N**
Reminders -	**1 0**

33. After you have made all of the entries, *click Week on the toolbar.* Your weekly calendar for the week of June 11, 2012 should look similar to AbacusLaw Exhibit 18. *Note:* The gray bars that separate the reminders, appointment, and things-to-do sections can be dragged up or down to adjust how the information appears on the screen (see AbacusLaw Exhibit 18).

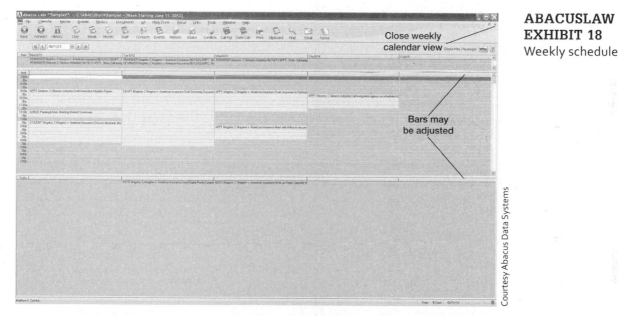

**ABACUSLAW
EXHIBIT 18**
Weekly schedule

Courtesy Abacus Data Systems

34. *Click the Close (X) icon for the Weekly calendar view.*
35. *Click the Close (X) icon for the Daily Organizer.*
36. *Click File on the menu bar and then click Exit* (the very last entry under the Recent Files Accessed list).
37. At the **"Please register now!"** window, *click OK.*

This concludes Lesson 4.

LESSON 5: CREATING EVENTS, PART 2

Rule-based entries are extremely efficient and can greatly enhance data entry. In this lesson, you will create a recurring event, make a rule-based entry, and work with the Date Calculator. This lesson assumes that you have completed Lessons 1 through 4 and that you are familiar with the AbacusLaw interface.

1. The first thing you will do in this lesson is populate AbacusLaw with sample data. *If you start AbacusLaw from the icon on the desktop, the sample data will not be loaded,* so please follow these directions.

2. Start Windows. *Click the Start button on the Windows desktop, point to Programs or All Programs, point to the AbacusLaw group, then click Sample Data.* This will populate Abacus with some sample data.

3. The "User Log on" window should now be displayed. Note that the AbacusLaw desktop should say **"Sample Data."**

4. In the "User Log on" window, in the User ID field, type the same initials you entered in Lesson 1. It is important that you enter the same initials each time you start Abacus. Do not type anything in the Password field. ***Click OK in the "User Log on" window.***

5. The "Tip of the Day" window should now be displayed on your screen. ***Click OK in the "Tip of the Day" window.*** You should now be at the Abacus desktop with the name plate that reads **"Your name appears here after registration."**

6. You will next make a recurring entry that will occur every day. Arthur Simon has decided that he would like to have a staff meeting with Diana Nita from 8:30 a.m. to 9:00 a.m. every morning through the month of June.

7. ***Click Day on the toolbar to see the Daily Organizer. Change the date on the Daily Organizer to 06/11/2012.***

8. ***Double-click on 8:30a.*** Create the events using the data in the following list. *Note:* You will need to add a new WHAT entry for the staff meeting. ***In the "Valid WHAT Entries" window, click Add.*** In the "New "WHAT" Code" window, type **STAFF MT,** ***click OK;*** then, in the "WHAT Code Description" window, type **Staff Meeting.** ***Click OK in the "WHAT Code Description" window.*** Finally, ***click on Staff Meeting in the "Valid WHAT Entries" window and click OK.***

Who	DIANA
What	STAFF MT
When	06/12/12 at 8:30a for .50 hours
Where	HERE
Description (open light yellow box)	
Name	
Matter	
Priority	
Type	A
Status	N
Reminders -	0 0

9. Once you have finished creating the entry, ***click Save in the "Adding a new Event" window.***

10. In the Daily Organizer, the STAFF MT entry you just created should be selected. ***Click Recur on the menu bar*** (see AbacusLaw Exhibit 19.) The "Recur Event: STAFF MT…" window should now be displayed. ***Click Daily under Interval, change the End entry to 06/29/12, click the box to the left of Omit weekend events, then click OK.***

11. The "Select an option" window should appear and ask **"Ready to schedule up to 18 events through 06/29/12. Are you sure?"** ***Click Yes.*** The "Linked Events Browse" window is then displayed (see AbacusLaw Exhibit 20). You can see all of the entries that the program is about to make. ***Click OK.***

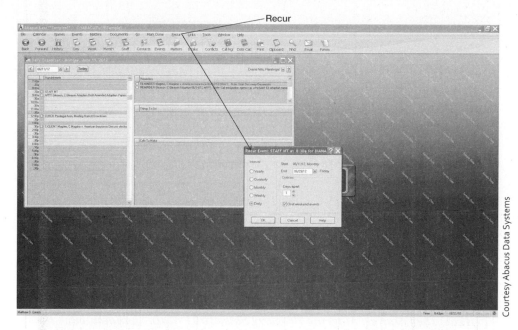

**ABACUSLAW
EXHIBIT 19**
Entering a recurring event

Courtesy Abacus Data Systems

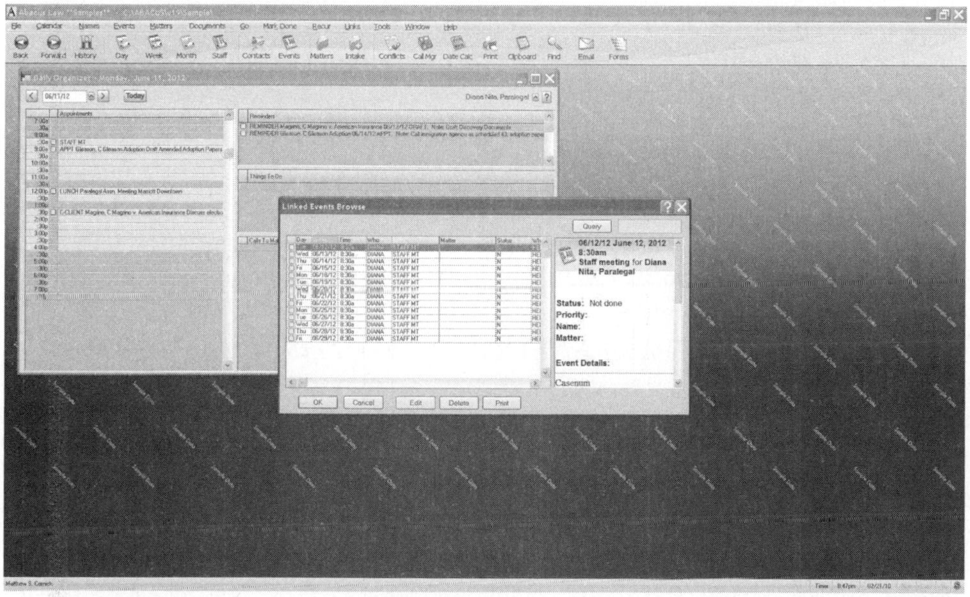

**ABACUSLAW
EXHIBIT 20**
Recurring event—"Linked
Events Browse" window

Courtesy Abacus Data Systems

HANDS-ON EXERCISES

12. *In the Daily Organizer, next to the date, click Next day > several times* and notice that the staff meeting has been added. *Click the Close (X) icon for the Daily Organizer.*

13. You will next enter a new matter and learn how to make a rule-based entry for the new matter. Arthur Simon has told you that the firm will be handling a new matter for Cathy Magrino regarding the sale of a piece of property and that he would like you to schedule the normal New Matter deadlines. The initial client meeting for the matter will be on 6/14/12.

14. *Click Matters on the toolbar, then click on Add.*

15. In the "Adding a new Matter" window, enter the data from the following list.

FIELD NAME	DATA TO ENTER
Matter	**Magrino Property Sale, 1001 Main**
File/case#	**1005**
Attorney	**AMS**
Case Code	**REA**
Court	
Opened	**06 11 12**
Closed	
User1	
User2	
User3	
User4	

16. When you are finished, *click Save in the "Adding a new Matter" window. From the "Matter: Magrino Property Sale, 1001 Main" window, click the Linked Names tab, click Add link, click Magrino, Cathy, and click OK in the "Names Browse" window.*

17. *In the "Name-to-Matter Link" window, click the up arrow next to Link Type. In the "Valid ATTACHTYPE Entries" window, click CLIENT and then click OK. Click OK in the "Name-to-Matter Link" window.*

18. An entry for "Magrino, Cathy" now appears in the "Matter: Magrino Property Sale, 1001 Main" window. ***Click the Close (X) icon in the "Matter: Magrino Property Sale, 1001 Main" window.***

19. You should be back at the Daily Organizer for 06/14/12. ***Right-click 1:00p. Click Add Events from a Rule.*** The "Rules" window should now be displayed (see AbacusLaw Exhibit 21).

20. *In the "Rules" window, click NEWCASE. Then, in the "Rules" window, click Edit.*

**ABACUSLAW
EXHIBIT 21**

Making a rule-based entry

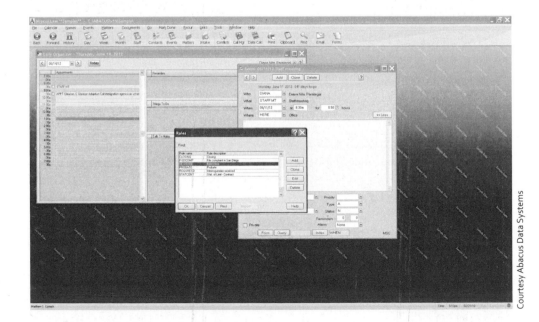

ABACUSLAW EXHIBIT 22
Rule-based entry—"Rule name" window

21. The "Rule name (Event #0): NEWCASE New case" window should be displayed (see AbacusLaw Exhibit 22). This screen shows the entries that will automatically be made. The Interval column refers to the number of days from the initial event (e.g., 0 days, 1 day, 1 day, 0 days, 7 days, or 14 days).

22. *Click OK in the "Rule name (Event #0): NEWCASE New case" window.*

23. *In the "Rules" window, click OK.* Notice that NEWCASE has now been added to the open Event on the screen. Enter the information from the following list in the "Event" window. Note that in the Matter field you will need to *click the Magrino Property Sale matter in the "Matters for Magrino, Cathy" window, then click OK.*

Who	**DIANA**
What	**NEWCASE**
When	**06/14/12 at 1:00p for 1.00 hours**
Where	**HERE**
Description (open light yellow box)	
Name	**Magrino, Cathy**
Matter	**Magrino Property Sale**
Priority	
Type	**A**
Status	**N**
Reminders -	**0 0**

24. When you are finished creating the entry, *click Save in the "Adding a new Event" window.*

25. The "Creating Events from Rule: NEWCASE" window is displayed. You are asked if you want the related events scheduled. *Click Yes.*

**ABACUSLAW
EXHIBIT 23**
Rule-based entry—"Linked
Events Browse" window

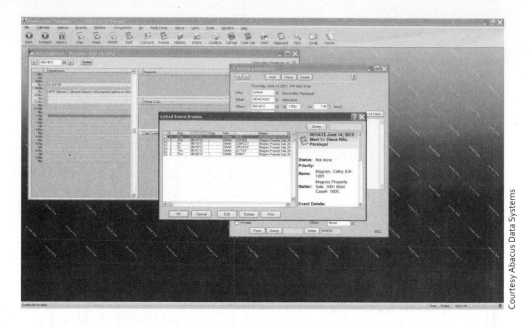

Courtesy Abacus Data Systems

26. The "Linked Events Browse" window should be displayed (see AbacusLaw Exhibit 23). ***Click OK in the "Linked Events Browse" window.*** Notice that the initial meeting is set at 1:00 and that in the Reminders section of the Daily Organizer there are some entries regarding the new case.

27. ***Click the Next Day icon (>) in the Daily Organizer until you come to 06/21/12.*** Notice that there is a reminder to do the Confirmation Letter.

28. ***Click the Next Day icon (>) in the Daily Organizer until you come to 06/28/12.*** Notice that there is a reminder to do the fee contract.

29. In the date field in the Daily Organizer, type **06/11/12** and press the **[ENTER]** key.

30. You will now use the Date Calculator feature. On 06/11/12 the office received a motion to dismiss that must be responded to, within 20 days. Arthur Simon asks you to let him know exactly what date the response is due using the AbacusLaw Date Calculator.

31. ***Click Date Calc on the toolbar.*** The "Date Calculator" window should now be displayed (see AbacusLaw Exhibit 24).

**ABACUSLAW
EXHIBIT 24**
Date Calculator

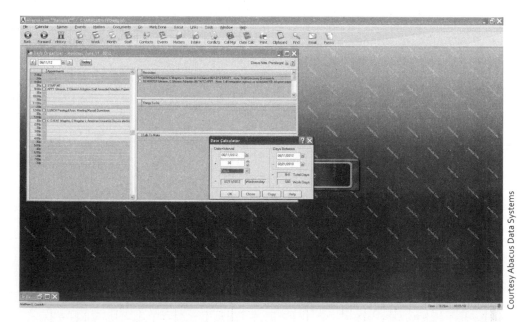

Courtesy Abacus Data Systems

32. Under Date+Interval, type **06/11/2012**, then enter **10** next to the plus sign (+). *Click the down arrow next to Days and select Days.* The Date Calculator should return a date of **"6/21/2012 (Thursday)."**

33. *Click OK to close the Date Calculator.*

34. *Click the Close (X) icon for the Daily Organizer.*

35. *Click File on the menu bar and then click on Exit* (the very last entry under the Recent Files Accessed list).

36. At the **"Please register now!"** window, *click OK.*

This concludes Lesson 5.

LESSON 6: CREATING LINKED NAMES AND LINKED NOTES, AND CHECKING FOR CONFLICTS

In this lesson, you will link a non-client to a case, create notes that are linked to contacts and matters, and run a conflict of interest search. This lesson assumes that you have completed Lessons 1 through 5 and that you are familiar with the AbacusLaw interface.

1. The first thing you will do in this lesson is populate AbacusLaw with sample data. *If you start AbacusLaw from the icon on the desktop, the sample data will not be loaded,* so please follow these directions.

2. Start Windows. *Click the Start button on the Windows desktop, point to Programs or All Programs, point to the AbacusLaw group, and click Sample Data.* This will populate Abacus with some sample data.

3. The "User Log on" window should now be displayed. Note that the AbacusLaw desktop should say **"Sample Data."**

4. In the "User Log on" window, in the User ID field, type the same initials you entered in Lesson 1. It is important that you enter the same initials each time you load Abacus. Do not type anything in the Password field. *Click OK in the "User Log on" window.*

5. The "Tip of the Day" window should now be displayed on your screen. *Click OK in the "Tip of the Day" window.* You should now be at the Abacus desktop with the name plate that reads **"Your name appears here after registration."**

6. The first thing you will do is link an opposing attorney to a case. Just as you can link clients to matters, you can link people who are not clients to other people and to matters.

7. *Click Matters on the toolbar. Double-click Magrino v. American Insurance.* The "Matter: Magrino v. American Insurance" window should now be displayed.

8. *Click the Linked Names tab. Click Add link. Click McKie, Dianne and then click OK.*

9. *In the "Name-to-Matter Link" window, click the up arrow next to Link Type and then in the "Valid ATTACHTYPE Entries" window click OPP-ATTY-Opposing Attorney. Click OK in the "Valid ATTACHTYPE Entries" window.*

10. *Click OK in the "Name-to-Matter Link" window.* Notice that Dianne McKie, the defendant's attorney, has now been linked to the case.

11. You have already added a number of events to the *Magrino v. American Insurance* case. *Click the Linked Events tab in the "Matter: Magrino v. American Insurance" window to see all of the items that are linked to the case.* Approximately 13 entries should be present (see AbacusLaw Exhibit 25).

12. You will now create two notes that will be linked to the case.

13. *Click the Notes tab in the "Matter: Magrino v. American Insurance" window. Click Add.*

**ABACUSLAW
EXHIBIT 25**
Listing of linked events

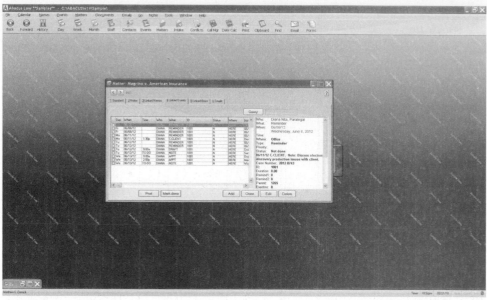

Courtesy Abacus Data Systems

**ABACUSLAW
EXHIBIT 26**
Adding a note

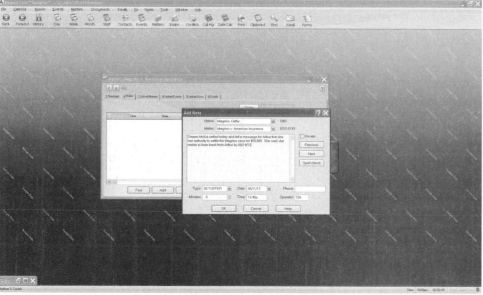

Courtesy Abacus Data Systems

14. The "Add Note" window should now be displayed (see AbacusLaw Exhibit 26). Notice that **"Magrino, Cathy"** has already been entered and linked to the Name field and that **"Magrino v. American Insurance"** has already been linked as the matter concerning the note.

15. *Click in the note description field.* Type **Dianne McKie called today and left a message for Arthur that she has authority to settle the Magrino case for $50,000. She said she needs to hear back from Arthur by 6/14/12.** (See AbacusLaw Exhibit 26.)

16. *Click the up arrow next to Type, click SETOFFER Settlement Offer, then click OK in the "Valid NOTETYPE Entries" window.*

17. In the Date field of the "Add Note" window, type **06/11/12.**

18. In the Operator field of the "Add Note" window, type **DN** and then *click OK.*

19. Notice that the note has now been added.

20. **Click Add** to add one more note. Create the note using the data in the following list.

Name	**Magrino, Cathy**
Matter	**Magrino v. American Insurance**
Description	**Cathy Magrino called and left a message for Arthur that she would accept the defendant's offer to settle the case for $50,000.**
Type:	**SETOFFER**
Date:	**06/12/12**
Operator:	**DN**

21. When you have finished creating the note, *click OK in the "Add Note" window.*

22. *Click the Close (X) icon in the "Matter: Magrino v. American Insurance" window.*

23. You will now run a conflict of interest search. Arthur Simon called and asked you to run the name of Margaret Krakes for conflicts of interest. A possible new client named John Krakes has asked the firm to handle a custody dispute with his former wife, Margaret. Arthur said that the name sounded familiar, but he did not know why.

24. *Click Conflicts on the toolbar.* The "Conflict of Interest Check" window should now be displayed (see AbacusLaw Exhibit 27). Under Enter last name, type **Krakes** and then press the **[ENTER]** key.

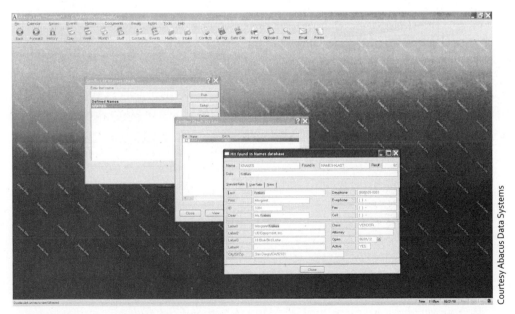

**ABACUSLAW
EXHIBIT 27**
Running a conflict of interest search

Courtesy Abacus Data Systems

25. *Click Run in the "Conflict of Interest Check" window* (see AbacusLaw Exhibit 27). The "Conflict Check Hit List" window is then displayed.

26. *Double-click KRAKES in the "Conflict Check Hit List" window.* The "Hit found in Names database" window is then displayed (see AbacusLaw Exhibit 27). Margaret Krakes is a vendor with whom the firm works.

27. *Click Close in the "Hit found in Names database" window and then click the Close (X) icons for the other open windows.*

28. *Click File on the menu bar and then click Exit* (the very last entry under the Recent Files Accessed list).

29. At the **"Please register now!"** window, *click OK.*

This concludes Lesson 6.

▶ ADVANCED LESSONS

LESSON 7: LINKING DOCUMENTS; USING THE CALL MANAGER AND THE FORM GENERATION FEATURE

In this lesson, you will link documents, use the Call Manager feature, use the Form Generation feature, and work with the Events Browse tool. This lesson assumes that you have completed Lessons 1 through 6 and that you are familiar with the AbacusLaw interface.

1. The first thing you will do in this lesson is populate AbacusLaw with sample data. *If you start AbacusLaw from the icon on the desktop, the sample data will not be loaded,* so please follow these directions.

2. Start Windows. ***Click the Start button on the Windows desktop, point to Programs or All Programs, point to the AbacusLaw group, then click Sample Data.*** This will populate Abacus with some sample data.

3. The "User Log on" window should now be displayed. Note that the AbacusLaw desktop should say **"Sample Data."**

4. In the "User Log on" window, in the User ID field, type the same initials you entered in Lesson 1. It is important that you enter the same initials each time you load Abacus. Do not type anything in the Password field. ***Click OK in the "User Log on" window.***

5. The "Tip of the Day" window should now be displayed on your screen. ***Click OK in the "Tip of the Day" window.*** You should now be at the Abacus desktop with the name plate that reads **"Your name appears here after registration."**

6. ***Click Matters on the toolbar.*** Press the **[HOME]** key to go the beginning of the matters in the "Matters Browse" window.

7. ***Double-click Cal. Computers v. Multimedia. In the "Matter: Cal. Computers v. Multimedia" window, click the Linked Docs tab. Click Edit*** to see the screen that is used to add/edit a link (see AbacusLaw Exhibit 28). The process is extremely easy: The user types the path of the document, links the document to a name and/or matter, and then completes the rest of the options in the screen, if desired (see AbacusLaw Exhibit 28). ***Click the Close (X) icon in the "Document Details" window.***

8. ***Click the Close (X) icon in the "Matter: Cal. Computers v. Multimedia" window.***

9. You will now learn to use the Call Manager feature. ***Click Call Mgr on the toolbar.***

10. Enter the call in the "Call Manager" window as shown in AbacusLaw Exhibit 29. Notice that you can indicate whether the call is an incoming call or an outgoing call. You can use the Call Manager to make a record of all incoming and outgoing calls.

11. In AbacusLaw Exhibit 29, in the "Call Manager" window, notice that there is a button for an option called Bill. If Abacus is set up to exchange information with a timekeeping and billing system, you can click the Bill button, the entry will be sent to timekeeping and billing, and the client will be billed for the time.

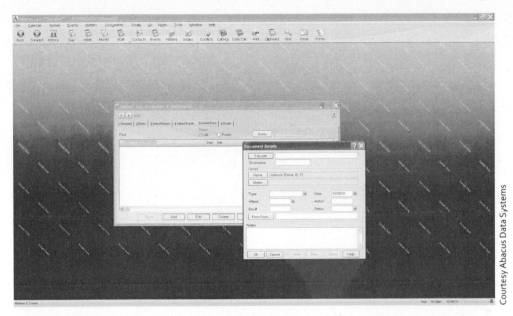

**ABACUSLAW
EXHIBIT 28**
Adding and editing a link to a document

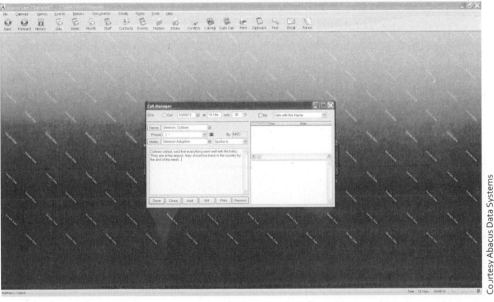

**ABACUSLAW
EXHIBIT 29**
Entering a call in the Call Manager

12. When you have entered the call, *click Save and then click Close in the "Call Manager" window.*

13. You can see all calls entered in the Call Manager in either the Matters or Contacts Notes tab. *Click Matters on the toolbar, double-click Gleason Adoption, and click the Notes tab.* You should now see the entry for the phone call.

14. *Click the Close (X) icon in the "Matter: Gleason Adoption" window.*

15. You will now learn how to use the Form Generation feature in AbacusLaw. (*Note:* This part of the lesson requires Microsoft Excel.) *Click Contacts on the toolbar, then scroll to and double-click on Magrino, Cathy.* The "Name: Magrino, Cathy" window should now be displayed.

16. *Click the Linked Events tab, then click the 06/08/12 1:30 p C-CLIENT entry.* The data from this entry will be referenced in the form you will generate.

17. *Click Print on the toolbar, click Form generation, then click MS Excel.*

**ABACUSLAW
EXHIBIT 30A**
Selecting a template to run
with the Form Generation
feature

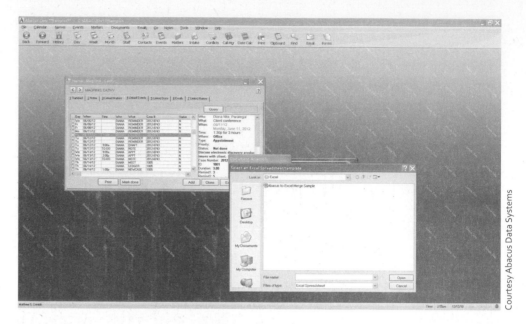

Courtesy Abacus Data Systems

**ABACUSLAW
EXHIBIT 30B**
Selecting a template to run
with the Form Generation
feature

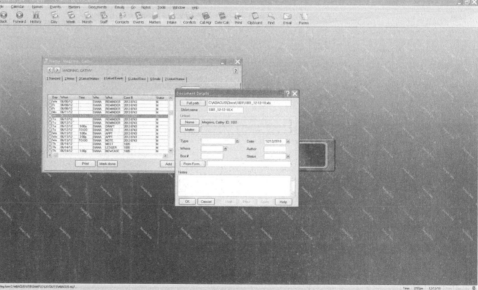

Courtesy Abacus Data Systems

18. The "Select an MSExcel Spreadsheet/template" window should now be displayed (see AbacusLaw Exhibit 30A). ***Double-click the file called Abacus to Excel Merge Sample*** (see AbacusLaw Exhibit 30A). The "Document Details" window will open; ***click OK*** (see AbacusLaw Exhibit 30B).

19. You should now be in Microsoft Excel with the template filled in (see AbacusLaw Exhibit 31). Notice that Abacus automatically inserted the client's address, case name, and date of the event in the form. ***Close the file in Excel.***

20. ***Click once more on the "AbacusLaw" window if it is not already shown. Close the "Name: Magrino, Cathy" window.***

21. ***Click Events on the toolbar.*** This feature shows you all of the events that have been entered into AbacusLaw (see AbacusLaw Exhibit 32). The default setting sorts events on the When (date) field. You can also sort the events by the What field by clicking in the What column heading. You can also use the Query feature

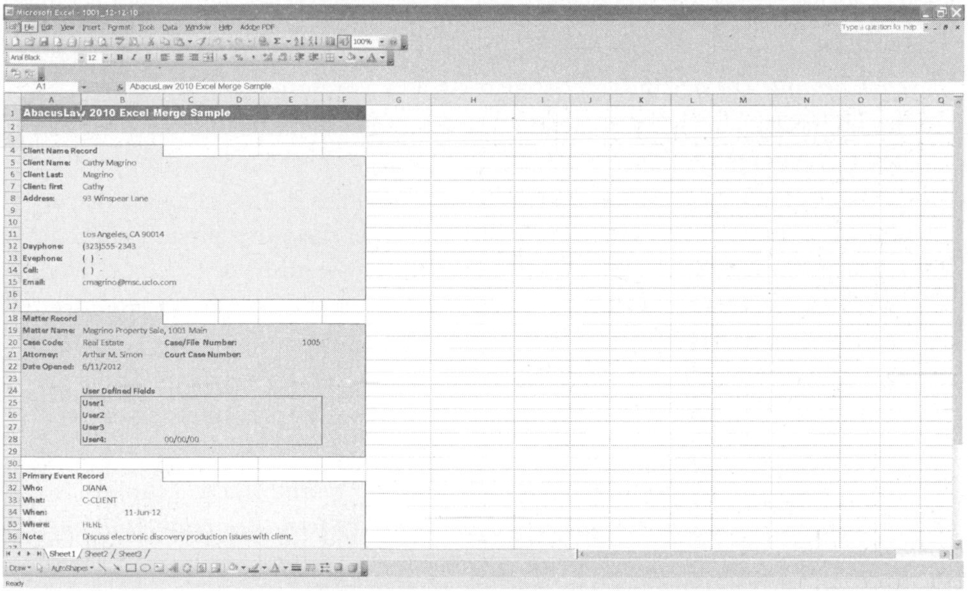

Courtesy Abacus Data Systems

ABACUSLAW EXHIBIT 31
Document generation—Completed form and template

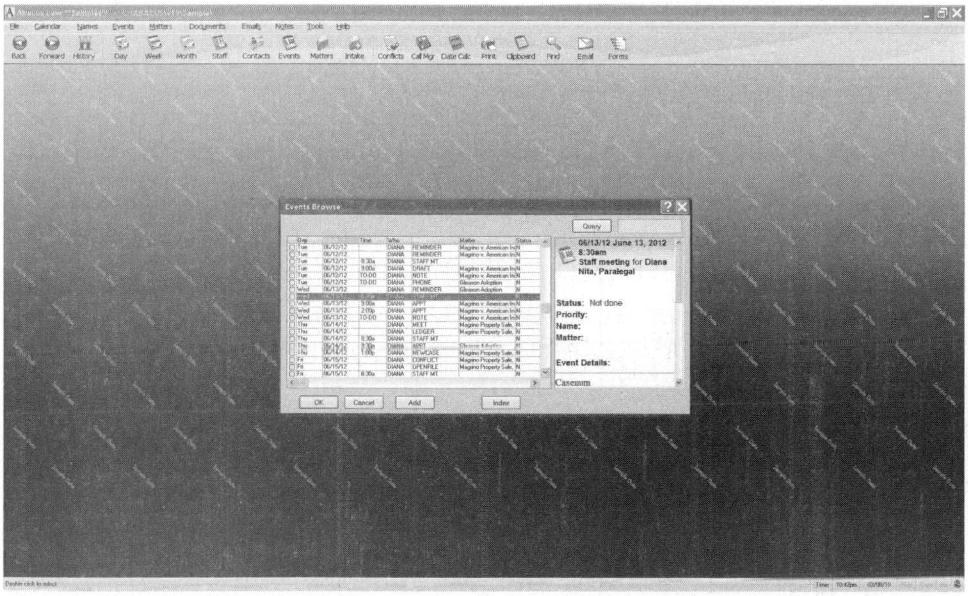

Courtesy Abacus Data Systems

ABACUSLAW EXHIBIT 32
"Events Browse" window

in the "Events Browse" window to select fewer than all events. The "Events Browse" window allows you to manage all events in a quick and easy interface. ***Click the Close (X) icon in the "Events Browse" window.***

22. ***Click File on the menu bar and then click Exit*** (the very last entry on the Recent Files Accessed list).
23. At the **"Please register now!"** window, ***click OK.***

This concludes Lesson 7.

LESSON 8: REPORTS

In this lesson, you will run a number of reports in AbacusLaw. This lesson assumes that you have completed Lessons 1 through 7 and that you are familiar with the AbacusLaw interface.

1. The first thing you will do in this lesson is populate AbacusLaw with sample data. *If you start AbacusLaw from the icon on the desktop, the sample data will not be loaded,* so please follow these directions.

2. Start Windows. ***Click the Start button on the Windows desktop, point the cursor to Programs or All Programs, point to the AbacusLaw group, then click Sample Data.*** This will populate Abacus with some sample data.

3. The "User Log on" window should now be displayed. Note that the AbacusLaw desktop should say **"Sample Data."**

4. In the "User Log on" window, in the User ID field, type the same initials you entered in Lesson 1. It is important that you enter the same initials each time you load Abacus. Do not type anything in the Password field. ***Click OK in the "User Log on" window.***

5. The "Tip of the Day" window should now be displayed on your screen. ***Click OK in the "Tip of the Day" window.*** You should now be at the Abacus desktop with the name plate that reads **"Your name appears here after registration."**

6. AbacusLaw comes with more than 100 standard reports. You will run just a few of them. ***Click File on the menu bar, point to Reports, then click All reports.***

7. ***In the "Report List:" window, click OK.*** The "Report Control" window should now be displayed. This report will run a matters or case list for the whole office. The default setting will print the reports to the screen. If you wanted to change that, you would click Output to and select a printer, but **"Screen"** is fine for this exercise.

8. ***Click Print in the "Report Control" window.*** A listing of all of the clients and names linked to the cases should be displayed (see AbacusLaw Exhibit 33).

9. ***Click the red X (Exit) on the toolbar in the "Report Viewer" window.***

10. The "Report Control" window is again displayed. This time you will run a report just of the cases on which Arthur Simon is the lead attorney.

11. ***In the "Report Control" window, click Query, then click Quick query.*** The "Quick Query for EVENTS" window is displayed.

12. ***Click the up arrow key next to Who and double-click AMS Arthur M. Simon. Click OK in the "Quick Query for EVENTS" window.***

13. ***In the "Report Control" window, click Print.*** If you would like to magnify the print on the screen, ***double-click the title bar.*** Scroll through the document and look at only the matters that Arthur Simon is managing. When you are

ABACUSLAW EXHIBIT 33
Report Viewer

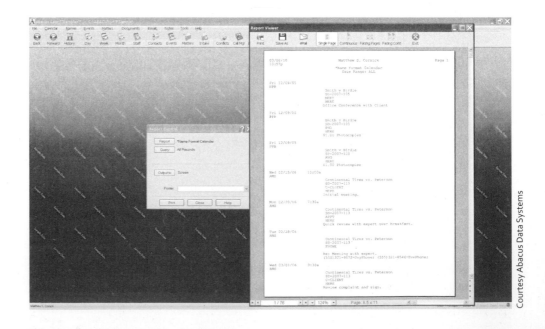

done viewing the report, *click the red X (Exit) on the toolbar in the "Report Viewer" window.*

14. The "Report Control" window should again be displayed. *Click Query and then click Clear current query.*

15. The "Report Control" window should again be displayed. *Click Report and then click Matter Format Calendar.* This will produce a list of calendar events for cases. Because this list could be long, you will just run this report for the *Magrino v. American Insurance* case.

16. *Click OK in the "Report List:" window. In the "Report Control" window, click Query and then click Quick query.* The "Quick Query for EVENTS" window should be displayed.

17. *Click the up arrow key next to Matter and double-click Magrino v. American Insurance. Click OK in the "Quick Query for EVENTS" window.*

18. *In the "Report Control" window, click Print.* If you would like to magnify the print on the screen, *double-click the title bar.* Scroll through the document and look at all of the events for the *Magrino v. American Insurance* case.

19. When you are done viewing the report, *click the red X (Exit) on the toolbar in the "Report Viewer" window.*

20. The "Report Control" window is again displayed. *Click Query and then click Clear current query.*

21. The "Report Control" window should again be displayed. *Click Close in the "Report Control" window.*

22. You will now print a report for a date range. *Click File on the menu bar, point to Reports, then click Events (Calendars).* In the "Events Report Control" window, under All, type **06/11/2012—06/15/2012** and then *click Print.*

23. When you are done viewing the report, *point and click on the red X (Exit) on the toolbar in the "Report Viewer" window.*

24. *Click Close in the "Events Report Control" window.*

25. *Click File in the menu bar and then click Exit* (the very last entry on the Recent Files Accessed list).

26. At the **"Please register now!"** window, *click OK.*

This concludes the AbacusLaw Hands-On Exercises.

CHAPTER 6

Electronic Discovery

There are no Hands-On Exercises for Chapter 6.

CHAPTER 7

Litigation Support Software

FEATURED SOFTWARE	
Discover FY™	241
LexisNexis CaseMap	260
LexisNexis TimeMap	293

DISCOVER FY™

I. INTRODUCTION–READ THIS!

Discover FY™ is an e-discovery/litigation support tool provided and supported by ILS Technologies. The ILS Technologies Discover FY™ demonstration version is a full working version of the program. This program demonstration version will not time out. However, it is still recommended that you do not install the program on your computer until you are actually ready to go through the Hands-On Exercises and learn the program. When you are ready to install the program, follow the instructions in Section III.

II. USING THE DISCOVER FY™ HANDS-ON EXERCISES

The Discover FY™ Hands-On Exercises are easy to use and contain step-by-step instructions. Each lesson builds on the previous exercise, so please complete the Hands-On Exercises in order. Discover FY™ comes with sample data, so you should be able to utilize many features of the program.

III. INSTALLATION INSTRUCTIONS

Following are step-by-step instructions for loading the ILS Technologies Discover FY™ demonstration version on your computer. Note that you will need to load two separate programs (a Microsoft program and Discover FY™).

1. Log onto your CengageBrain.com account.
2. Under **"My Courses and Materials,"** find the Premium website for Using Computers in the Law Office.
3. *Click Open* to go to the Premium Website.
4. Locate **"Book -Level Resources"** in the left navigation bar.
5. *Click the link for Discover FY.*

6. ***Click the link for the Microsoft .NET Framework 4.*** If necessary, ***change the language to English and click Download.***

7. The "File Download—Security Warning" window will open. ***Click Run.*** An "Internet Explorer—Security Warning" window will open. ***Click Run.***

8. The "Microsoft .NET Framework 4 Setup" window will open. ***Click the box to accept the license terms and click Install.***

9. The program will load onto your computer.

10. When the installation is complete, ***click Finish; close the Microsoft Download page and return to the Premium Website and click on the link for Access Discover FY.***

11. The "File Download—Security Warning" window will open. See Discover FY™ Installation Exhibit 1. ***Click Save; then***

    a. Navigate to the folder where you saved the ZIP file.

    b. Double click the file. Your default ZIP program (e.g., WinZip, 7-Zip, or Windows Explorer) should open, displaying the contents of the zip file. Extract the contents of the ZIP file.

    c. Double-click the file DFY_6.3.9_singleuser_demo.exe to begin installation.

12. The Discover FY™ Single User Demo Setup: License Page window will open. See Discover FY™ Installation Exhibit 2. ***Click I Agree.***

**DISCOVER FY™
INSTALLATION
EXHIBIT 1**

Courtesy of Webig Development, LLC in conjunction with ILS Technologies, LLC.

13. The Discover FY™ Single User Demo Setup: Installation Options window will open. See Discover FY™ Installation Exhibit 3. ***Select the DiscoverFY Single User Demo and click Install.***

**DISCOVER FY™
INSTALLATION
EXHIBIT 2**

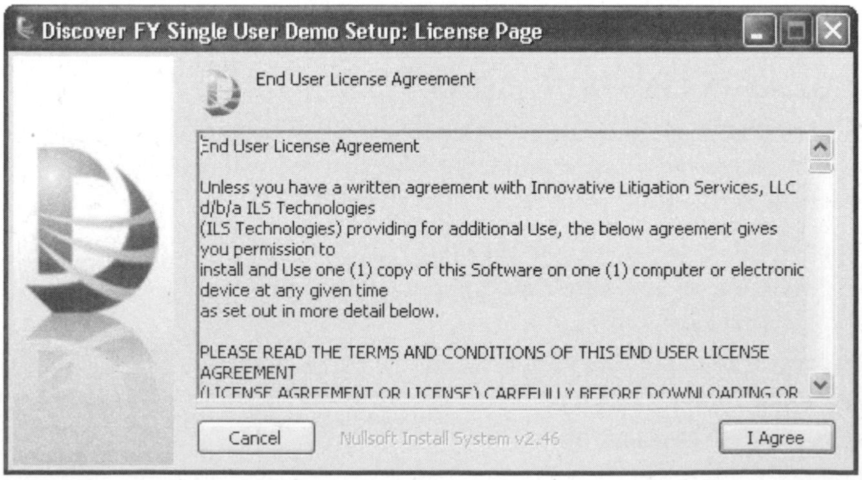

Courtesy of Webig Development, LLC in conjunction with ILS Technologies, LLC.

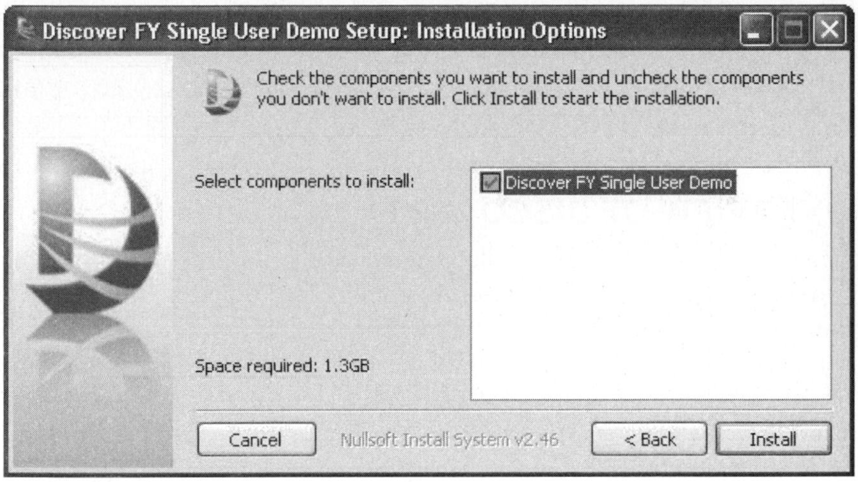

**DISCOVER FY™
INSTALLATION
EXHIBIT 3**

14. When the program has been installed on your computer, ***click Close*** on the Discover FY™ Single User Demo Setup: Completed window.

IV. INSTALLATION TECHNICAL SUPPORT

If you have problems installing the demonstration version of Discover FY™, please contact Delmar Cengage Learning Technical Support first at http://cengage.com/support. If Delmar Cengage Learning Technical Support is unable to resolve your installation question, or if you have a noninstallation-related question, you will need to contact ILS Technologies directly at (855) 300-0632.

GETTING STARTED

Number	Lesson Title	Concepts Covered
BASIC		
Lesson 1	Introduction to Discover FY™	Explanation and introduction to the Discover FY™ interfaces
INTERMEDIATE		
Lesson 2	Searching for Documents in the Datastore	Search for documents; native format; metadata; create folders
ADVANCED		
Lesson 3	Document Images	HTML images, native format images, Image Viewer, creating a TIFF, redacting a TIFF, clearing and saving redactions, print options

Introduction

Throughout these exercises, information you need to enter into the program will be designated in several different ways:

- Keys to be pressed on the keyboard are designated in brackets, in all caps, and in bold (e.g., press the **[ENTER]** key).
- Movements with the mouse pointer are designated in bold and italics (e.g., ***point to File and click***).
- Words or letters that should be typed are designated in bold (e.g., type **Training Program**).

HANDS-ON EXERCISES

- Information that is or should be displayed on your computer screen is shown in bold, with quotation marks (e.g., "**Press ENTER to continue**.").
- Specific menu items and commands are designated with an initial capital letter (e.g., click Open).

OVERVIEW OF DISCOVER FY™

Discover FY™ is a powerful e-discovery and litigation support tool. Discover FY™ is designed for anyone who needs to search, view, examine, or categorize volumes of electronic documents. Beyond these fundamental functions, Discover FY™ allows users to generate customized productions of subsets of documents in universally readable formats for opposing counsel, government agencies, or anyone to whom relevant documents are due. The sample data used in the demonstration program consists of real emails and documents generated by Enron Corporation.

▶ BASIC

LESSON 1: INTRODUCTION TO DISCOVER FY™

This lesson introduces you to the Discover FY™ litigation support program. It explains basic information about the Discover FY™ interface, including information about the Fact, Object, Issue, Question, and Research spreadsheets.

1. Start Windows. Then, ***double-click the Discover FY™ icon on the desktop.*** Discover FY™ will then start.

2. When you start Discover FY™, the "Login" dialog box will open and you will be asked to enter your user ID and password. Type **admin** in the User ID text box and type **password** in the Password text box. (Note: The password will appear as a series of dots. See Discover FY™ Exhibit 1.) ***Click Login.***

**DISCOVER FY™
EXHIBIT 1**

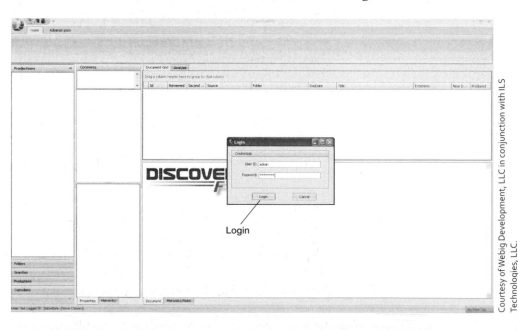

Login

Courtesy of Webig Development, LLC in conjunction with ILS Technologies, LLC.

3. The "Choose Datastore" box will appear. We have not yet created any Datastores, so ***click DISCOVER FY™ DEMO to highlight it and click Select.*** (See Discover FY™ Exhibit 2.)

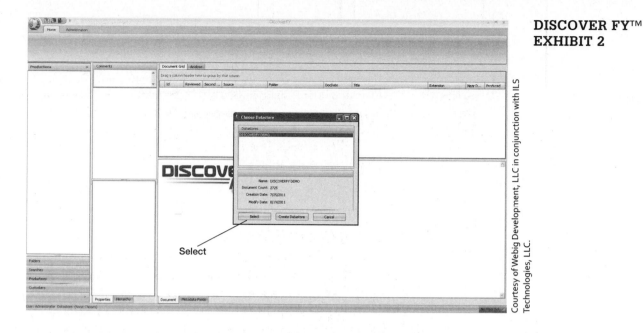

DISCOVER FY™ EXHIBIT 2

Select

4. All of the sections of the Discover FY™ screen are empty because we have not yet selected any data. To access the sample data provided with the application, we need to select a Custodian. *Click Custodians in the lower left part of the screen and then click the only name provided, Chris Germany.* When you do so, the sample data will load. See Discover FY™ Exhibit 3.

Home tab

Chris Germany

Custodians

DISCOVER FY™ EXHIBIT 3

5. We will explore the various sections of the Discover FY™ screen. Running across the top of the screen is the Ribbon Bar. (See Discover FY™ Exhibit 3.) You should be in the Home tab, but if you are not, *click Home.* Within the Home tab, there are option groups: Search, Tagging, View, Reports, and Images.

6. The Search group enables you to search the datastore for specific documents. A number of search methods are available. *Click Search* (its icon looks like a blue square with a magnifying glass on it). The "Define Search" box will open. (See

Discover FY™ Exhibit 4). This enables you to search for documents by entering specific search terms within the full text of the document or by searching the metadata of the documents. You can refine your searches by using filters to search for documents of a specific custodian, documents created within a specific date range, or documents held within a specific folder. We will explore these search options in a later exercise, but now *click Cancel* at the bottom of the "Define Search" box.

**DISCOVER FY™
EXHIBIT 4**

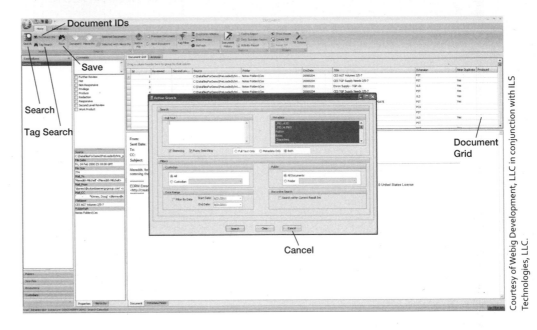

7. ***Click the Document IDs*** to the right of the Search icon. The "Search—Document ID" box opens. This allows you to search for a document by its Document ID (a specific identification number). ***Click Cancel in the "Search-Document ID" box.***

8. ***Click the Tag Search,*** which is found below the Document ID icon. The "Coding Tag Search" box opens. This enables you to search for a document that has been given a specific tag, such as Privilege or Work Product. ***Click Cancel in the "Coding Tag Search" box.***

9. ***Click Save*** (its icon looks like a pair of binocular with a green pointer on it). The "Save Search" box opens. This allows you to name and save the results of a search for later use. ***Click Cancel in the "Save Search" box.***

10. The Tagging option group allows users to apply tags to documents in the Datastore. This facilitates the process of organizing and retrieving documents. You may apply a tag to just the selected document by clicking Selected Documents. If you also wish to tag any attachments or other documents connected to the selected document, you would click Selected With Hierarchy. (Note: The term *hierarchy* refers to the attachments that may accompany an email.) We will explore tagging options in a later exercise.

11. The View group on the Home tab gives you different options for viewing documents. ***Click the third line of the Document Grid pane.*** This document is a spreadsheet, and you can see a representation of that spreadsheet in the Document Display pane. (See Discover FY™ Exhibit 5.) ***Click Native File.*** See Discover FY Exhibit 5. A new window will open and display the spreadsheet as a native file; that is, it will show the spreadsheet within a spreadsheet program. If you have Microsoft Excel on your computer, Discover FY™ will open Excel to display the spreadsheet. (See Discover FY™ Exhibit 6.) This option allows you to see the formulas used in

the spreadsheet and to manipulate the data, if desired. *Close the spreadsheet; if you are asked whether you want to save any changes to the file, click No.*

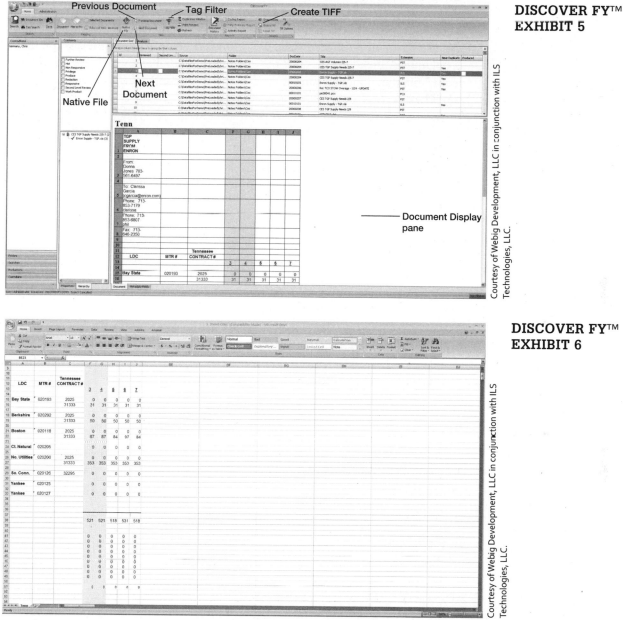

DISCOVER FY™ EXHIBIT 5

Courtesy of Webig Development, LLC in conjunction with ILS Technologies, LLC.

DISCOVER FY™ EXHIBIT 6

Courtesy of Webig Development, LLC in conjunction with ILS Technologies, LLC.

HANDS-ON EXERCISES

12. You can navigate between different documents listed in the Document Grid by clicking on the Next Document and Previous Document icons. The Tag Filter allows you to specify specific types of documents when executing a search. The Duplicate Window allows you to see any documents that are duplicates of the selected document. The Print Preview command permits you to see what a document will look like when printed.

13. The Reports group on the Home tab gives you the ability to generate a variety of reports. The Document History report details activity related to the selected document. The Coding report shows the Document ID, Document Date, Title, and a column for each available flag for every document displayed in the Document Grid. The Daily Summary report summarizes activity during

a specified time interval. The Activity report shows a selected user's coding activity within a specified time range. We will explore these various reports in a later exercise.

14. The final group on the Home tab is the Images group. This option group allows you to create, view, and manipulate TIFF images of documents in the Datastore. A TIFF (Tagged Image File Format) is essentially a photograph of a document. It shows you what the document looks like, but, unlike with the native file function, you cannot modify the document. ***Click the first line of the Document Grid and then Click Create TIFF***. Discover FY™ will now create a TIFF of the selected document. To see the TIFF, click Show Viewer. The TIFF will appear within the Image Viewer. (See Discover FY™ Exhibit 7.)

**DISCOVER FY™
EXHIBIT 7**

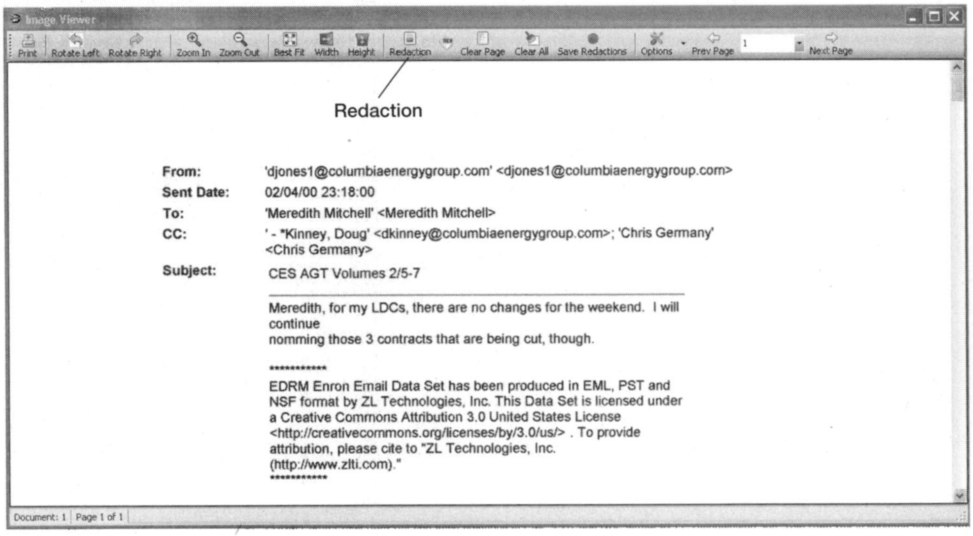

15. Within the Image Viewer, it is possible to redact a TIFF. We will now redact this TIFF.

16. To redact a TIFF, ***click Redaction Tool at the top of the Image Viewer screen. Move your cursor to the message portion of the email. Drag the cursor (+) so that the entire message portion is obscured by a black rectangle and release the cursor.*** Your screen should now look like Discover FY™ Exhibit 8. ***Click***

**DISCOVER FY™
EXHIBIT 8**

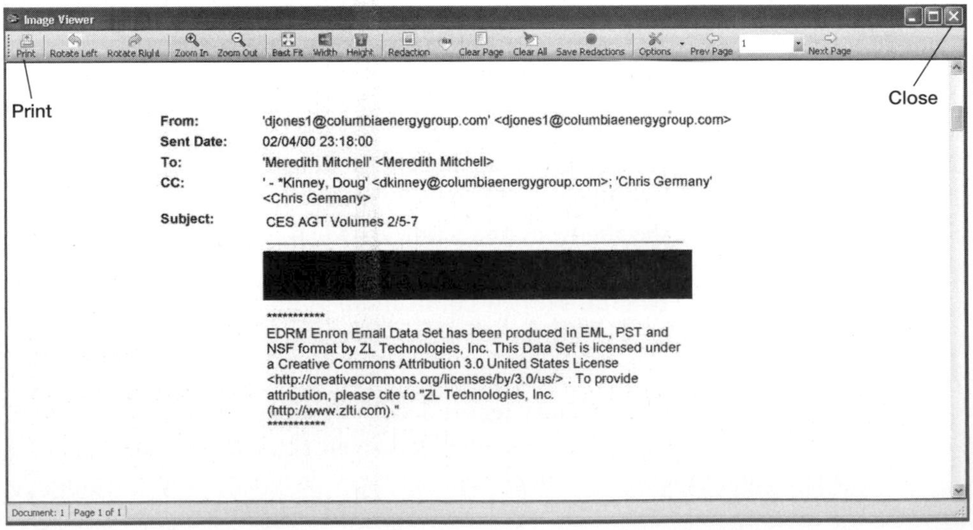

Print in the Image Viewer toolbar to print the redacted TIFF. If instructed to do so, turn the printed TIFF image in to your teacher. ***Click the Close button (the X in the upper right corner of the Image Viewer window) to close the Image Viewer.***

17. We will now explore the options available in the Administrator tab. ***Click Administration.*** There are four option groups in the Administration tab: Admin, Datastore, Processing, and Production. See Discover FY™ Exhibit 9.

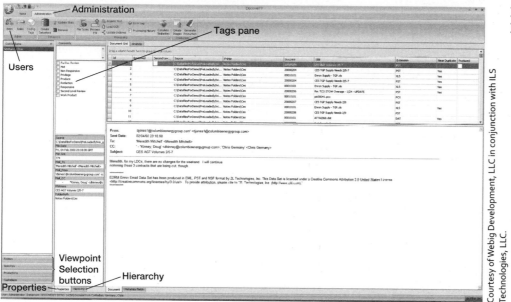

Courtesy of Webig Development, LLC in conjunction with ILS Technologies, LLC.

DISCOVER FY™ EXHIBIT 9

18. The Admin group provides options for managing who has access to which options available in Discover FY™. ***Click Users.*** The "User Maintenance" box will open. This gives the administrator the ability to set users' User IDs, passwords, and assigned roles. ***Click Close in the "User Maintenance" box.***

19. The Coding Tags tool allows you to adjust the definitions of the tags that are used to code (or organize) documents.

20. The Datastore group allows you to create, delete, and update datastores.

21. The Processing group is used to work with files as part of the electronic discovery process. These features are beyond the scope of these Hands-On Exercises, which focus on the litigation support features of Discover FY™.

22. The Production group allows you to generate the documents required for production. We will explore the production utilities in a later exercise.

23. In the window under the Ribbon Bar are a number of panes. The pane on the far left side of the screen shows the current viewpoint. For example, we have been looking at the Custodians view. The Viewpoint Selection buttons at the bottom of that screen show that you have the option of Folders, Searches, Productions, as well as Custodians.

24. To the right of the Viewpoint screen is the Tags pane. By clicking on one or more of the available tags, you can apply those tags to the selected documents. The application of tags to documents makes it easier to organize and retrieve documents.

25. Under the Tags pane, there is a tabbed pane that gives you the option to see the hierarchy or properties of the selected document. For example, ***with the first document selected in the Document Grid, click the Properties tab.*** You can now see the specific properties of the selected email, such as the persons who sent and received the email, and the date, size, and file name of the selected email. ***Click the Hierarchy tab*** and you can see that this email does not have any related attachments.

26. To the right of the Tags pane is the Document Grid pane. This is where the files contained in the selected Datastore are listed. Under the Document Grid pane is the Document Display pane. This is where you can see an HTML representation of the selected document. By clicking the Metadata Fields tab at the bottom of the Document Display pane, you can view the metadata of the selected document.

27. On the far left portion of the screen, you can choose different viewpoints for the Datastore.

This concludes Lesson 1. ***To close Discover FY™, click the Close button (the X in the upper right corner of the screen)*** or you may continue to Lesson 2.

▶ INTERMEDIATE

LESSON 2: SEARCHING FOR DOCUMENTS IN THE DATASTORE

1. If you need to open Discover FY™, follow the instructions in Steps 2–5. If the program is already open and running on your computer, you may begin this exercise with Step 6.

2. Start Windows. Then, ***double-click the Discover FY™ icon on the desktop.*** Discover FY™ will then start.

3. When you start Discover FY™, the "Login" box will open and you will be asked to enter your user ID and password. Type **admin** in the User ID text box and type **password** in the Password text box. (Note: The password will appear as a series of dots. See Discover FY™ Exhibit 1.) Then ***click Login.***

4. The "Choose Datastore" box will appear. We have not yet created any Datastores, so ***click DISCOVER FY™ DEMO to highlight it and click Select.*** See Discover FY™ Exhibit 2.

5. All of the sections of the Discover FY™ screen are empty, because we have not yet selected any data. To access the sample data provided with the application, we need to select a Custodian. ***Click Custodians and then click the only name provided, Chris Germany.*** When you do so, the sample data will load. See Discover FY™ Exhibit 3.

6. Discover FY™ can be used to sort and organize files in preparation for depositions, trial, and other purposes. We will now search for specific documents, create a new folder, and place those documents in that folder.

7. Assume that your firm is about to conduct the deposition of a witness regarding business transactions between Enron and Columbia Energy Systems. Discover FY™ allows you to search for files that name Columbia Energy Systems and then to further search within those documents. To begin a search, with the Home tab selected, ***click Search*** in the upper left corner of the screen. The "Define Search" box will open. (See Discover FY™ Exhibit 10). Type **Columbia** under Full Text. (See Discover FY™ Exhibit 10). Notice that there are a number of boxes and buttons. You can choose to conduct a search with Stemming and

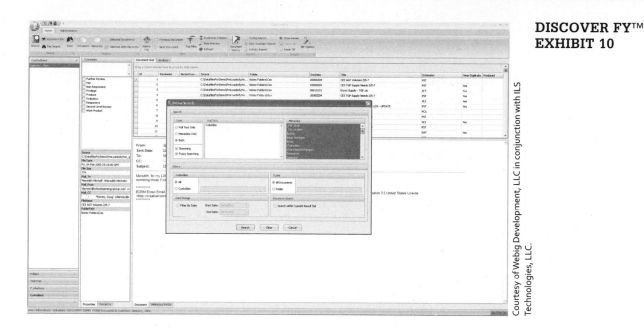

Fuzzy Searching. *Stemming* enables the search engine to look for documents containing terms that use the search term as a stem; for example, using stemming with the search term "contract" can find documents with "contracts," "contracted," "contracting," and so on. *Fuzzy searches* enable the search engine to locate documents with terms that are very similar to the specified search term; it compensates for the fact that some documents may contain a misspelled version of the specified search term. It is generally a good idea to select both of these options.

8. You can limit the scope of the search to the contents of the documents or the metadata of the documents. Selecting the Full Text Only option will limit the search results to documents that actually contain the specified search term(s) within the document. For example, if you selected Full Text Only, your search results would be limited to those documents that contain the word *Columbia* in the text of the document; if there is an email with *Columbia* in the "To" or "From" line, that document would not be included in the search results unless the term *Columbia* also appeared in the body of the document. In contrast, by choosing Metadata Only and then selecting the desired types of metadata (they appear in the box marked "Metadata"; see Discover FY™ Exhibit 10), the search results would be limited to documents that contain the specified search term(s) in the metadata. So, if you were to select Metadata Only, your search results would not include any documents that include the term *Columbia* in the text of the document unless it also appeared in the metadata. To begin, we will not limit our search, so **click Both and then click Search.**

9. Your screen should now look like Discover FY™ Exhibit 11. Notice that the search term (*Columbia*) is highlighted. The Document Grid pane now contains only those documents that satisfied the search query. **Click a few different documents.** As you do, you will notice that the document image appears in the Document Display pane with the search term highlighted. Clicking on the brackets to either side of the search hit allows you to jump from hit to hit within the document. **Click the first document in the Grid, Document ID 19. Click the brackets to the right of the highlighted search term** and you will be taken to the next hit (next appearance of the search term). Now, **click the**

DISCOVER FY™ EXHIBIT 11

Courtesy of Webig Development, LLC in conjunction with ILS Technologies, LLC.

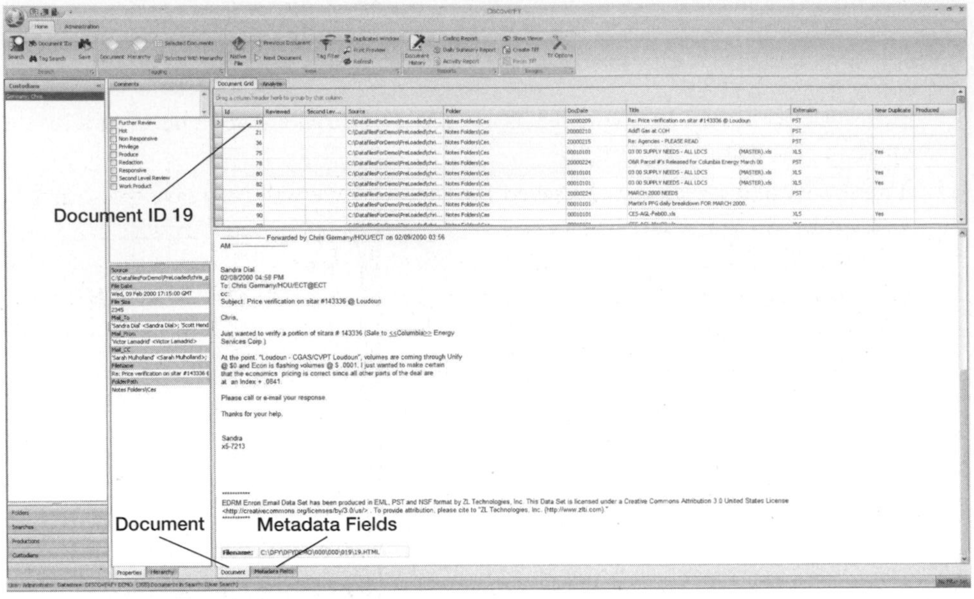

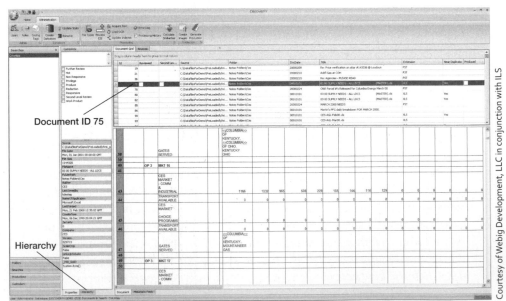

Metadata Fields ***tab at the bottom of the Document Display pane.*** You can now see the metadata associated with this document (Title, Folder, Mail To, Mail From, Mail CC, Mail BCC, and Comments). ***Click the Document tab again.***

10. ***Click the fourth item in the Document Grid, Document ID 75.*** Notice that a spreadsheet now appears in the Document Display pane with the search term *Columbia* highlighted. See Discover FY Exhibit 12. ***Click the Properties tab*** in the pane to the left of the Document Display pane. The Properties pane displays useful information about the document currently displayed in the Document Display pane. Any available metadata for the selected document will be displayed here. Now ***click the Hierarchy tab***. A *Hierarchy* refers to an email item and its attachment(s). The Hierarchy tab identifies the document currently shown in the Document Display pane with a red checkmark. If the document is part of an email hierarchy, all the other attachments and the email

DISCOVER FY™ EXHIBIT 12

Courtesy of Webig Development, LLC in conjunction with ILS Technologies, LLC.

that make up the hierarchy will be displayed and can be examined by clicking on them. To see the email to which this spreadsheet is attached, **click the line that says "CES March Needs-Preliminary (ID 74)".** Notice that now the email appears in the Document Display pane and that the red checkmark now appears next to this document.

11. The results of a search may be saved for later use. We will now save this search. **Click Save in the Search group** (it looks like a pair of binoculars with a green pointer). (See Discover FY™ Exhibit 13). The "Save Search" box will open. Type **Columbia** next to Search Name and **click Save in the "Save Search" box.** See Discover FY™ Exhibit 13. **Click the Searches button** at the lower left corner of the screen. You should now see your saved search, **"Columbia."**

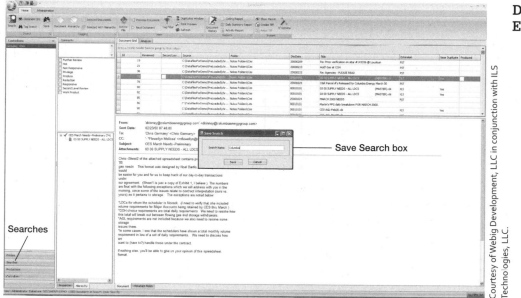

**DISCOVER FY™
EXHIBIT 13**

12. Another way to search for documents is to use the Analyze Tab pane next to the Document Grid pane. **Click the Analyze Tab.** Your screen should now look like Discover FY™ Exhibit 14. When documents are processed into Discover FY™, keywords for each document are identified. The Analyze tab gives you a quick and easy way to find documents based upon the keywords they contain. A review of the keywords list allows you to identify words or concepts contained within the document set that are of interest or importance to the review. Once keywords of interest are identified, documents containing these words can be quickly located and examined. There are a number of options within the Analyze Tab pane. Populate brings keywords into the tab for analysis. The Populate All option adds all keywords from all Custodians. The Populate from Grid option only adds keywords from documents currently displayed in the Document Grid. After keywords are added, you can click to select any combination of Custodian(s), Keyword(s), or Content Type(s) that are of interest. The Apply option applies your selections and produces a set of documents that meet the keyword criteria. The Clear Selections option allows you to clear any selected items and start over. The Clear Grid option clears the Document Grid of any documents, so that you can Add to Grid to see the documents you've selected. The Add to Grid option adds the documents from the Keyword selections to the Grid.

13. We will now conduct a search similar to the one we did in Step 8, except that this time we will limit our search to only Word documents. To begin, *click Clear Grid.* (See Discover FY™ Exhibit 14.) This will remove all of the documents now in the Document Grid. Once we have concluded the search, we will add the documents found in this search to the Document Grid. *Click Populate All.* (See Discover FY™ Exhibit 14.) The "Custodians," "Keywords," and "Content Type" boxes now show the available search terms. Chris Germany is the only available Custodian, so we will not change the Custodian. The "Keywords" box contains all of the keywords from all of the documents in the Datastore. *Scroll down and look at the available keywords.* This gives you a good idea of the specific terms used in the documents. *Scroll down until you come to "Columbia," and then click Columbia to highlight it.* Then, in the "Content Type" box, *click Doc to highlight it. Click Apply, then click Add to Grid.* A document will appear in the Document Display pane. *Click Document Grid.* Your screen should look like Discover FY™ Exhibit 15.

DISCOVER FY™ EXHIBIT 14

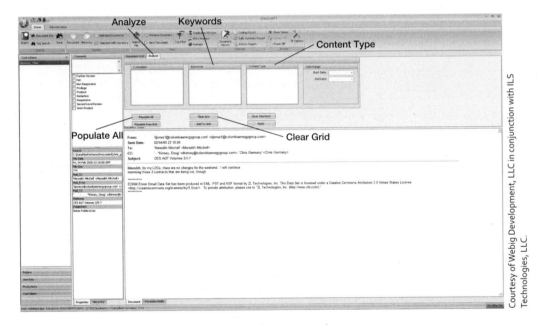

Courtesy of Webig Development, LLC in conjunction with ILS Technologies, LLC.

14. Notice that there are six items listed in the Document Grid. The first document in the Document Display Grid is ID 337 and is a press release titled "Columbia Energy Group To Sell Retail Energy Marketing Operations, Will Maintain Equity Interest". Now, *click the fourth item in the Document Grid, ID 1148.* It appears to be the same document. Now *click the Hierarchy tab* (see Discover FY™ Exhibit 15). The red checkmark next to Press Release indicates that this is the document currently displayed in the Document Display pane. *Click the document above, titled* "Sale of Columbia Energy Services' Mass Markets." The Document Display pane now shows an email dated 07/05/00 from Chris Germany. *Click the first item on the Document Grid, ID 337, and then, in the "Hierarchy" pane, click the document titled* "Sale of Columbia Energy Services' Mass Markets." Notice that the Document Display pane now shows an email dated 07/03/00 from jporte1@columbiaenergygroup.com. Both ID 337 and 1148 (which are two different emails) were included in the search results because both contain as attachments a Word document with the specified search term within it.

15. We will now tag the documents produced by our search. *Tagging* simply refers to the process of attaching (or "tagging") a word or phrase to a document or

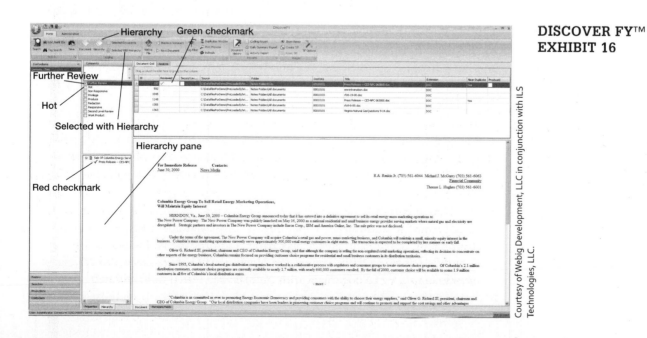

DISCOVER FY™
EXHIBIT 15

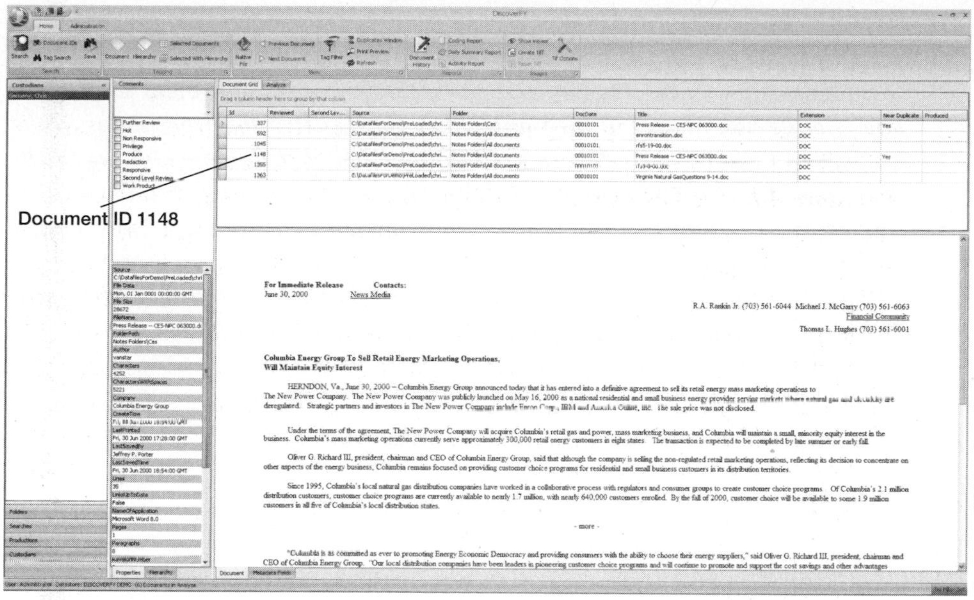

Document ID 1148

set of documents. Among other purposes, tagging facilitates later searches and provides a degree of organization to otherwise unorganized data. Documents may be tagged individually or as a group. We will first apply a tag to a single document. Assume that the first document in the Document Grid requires further review and we want to tag it accordingly. If you click Document in the Tagging group options, that will save the tag selection only to the document that is currently displayed on screen. If you click Hierarchy in the Tagging options, that will save the tag selection with the document displayed on the screen, and also all other elements of an email hierarchy to which the document may belong. We want to save the tag selection to all elements of the email hierarchy, so ***with the first item (ID 337) selected in the Document Grid, click the Further Review tag in the Tag pane, and then click the Hierarchy icon.*** Notice that a green checkmark now appears under Reviewed for that item. (See Discover FY™ Exhibit 16.)

DISCOVER FY™
EXHIBIT 16

Hierarchy   Green checkmark

Further Review

Hot

Selected with Hierarchy

Hierarchy pane

Red checkmark

16. Now assume that the remaining documents in the Document Grid are deemed to be especially important, so we want to tag them as "Hot". To tag multiple documents simultaneously, first *click the second item in Document Grid. Then, while holding down the Control key (Ctrl), click the other items in the Document Grid (IDs 1045, 1148, 1355, and 1363). Click the Hot tag in the Tag pane, then click Selected With Hierarchy in the Tagging options.* (See Discover FY™ Exhibit 16.) All of the documents in the Document Grid should now have a checkmark in the Reviewed column.

This concludes Lesson 2. To close Discover FY™, *click Close (the X in the upper right corner of the window)* or you may continue on to Lesson 3.

⏵ ADVANCED

LESSON 3: DOCUMENT IMAGES

Discover FY™ allows three views of a document: the Document Display pane, Native View, and TIFF Viewer. The Document Display pane is an HTML representation of the document. This is the document view used most often. The text extracted from the document is displayed here and whenever possible text formatting is preserved. Native View brings up the native application used to create the document if it is installed on the local machine. Note that the native application must be installed on a computer as the default application for the specified file type in order for Native View to open. The TIFF Viewer displays TIFF images of the documents. Use the TIFF Viewer if you need to redact a document. Discover FY™ does not create TIFFs of documents up front.

You will now have the opportunity create a TIFF that you can view in the TIFF Viewer or redact.

1. If you need to open Discover FY™, follow the instructions in Steps 2–5. If the program is already open and running on your computer, you may begin this exercise with Step 6.

2. Start Windows. Then, *double-click the Discover FY™ icon on the desktop.* Discover FY™ will then start.

3. When you start Discover FY™, the "Login" box will open and you will be asked to enter your user ID and password. Type **admin** in the User ID text box and type **password** in the Password text box. (Note: The password will appear as a series of dots. See Discover FY™ Exhibit 1.) Then *click Login.*

4. The "Choose Datastore" box will appear. We have not yet created any Datastores, so *click DISCOVER FY™ DEMO to highlight it and click Select.* See Discover FY™ Exhibit 2.

5. All of the sections of the Discover FY™ screen are empty, because we have not yet selected any data. To access the sample data provided with the application, we need to select a Custodian. *Click Custodians and then click the only name provided, Chris Germany.* When you do so, the sample data will load. See Discover FY™ Exhibit 3.

6. The Document Display pane is an HTML representation of the contents of each document. You can search within the displayed document by clicking anywhere in the Document Display pane, and pressing [**CTRL-F**] to open a Find box. *Click the fifth item on the Document Display Grid (ID No. 5) – Enron Supply - TGP.xls, then press* [**CTRL-F**]. The "Find" box will open. Type **Yankee** in the text box. Notice that as you type the search term, possible

matches ("hits") are highlighted. ***Click Next to see the next hit. Click the Close button to close the Find box.***

7. To view a document in its native application, users can press **CTRL-N** with that document highlighted in the Document Display Pane or click on the Native File icon on the Ribbon bar. We have already used the Native File icon, so with Document ID 5 still in the Document Display pane, ***press* [CTRL-N].** The document will open in a separate window as a Microsoft Excel spreadsheet. ***Click the spreadsheet's Close button. Click No*** if any windows open asking if you want to save any changes to the document.

8. The Show Viewer in the Images option group displays the TIFF of any document in a new window. This Image Viewer will remain open until you click Show Viewer again to toggle it off. You can resize and reposition the window as needed. If the "Image Viewer" window is blank when a document is selected in the Grid, that means the document does not yet have a TIFF image. With Document ID 5 still in the Document Display pane, ***click Show Viewer.*** The "Image Viewer" window will open, but it will be blank. ***Click Show Viewer again to close the viewer. Click Create Tiff in the Images option group and then click Show Viewer.*** Your screen should now look like Discover FY™ Exhibit 17. Note that the document is rather large so it may take a few seconds to load.

9. The content of Document ID 5 is larger than the Image Viewer can display. To see additional content, ***click Next Page*** to see page 2 of the TIFF. ***Click Prev Page*** to return to the first page of the TIFF. (See Discover FY™ Exhibit 17.) There are various page display control options. ***Click Best Fit*** (see Discover FY™ Exhibit 17). This shows the entire page of the document sized to fit the width and height of the current "Image Viewer" window. (Note: The image may already be properly sized, so you may not notice any change.) ***Click Width.*** This shows the document sized to fit the width of the current "Image Viewer" window. ***Click Height.*** This shows the document sized to fit the height of the current "Image Viewer" window.

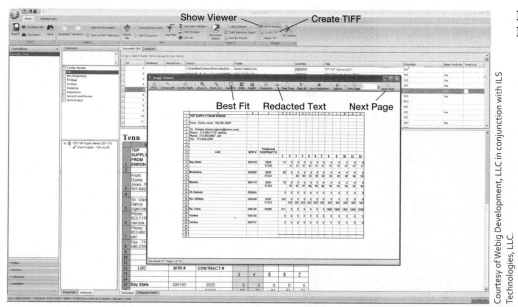

DISCOVER FY™ EXHIBIT 17

HANDS-ON EXERCISES

10. It is possible to zoom in and zoom out as necessary to better view a document. **In the *Images group click the Zoom In icon twice*** to magnify the image. (See Discover FY™ Exhibit 17.) ***Click Zoom Out twice*** to return the document image to its original size.

11. It is possible for to make redactions in an image in the Image Viewer. Several selections are available for creating and managing redactions. ***Click Redaction*** (see Discover FY™ Exhibit 17). Your cursor should now look like a plus sign: (+). Use the cursor to cover the information on line 3. This allows you to draw a plain black box on the document page. If necessary, you can left-click the black box to move and resize the box as needed.

12. ***Click Clear Page and if you are asked if you are sure you want to remove all redactions from this page, click Yes.*** This clears all redactions from the current page. If there were other redactions on other pages of the document, you could use the Clear All option to clear all of the redactions from the entire document.

13. Another option is to place a black box bearing the default text "Redacted" on the redacted material. ***Click Redacted Text*** (it looks like a diamond with some text on it, just to the right of Redaction). (See Discover FY™ Exhibit 17.) The Input dialog box will open. We will use the default text (REDACTED), so ***click OK.*** Your cursor should now look like a plus sign: "+". ***Use the cursor to cover the information on lines 5 through 8.*** (See Discover FY™ Exhibit 18.) The redaction text box can be moved, sized, or deleted in the same fashion as the regular redaction boxes.

DISCOVER FY™ EXHIBIT 18

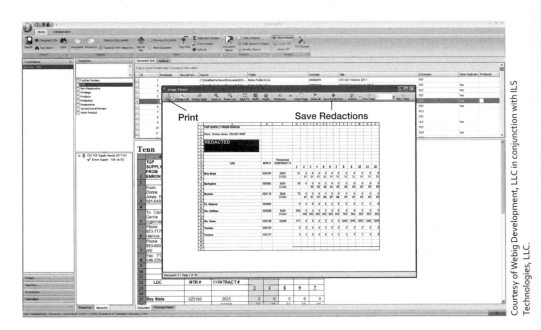

14. You can print a copy of a TIFF. ***Click Print in the Image Viewer toolbar.*** (See Discover FY™ Exhibit 18.) The "Print" window will open. This spreadsheet is a large document, so *be sure to print only the first page.* ***Select the desired printer and click Print.***

15. ***Click Save Redactions.*** This saves the redactions with the document. You will be prompted to save redactions if you move to another document without first clicking on Save.

This concludes the Discover FY™ Hands-On Exercises. To exit Discover FY™, ***click the Close button*** in the upper right corner of the screen.

HANDS-ON EXERCISES

▶ LEXISNEXIS CASEMAP

I. INTRODUCTION–READ THIS

LexisNexis CaseMap is a litigation support analytical tool. CaseMap lets you manage, organize, and connect case facts, legal issues and key players through in-depth research integration. The LexisNexis CaseMap demonstration version is a full working version of the program (with a few limitations). The program demonstration version times out 120 days after installation. This means that the program will only work for 120 days once you install it. So, it is highly recommended that you do not install the program on your computer until you are actually ready to go through the Hands-On Exercises and learn the program. When you are ready to install the program, follow the instructions below.

II. USING THE LEXISNEXIS CASEMAP HANDS-ON EXERCISES

The LexisNexis CaseMap Hands-On Exercises are easy to use and contain step-by-step instructions. Each lesson builds on the previous exercise so please complete the Hands-On Exercises in order. CaseMap comes with sample data so you should be able to utilize many features of the program.

III. INSTALLATION INSTRUCTIONS

Below are step-by-step instructions for loading the LexisNexis CaseMap demonstration version on your computer.

1. Log in to your CengageBrain.com account.
2. Under "My Courses & Materials," find the Premium Website for Using Computers in the Law Office.
3. ***Click "Open" to go to the Premium Website.***
4. Locate "Book Resources" in the left navigation menu.
5. ***Click on the link for "CaseMap 8."***
6. You may get a File Download – Security Warning. **Click "Run."** See CaseMap Installation Exhibit 1. The file will begin to download.

CASEMAP INSTALLATION EXHIBIT 1

7. You may get an Internet Explorer – Security Warning. **Click "Run."** See CaseMap Installation Exhibit 2.

CASEMAP INSTALLATION EXHIBIT 2

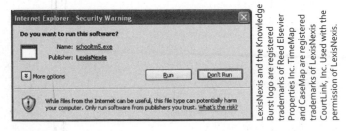

8. Your screen will look like CaseMap Installation Exhibit 3. **Click "Next."**

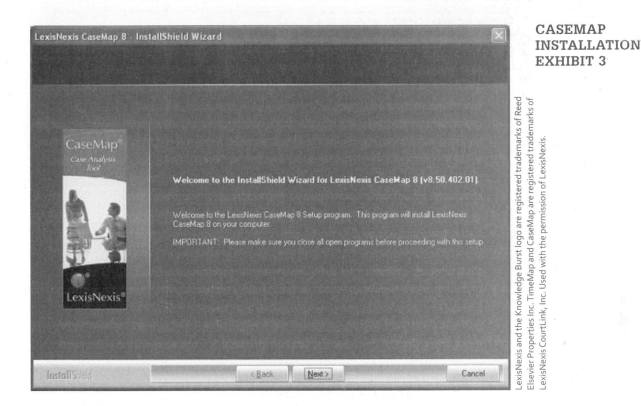

**CASEMAP
INSTALLATION
EXHIBIT 3**

9. Your screen will look like CaseMap Installation Exhibit 4. **Click "Yes"** to agree to the License Agreement.

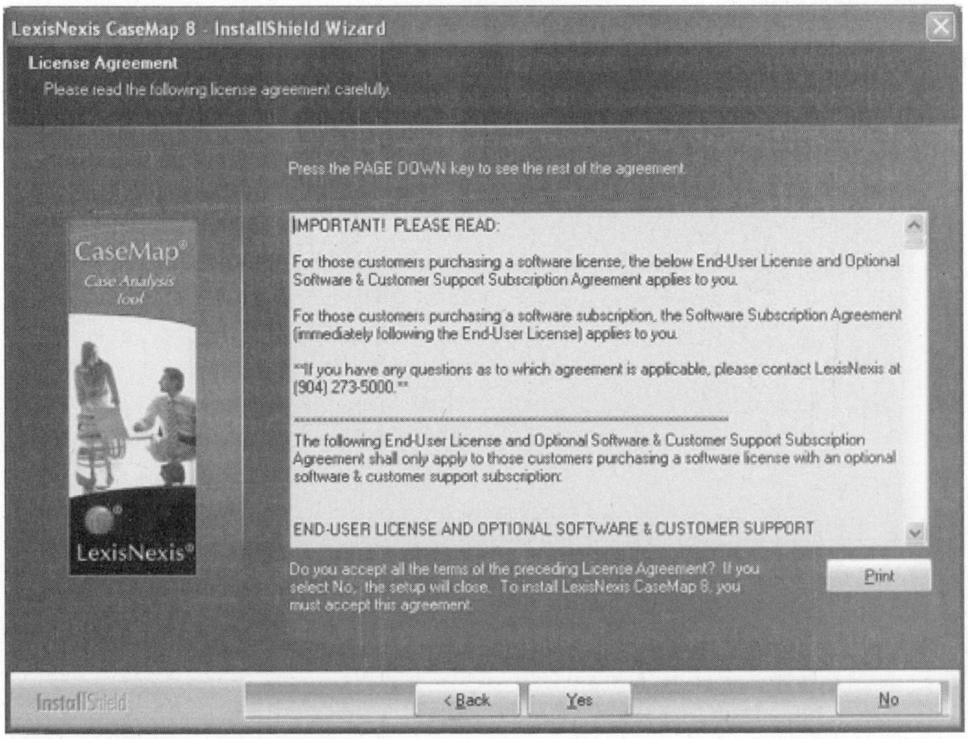

**CASEMAP
INSTALLATION
EXHIBIT 4**

HANDS-ON EXERCISES

10. Your screen will look like CaseMap Installation Exhibit 5. **Click "Next."**

**CASEMAP
INSTALLATION
EXHIBIT 5**

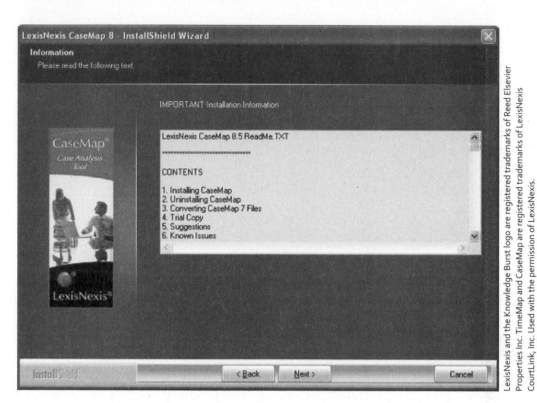

11. Your screen will look like CaseMap Installation Exhibit 6. If you wish to change the default installation location, click on Browse to navigate to the desired location. Otherwise, **click "Next"** to install CaseMap to the default directory.

**CASEMAP
INSTALLATION
EXHIBIT 6**

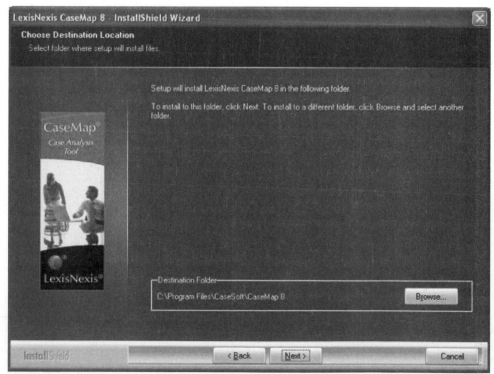

12. Your screen will look like CaseMap Installation Exhibit 7. **Click "Next."**

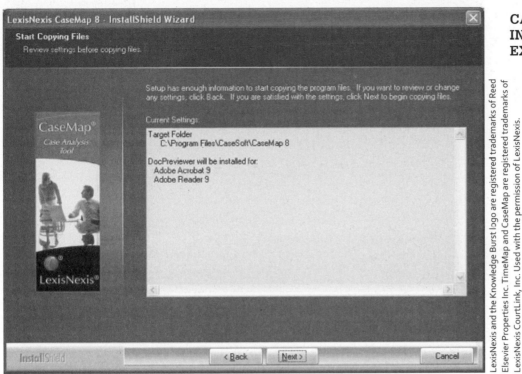

CASEMAP INSTALLATION EXHIBIT 7

13. When the program is through copying files, the screen will look like CaseMap Installation Exhibit 8. **Click "Finish"** to finish installation and launch the program.

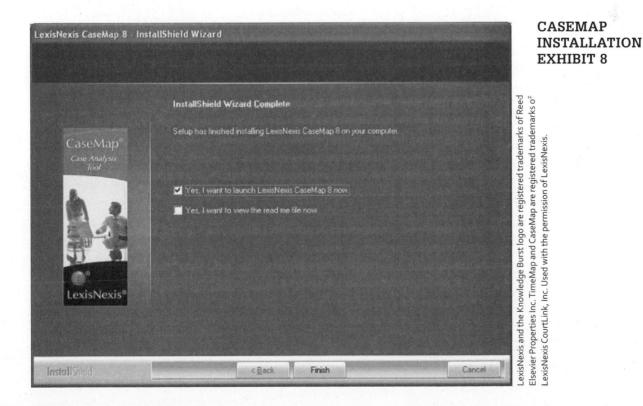

CASEMAP INSTALLATION EXHIBIT 8

HANDS-ON EXERCISES

14. Your screen will look like CaseMap Installation Exhibit 9. **Click "Continue."**

CASEMAP
INSTALLATION
EXHIBIT 9

15. Your screen will look like CaseMap Installation Exhibit 10.

CASEMAP
INSTALLATION
EXHIBIT 10

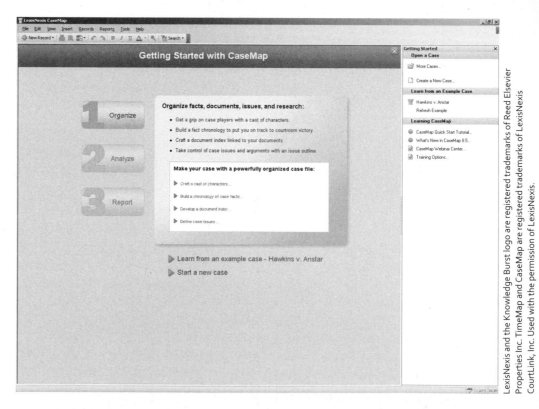

IV. INSTALLATION TECHNICAL SUPPORT

If you have problems installing the demonstration version of LexisNexis CaseMap, you will need to contact LexisNexis CaseMap directly at (904) 273-5000.

Number	Lesson Title	Concepts Covered
BASIC LESSONS		
Lesson 1	Introduction to CaseMap	Explanation and introduction to the CaseMap interface, including the Fact, Object, Issue, Question, and Research spreadsheets.
Lesson 2	Working with the Facts Spreadsheet	Introduction to entering information, fuzzy dating, date stamping, data format options, auto-sizing cell widths, correcting spelling errors, linking files, short names, sorting, linking issues (Link Assistant), Filter by Selection, Filter Tagging, and evaluating facts.
INTERMEDIATE LESSONS		
Lesson 3	Working with the Objects Spreadsheet	Entering objects, executing primary and secondary sorts, expanding and contracting column widths, the meaning of columns in the Objects spreadsheet, the different views in the Objects spreadsheet, and using the Objects spreadsheet in litigation.
Lesson 4	Working with the Issues Spreadsheet	Entering issues, promoting issues, demoting issues, and deleting issues.
Lesson 5	Working with Advanced Features	Using the Viewing CaseWide command, hiding columns, inserting columns, adjusting rows, moving columns, printing and viewing reports, adding objects on the fly, hiding shortcuts, and viewing the detail of a record.
ADVANCED LESSONS		
Lesson 6	Creating a New Case	Setting up/creating a new case in CaseMap and entering new objects, including people, organizations, and documents.
Lesson 7	Entering Issues and Facts in a New Case	Entering new issues in a case, entering new facts in a case, and copying data automatically from one cell to another.
Lesson 8	Using CaseMap for a New Case	Using CaseMap for a new case, including printing reports, viewing case data in a variety of ways, exporting to a PDF file, exporting a summary judgment report to a word processor, using the CaseWide tool, and searching/filtering data.

HANDS-ON EXERCISES

GETTING STARTED

Introduction

Throughout these lessons and exercises, information you need to type into the software will be designated in several different ways:

- Keys to be pressed on the keyboard are designated in brackets, in all caps, and in bold (e.g., press the **[ENTER]** key).
- Movements with the mouse pointer are designated in bold and italics (e.g., ***point to File on the menu bar and click***).
- Words or letters that should be typed are designated in bold (e.g., type **Training Program**).
- Information that is or should be displayed on your computer screen is shown in bold, with quotation marks (e.g., **"Press ENTER to continue."**).
- Specific menu items and commands are designated with an initial capital letter (e.g., ***click Open***).

OVERVIEW OF CASEMAP

CaseMap is a powerful knowledge management and litigation support tool. CaseMap helps legal professionals organize and understand facts, issues, people, documents, and other information about a case. Using CaseMap, a legal professional can prepare detailed chronologies of the facts and events in a case, a cast of characters (people) in a case, a list of important factual and legal issues in a case, a list of documents in a case, and much more. In addition, CaseMap can link all of this information together. The program is very flexible, and allows you to change views and change how information is sorted "on the fly." CaseMap also allows the legal professional to evaluate the strength of a case, to track what data/information in the case is agreed on by the parties or is disputed (and by whom), and allows the images or text of documents to be attached or linked to information stored in CaseMap.

CaseMap fills a unique niche in the litigation support market. It is not designed to be a full litigation support tool (like Summation iBlaze, which can handle millions of document abstracts, transcripts, full-text documents, etc.). Rather, it is designed to be a strategy/knowledge management tool that helps legal professionals think, prepare, and strategize about their cases. It is somewhat similar to (though still different from) the Case Organizer, People database, and Event database in Summation iBlaze. CaseMap is a database program, but looks more like a spreadsheet because it stores data in columns and rows.

The purpose of these exercises is to give you a general introduction to CaseMap and how it is used in litigation. CaseMap, like Summation iBlaze, is a very popular litigation support program that is used extensively in all types of legal organizations throughout the country. A fully functioning demonstration version of CaseMap is used. The demonstration version of CaseMap includes a sample case, *Hawkins v. Anstar*. This hypothetical case is ready for trial and most of the information about the case has already been entered into CaseMap. In addition, this tutorial includes exercises in which you will create a new file in CaseMap for the sample case of *Richards v. EZ Pest Control*.

The *Philip Hawkins v. Anstar Biotech Industries* Case

An overview of the facts of the *Philip Hawkins v. Anstar Biotech Industries* case follows. Philip Hawkins (the plaintiff) was hired to be a sales manager by William Lang, the CEO of Anstar Biotech Industries (the defendant), in early 2003. In late 2003, Hawkins was promoted to vice president of sales. In May 2005, Hawkins received an outstanding performance review from Lang. In June 2005, Lang made the decision to lay off some of the company's staff. In early July 2005, Anstar's second-quarter sales were announced: Sales had dropped by 8 percent. In late July, Hawkins was demoted to the position of sales manager. Hawkins alleges that in August 2005, Lang told him that "old wood must be trimmed back hard." Hawkins claims that this was a reference to him being over the age of 40, and implied that he was "old wood" that must be "trimmed." Hawkins was transferred to another office a few weeks later. In September, Hawkins wrote Lang and complained about the way he was being treated and that the purpose of the layoffs was to eliminate older staff. In November, Anstar laid off 55 employees, including Hawkins, who turned 51 years old that month. Ten days later, Hawkins sued Anstar for age discrimination, wrongful termination, and retaliation. Anstar claims that the layoffs were due to poor sales and were completely lawful. You are acting on behalf of the law firm representing the defendant, Anstar Biotech Industries.

The *Sherry Richards v. EZ Pest Control* Case

Here are the facts of the *Richards v. EZ Pest Control* case: Sherry Richards had a contract with EZ Pest Control to conduct periodic reviews of her house several times a year and to provide preventative pest control maintenance to keep termites out.

John Lincoln of EZ Pest Control came out several times and inspected the house. Nonetheless, Sherry Richards discovered several colonies of termites in her house, and found that massive damage was being done. She called a contractor, Tim Stewart, to look at the house, and he determined that there was damage to the house and that repairs would have to be done as soon as the termites were removed. Sherry Richards is suing EZ Pest Control for breach of contract and negligence. You are acting on behalf of the law firm representing the plaintiff, Sherry Richards.

▶ BASIC LESSONS

LESSON 1: INTRODUCTION TO CASEMAP

This lesson introduces you to the CaseMap litigation support program. It explains basic information about the CaseMap interface, including information about the Fact, Object, Issue, Question, and Research spreadsheets.

Install the CaseMap demonstration version on your computer following the instructions in section I, "Introduction—Read This!," and section III, "Installation Instructions." *Note*: The CaseMap demonstration version times out (stops working) **120 days after installation.** It is highly recommended that you do not install the program on your computer until you are ready to complete these Hands-On Exercises.

1. Start Windows. After it has loaded, ***double-click the LexisNexis CaseMap 8 icon on the desktop,*** or ***click the Start button on the Windows desktop, point to Programs or All Programs, point to the LexisNexis CaseMap Suite, then click LexisNexis CaseMap 8.*** LexisNexis CaseMap 8 will then start.

2. When you start CaseMap, you will see a small window in the middle of the screen that says **"CaseMap"** and adds some information about a grace period. ***Click Continue in the "CaseMap" window.*** CaseMap will then start, with several options listed to the right of the screen.

3. Your screen should now look similar to CaseMap Exhibit 1. The Getting Started task pane should be displayed on the right side of the screen. ***Under Learn from an Example Case, click*** **Hawkins v. Anstar.**

CASEMAP EXHIBIT 1

Hawkins v. Anstar

4. The "Case Log On" window should now be displayed. ***Click the down arrow icon to the right of Staff Member: Chris Attorney.*** A dropdown list should now be displayed with the name of several staff members. This is actually a very useful function in CaseMap. Using a network, many staff members can access a CaseMap case/database. In addition, because each staff member must log in with his or her own name, CaseMap can track the new information that has been entered since each staff member logged in. Using a feature called What's New, a staff member can get a summary of what new information has been entered into CaseMap since she or he last logged in.

5. ***Click Dave Paralegal, then click OK.***

6. The CaseMap Fact spreadsheet for the *Hawkins* case should now be displayed (see CaseMap Exhibit 2). CaseMap uses a series of spreadsheets to organize a case. The primary (Favorite) spreadsheets are Facts, All Objects, Persons, Documents, and Issues. CaseMap refers to these screens as spreadsheets because it uses an interface that has rows and columns, and thus looks like a spreadsheet.

7. Each of the five Favorite spreadsheets tracks different data about a case. The Fact spreadsheet allows you to build a chronology of case facts. The Fact spreadsheet contains separate facts about the *Hawkins v. Anstar Biotech Industries* case.

8. ***Click the All Objects icon to the left of the screen under the Case Shortcuts > Favorites heading.*** Your screen should now look like CaseMap Exhibit 3.

9. The Objects spreadsheet tracks a number of items, including people (this allows you to create a cast of characters in a case), documents (this allows you to create a document abstract database and document index), organizations (to track the different organizations/parties in a case), and pleadings (to track pleadings in a case), as well as other information (see CaseMap Exhibit 3). You can also attach document images to any information or record in the Objects spreadsheet. In the Objects spreadsheet, you can see all of the objects (notice in CaseMap Exhibit 3 that you can see Person, Organization, and Document), or you can select another view and see just one specific type of object, such as all Persons or all Documents.

CASEMAP EXHIBIT 2

CASEMAP EXHIBIT 3

Issues

10. *Click the Issues icon to the left of the screen under the Case Shortcuts > Favorites heading.* Your screen should now look like CaseMap Exhibit 4.

CASEMAP EXHIBIT 4

Documents   **New Record**   **Outline**

11. The Issues spreadsheet tracks all of the different issues in a case (see CaseMap Exhibit 4). This usually includes all of the causes of action in a lawsuit, and may also include the specific elements of each cause of action. Notice in CaseMap Exhibit 4 that there are five main issues/causes of action or controversies in the case, including wrongful termination, age discrimination, retaliation, whether the plaintiff deserved to be terminated, and damages.

HANDS-ON EXERCISES

12. *Click the Documents icon to the left of the screen under the Case Shortcuts > Favorites heading.* Your screen should now look like CaseMap Exhibit 5.

CASEMAP EXHIBIT 5

13. Notice that the heading in CaseMap Exhibit 5 says **"Objects – Documents."** These are the same documents listed previously in the All Objects spreadsheet, but in this screen the information is more complete and other objects (such as people and organizations) are not shown.

14. *Click the Persons icon to the left of the screen under the Case Shortcuts > Favorites heading.* Your screen should now look like CaseMap Exhibit 6.

15. The Persons spreadsheet tracks all of the different persons in a case (see CaseMap Exhibit 6). Notice that this spreadsheet includes headings for each person's full names, short names, the person's role in the case, and the type of person (fact witness, expert witness, etc.). It also links the persons to relevant facts and documents.

16. There are two other spreadsheets in CaseMap that are not listed in the Case Shortcuts Favorites.

CASEMAP EXHIBIT 6

17. *Click All Shortcuts in the lower part of the Case Shortcuts task pane.*

18. A full list of shortcuts appears, including all of the Favorites described earlier as well as two more, Questions and Research.

19. *Click Questions.* The Questions spreadsheet should now be displayed (see CaseMap Exhibit 7).

CASEMAP EXHIBIT 7

LexisNexis and the Knowledge Burst logo are registered trademarks of Reed Elsevier Properties Inc. TimeMap and CaseMap are registered trademarks of LexisNexis CourtLink, Inc. Used with the permission of LexisNexis.

20. The Questions spreadsheet allows you to enter questions that you need to answer, gives you the opportunity to assign the responsibility for finding the answer to the question, allows you to assign a due date for completion of that task, allows you to assign the degree of criticality (importance), and provides a place to put the answer to the question (see CaseMap Exhibit 7). The Questions spreadsheet is somewhat similar to a things-to-do list, and helps to make sure that you discover everything you need to know about a case.

21. Notice that the Research icon has three subelements: Authorities, Extracts from Authorities, and Authorities and Extracts. *Click Authorities.* The Research – Authorities spreadsheet should now be displayed (see CaseMap Exhibit 8).

CASEMAP EXHIBIT 8

LexisNexis and the Knowledge Burst logo are registered trademarks of Reed Elsevier Properties Inc. TimeMap and CaseMap are registered trademarks of LexisNexis CourtLink, Inc. Used with the permission of LexisNexis.

HANDS-ON EXERCISES

22. The Research – Authorities spreadsheet allows you to track legal citations and legal references relevant to your case. CaseMap Exhibit 8 shows the Research – Authorities spreadsheet, which lists the major statutes and cases involved in the *Hawkins* case.

23. **Click Extracts from Authorities.**

24. **Click in the second column of the first row.** Your screen should now look similar to CaseMap Exhibit 9.

CASEMAP EXHIBIT 9

25. Notice that this is a long quote from Section 102, Part A of the Americans with Disabilities Act. The Extracts from Authorities option is where you can store long sections from authorities. It is a subelement of the Research spreadsheet that has the ability to display in-depth excerpts, quotations, and other more detailed information from other cases, statutes, and so on. You can also link the research to the specific legal issues in the Issues spreadsheet.

26. **Click Authorities and Extracts.** Your screen should look like CaseMap Exhibit 10. Notice that the screen now splits to show a research filter on top and the list of authorities below. The Authority Filter feature allows you to search more efficiently.

CASEMAP EXHIBIT 10

27. ***Click the Facts icon*** to go back to the Facts spreadsheet.

This concludes Lesson 1. To exit CaseMap, ***click File on the menu bar, then click Exit,*** or go to Lesson 2.

LESSON 2: WORKING WITH THE FACTS SPREADSHEET

This lesson introduces you to the CaseMap Facts spreadsheet, including how to enter information in CaseMap. This lesson also provides information about a variety of CaseMap features, including fuzzy dating, date stamping, data format options, auto-sizing cell widths, correcting spelling errors, linking files, short names, sorting, linking issues (Link Assistant), filtering by Selection, filter tagging, and evaluating facts.

If you did not exit CaseMap after Lesson 1, then skip Steps 1–5 and go directly to Step 6.

1. Start Windows. ***Double-click the LexisNexis CaseMap 8 icon on the desktop,*** or ***click the Start button on the Windows desktop, point to Programs or All Programs, point to the LexisNexis CaseMap Suite, and click LexisNexis CaseMap 8.*** LexisNexis CaseMap 8 will then start.

2. When you start CaseMap, you will see a small window in the middle of the screen that says **"CaseMap"** and adds some information about a grace period. ***Click Continue in the "CaseMap" window.*** CaseMap will then start, with several options listed to the right of the screen.

3. Your screen should now look similar to CaseMap Exhibit 1. The Getting Started task pane should be displayed on the right side of the screen. ***Under Learn from an Example Case, click*** **Hawkins v. Anstar.**

4. The "Case Log On" window should now be displayed. ***Click the down arrow icon to the right of Staff Member: Chris Attorney. Click Dave Paralegal and then click OK.***

5. CaseMap should put you back at the last spreadsheet you were using when you exited the program. Thus, the Facts spreadsheet for the *Hawkins* case should be displayed.

6. As indicated previously, the Facts spreadsheet gives you a chronology of a case. Chronologies are very useful when litigating a case. They are a great tool for refreshing the recollection of the legal professionals who are assigned to a case (particularly if it has been a while since they worked on that particular case). They are useful for sharing knowledge with everyone on the legal team, working with clients, aiding in preparation of depositions, preparing summary judgment motions, and preparing for trial. The chronologies that CaseMap can produce are particularly helpful because they also help a legal professional evaluate the strength of the case and link facts to central issues in the case. Chronologies are also extremely helpful when attorneys or legal professionals on a case change, such as when an attorney leaves the firm and another attorney takes over the case.

7. Notice in the Facts spreadsheet that the first column is Date & Time. Also, notice in the second entry, 12/??/2002 (see CaseMap Exhibit 2), that there are question marks where the day should be.

8. CaseMap comes with a feature called "fuzzy dating." Many times, parties or witnesses to a lawsuit cannot remember exactly when something happened. When you do not know exactly when an event or fact happened, just put in question marks. When you see a fuzzy date, you immediately know that additional research is needed, that the date is not completely set, or that the party or witness cannot remember the date with certainty. The 12/??/2002 date

means that the event occurred sometime during the month of December 2002. CaseMap reads the date as 12/01/02 for the purpose of sorting by date.

9. ***Click in the third record on the date 01/??/2003.*** Notice that there is a gray box to the right of the date in the Date and Time field (see CaseMap Exhibit 11). This is called the Date Stamper.

10. ***Click the gray Date Stamper box next to the date 01/??/2003 in the third record*** (see CaseMap Exhibit 11).

11. You should now see the "Date Stamper (Date & Time)" window displayed (see CaseMap Exhibit 11). Notice that a calendar is displayed. Using the Date Stamper, you can change the date interactively while you view the calendar. ***Click Cancel in the "Date Stamper" window.***

12. In the fourth record from the top in the Date & Time column, Mon 01/13/2003, notice that the day of the week, **"Mon,"** is shown. See CaseMap Exhibit 11. It is sometimes helpful to know the day of the week on which a particular event occurred. CaseMap does this automatically for you. When you enter a date (e.g., 01/13/2003), CaseMap automatically calculates and enters the day of the week for you if that is how the Date & Time column has been configured.

13. You can change how the Date & Time column is formatted. ***Click Tools on the menu bar, then click Options.*** See CaseMap Exhibit 11. The "Options" window should now be displayed. ***Click the Date tab.***

14. ***Click the down arrow just to the right of Style: MM/dd/yyyy.*** Notice that many different date formatting options are available.

15. ***Click the first style, MM/dd/yyyy***.

16. Notice under Style that there is a check mark in the box next to **"Show Day of Week."** If you did not want CaseMap to show the day of the week in the Date & Time column, you could click in that check box to turn the feature off.

17. ***Click Cancel on the Options menu.***

CASEMAP EXHIBIT 11

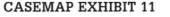

LexisNexis and the Knowledge Burst logo are registered trademarks of Reed Elsevier Properties Inc. TimeMap and CaseMap are registered trademarks of LexisNexis CourtLink, Inc. Used with the permission of LexisNexis.

18. Notice in the sixth record from the top that a date range is listed (**"Fri 01/09/2004 to Wed 01/21/2004"**). See CaseMap Exhibit 11. CaseMap is very flexible and can even handle date ranges. Date ranges are sorted by the first date in the range. This is a very useful feature because witnesses often do not remember exact dates of events that happened over several days, though they may be able to narrow it down to a certain range of dates.

19. *Click in the seventh record in the Fact Text column (which begins "William Lang tells Philip Hawkins that he has changed his mind ... ."* Notice that the cell expanded so that you could read the full text in the cell. This is CaseMap's auto-sizing feature.

20. *Click on any other cell.* The expanded cell will collapse back to its normal size.

21. *Click the first record from the top* **"William Lang meets Philip Hawkins while touring Converse Chemical Labs plant in Bakersfield".** See CaseMap Exhibit 11. Notice that there is a paper clip just to the left of the date 11/25/02. The paper clip means that there is a file linked to this fact.

22. *Click the paper-clip icon just to the left of 11/25/02 in the first record from the top. Then click on the P001401 file (this is a PDF file).* As long as you have Adobe Reader or some other PDF file reader, you should see an email from Philip Hawkins to William Lang.

23. *Click the Close icon* (a red box with a white X) *in the "P001401" window.*

24. Notice in the first record from the top in the Fact Text column, where it says "William Lang meets Philip Hawkins …" that "William Lang," "Philip Hawkins," and "Converse Chemical Labs" have small dotted lines under them. The dotted lines mean that these entities are in the database. Lang and Hawkins are listed as persons and Converse Chemical Labs is listed as an organization.

25. *Click in the first record from the top in the Fact Text column where it says* **"William Lang meets Philip Hawkins ... ."** Notice that once you click on the cell, it says **"LangW meets HawkinsP while touring CCL plant in Bakersfield."** LangW, Hawkins P, and CCL are short names for William Lang, Philip Hawkins, and Converse Chemical Labs. Short names are critical in a database because there are many times in a case when someone is referred to by a nickname, a first name but no last name, only by initials, and so on. If one person was referred to in all of these different ways, it would be difficult to do searches that were even close to exhaustive. The Short names feature standardizes names (short names can actually apply to any Object in CaseMap) so that all names referring to the same person are entered exactly the same.

26. Notice that the third column in the Facts spreadsheet is Source(s). See CaseMap Exhibit 11. The Sources column allows you to enter notes about where the information came from. In the first record from the top in the Sources column, it says **"Deposition of William Lang, 25:14"**; this is a reference to that deposition at page 25, line 14. This is very important because in a summary judgment motion, for example, you must include a citation for every fact submitted in the motion. Also, during trial, if a witness contradicts what he or she previously said in a deposition, the attorney can use this information to immediately find the page in the deposition where the prior testimony is recorded, read the prior testimony from the deposition, and impeach the witness.

27. The fourth column in the Facts spreadsheet is the Material + column, which classifies facts as *material*, or particularly important, to the case. See CaseMap Exhibit 11. This field allows a legal professional to quickly see whether a specific fact is particularly important to the case. You can also sort material

facts, and thus see all at once the facts in the case that are the most important. This keeps legal professionals from forgetting important evidence.

28. **Right-click the Material heading at the top of the fourth column. Click Sort Descending.**

29. Notice that all of the facts that have "Yes" in the Material + column have now been sorted and are at the top of the screen. This allows you to see all of the material facts in the case at one time. When you have hundreds of facts in a case, this feature can be very helpful.

30. To sort the facts by date (the way it was before the sort on material facts), **right-click the word Date & Time at the top of the first column, then click Sort Ascending.** Notice that the Fact spreadsheet is now sorted the way it was previously.

31. Look carefully at the Date & Time header. Notice that there is a small, faint outline of a triangle pointing up. Whenever you see such a triangle in a CaseMap column header, it means that column is being used to sort the spreadsheet. In addition, a triangle pointing up means that the sort is ascending (A to Z), whereas a triangle pointing down means the sort is descending (Z to A).

32. The fifth column in the Facts spreadsheet is headed Status +. See CaseMap Exhibit 11. **Click the word Undisputed in the third record from the top ("01/??/2003 – William Lang offers Philip Hawkins Sales Manager position …") in the Status + column. Click the down arrow next to Undisputed.** A list of options is now displayed.

33. The list of options allows you to identify whether the fact is undisputed, disputed by opposition, disputed by us, unsure, or prospective. A *prospective fact* is one that you would like to be true, but requires further investigation.

34. **Click Undisputed** to leave the status unchanged and to close the option list.

35. The sixth column in the Facts spreadsheet is the Linked Issues column. See CaseMap Exhibit 11. This is where you can connect (or link) a specific fact to an issue. This is very helpful when you are making legal arguments about specific legal causes of action or legal issues, because you can display only the facts that are related to the legal issue you are addressing.

36. **Click the third record from the top ("01/??/2003 — William Lang offers Philip Hawkins Sales Manager position …") in the Linked Issues column.**

37. **Click the left facing arrow in the selected cell, (see CaseMap Exhibit 11).** The "Issue Linking" window opens to the right of the screen (see CaseMap Exhibit 12). To delete the current issue, click on another issue. To add another issue, click Add a new Issue at the top of the "Issue Linking" window.

38. **Click on Retaliation** to keep the selection. **Click the small x at the upper right corner of the "Issues Linking" window** to close this window.

39. Suppose, for example, that you are writing a summary judgment motion and you would like to see all of the facts regarding the issue of retaliation.

40. **Point to the word Retaliation in the third record and right-click anywhere in that cell. Then, click the Filter by Selection icon. It looks like a funnel with a lightning bolt next to it.)**

41. A small LexisNexis CaseMap window should appear, stating that the issue you selected has subissues and asking whether you want to include the subissues in the search. **Click No.** Notice that only the facts with "retaliation" somewhere in the Linked Issues are listed.

42. To cancel the filter, **click the Cancel Search icon at the top right corner of the screen.**

CASEMAP EXHIBIT 12

43. The screen should now return to what it looked like before you engaged the filter. Using the Filter by Selection tool, you can click a cell and right-click the cell and select Filter by Selection, and CaseMap will then search for the item in the cell you selected.

44. Now, suppose that you are writing a summary judgment motion and you want to see all of the facts in chronological order, but you would like the undisputed facts tagged or marked so you can easily identify them.

45. *Click the word Undisputed in the third record from the top* ("**William Lang offers Philip Hawkins Sales Manager position …**") *in the fifth column* (Status +).

46. *Right-click the same cell and select Tag by Selection.* Notice in the far left column that there are now red vertical ovals ("tags") next to every cell that has Undisputed in the Status + column.

47. To cancel the tag, *click Cancel Search.*

48. The tags should now have disappeared.

This concludes Lesson 2. To exit CaseMap, *click File on the menu bar, then click Exit, then click OK* to acknowledge the need to back up your files (if it asks), or go to Lesson 3.

▶ INTERMEDIATE LESSONS

LESSON 3: WORKING WITH THE OBJECTS SPREADSHEET

This lesson introduces you to the CaseMap Objects spreadsheet. It covers entering objects, executing primary and secondary sorts, expanding and contracting column widths; reviews what the columns mean in the Objects spreadsheet; explains the different views in the Objects spreadsheet; and gives tips on how to use the Objects spreadsheet to its full potential.

If you did not exit CaseMap after Lesson 2, then skip Steps 1–5 and go directly to Step 6.

1. Start Windows. *Double-click on the LexisNexis CaseMap 8 icon on the desktop, or click the Start button on the Windows desktop, point to Programs or All Programs, point to the LexisNexis CaseMap Suite, and point and click on LexisNexis CaseMap 8.* LexisNexis CaseMap 8 will then start.

2. When you start CaseMap, you will see a small window in the middle of the screen that says **"CaseMap"** and adds some information about a grace period. *Click Continue in the "CaseMap" window.* CaseMap will then start, with several options listed to the right of the screen.

3. Your screen should now look similar to CaseMap Exhibit 1. The Getting Started task pane should be displayed on the right side of the screen. *Under Learn from an Example Case, click* Hawkins v. Anstar.

4. The "Case Log On" window should now be displayed. *Click the down arrow icon to the right of Staff Member: Chris Attorney. Click Dave Paralegal, then click OK.*

5. CaseMap should put you back at the last spreadsheet you were using when you exited the program. Thus, the Facts spreadsheet for the *Hawkins* case should be displayed.

6. *Click the All Objects icon on the left side of the screen under Case Shortcuts > Favorites.*

7. Notice, in the header of the Object Type column, that there is a **"1"** next to a triangle pointing up. Also notice that in the header of the Full Name column, there is a **"2"** next to a triangle pointing up. As indicated previously, the triangle shows which column is being used to sort the spreadsheet, and the direction of the triangle (pointing up) means that it is an ascending sort. The **"1"** indicates the primary sort column and the **"2"** indicates the secondary sort column. CaseMap first sorts the spreadsheet by object (not alphabetically, however; CaseMap prioritizes objects based on Persons first, then Organizations, then Documents, etc.) and then sorts the spreadsheet by the Full Name field. By right-clicking in the header of any column, you can sort a spreadsheet by that column; however, if you want to do a primary and secondary sort, you must use a menu option.

8. *Click Records in the menu bar, click Sort, then click Advanced Sort.* The "Advanced Sort: Object" window is now displayed. Notice that in the Sort By field it says **"Object Type."** Under that, it says **"Then By,"** and **"Full Name."** Under that, it says **"Then By"** and displays a drop-down menu with the option to choose a key or short name. Thus, using the Advanced Sort option, you can create a primary, secondary, and even tertiary sorts. Notice that if you did not have a secondary sort, the Object Types would be sorted, but there would be no order beyond that.

9. *Click Cancel in the "Advanced Sort: Objects" window.*

10. Notice the title **"Objects – All Objects"** just under the toolbar. Also, notice in the first column of the spreadsheet (Object type), that there are several different kinds of object types, including Person, Organization, Document, and others.

11. CaseMap is currently combining all of the objects into one view. This is the All Objects view. However, you can change this so that you see only Persons, or Organizations, or another object type. The reason for doing this is that additional fields are shown when you do.

12. For example, notice on your screen that no Type field is shown for the object type (e.g., whether the witness is a fact witness or an expert witness). When you view only the Persons object list, you will be able to see the Type column.

13. Toward the bottom of the Case Shortcuts window list (on the left side of the screen), notice that the topic of Objects has 12 subtopics. Notice also that next to each of the subtopics is the number of objects present in the case for that category.

14. ***Click Persons on the left side of the screen under Objects.***

15. The title directly under the menu bar should now read **"Objects – Persons"** (see CaseMap Exhibit 13). You should now see only People objects displayed on the screen. Notice that in the fourth column from the left (the "Type +" column), you can see whether the person is a fact witness or an expert witness. This column was not visible in the All Objects view. Notice that there is a column for Short Name. Also, notice the Role in Case column, where you can see a short description about the role or function of each person in the case.

16. The Objects – Persons view also has a Key column so you can identify whether a person is a key player in the case.

17. In the column called Facts, the fifth record from the top is Philip Hawkins. Notice that the Facts column tells you that he was referenced in 24 separate Fact records.

18. ***Click Documents on the left side of the screen under Objects.*** The Objects – Documents view should now be displayed (see CaseMap Exhibit 14). *Note:* You can also access the Objects – Documents view from the Case Shortcuts > Favorites list.

19. In the Objects – Documents view, the first and second columns are called **"Bates – Begin"** and **"Bates – End."** Bates numbers are important because they allow you to track and find documents numerically (assuming that every document in the case has a Bates number).

20. ***Click the second record from the top*** **("Hawkins Letter of 8/2/2005")** *in the Type + column. Click the down arrow icon next to Letter.* The box lists document types, including Contract, Deposition, E-mail, Internal memo, Letter, and Performance Review.

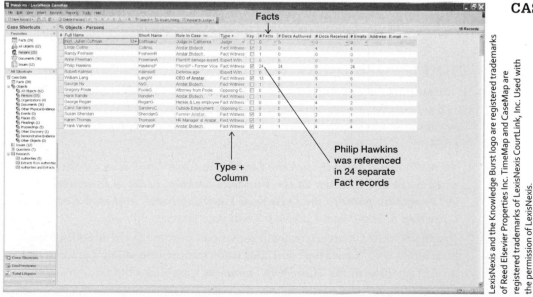

CASEMAP EXHIBIT 13

CASEMAP EXHIBIT 14

21. ***Click Letter*** to keep the current selection.

22. ***Scroll to the right using the right cursor key on the keyboard*** or ***use the horizontal scroll bar.*** There are columns for the document author(s) and recipients. Also, there is a Linked Issues column for linking the document to a specific legal issue and a Linked File column so you can see the actual image, or full text, of the document and evaluation columns.

23. ***Click Organizations on the left side of the screen under Objects.*** The Objects – Organizations view should now be displayed. The Organization columns are similar to the columns in other Object spreadsheet views.

24. ***Click the All Objects icon to the left side of the screen*** to display all of the objects again.

25. ***Click Case Shortcuts > Favorites, then click Facts*** to return to the Fact spreadsheet.

This concludes Lesson 3. To exit CaseMap, ***click File on the menu bar, then click Exit, then click OK*** to acknowledge the need to back up your files (if it asks), or go to Lesson 4.

LESSON 4: WORKING WITH THE ISSUES SPREADSHEET

This lesson introduces you to the CaseMap Issues spreadsheet, including how to enter new issues, promote and demote issues, and delete issues.

If you did not exit CaseMap after Lesson 3, then skip Steps 1–5 and go directly to Step 6.

1. Start Windows. ***Double-click the LexisNexis CaseMap 8 icon on the desktop,*** or ***click the Start button on the Windows desktop, point to Programs or All Programs, point to the LexisNexis CaseMap Suite, and click LexisNexis CaseMap 8.*** LexisNexis CaseMap 8 will then start.

2. When you start CaseMap, you will see a small window in the middle of the screen that says **"CaseMap"** and adds some information about a grace period. ***Click Continue in the "CaseMap" window.*** CaseMap will then start, with several options listed to the right of the screen.

3. Your screen should now look similar to CaseMap Exhibit 1. The Getting Started task pane should be displayed on the right side of the screen. ***Under Learn from an Example Case, click*** **Hawkins v. Anstar**.

4. The "Case Log On" window should now be displayed. ***Click the down arrow icon to the right of Staff Member: Chris Attorney. Click Dave Paralegal, then click OK.***

5. CaseMap should put you back at the last spreadsheet you were using when you exited the program. Thus, the Facts spreadsheet for the *Hawkins* case should be displayed.

6. ***Click the Issues icon on the left side of the screen under Case Shortcuts > Favorites.*** The Issues spreadsheet should be displayed (see CaseMap Exhibit 4). The Issues spreadsheet is where you enter the legal issues around which the case will revolve.

7. Notice that in the Full Name column there are issues with whole numbers (e.g., 1, 2), and then there are subissues with decimals (e.g., 2.1, 2.2,). CaseMap allows you to categorize whether an issue is a stand-alone issue, or is part of a more detailed issue.

8. ***Click the first record, "1 Wrongful Termination," in the Full Name column.***

9. On the toolbar, there is an icon called New Record. See CaseMap Exhibit 4. Directly next to this icon is a down arrow. ***Click the Down arrow icon.*** When you click the down arrow, you can select the type of item you want to enter, such as New Fact, New Object, and so on.

10. ***Click Issue.***

11. A blank record with the number "2" has been created. Just to the left of the "2," notice that there is a line with an up arrow, right arrow, and down arrow. ***Point to the up arrow*** and notice that it displays Move Up. ***Click the up arrow.*** The entry has now been moved up and is listed as 1.

12. Now, notice that the line next to the "1" only has a down arrow. ***Point to the down arrow*** and notice that it displays Move Down. ***Click the down arrow.*** The issue has reverted to number 2.

13. ***Point to the right arrow next to 2***, and notice that it displays **"Demote." *Click the right arrow next to 2.*** It now becomes 1.1. Using these arrows, you can control where each issue in the Issues list is displayed.

14. ***Click Outline on the menu bar.*** See CaseMap Exhibit 4. A list of options is displayed, including the ability to promote, demote, move up, or move down any issue in the outline hierarchy.

15. Press the [ESC] key to make the menu list go away.

16. With the pointer still on 1.1, type **Against Public Policy** and press the [TAB] key. Notice that CaseMap has entered AgainstPublicPolicy in the Short Name field. It is best to keep all Short Name entries as short as possible.

17. Press the [DELETE] key, type **AgPubPolicy,** and then press the [ENTER] key.

18. To delete the issue, ***click the Delete Record icon on the toolbar.*** (It looks like a red script X with a red left arrow next to it).

19. ***Click Yes*** when CaseMap asks if you are sure if you want to delete this issue. The issue is now deleted.

20. ***Click Case Shortcuts > Favorites and then click Facts*** to return to the Facts spreadsheet.

This concludes Lesson 4. To exit CaseMap, ***click File on the menu bar, click Exit, then click OK*** to acknowledge the need to back up your files (if it asks), or go to Lesson 5.

LESSON 5: WORKING WITH ADVANCED FEATURES

This lesson introduces you to some advanced features in CaseMap, including using the View CaseWide command, hiding columns, inserting columns, adjusting rows, moving columns, printing and viewing reports, adding objects on the fly, hiding shortcuts, and viewing the detail of a record.

If you did not exit CaseMap after Lesson 4, then skip Steps 1–5 and go directly to Step 6.

1. Start Windows. *Double-click the LexisNexis CaseMap 8 icon on the desktop, or click the Start button on the Windows desktop, point to Programs or All Programs, point to the LexisNexis CaseMap Suite, and click LexisNexis CaseMap 8.* LexisNexis CaseMap 8 will then start.

2. When you start CaseMap, you will see a small window in the middle of the screen that says **"CaseMap"** and adds some information about a grace period. *Click Run in the "CaseMap" window.* CaseMap will then start, with several options listed to the right of the screen.

3. Your screen should now look similar to CaseMap Exhibit 1. The Getting Started task pane should be displayed on the right side of the screen. *Under Learn from an Example Case, click Hawkins v. Anstar*.

4. The "Case Log On" window should now be displayed. *Click the down arrow icon to the right of Staff Member: Chris Attorney. Click Dave Paralegal, then click OK.*

5. CaseMap should put you back at the last spreadsheet you were using when you exited the program. Thus, the Facts spreadsheet for the *Hawkins* case should be displayed.

6. *Click the View CaseWide icon on the toolbar* (it looks like a graph; see CaseMap Exhibit 15).

7. The CaseWide view allows you to see a timeline of when the facts of the case occurred. Notice in the right corner of the graph that the "Y" is selected (see CaseMap Exhibit 15). The current graph in the CaseWide view is by year. Notice that the largest number of events occurred in 2005 (see CaseMap Exhibit 15).

CASEMAP EXHIBIT 15

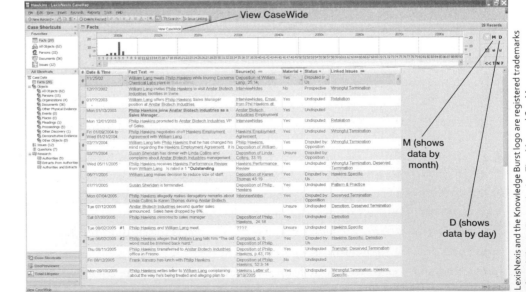

8. *Click M to the right of the CaseWide graph.* See CaseMap Exhibit 15. CaseMap responds by displaying the same data on a monthly basis.

9. *Using the horizontal scroll bar under the CaseWide graph, scroll to the right.* You can see that the largest number of events occurred in July and August 2005.

10. *Click D to the right of the CaseWide graph.* See CaseMap Exhibit 15. CaseMap responds by displaying the same data on a daily basis.

11. *Use the horizontal scroll bar under the CaseWide graph to scroll to the right* until you see some blue bars showing daily activity.

12. The CaseWide view gives you an overview of the general timing involved in a case.

13. *Click the View CaseWide icon on the toolbar* (it is now highlighted) to close the CaseWide view. Notice that the CaseWide icon is no longer highlighted.

14. If necessary, *scroll to the right until you see the Linked Issues column.* Suppose that this column is no longer important and is just taking up space in the spreadsheet view. *Right-click the header of the Linked Issues column, then click Hide Field.*

15. Notice that the column can no longer be seen on the spreadsheet. *Note*: The data in the column/database have not been deleted; they have just been hidden and are no longer in the current view.

16. *Right-click the header of the Status + column, then click Insert Fields.*

17. The "Selected Field(s) to Insert" window should now be displayed. Notice that a number of fields are listed, including the field that was just deleted (Linked Issues). You can use the Insert Field command to customize the views of your spreadsheets and to add other columns that include additional data. *Scroll down and click Linked Issues, then click OK.*

18. *Scroll to the right to see the Linked Issues column.* If the Linked Issues column is to the left of the Status + column, *click the Linked Issues column header and drag it to the right of the Status + column.* The column has now been added back to the Facts spreadsheet view.

19. If necessary, *scroll back to the left to see the first columns of the Facts spreadsheet.*

20. *Click File and then click Print Preview* to see how the Facts spreadsheet would look printed. *Click Print* if you would like to print the report, or *click Close* to close the "Print Preview" window.

21. *Click File and Page Setup, then click the Report Options tab.* Sometimes the spreadsheets are too long to print on one page, but by changing the size of the type and other options, you can manipulate the reports to print on one page. You can also hide columns to get your reports to print on one page.

22. *Click Cancel in the "Page Setup" window.*

23. Suppose that you are entering a new fact in the Facts spreadsheet and you need to reference a new person. You do not have to go to the Object spreadsheet to enter it.

24. *Click New Record on the toolbar and then Fact on the drop-down menu.* A new record should now be displayed at the bottom of the Facts spreadsheet.

25. In the Date & Time column, type **10/1/05** and press the [**TAB**] key. Notice that CaseMap converted the date to Sat 10/01/2005.

26. The cursor should now be in the Fact Text column of the new record. Type **John Allen admitted HawkinsP to Laketown Hospital.**

27. *Drag the mouse over the name* **John Allen** *until it is highlighted. Right-click in the highlighted area and click Add Object.* The "Add Object" window is

now displayed. Everything in the "Add Object" window is correct, but if it were not, it could be edited.

28. ***Click OK in the "Add Object" window.*** The name "AllenJ" should now have a dotted line underneath it, showing that it has been listed as a Person in the Object spreadsheet, and that a Short Name has been made for the person.

29. ***Click the All Objects icon on the left side of the screen.*** Notice that John Allen has been added.

30. ***Click the Role in Case column in the row for John Allen.*** Type **Doctor for Philip Hawkins**, and then ***click any cell*** to enter the text.

31. ***Click Linda Collins in the third record from the top of the Objects – All Objects spreadsheet, in the Full Name column. Click Records on the menu bar and then click Record Detail.*** The "Object Detail" window has now been displayed. (If the window is too small, you can adjust its size by ***placing the cursor over the borders and dragging the window to the desired size.***) Notice that you can now collect and/or view a wide variety of other information about the person, including how to contact the person and other information. This is extremely helpful at trial when it is necessary to schedule witness testimony.

32. ***Click Close in the "Object Detail" window.***

33. ***Scroll down and click the document "Hawkins Performance Review (P001357)" in the Objects – All Objects spreadsheet.***

34. ***Click Records on the menu bar and then click Record Detail.*** Notice that the "Object Detail" window, which shows a number of additional fields about the document, is displayed. ***Scroll down in the "Object Detail" window to see all of these fields.*** Some of the additional fields include Privilege, Producing Party, Trial Ex(hibit) #, and others. *Note:* Any of these additional fields that are listed can be included in the spreadsheet view at any time by ***clicking in a header and selecting Insert Field.*** For Objects, you will need to go to the specific object spreadsheet (e.g., the Objects – Documents spreadsheet rather than the Objects – All Objects spreadsheet).

35. ***Click Close in the "Object Detail" window.***

36. ***Click Case Shortcuts > Favorites and then click on Facts*** to return to the Facts spreadsheet.

This concludes Lesson 5. To exit CaseMap, ***click File on the menu bar, click Exit, then click OK*** to acknowledge the need to back up your files (if it asks), or go to Lesson 6.

▶ ADVANCED LESSONS

LESSON 6: CREATING A NEW CASE

This lesson introduces you to setting up (creating) a new case in CaseMap and entering new Objects, including people, organizations, and documents.

If you did not exit CaseMap after Lesson 5, then skip Steps 1–5 and go directly to Step 6.

1. Start Windows. ***Double-click the LexisNexis CaseMap 8 icon on the desktop,*** or ***click the Start button on the Windows desktop, point to Programs or All Programs, point to the LexisNexis CaseMap Suite, then click LexisNexis CaseMap 8.*** LexisNexis CaseMap 8 will then start.

2. When you start CaseMap, you will see a small window in the middle of the screen that says **"CaseMap"** and adds some information about a grace period.

Click Run in the "CaseMap" window. CaseMap will then start, with several options listed to the right of the screen.

3. Your screen should now look similar to CaseMap Exhibit 1. The Getting Started task pane should be displayed on the right side of the screen. ***Under Learn from an Example Case, click* Hawkins v. Anstar.**

4. The "Case Log On" window should now be displayed. ***Click the down arrow icon to the right of Staff Member: Chris Attorney. Click Dave Paralegal, then click OK.***

5. CaseMap should put you back at the last spreadsheet you were using when you exited the program. Thus, the Facts spreadsheet for the *Hawkins* case should be displayed.

6. You will now create a new case. ***Click File on the menu bar and then click New.***

7. The "New Case Wizard" window should now be displayed. ***Click Next.***

8. The "Case Setup" window should now be displayed (see CaseMap Exhibit 16).

9. In the "Case name:" box, type **Richards v. EZ Pest Control.** ***Then select your time zone as the default time zone and click Next.*** (For demonstration purposes, the example in the text will use GMT -5:00 Eastern Time.)

10. At the "Case Staff Information" window, under Enter your name:, type **your name**; in the Enter your firm or organization: field, type **Johnson Beck and Taylor**; and when it asks **"Do you want to set up additional staff members for this case now?"** ***click Yes. Then click Next.***

11. At the "Manage Staff Members" window, to the right of Staff name, type **Dave Paralegal** and ***click Add; then click Next.***

12. At the "Case File" window, to the right of File name, **"Richards v. EZ Pest Control"** should already be typed in. We will use the default location for this file on the computer, so ***click Next.***

13. CaseMap will then tell you that it has enough information to create your new file and that the case is not password protected. Be sure that the box next to Launch Case Jumpstart Wizard is checked and ***click Finish.***

CASEMAP EXHIBIT 16

HANDS-ON EXERCISES

14. The "Welcome to the Case Jumpstart Wizard" window will open. This tool will help us populate the cast of characters in our case. Notice also that the wizard window is opened on top of an empty Objects – All Objects spreadsheet and that all of the numbers next to the Case Shortcuts are zero (0). *Click Next* (see CaseMap Exhibit 17).

CASEMAP EXHIBIT 17

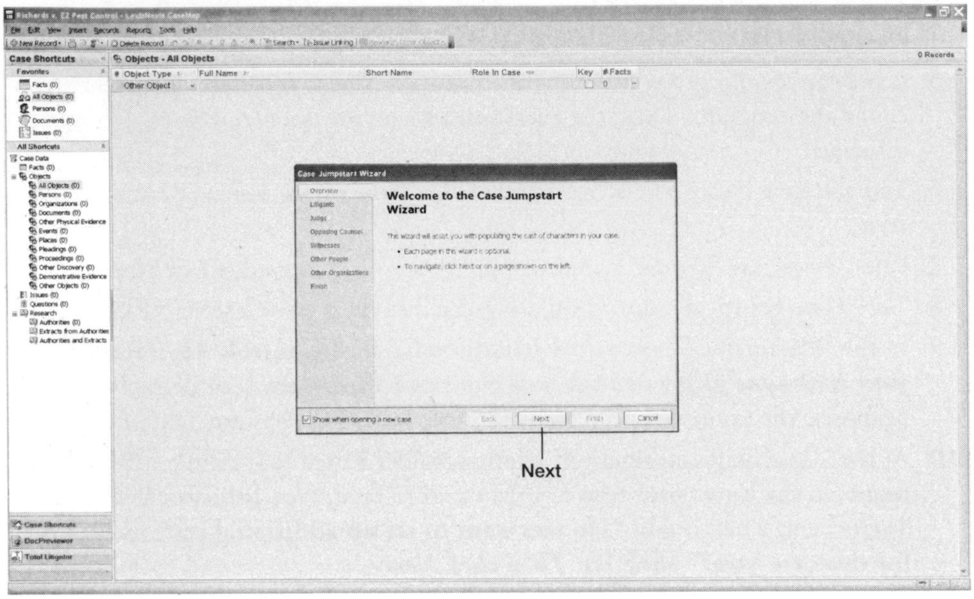

Next

15. At the "Who are the parties in this case?" window, under Type: *click Person* from the drop down list and under Party:, type **Sherry Richards.** Then *click Add Another.* Under Type:, *click Organization* and under Party:, type **EZ Pest Control.** Then *click Next* (see CaseMap Exhibit 18).

16. At the "Who is presiding over this case?" window, *click Next.* (The windows in this wizard are all optional and should be skipped if you do not know the names of the appropriate parties. We will assume that we do not yet know the name of the judge assigned to this case.)

CASEMAP EXHIBIT 18

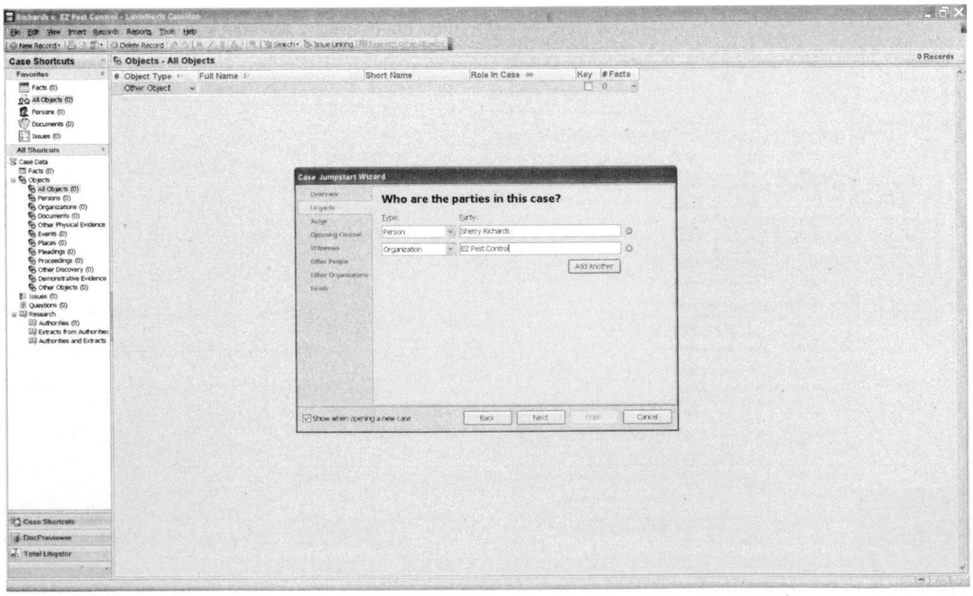

17. At the "Who are the opposing counsel?" window, under Attorney: type **Peter Gibbons** and under Firm: type **Gibbons and Kilgo**. *Click Next.*

18. At the "Who are the witnesses in this case?" window, type **John Lincoln.** Do not check the box next to Expert. *Click Next.*

19. At the "Who are the other people involved?" window, *click Next.* You could add the names of the other people later.

20. At the "What other organizations are involved?" window, *click Next.* You could add the names of the other organizations later.

21. At the "Completing the Case Jumpstart Wizard" window, *click Finish.*

22. You should now see the Objects – All Objects screen for *Richards v. EZ Pest Control.* Notice that the persons and organization we already added have Short Names assigned to them. We now need to fill in the remaining fields.

23. *Move your cursor to the Role in Case field for Sherry Richards.* Type **Plaintiff — homeowner of house at 7788 SW 52nd Street that is full of termites** and then press the [**TAB**] key.

24. *Double-click in the check box under Key in the Sherry Richards record.*

25. *Move your cursor to the Role in Case field for EZ Pest Control.* Type **Defendant** and then press the [**TAB**] key.

26. *Double-click in the check box under Key in the EZ Pest Control record.*

27. *Move your cursor to the Role in Case field for John Lincoln.* Type **EZ Pest Control Branch Manager and Head Inspector; has prepared many reports to the effect that the property has no visible evidence of termites.** Leave the box under Key empty. Press the [**TAB**] key to go to the Full Name field.

28. You will now add a few new objects to this case.

29. *Click New Record on the toolbar and then click Person.* The Objects – Persons screen and a new blank record should be displayed.

30. *Move your cursor to the Full Name field.* Type **Tim Stewart** and then press the [**TAB**] key. The pointer should now be in the Short Name column. Press the [**TAB**] key to accept the default entry of StewartT. The pointer should now be in the Role in Case field.

31. Type **Contractor hired by RichardsS to repair the immense termite damage to the house; will testify about the extensive damage to the house.** Press the [**TAB**] key.

32. *Double-click in the check box under Key in the Tim Stewart record.*

33. *Click New Record on the toolbar and then click Document.* The Objects – Documents screen and a new blank record are displayed.

34. *Move your cursor to the Full Name field.* Type **Termite Agreement** and then press the [**TAB**] key. The pointer should now be in the Short Name column. Press the [**TAB**] key to accept the default entry of TermiteAgreement. The pointer should now be in the Role in Case field.

35. Type **Contract between RichardsS and EPC for termite inspections and preventative maintenance** and then press the [**TAB**] key. Press the [**ENTER**] key to accept the short name.

36. *Double-click in the check box under Key in the Termite Agreement record.*

37. *Click Case Shortcuts > Favorites and then click Facts* to return to the Facts spreadsheet, which is blank.

This concludes Lesson 6. To exit CaseMap, *click File on the menu bar, then click Exit, then click OK* to acknowledge the need to back up your files (if it asks), or go to Lesson 7.

LESSON 7: ENTERING ISSUES AND FACTS IN A NEW CASE

This lesson introduces you to entering issues and facts in a new case and automatically copying data from one cell to another.

If you did not exit CaseMap after Lesson 1, then skip Steps 1–5 and go directly to Step 6.

1. Start Windows. ***Double-click on the LexisNexis CaseMap 8 icon on the desktop,*** or ***click the Start button on the Windows desktop, point to Programs or All Programs, point to the LexisNexis CaseMap Suite, and click LexisNexis CaseMap 8.*** LexisNexis CaseMap 8 will then start.

2. When you start CaseMap, you will see a small window in the middle of the screen that says **"CaseMap"** and adds some information about a grace period. ***Click Continue in the "CaseMap" window.*** CaseMap will then start, with several options listed to the right of the screen.

3. Your screen should now look similar to CaseMap Exhibit 1. The Getting Started task pane should be displayed on the right side of the screen. ***Under Open a Case, click*** Richards v. EZ Pest Control.cm8.

4. The "Case Log On" window should now be displayed. **"Dave Paralegal"** should be the default selection, so ***click OK.***

5. CaseMap should put you back at the Facts spreadsheet.

6. ***Click the Issues icon on the left side of the screen.*** The Issues spreadsheet should now be displayed and the pointer should be in a blank record.

7. In the Full Name column, type **Breach of Contract** and then press the [**TAB**] key.

8. Press the [**TAB**] key to accept the default entry of BreachOfContract in the Short Name field. Press the [**TAB**] key until the pointer is in the Description field.

9. Type **Defendant had maintenance contract to spray the house preventively for termites for five years prior to discovery of extensive termite damage.**

10. ***Double-click in the check box under Key in the Breach of Contract record.***

11. Press the [**TAB**] key until you are in a new record. In the Full Name column, type **Negligence** and then press the [**TAB**] key.

12. Press the [**TAB**] key to accept the default entry of Negligence in the Short Name field. Press the [**TAB**] key until the pointer is in the Description field. Type **Defendant negligently failed to discover enormous termite colony that did extensive damage to the house.**

13. ***Double-click in the check box under Key in the Negligence record.***

14. ***Click Facts on the left side of the screen.*** The Facts spreadsheet should now be displayed and the cursor should be in a blank record.

15. In the Date & Time column, type **01/02/2006** and then press the [**TAB**] key to go to the Fact Text field.

16. Type **RichardsS and EPC sign TermiteAgreement** and then press the [**TAB**] key to go to the Source(s) column.

17. Type **Ter** and then press the [**ENTER**] key to accept this short name for "Termite Agreement."

18. Press the [**TAB**] key. The pointer should now be in the Material + field.

19. ***Click the down arrow in the Material + field. Click Yes,*** then press the [**TAB**] key.

20. ***Click in the Status + column in the record, click the down arrow icon, then click Undisputed.***

21. Press the [TAB] key.

22. *Right-click in the Linked Issues column in the record, click Link Assistant, then click BreachOfContract.*

23. Press the [TAB] key. You should now be in a blank Fact record.

24. In the Date & Time column, type **5/15/2006** and then press the [TAB] key to go to the Fact Text field.

25. Type **LincolnJ completes full termite inspection of house** and then press the [TAB] key to go to the Source(s) column.

26. Type **Deposition of RichardsS, 32:18 and Deposition of LincolnJ, 45:9** and then press the [TAB] key.

27. The pointer should now be in the Material + column. *Click the down arrow and click Yes.* Then press the [TAB] key.

28. The pointer should now be in the Status + column. *Click the down arrow icon, then click Undisputed.*

29. Press the [TAB] key. The pointer should now be in the Linked Issues column.

30. *Right-click in the Linked Issues column in the record, click Link Assistant, then click BreachofContract.*

31. Type **;** (a semi-colon).

32. *Right-click again in the Linked Issues column in the record, click Link Assistant, then click Negligence.*

33. Press the [TAB] key. You should now be at a blank Fact record.

34. In the Date & Time column, type **8/??/2006** and then press the [TAB] key to go to the Fact Text field.

35. Type **RichardsS hears noise inside walls at night; later discovered to be termites** and then press the [TAB] key to go to the Source(s) column.

36. Type **Deposition of RichardsS, 45:6**, and then press the [TAB] key.

37. *Click the down arrow in the Material + column and click Yes.* Then press the [TAB] key.

38. *Click the down arrow in the Status + column and then click Undisputed.*

39. Press the [TAB] key.

40. Press the [CTRL]+["] (quotation mark) keys on the keyboard. [CTRL]+["] copies the value from the cell above. Notice that "Breach of Contract, Negligence" was copied from the cell above to the current cell. Using this command will greatly decrease data entry time if there are a number of duplicate entries; it will also lessen the possibility of making an error.

41. Press the [TAB] key. You should now be at a blank Fact record.

42. In the Date & Time column, type **10/15/2006** and then press the [TAB] key to go to the Fact Text field.

43. Type **StewartT inspects house to make a bid on repairs and finds massive termite damage**, then press the [TAB] key to go to the Source(s) column.

44. Type **Deposition of StewartT, 14:12**, then press the [TAB] key.

45. *Click the down arrow in the Material + column and click Yes.* Then press the [TAB] key.

46. *Click the down arrow in the Status + column and then click Undisputed.*

47. Press the [TAB] key.

48. Press the [CTRL]+["] (quotation) keys on the keyboard to copy the cell above to the current cell.

49. Press the [**TAB**] key. You should now be at a blank Fact record.

50. In the Date & Time column, type **11/01/2006** and then press the [**TAB**] key to go to the Fact Text field.

51. Type **RichardsS hires another pest control service to look at the property; confirms massive termite damage** and then press the [**TAB**] key to go to the Source(s) column.

52. Type **Deposition of RichardsS, 22:7** and then press the [**TAB**] key.

53. *Click the down arrow in the Material + column and click Yes.* Then press the [**TAB**] key.

54. *Click the down arrow icon in the Status + column, then click Undisputed.*

55. Press the [**TAB**] key.

56. Press the [**CTRL**]+[**"**] (quotation) keys on the keyboard to copy the cell above to the current cell.

57. Press the [**TAB**] key. You should now be at a blank Fact record.

58. In the Date & Time column, type **07/15/2006** and then press the [**TAB**] key to go to the Fact Text field.

59. Type **LincolnJ attempts to inspect property; sees RichardsS in the house, but she will not open the door. LincolnJ is not able to inspect house.** Then press the [**TAB**] key to go to the Source(s) column.

60. Type **Deposition of LincolnJ, 52:20** and then press the [**TAB**] key.

61. *Click the down arrow in the Material + column and click Yes.* Then press the [**TAB**] key.

62. *Click the down arrow in the Status + column and then click Disputed by: Us.*

63. Press the [**TAB**] key.

64. Press the [**CTRL**]+[**"**] (quotation) keys on the keyboard to copy the cell above to the current cell.

This concludes Lesson 7. To exit CaseMap, *click File on the menu bar, click Exit, then click OK* to acknowledge the need to back up your files (if it asks), or go to Lesson 8.

LESSON 8: USING CASEMAP FOR A NEW CASE

This lesson introduces using CaseMap for a new case, including printing reports, viewing case data in a variety of ways, exporting to a PDF file, exporting a summary judgment report to a word processor, using the CaseWide tool, and searching/filtering data. This lesson assumes that you have completed all of the prior exercises, and that step-by-step directions are therefore not necessary.

If you did not exit CaseMap after Lesson 7, then skip Steps 1–5 and go directly to Step 6.

1. Start Windows. *Double-click the LexisNexis CaseMap 8 icon on the desktop,* or *click the Start button on the Windows desktop, point to Programs or All Programs, point to the LexisNexis CaseMap Suite, and click LexisNexis CaseMap 8.* LexisNexis CaseMap 8 will then start.

2. When you start CaseMap, you will see a small window in the middle of the screen that says **"CaseMap"** and adds some information about a grace period. *Click Run in the "CaseMap" window.* CaseMap will then start, with several options listed to the right of the screen.

3. Your screen should now look similar to CaseMap Exhibit 1. The Getting Started task pane should be displayed on the right side of the screen. *Under Open a Case, click* **Richards v. EZ Pest Control.cm8**.

4. The "Case Log On" window should now be displayed. **Dave Paralegal** should be the default selection, so *click OK.*

5. CaseMap should put you back at the Facts spreadsheet.

6. *Right-click in the header of the Date & Time field in the Facts spreadsheet, and sort the column in descending order.*

7. Print the Facts spreadsheet *(click File on the menu bar, then click Print),* or view it on the screen *(click File on the menu bar, then click Print Preview).*

8. *Click the record that has "Disputed by: Us" in the Status + column, and filter the selection by right-clicking on the entry.*

9. *Cancel the filter using the Cancel Search icon on the toolbar.*

10. In the Issues spreadsheet, move the Description column to the third column by *clicking in the column header and dragging it to the new location.*

11. Print a report that contains only Persons in the Object spreadsheet. First, *click Persons on the left side of the screen, click File on the menu bar, then click Print.*

12. Print a report of All Objects using the Objects – All Objects spreadsheet view.

13. *Return to the Facts spreadsheet on the left side of the screen.*

14. Using CaseMap, you can automatically print any CaseMap report to a PDF file that can then be emailed to a client. *Click the Print to PDF icon on the toolbar* (the fourth icon from the left). *Click Print to PDF.*

15. At the "Save As Adobe PDF" window, *click Save* to save the document to the default directory with the default file name.

16. A window should now be displayed that says **"The report has been saved as an Adobe PDF file. Do you want to open it now?"** *Click Yes.*

17. If Adobe Reader is installed on your computer, the Fact Chronology report should now be displayed.

18. *Click the Close icon* (a red box with a white X) *in the "Adobe Reader" window.*

19. You will now print the Case Summary Report, which prints out each of the key spreadsheets automatically. *Click Reports on the menu bar, then click ReportBooks, then click Case Summary and click Preview* (see CaseMap Exhibit 19). CaseMap will then display a window stating that some spreadsheets are empty. *Click Yes* to indicate that you want to continue.

20. Page down through the report. When you are done, *click Close.*

CASEMAP EXHIBIT 19

21. CaseMap has a convenient feature specifically related to summary judgment motions. CaseMap can export a word-processing file directly to Word or WordPerfect that will assist in creating a summary judgment motion or response. *In the Facts spreadsheet, click Reports on the menu bar and then click Summary Judgment Wizard.*

22. *In the "Welcome to the Summary Judgment Wizard" window, click Next.*

23. When the "Customize Report" window asks, **"Do you want to customize the report?"** *click* **"No, I want to use CaseMap's default options button"** *and then click Next.*

24. *In the "Report Format" window, select either Microsoft Word, Corel WordPerfect, or HTML; then click Next.*

25. *In the "Completing the Summary Judgment Wizard" window, click Finish.*

26. Notice that a table has been created showing all of the facts that relate to each legal issue, as well as the citation for each factual reference (see CaseMap Exhibit 20).

27. After reading the document, *close the word-processing file.*

28. *Click the View CaseWide icon on the toolbar.* (It looks like a chart.)

29. *Click M (for Month) in the upper right of the screen.*

30. *Click the View CaseWide icon on the toolbar again* to make the CaseWide view disappear.

31. Suppose that you are assisting your supervising attorney in preparing for the deposition of John Lincoln and that you would like to retrieve all of the Fact records that have his name.

32. *Right-click any occurrence of John Lincoln's name in the Facts spreadsheet.* Notice that the first option in the menu is Selection: LincolnJ. *Click Filter by Selection.*

33. Notice that only the records for John Lincoln are shown. *Click Cancel Search on the toolbar.* (It looks like a funnel next to a red ball.)

34. If you would like additional training on CaseMap, *click Help on the menu bar and then click CaseMap Webinar Center.* Numerous free "webinars" (web seminars) are available on the Internet that will further assist you in learning CaseMap.

35. This concludes Lesson 8. To exit CaseMap, *click File on the menu bar, then click Exit, then click OK* to acknowledge the need to back up your files (if it asks).

This concludes the CaseMap exercises.

CASEMAP EXHIBIT 20

▶ TIMEMAP

I. INTRODUCTION – READ THIS!

LexisNexis TimeMap is a litigation support analytical tool that creates time maps or time-lines. The LexisNexis TimeMap demonstration version is a full working version of the program (with a few limitations). The program demonstration version times out 120 days after installation. This means that the program will only work for 120 days after you install it. So, it is highly recommended that you do not install the program on your computer until you are actually ready to go through the Hands-On Exercises and learn the program. When you are ready to install the program, follow the instructions below.

II. USING THE LEXISNEXIS TIMEMAP HANDS-ON EXERCISES

The LexisNexis TimeMap Hands-On Exercises are easy to use and contain step-by-step instructions. Each lesson builds on the previous exercise, so please complete the Hands-On Exercises in order. TimeMap comes with sample data, so you should be able to utilize many features of the program.

III. INSTALLATION INSTRUCTIONS

Below are step by step instructions for loading the LexisNexis TimeMap demonstration version on your computer.

1. Log in to your CengageBrain.com account.

2. Under "My Courses & Materials," find the Premium Website for Using Computers in the Law Office.

3. *Click "Open" to go to the Premium Website.*

4. Locate "Book Resources" in the left navigation menu.

5. *Click on the link for "TimeMap 5."*

6. You may get a File Download – Security Warning. **Click Run.** See TimeMap Installation Exhibit 1. You may get an Internet Explorer – Security Warning. **Click Run.** See TimeMap Installation Exhibit 2.

LexisNexis and the Knowledge Burst logo are registered trademarks of Reed Elsevier Properties Inc. TimeMap and CaseMap are registered trademarks of LexisNexis CourtLink, Inc. Used with the permission of LexisNexis.

TIMEMAP INSTALLATION EXHIBIT 1

LexisNexis and the Knowledge Burst logo are registered trademarks of Reed Elsevier Properties Inc. TimeMap and CaseMap are registered trademarks of LexisNexis CourtLink, Inc. Used with the permission of LexisNexis.

TIMEMAP INSTALLATION EXHIBIT 2

7. Your screen will look like TimeMap Installation Exhibit 3. **Click Next.**

**TIMEMAP
INSTALLATION
EXHIBIT 3**

LexisNexis and the Knowledge Burst logo are registered trademarks of Reed Elsevier Properties Inc. TimeMap and CaseMap are registered trademarks of LexisNexis CourtLink, Inc. Used with the permission of LexisNexis.

8. Your screen will look like TimeMap Installation Exhibit 4. **Click Yes.**

**TIMEMAP
INSTALLATION
EXHIBIT 4**

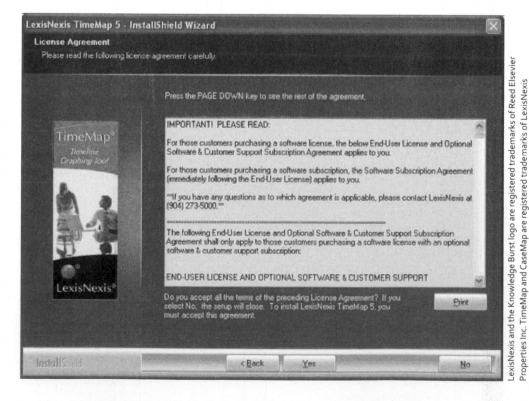

LexisNexis and the Knowledge Burst logo are registered trademarks of Reed Elsevier Properties Inc. TimeMap and CaseMap are registered trademarks of LexisNexis CourtLink, Inc. Used with the permission of LexisNexis.

9. Your screen will look like TimeMap Installation Exhibit 5. **Click Next.**

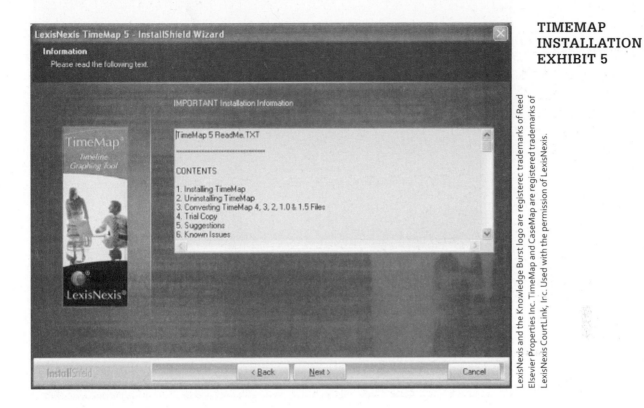

TIMEMAP INSTALLATION EXHIBIT 5

10. Your screen will look like TimeMap Installation Exhibit 6. If you wish to change the default installation location, click on Browse to navigate to the desired location. Otherwise, **click Next.**

TIMEMAP INSTALLATION EXHIBIT 6

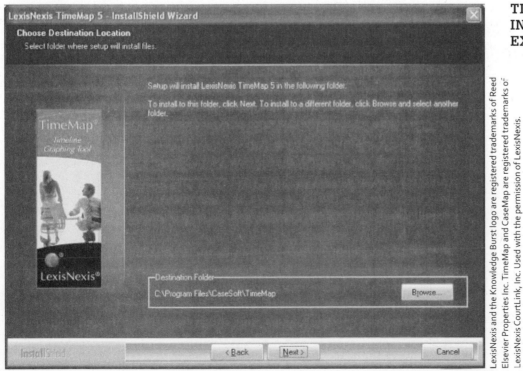

HANDS-ON EXERCISES

11. Your screen will look like TimeMap Installation Exhibit 7. **Click Next.**

TIMEMAP INSTALLATION EXHIBIT 7

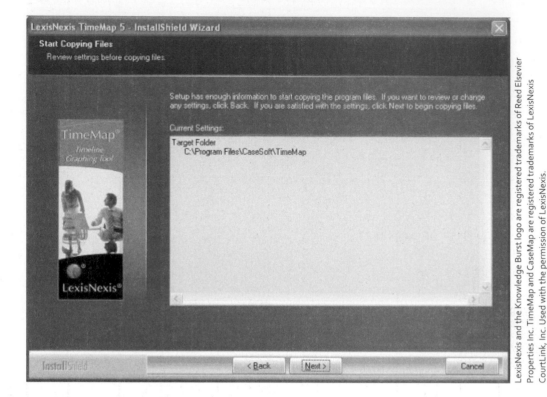

12. Your screen will look like TimeMap Installation Exhibit 8. **Click Finish** to finish installation and launch the program.

TIMEMAP INSTALLATION EXHIBIT 8

13. When you launch TimeMap you will see the screen shown in TimeMap Installation Exhibit 9. **Click Continue.**

**TIMEMAP
INSTALLATION
EXHIBIT 9**

14. You will now see a screen like the one in TimeMap Installation Exhibit 10.

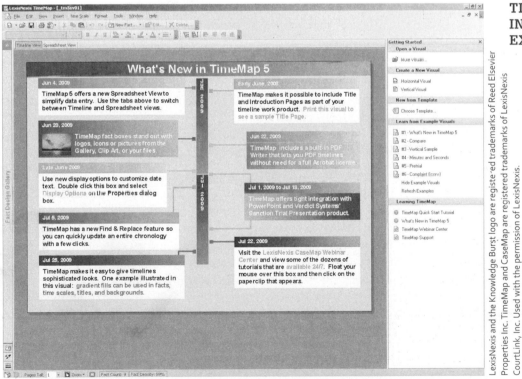

**TIMEMAP
INSTALLATION
EXHIBIT 10**

HANDS-ON EXERCISES

IV. INSTALLATION TECHNICAL SUPPORT

LexisNexis TimeMap is a licensed product of LexisNexis. If you have problems installing the demonstration version of LexisNexis TimeMap, you will need to contact LexisNexis TimeMap directly at (904) 273–5000.

Number	Lesson Title	Concepts Covered
BASIC LESSON		
Lesson 1	Introduction to TimeMap	Explanation and introduction to the TimeMap interface.
INTERMEDIATE LESSON		
Lesson 2	Creating a new timeline in TimeMap	Entering new fact boxes and customizing the chronology.
ADVANCED LESSON		
Lesson 3	Exporting CaseMap Entries to TimeMap	Exporting entries from CaseMap into TimeMap.

GETTING STARTED

Introduction

Throughout these lessons and exercises, information you need to type into the software will be designated in several different ways:

- Keys to be pressed on the keyboard are designated in brackets, in all caps, and in bold (e.g., press the [**ENTER**] key).
- Movements with the mouse pointer are designated in bold and italics (e.g., *point to File on the menu bar and click*).
- Words or letters that should be typed are designated in bold (e.g., type **Training Program**).
- Information that is or should be displayed on your computer screen is shown in bold, with quotation marks (e.g., **"Press ENTER to continue."**).
- Specific menu items and commands are designated with an initial capital letter (e.g., click Open).

OVERVIEW OF TIMEMAP

TimeMap is a litigation support product that creates timelines or time maps. A *timeline* or *time map* is a visual representation of time, showing when events occurred and in what sequence. TimeMap computerizes this process. Timelines are extremely helpful in a litigation context because they allow a jury or other factfinder to visualize how the events in the case occurred. TimeMap is straightforward and easy to use. It can accept entries imported directly from a CaseMap chronology, so that you do not have to retype or re-enter information into the computer.

▶ BASIC LESSON

LESSON 1: INTRODUCTION TO TIMEMAP

This lesson introduces you to the TimeMap litigation support program. It explains basic information about the TimeMap interface.

1. Start Windows. After it has loaded, *double-click on the LexisNexis TimeMap icon on the desktop,* or *click the Start button on the Windows desktop, point to Programs or All Programs, point to the LexisNexis CaseMap Suite, then point and click on LexisNexis TimeMap.* LexisNexis TimeMap will start.

2. When you start TimeMap, you may intermittently see a small window in the middle of the screen that says **"TimeMap"** and adds some information about a grace period. If this occurs, *click Continue.*

3. Your screen should now look similar to TimeMap Exhibit 1. On the right side of the screen is the Getting Started task pane.

TIMEMAP EXHIBIT 1

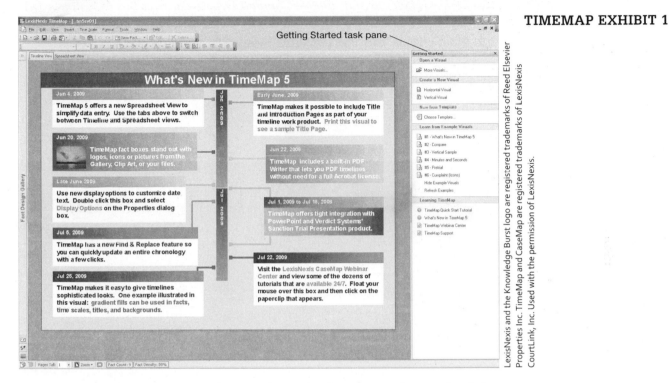

4. *In the Getting Started task pane, under Learn from Example Visuals, click #5 – Pretrial.*

5. The Key Events Before Trial time map should now be displayed (see TimeMap Exhibit 2).

TIMEMAP EXHIBIT 2

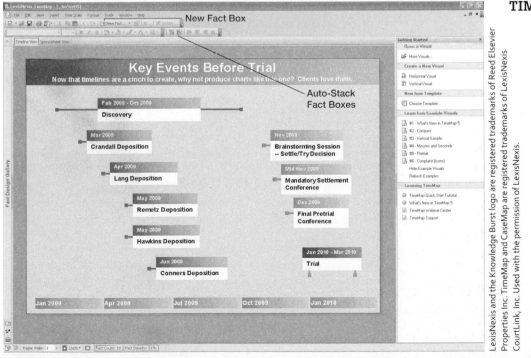

HANDS-ON EXERCISES

6. In TimeMap, there are three types of visual elements: Fact Boxes, Text Boxes, and the Time Scale.

7. Notice in TimeMap Exhibit 2 that 10 entries are displayed in the timeline (10 rectangular boxes that contain dates and descriptive information). These are called Fact Boxes.

8. ***Double-click the Mar 2009—Crandall Deposition Fact Box*** (it is the second Fact Box from the top on the left side of the screen).

9. Notice that a "Fact Box Properties" window is now displayed (see TimeMap Exhibit 3). ***Click the date*** and edit it so that it reads **03/15/2009.** Then change **"Crandall Deposition"** so that it reads **John Crandall Deposition,** and ***click OK in the "Fact Box Properties" window.***

TIMEMAP EXHIBIT 3

10. You will now create a new Fact Box. ***Click the New Fact Box (Ins) icon on the toolbar.*** (It looks like a yellow file folder with an "F" on it and a star in the upper left corner; see TimeMap Exhibit 2.)

11. The "New Fact Box" window is displayed. ***Click in the white box to the right of the Date & Time field,*** and type **10/01/2009.**

12. ***Click in the large white box in the "New Fact Box" window.*** Type **Client Discovery Meeting** and then ***click OK in the "New Fact Box" window.***

13. Notice that TimeMap has placed the Fact Box in the middle of the screen (see TimeMap Exhibit 4).

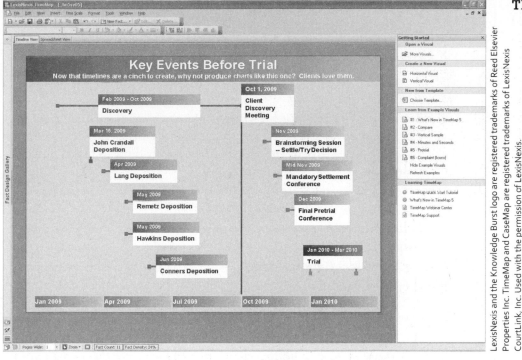

14. *Double-click on the* "Oct 1, 2009" *Fact Box.*

15. *Click the Colors and Lines tab in the "Fact Box Properties" window.*

16. *Click the down arrow to the right of Date under the Fill section. Click Plum* (medium purple). Notice that under the Fill section, next to Box, the color selected is white. This is the color for the lower part of the Fact Box where the text goes. You can control the font, color, lines, and all other aspects of Fact Boxes. *Click OK in the "Fact Box Properties" window.*

17. On the left side of the screen is the Fact Design Gallery task pane (see TimeMap Exhibit 5). To access this window, *click the double right-facing arrow at the top of the pane.* And if you have not already closed the Getting Started window on the right of the screen, do so now by *clicking the small x at the top of that pane.* Notice that in TimeMap Exhibit 5 there are several different box styles. For example, if you want to add a blue box, *click the blue style fact box.* Notice that the "New Fact Box" window is now displayed. You can now enter a new Fact Box in the blue style quickly and easily.

18. *Click Cancel in the "New Fact Box" window.*

19. In the Fact Design Gallery task pane, notice that there is a plum style Fact Box (the one you previously created). You can now add Fact Boxes with this style by clicking on the style.

20. *Double-click anywhere in the title* "Key Events Before Trial." This is a Text Box. Notice that the "Text Box Properties" window is now displayed. You can create a text box anywhere in a time map.

21. Edit the Text Box Properties so that instead of saying "**Key Events Before Trial,**" it says **Key Dates—Crandall v. Conners.**

22. *Click the Colors and Lines tab of the "Text Box Properties" window.*

23. *Under Fill—Box, click the down arrow and select yellow.*

HANDS-ON EXERCISES

24. ***Click the Text tab. Drag the mouse pointer so that*** "Key Dates—Crandall v. Conners" ***is highlighted. Click the Font Color icon.*** (It looks like the letter "A".) It should already be black.

25. ***Click OK.*** Notice that the title of the time map has now been changed.

26. The time scale in TimeMap can be adjusted easily. ***Click Time Scale on the menu bar, then click Expand.***

27. ***Click Time Scale on the menu bar and then click Expand one more time.*** Notice that the scale has expanded and that it is now on two screens. You can make the time scale as large as you wish. This is usually done to make room for more Fact Boxes.

28. You can also compress the scale width. ***Click Time Scale on the menu bar and then click Compress. Do this a total of three times.***

29. ***Click Time Scale on the menu bar and then click Expand*** to put the scale back to where it started.

30. ***Click the*** "Nov 2009 Brainstorming Session —Settle/Try Decision" ***Fact Box.*** Notice that the entire box is now surrounded by small white squares. These are called *handles.* If you point to one of the handles that are in the middle, on either side, or on the bottom in the middle, the cursor will change to a double-sided arrow and you can expand or contract the box.

31. ***Point to the middle handle on the right side and then drag the mouse pointer to the left toward the center of the box about a quarter of an inch.*** Notice that the box just got smaller.

32. You can also easily delete a Fact or Text Box by ***clicking to select it*** and then pressing the [**DELETE**] key, or by ***clicking the Delete icon on the toolbar.***

33. ***Click Time Scale on the menu bar and then select Increase Pages Wide.*** TimeMap responds by expanding the time map out by a whole page. It is possible to expand the time map out over many pages.

34. ***Click Time Scale on the menu bar and then click Decrease Pages Wide*** to restore the time map to its original size.

35. ***Click the Auto-Stack fact boxes icon on the toolbar.*** (It looks like three stacked boxes with a single vertical line to the right; see TimeMap Exhibit 2.) TimeMap will condense the Fact Boxes so that they are arranged more tightly.

36. ***Drag the timeline dates at the bottom of the screen*** (the gray bar with the months on it) ***up. Drag the timeline straight up to the top of the page.*** Notice that you can change the position of the timeline by dragging it.

37. Press the [**CTRL**]+[**Z**] keys to undo the move. If you change something in TimeMap and then do not like how it looks, just press [**CTRL**]+[**Z**] (or ***click Edit > Undo)*** and TimeMap will put it back the way it was.

38. In TimeMap, you do not have to change items one at a time; you may select a number of Fact Boxes and make a change to all of them at the same time. Press the [**CTRL**]+[**A**] keys. Notice that all of the Fact Boxes are selected.

39. ***Double-click on any Fact Box.*** The "Fact Box Properties" window is now displayed.

40. ***Click the Date Font tab. Click Italic at the bottom of the "Fact Box Properties" window to change all of the dates to italics. Click OK.*** Notice that all of the dates have been changed to italics.

41. Press the [**CTRL**]+[**Z**] keys on the keyboard to undo the font change.

42. ***Click Tools.*** Notice that one of the options is Spelling. This allows you to run a spell check on your document. ***Click anywhere outside of the drop-down menu*** to make it disappear.

43. Notice that the primary window of TimeMap has two different views. So far, we have only used the Timeline View. Now, ***click Spreadsheet View.*** See TimeMap Exhibit 5. Now you can see the same facts listed in a spreadsheet. You can also enter new facts in this view and they will appear in the Timeline View.

44. ***Click on the line where it says "Click here to add a new fact".*** In the first column, under Date & Time, **type 07/01/09.** In the second column, under Fact Text, **type Prepare Motion for Summary Judgment.**

45. ***Click on Timeline View.*** You can now see the newly added fact on the timeline.

TIMEMAP EXHIBIT 5

LexisNexis and the Knowledge Burst logo are registered trademarks of Reed Elsevier Properties Inc. TimeMap and CaseMap are registered trademarks of LexisNexis CourtLink, Inc. Used with the permission of LexisNexis.

This concludes Lesson 1. ***Click File and then click Exit.*** You do not want to save your changes, so ***click No.***

▶ INTERMEDIATE LESSON

LESSON 2: CREATING A NEW TIMELINE IN TIMEMAP

This lesson allows you to create a completely new timeline, and assumes that you have successfully completed Lesson 1.

1. Start Windows. Then, ***double-click the LexisNexis TimeMap icon on the desktop, or click the Start button on the Windows desktop, point with the mouse to Programs or All Programs, point to the LexisNexis CaseMap Suite, and then click LexisNexis TimeMap.*** LexisNexis TimeMap will start.

2. When you start TimeMap, you may intermittently see a small window in the middle of the screen that says **"TimeMap"** and adds some information about

a grace period. If you get this message, *click Continue in the "TimeMap" window.* If you do not get this message, go to the next step.

3. Your screen should now look similar to TimeMap Exhibit 1. On the right side of the screen is the Getting Started task pane.

4. *In the Getting Started task pane, under Create a New Visual, click Horizontal visual.*

5. A blank time map should be displayed.

6. *Double-click* "**Double-click to add title**" *at the top of the page.* Edit the text box so that it says **John R. Ewing Zoning Dispute** and then *click OK* to enter the title in the Text Box.

7. Using the Spreadsheet View, enter the following fact boxes:

Date & Time	Fact Text
01/29/12	Application for Zoning Change Filed
03/04/12	Additional Plats Filed
03/15/12	Initial Zoning Commission Hearing
03/18/12	Opposition to Zoning Change Filed by Druid Hills Homeowners Association
04/25/12	Response to Opposition to Zoning Change Filed
04/29/12	Newspaper Story on Zoning Change
05/17/12	Town Hall Meeting Druid Hills Homeowners
06/06/12	Zoning Change on County Commission Agenda
06/15/12	Zoning Commission Votes to Deny Change

See TimeMap Exhibit 6.

TIMEMAP EXHIBIT 6

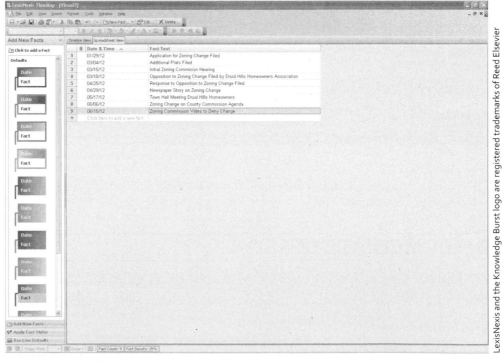

8. *Click Timeline View.* Your screen should now look similar to TimeMap Exhibit 7.

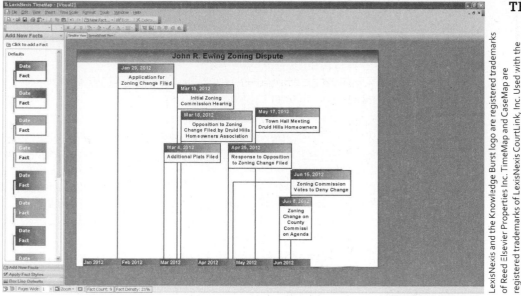

9. Press the **[CTRL]+[A]** keys on the keyboard to select all of the Fact Boxes. ***Double-click on any Fact Box*** and format the Date Font, Colors and Lines to your liking.

10. Experiment with the features discussed in Lesson 1 to manipulate your time map, including Expand/Compress Scale Width, Increase/Decrease Pages Wide, Time Scale Break, Fit to Pages Wide, and Snap Flag Left/Right Side of Line.

11. Print your timeline by ***clicking the printer icon on the toolbar*** or by ***selecting File from the menu bar and then clicking Print.***

12. ***Click File and Save.*** Type **your name TimeMap** (e.g., Jones TimeMap), and then ***click Save.***

13. ***Click File on the menu bar, click Open, then double-click one of the example time maps*** (e.g., tm5sv01, tm5sv01). *Note*: You can switch between the open time maps by ***clicking Window on the menu bar and selecting a different TimeMap file.***

14. Use the example files to get ideas for making your time map more visually appealing. If you make any changes to the sample files, do not save them.

15. When you are done working on your time map, save it, print it, ***click File, and then click Exit*** to exit TimeMap.

This concludes Lesson 2.

ADVANCED LESSON

LESSON 3: EXPORTING CASEMAP ENTRIES TO TIMEMAP

This lesson shows you how to automatically export entries from CaseMap to Time-Map using the *Richards v. EZ Pest Control Case* (or the *Hawkins* case) that you entered into CaseMap.

1. Start Windows. ***Double-click the LexisNexis TimeMap icon on the desktop, or click the Start button on the Windows desktop, point to Programs or All Programs, point to the LexisNexis CaseMap Suite, then click LexisNexis TimeMap.*** LexisNexis TimeMap will then start.

2. When you start TimeMap, you may intermittently see a small window in the middle of the screen that says **"TimeMap"** and adds some information about a grace period. If you get this message, ***click Continue in the "TimeMap" window.*** If you do not get this message, go to the next step.

3. A blank time map should now be displayed. The right side of the screen should have the Getting Started task pane open.

4. You will now start LexisNexis CaseMap so that you can export the CaseMap entries into TimeMap. ***Click start, point to Programs or All Programs, point to the LexisNexis CaseMap Suite, then click LexisNexis CaseMap.*** When you load CaseMap, you may see a small window in the middle of the screen that says **"CaseMap"** and adds some information about a grace period. If you see this message, ***click Continue in the "CaseMap" window.*** CaseMap will then start, with several options listed on the right of the screen. If you do not see this message, go to the next step.

5. ***Under Open a Case in the Getting Started task pane, click Richards v. EZ Pest Control.cm8.*** If the file is not there, ***click Hawkins v. Anstar under Open the example case.***

6. The "Case Log On" window should now be displayed. ***Click the down arrow, click Dave Paralegal, then click OK.***

7. The CaseMap Fact spreadsheet should now be displayed. ***Click File on the menu bar, click Send To, then click LexisNexis TimeMap and click Spreadsheet.***

8. The chronology from CaseMap should now be exported into TimeMap and the Richards time line should be displayed (see TimeMap Exhibit 8).

9. If you loaded the *Hawkins* case, you may need to select some of the longer entries and edit them down. Regardless of the case you choose, you can see how entries in CaseMap can be automatically sent to TimeMap.

TIMEMAP EXHIBIT 8

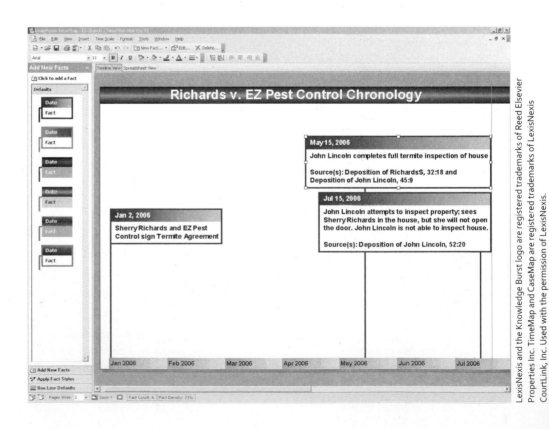

10. Note that instead of sending all entries from CaseMap to TimeMap, you can also choose to send only one entry at a time.

11. ***Click CaseMap*** at the bottom of the screen to switch to CaseMap.

12. ***Right-click any record in the Fact Text field.***

13. ***Point to Send to, then LexisNexis TimeMap, then Current Record.*** By choosing Current Record, only the specific record is sent to TimeMap, rather than the entire spreadsheet.

14. ***Click TimeMap*** at the bottom of the screen to switch to TimeMap.

15. In LexisNexis TimeMap 5, you can export time maps to other programs, such as Microsoft PowerPoint. It works best when Fact Boxes are not split across pages. ***Drag the July 15, 2006 Fact Box to the left so that it fits on page 1 of the time map.*** Do the same thing for the Aug ??, 2006 Fact Box.

16. ***Click File on the menu bar and then point to Send to.*** Notice that one of the options is Microsoft PowerPoint.

17. If you have Microsoft PowerPoint installed on your computer, ***point to Send to Microsoft PowerPoint.***

18. ***Click One Slide per Page.***

19. Microsoft PowerPoint should now open with the time map displayed.

20. ***In the Microsoft PowerPoint window, click the Close icon*** (the X) to close Microsoft PowerPoint.

21. When a Microsoft PowerPoint dialog box opens, ***click No,*** because you do not want to save the file.

22. You can also convert time maps to PDF files. ***Click File the menu bar, point to Print to PDF, then click Print to PDF (File).***

23. ***In the Save As dialog box, click Save*** to accept the default directory and default file name. ***Click Yes*** to indicate that you would like to open the file.

24. ***In the "PDF Viewer" window, click the Close*** (X) ***icon to close PDF Viewer.***

25. The time map currently spans two pages, but you can only see one page at a time. To see both pages at the same time, ***click View on the menu bar, then select Zoom, and then click Fit in Window.*** Although the text may be too small to edit in this mode, it does give you a good overview of the time map for formatting purposes.

26. ***Click View on the menu bar, then select Zoom, then click Fit Height*** to bring the view back to one page at a time.

27. ***Click View on the menu bar and then click Full Screen*** to see the time map in full-screen mode.

28. Press the **[ESC]** key to turn off full-screen mode.

29. If you wish, revise the timeline to make it more visually appealing. When you are done working in TimeMap, print the timeline, but do not save it.

30. If you would like additional training on TimeMap, ***click Help on the menu bar and then click TimeMap Webinar Center.*** Numerous free webinars are available on the Internet that will further assist you in learning TimeMap.

31. ***Click File and then click Exit*** to exit TimeMap.

This concludes the TimeMap tutorial.

HANDS-ON EXERCISES

CHAPTER 8

The Internet, Computer-Assisted Legal Research, and Electronic Mail

HANDS-ON EXERCISES

FEATURED SOFTWARE
Legal and Factual Research on the Internet
Westlaw Computer-Assisted Legal Research
LexisNexis Computer-Assisted Legal Research

LEGAL AND FACTUAL RESEARCH ON THE INTERNET

Number	Lesson Title	Concepts Covered
BASIC LESSONS		
Lesson 1	Using a Legal Search Engine, Part 1	Find practice/subject matter indexes on FindLaw. com; locate free legal forms in the Internet Legal Research Group; find free legal-related news articles in Alllaw.com
Lesson 2	Using a Legal Search Engine, Part 2	Find a legal dictionary in Lawguru.com; find a large number of law journals using the Internet Legal Research Group and Lawguru.com
INTERMEDIATE LESSONS		
Lesson 3	Conducting Legal Research on the Internet, Part 1 U.S. Supreme Court State/Federal Rules	Find United States Supreme Court cases, state court rules, and federal court rules
Lesson 4	Conducting Legal Research on the Internet, Part 2 State statutes U.S. Code Code of Federal Regulations	Do keyword searching for state statutes, in the U.S. Code, and in the Code of Federal Regulations
Lesson 5	Conducting Legal Research on the Internet, Part 3 Current Congressional Record State Appellate Court opinions	Perform keyword searches in and for current congressional legislation; keyword-search federal legislative history in the Congressional Record; keyword-search state appellate court opinions

Lesson 6	Conducting Factual Research on the Internet, Part 1 Expert witnesses Attorneys Satellite and street level images	Find expert witnesses using ExpertPages.com; find attorneys in particular specialties by city/state using Martindale.com; find satellite and street level images using Google
Lesson 7	Conducting Factual Research on the Internet, Part 2 Federal Bureau of Prisons Inmate Locator State criminal records search	Find federal inmates using the Federal Bureau of Prisons Inmate Locator; conduct state criminal background checks
Lesson 8	Conducting Factual Research on the Internet, Part 3 Real estate/appraisal searches State vital record searches Federal statistic searches	Find county real estate appraisal records; find state vital records (birth, death, marriage, divorce); find statistics from the federal government
ADVANCED LESSONS		
Lesson 9	Conducting Factual Research on the Internet, Part 4 SEC filings (EDGAR) PDRHealth.com Prescription drug search Library Gateway—Aviation	Find Securities and Exchange Commission filings using the EDGAR database; find the side effects of a prescription drug using PDRHealth.com; find aviation-related information using a library gateway
Lesson 10	Conducting Factual Research on the Internet, Part 5 Pipl.com Salary.com	Find individuals using Pipl.com; find salary information using Salary.com

GETTING STARTED

Introduction

Throughout these lessons and exercises, information you need to type into the software will be designated in several different ways:

- Keys to be pressed on the keyboard are designated in brackets, in all caps, and in bold (e.g., press the **[ENTER]** key).
- Movements with the mouse pointer are designated in bold and italics (e.g., *point to File on the menu bar and click*).
- Words or letters that should be typed are designated in bold (e.g., type **Training Program**).
- Information that is or should be displayed on your computer screen is shown in bold, with quotation marks (e.g., **"Press ENTER to continue."**).
- Specific menu items and commands are designated with an initial capital letter (e.g., click Open).

OVERVIEW

These Hands-On Exercises assume that you have a web browser, that you are generally familiar with it, and that you have access to the Internet. The exercises are designed to give you experience in using a number of different websites and practice at finding different kinds of information. Because the use of web browsers is straightforward and routine, only summary instructions are included in these exercises. The instructions are current as of this writing, but websites change from time to time, so it is possible that the instructions will not work on sites that have been significantly changed. If you encounter this problem, just skip that assignment and go to the next.

▶ BASIC LESSONS

LESSON 1: USING A LEGAL SEARCH ENGINE, PART 1

Exercise 1.a.   The objective of this exercise is to use the practice/subject indexes on FindLaw.com to find an article related to the state of California and the need for employees to use an organization's internal grievance procedures before suing in court.

Notice that FindLaw has more than 40 subject-matter practice areas. Searching subject matter indexes in legal search engines may produce useful information.

Instructions:

1. Go to www.findlaw.com.
2. *Click* "Visit our professional site" *at the top of the page.*
3. *Go to Browse Research Materials by Practice Area and click More.*
4. *Click Administrative Law.*
5. *Click FindLaw Library – Administrative Law Documents, Articles and Books.*
6. *Click Judicial Review.*
7. *Click Decisions Reviewable.*
8. *Click Exhaustion of Administrative Remedies.*
9. *Click California Employers Gain Yet One More Reason for Internal Grievance Policies and Procedures.*
10. Print the article.

Exercise 1.b.   The objective of this exercise is to find a free residential lease agreement valid in the State of New York using the Internet Legal Research Group (ilrg.com).

The Internet Legal Research Group has an excellent forms archive. Many websites have legal forms for sale, but this site provides many different forms for free.

Instructions:

1. Go to http://ilrg.com.
2. *Click ILRG Legal Forms Archive.*
3. *Click Leases and Real Estate.*
4. *Click Agreement to Lease (Residential Lease).*
5. *Click New York.*
6. *Scroll down* to see/read the "New York Residential Lease Agreement."
7. Copy the text of the lease and paste it into a document in your word processor.
8. Print the lease agreement.

Exercise 1.c.   The objective of this exercise is to find a free, law-related news site using Alllaw.com.

Instructions:

1. Go to www.alllaw.com.
2. *Click Reference and News.*
3. *Click Legal eNews.*
4. Read the table of contents.
5. Visit one of the sites listed and read and print out an article of interest.

LESSON 2: USING A LEGAL SEARCH ENGINE, PART 2

Exercise 2.a.   The objective of this exercise is to find a legal term or phrase in Lawguru's legal search engine.

Instructions:

1. Go to www.lawguru.com.
2. *Click Legal Dictionary under LawGuru Tools.*
3. Search for "easements" and print out the definition.

Exercise 2.b.   The objective of this exercise is to find access to law review articles using Internet Legal Research Group.

You can also read the full text of an article by clicking on the article title.

Instructions:

1. Go to http://ilrg.com.
2. *Under ILRG Web Index in the Academia section, click on Law Journals.*
3. Scroll down the list of law journals and *click on Harvard Law Review.*
4. Print the table of contents for the current issue.

▶ INTERMEDIATE LESSONS

LESSON 3: CONDUCTING LEGAL RESEARCH ON THE INTERNET, PART 1

Exercise 3.a.   The objective of this exercise is to find the full text of the U.S. Supreme Court decision *in Faragher v. City of Boca Raton* using the Legal Information Institute at Cornell Law School.

When you know the case name, year of decision, and name of the court, it is easy to find the full text of a case on the Internet for free (especially if it is a U.S. Supreme Court case).

Instructions:

1. Go to www.law.cornell.edu.
2. *Point to Court Opinions.*
3. *Click US Supreme Court Opinions.*
4. *Under Archive of decisions, point to By party and click 1990-present.*
5. *Next to 1997–1998, click 1st party.*
6. *Click* Faragher v. City of Boca Raton.
7. The syllabus of the court is then displayed, and you can *click the HTML or PDF version under Opinion* to read the full opinion.

Another method: Using a search engine such as Google.com, type **Faragher v. City of Boca Raton** in the search box. You will find numerous links to the full text of the opinion.

Exercise 3.b.   The objective of this exercise is to find the Rules of Criminal Procedure for the state of Alaska using Washlaw.edu (search by keyword).

Washlaw.edu has a large index that includes references to all 50 states and many federal resources.

Instructions:

1. Go to www.washlaw.edu.
2. *Click Alaska.*
3. *Under Court Rules, click Rules of Court.*
4. Print the listing of the Alaska Rules of Court.
5. *Click Criminal Procedure* to see the Alaska Rules of Criminal Procedure.

Exercise 3.c.   The objective of this exercise is to find the Federal Rules of Civil Procedure using Washlaw.edu.

Many rules for the federal courts are listed on this site.

Instructions:

1. Go to www.washlaw.edu.
2. *Click Federal Courts.*
3. *Under Court Rules, click Federal Rules of Civil Procedure.*
4. Print the table of contents.

LESSON 4: CONDUCTING LEGAL RESEARCH ON THE INTERNET, PART 2

Exercise 4.a.   The objective of this exercise is to access the New Hampshire Revised Statutes, using Washlaw.edu, and find the statutes related to criminal theft.

When searching for specific state statutes, you can often enter search terms and find the relevant statutes. Although this technique works well when searching statutes, it often does not work for case law.

Instructions:

1. Go to www.washlaw.edu.
2. *Click on New Hampshire.*
3. *Under Statutes, click New Hampshire Revised Statutes.*
4. *Under Full-Text Searching, click Search.*
5. Search for **Theft**.
6. *Click Chapter 637 Theft.*
7. Print the first page of the statute.

Exercise 4.b.   The objective of this exercise is to access the United States Code using the U.S. House of Representatives site (search by keyword).

The U.S. House of Representatives site is an excellent and efficient place to search the U.S. Code.

Instructions:

1. Go to http://uscode.house.gov.
2. *Click Search the U.S. Code.*
3. In the Search Word(s) field, type **Racketeer-Influenced and Corrupt Organizations** (do not use quotation marks). *Click Search.*
4. *Click 18 USC Sec. 1961.* (*Note:* There may be more than one listing; if so, choose the first one.)
5. Print the first page of the statute.

Exercise 4.c.   The objective of this exercise is to access the *Code of Federal Regulations* using the Government Printing Office (GPO) website (search by keyword).

Instructions:

1. Go to www.gpoaccess.gov/cfr.
2. In the Quick Search box, type **Canned fruit cocktail,** then *click Submit.*
3. *Find* **21CFR145.135-- Sec. 145.135 Canned fruit cocktail** and *click* **TEXT.** *You may need to scroll down the list of results to find this.*
4. Print the definition of *fruit cocktail.*

LESSON 5: CONDUCTING LEGAL RESEARCH ON THE INTERNET, PART 3

Exercise 5.a.   The objective of this exercise is to search for a current bill in Congress using the Library of Congress's Thomas site.

Instructions:

1. Go to http://thomas.loc.gov.
2. In the Legislation in Current Congress section, in the Search Bill Summary & Status Text field, type **Tax.** *Click SEARCH.* You will then see all of the bills with "Tax" in the title.
3. Print the first page.
4. *Click the Back button.*
5. At the Thomas main page, *under Browse Bills by Sponsor, select* a member of Congress and view the bills that member has sponsored or co-sponsored.
6. Print the first page of one of those bills.

Exercise 5.b.   The objective of this exercise is to search the *Congressional Record* for legislative history using the Library of Congress's Thomas site (search by keyword).

Instructions:

1. Go to http://thomas.loc.gov.
2. *Click Congressional Record on the left side of the page.*
3. *Click 109* (for the 109th Congress).
4. Under Enter Search, type **Pension Protection Act of 2006.** *Click Search.*
5. *Click PENSION PROTECTION Act of 2006 – (Senate – September 05, 2006) to read a speech by Senator Clinton.*
6. Print the first page.

Exercise 5.c.   The objective of this exercise is to search for a case using a search query.

Google Scholar allows you to search for cases in much the same way that you would using Westlaw or Lexis. As of this writing, only cases are available, but it is likely that statutes and regulations will become available at some point in the future.

Instructions:

1. Go to www.google.com.
2. *Click on Scholar* (you may have to first *click on More* to see the link for Scholar).
3. *Click the button for Legal opinions and journals, then click Advanced Scholar Search.*
4. In the search box for Find articles with **all** of the words:, type **negligence trespassing child swimming pool.**

5. *At the bottom of the page, under Legal opinions and journals, click the box next to Georgia.*

6. *Click Search Scholar.* You should see links to the case of *Gregory v. Johnson.*

LESSON 6: CONDUCTING FACTUAL RESEARCH ON THE INTERNET, PART 1

Exercise 6.a.   The objective of this exercise is to find a dental expert using ExpertPages.com.

This site has a wide array of specialty areas to choose from.

Instructions:

1. Go to www.expertpages.com.
2. *Click Medical/Surgical Specialties.*
3. *Click on Dentistry and Oral Surgery.*
4. *Click your state.*
5. Review the experts listed by visiting their websites.
6. Print the first page of the results.

Exercise 6.b.   The objective of this exercise is to find an attorney who specializes in divorce cases using Martindale.com.

This assignment can serve two purposes: it can provide experience doing factual research on the Internet, and it can provide a list of firms to consider when you commence your job search.

Instructions:

1. Go to www.martindale.com.
2. *Click Advanced search.*
3. *Choose the Law Firms tab.*
4. *In the City field, choose your city.*
5. *In the State field, choose your state.*
6. *Under Practice Area,* type **Family Law.**
7. *Click Search.*
8. Review the list of firms by visiting their websites.
9. Print the first page of the results.

Exercise 6.c.   The objective of this exercise is to find a satellite image of your home town. The satellite map tool is a free and useful feature of Google.

Instructions:

1. Go to www.google.com.
2. *Click Maps.*
3. *Double-click on your home town.*
4. *Continue double-clicking the map. When street names are displayed, click Satellite.*
5. You can use the + (plus) and – (minus) signs on the left side of the map to increase and decrease the magnification, and you can use the arrows just above the magnification tools to move the image in any direction.

Exercise 6.d.   The objective of this exercise is to find a street-level image of your home town.

Instructions:

1. Go to www.google.com.
2. *Click Maps.*
3. In the search box, type your address.
4. When the map appears, *use the cursor to drag and drop the figure that looks like the silhouette of a person on your exact location.*
5. In many cases, you should now see a street-level image of your home (this is known as "Street View").
6. If you are unable to see the image, try another address.

LESSON 7: CONDUCTING FACTUAL RESEARCH ON THE INTERNET, PART 2

Exercise 7.a.   The objective of this exercise is to perform a search for a federal inmate using the Federal Bureau of Prisons website.

Instructions:

1. Go to www.bop.gov.
2. *Click Inmate Locator* on the left side of the screen.
3. In the Search By Name section, under Last Name, type **Kaczynski.**
4. Under First Name, type **Theodore.**
5. *Under Race, click White.*
6. *Under Sex, click Male.*
7. *Click Search.*
8. The record for Theodore John Kaczynski (a/k/a/ the Unabomber) should be displayed.
9. Print the page.

Exercise 7.b.   The objective of this exercise is to do a state criminal background search using VirtualChase.com.

Instructions:

1. Go to www.virtualchase.com.
2. *Click Legal Research.*
3. *Click State Government and Legal Resources.*
4. *Under Criminal Records on the right side of the screen, click State.*
5. *Click Georgia.*
6. *Click the link for Georgia Inmate Query.* You can search this database for current and past inmates.
7. *Close the "Georgia Inmate Query" window and go back to the State Government and Legal Resources page.*
8. *Click the link for your state* and see if there is a link to find criminal records in your state.

LESSON 8: CONDUCTING FACTUAL RESEARCH ON THE INTERNET, PART 3

Exercise 8.a.   The objective of this exercise is to find real estate records and information.

Instructions:

1. Go to www.zillow.com.
2. Type in the address of a private home (yours or someone else's).
3. You should see an estimate (Zillow refers to it as a "Zestimate") of the property's dollar value.
4. Click on the link for the address to see detailed information about the property (square footage, taxes, etc.).

Exercise 8.b.   The objective of this exercise is to do a vital record search (birth, death, marriage, divorce).

Instructions:

1. Go to www.cdc.gov/nchs/nvss/state_health_departments.htm.
2. *Click Minnesota.*
3. *Under Certificates & Records, click death record.* The screen should now display information on how to get a death certificate from the state of Minnesota.
4. Print the page.

Exercise 8.c.   The objective of this exercise is to retrieve statistical records using Fedstats.gov.

Fedstats.gov gives users access to an enormous amount of data. However, finding the data you want may require time and patience. If you cannot find the data you need, a quick call to the responsible government agency can often prove helpful.

Instructions:

1. Go to www.fedstats.gov.
2. On the left side of the screen, *click the down arrow, select South Carolina, and then click Submit.*
3. Scroll down through the list and look at all of the statistical information regarding the state of South Carolina.
4. Print the list.
5. *Click Back* to go back to www.fedstats.gov.
6. On the right side of the screen, *click the down arrow and select Labor, then click Submit.*
7. *Under Bureau Of Labor Statistics, click Unemployment.*
8. Scroll down and notice that the unemployment rate for each state is listed on the right side of the screen.

▶ ADVANCED LESSONS

LESSON 9: CONDUCTING FACTUAL RESEARCH ON THE INTERNET, PART 4

Exercise 9.a.   The objective of this exercise is to find current Securities and Exchange Commission (SEC) filings for the Coca-Cola Company, using the SEC's EDGAR site.

Once you get comfortable with searching SEC filings, you will find that the EDGAR database contains a great deal of detailed information, including compensation plans, detailed financials, and other product/sales information.

Instructions:

1. Go to www.sec.gov.
2. *Under Filings & Forms, click Search for Company Filings.*
3. *Click Company or fund name, ticker symbol, CIK (Central Index Key), file number, state, country, or SIC (Standard Industrial Classification).*
4. At Company name, **type Coca Cola,** *click the button next to Contains and click Find Companies.*
5. *Click the link next to Coca Cola Co.*
6. Print the first page of the SEC filings for this company.

Exercise 9.b.   The objective of this exercise is to use the Digital Librarian library gateway to find a list of the top 300 drugs used in the United States.

Library gateway sites offer users a large number of access points to relevant sites on the Web.

Instructions:

1. Go to www.pdrhealth.com.
2. In the text box under Search All Drugs A-Z, type **Zoloft** and *click Search.*
3. Under Search results for Zoloft, *click the link for Zoloft.*
4. *Scroll down the page until you find the section titled "What are the possible side effects of Zoloft?"*
5. Print that page.

Exercise 9.c.   The objective of this exercise is to use the Digital Librarian library gateway to find a list of major airlines worldwide and other airline-related information.

Instructions:

1. Go to www.digital-librarian.com.
2. *Click Statistics.*
3. *Click Aviation Safety Statistics.*
4. *Click Most Recent Monthly Statistics.*
5. Print the first page of the statistics.

LESSON 10: CONDUCTING FACTUAL RESEARCH ON THE INTERNET, PART 5

Exercise 10.a.   The objective of this exercise is to find people using the Internet.

Instructions:

1. Go to www.pipl.com.
2. Type your name and state in the appropriate boxes and *click Search.*
3. Print the results page.

Exercise 10.b.   The objective of this exercise is to find salary data.

Instructions:
1. Go to www.salary.com.
2. Under Job Title, type **Paralegal.**
3. At Zip Code, enter your Zip Code and then *click Search.*
4. *Click on Paralegal I* and print the report.
5. *Click on Paralegal II, III, and IV* to see the full range of paralegal salaries in your area.

HANDS-ON EXERCISES

WESTLAW COMPUTER-ASSISTED LEGAL RESEARCH

Number	Lesson Title	Concepts Covered
BASIC LESSONS		
Lesson 1	Introduction to Westlaw	Signing on; introduction to the Westlaw interface; working with Westlaw tabs
Lesson 2	Find by Citation, Find by Party Name, and Exploring Retrieved Cases	Find by Citation; Find by Party Name; Star paging; Reporter Image; KeyCite overview; Case Outline; ResultsPlus
INTERMEDIATE LESSONS		
Lesson 3	Natural Language Search; Editing Searches; Changing Databases; Using the Term, Doc, and Best Features	Selecting a database; doing a Natural Language search; finding the scope of a database; editing a search; changing to a different database; using date restriction when searching; using the Require/Exclude Terms feature; using the Term, Doc, and Best features
Lesson 4	Terms and Connectors Searching	Searching using Terms and Connectors; using Thesaurus; printing a list of cases; using the Locate in Result tool; using WestClip
Lesson 5	KeyCite	KeyCite; depth-of-treatment stars; quotations; citing references; using the Limit KeyCite display; using the Research Trail feature
ADVANCED LESSON		
Lesson 6	KeySearch, Headnotes, and Key Numbers	Using KeySearch, Headnotes, Key Numbers, Most Recent Cases, and Most Cited Cases

GETTING STARTED

Introduction

Throughout these lessons and exercises, information you need to type into the software will be designated in several different ways:

- Keys to be pressed on the keyboard are designated in brackets, in all caps, and in bold (e.g., press the **[ENTER]** key).
- Movements with the mouse pointer are designated in bold and italics (e.g., ***point to File on the menu bar and click***).
- Words or letters that should be typed are designated in bold (e.g., type **Training Program**).
- Information that is or should be displayed on your computer screen is shown in bold, with quotation marks (e.g., **"Press ENTER to continue."**).
- Specific menu items and commands are designated with an initial capital letter (e.g., click Open).

▶ BASIC LESSONS

LESSON 1: INTRODUCTION TO WESTLAW

This lesson introduces you to Westlaw. It includes instructions for signing on to Westlaw, taking a tour of Westlaw and becoming familiar with the Westlaw interface, and working with Westlaw tabs. For an overview of the features available in Westlaw, read the section on Westlaw in Chapter 8 of the text.

1. Start Windows.

2. Start your Internet browser. Type **www.westlaw.com** in the browser and press the **[ENTER]** key.

3. Your screen should look similar to Westlaw Exhibit 1. *Click Switch to OnePass Sign On.* At the Westlaw Password field, enter your Westlaw ID and the Westlaw password supplied by your instructor.

WESTLAW EXHIBIT 1

4. In the Client ID field, enter **Hands-On Exercises 1** (or whatever your instructor tells you to enter; see Westlaw Exhibit 1). If you are using your own computer, you may also want to *click Save this Password.* Doing so will save you the time and trouble of reentering your password every time you log on to Westlaw. You should not use this feature if you are using a public computer (e.g., a library computer).

5. *Click Sign On* to sign on to Westlaw. If you are asked to agree to the terms of use, *click I Agree and then click Go.*

6. Your screen should now look similar to Westlaw Exhibit 2. This is the Welcome to Westlaw screen. *Note:* If your screen does not look like Westlaw Exhibit 2, try clicking the Westlaw tab (see Westlaw Exhibit 2) in the upper left section of the screen.

7. You will now take a brief tour of Westlaw. *Note:* In the middle of the Welcome to Westlaw screen, there may be notices or news items about new services or changes to Westlaw.

8. Notice the **Find** this document by citation: field in the upper left section of the screen (see Westlaw Exhibit 2). This is where you can enter a case or statutory citation and be taken directly to the case or statute.

9. Notice the **KeyCite** this citation: field in the middle left of the screen (see Westlaw Exhibit 2). This is where you can enter a case or statutory citation and have the history of the specified material displayed, including whether the document is still good law and other documents that cite the specified case or statute.

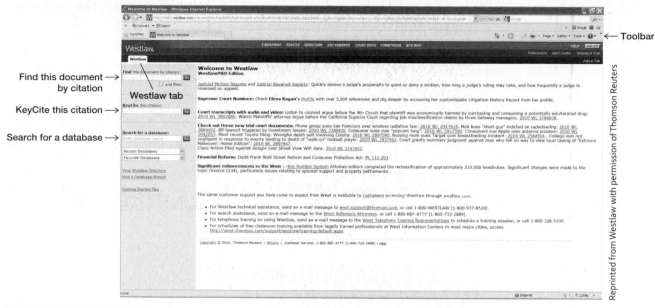

Find this document → by citation

KeyCite this citation →

Search for a database →

← Toolbar

Reprinted from Westlaw with permission of Thomson Reuters

WESTLAW EXHIBIT 2

10. Notice the **Search for a database:** field in the lower left of the screen (see Westlaw Exhibit 2). This is where you can enter the name of a specific database and be taken to that database to search or query it.

11. Notice the words **"Recent Databases"** in the lower left of the screen, just below the **Search for a database:** field (see Westlaw Exhibit 2). *Click the down arrow next to Recent Databases.* You may or may not have anything listed, depending on whether you or other users have recently used Westlaw. If you recently used a database that you want to go back to, you can click here, see the database, select it from the list, and return to it immediately.

12. If a pop-up window appears, press the **[ESC]** key to make it disappear.

13. Notice the toolbar at the top of the Westlaw screen (see Westlaw Exhibit 2). This toolbar is static, meaning that it always stays the same. Hence, you can access Find&Print, KeyCite, Directory, Key Numbers, Court Docs, FormFinder, Site Map, Help, and SIGN OFF at any time.

14. *Click Find&Print on the toolbar.* Westlaw's Find&Print feature lets you enter multiple citations and automatically send them to a printer, download them to a word processor, such as Word or WordPerfect, email the document to whomever you choose, or fax the citation to a fax number you supply. You can also include the citation's KeyCite history or citing-references information. Find&Print can be a good tool and a tremendous timesaver if you know exactly what you want.

15. *Click the Westlaw tab* (see Westlaw Exhibit 2). The Welcome to Westlaw screen should now be displayed.

16. *Click KeyCite on the toolbar.* As discussed in the main text, KeyCite is Westlaw's citation tool; using KeyCite, you can get the history of a case, including information on whether the case has been overruled or reversed, or a list of other documents that have cited your case.

17. You should now be at the KeyCite information screen. *Use the vertical scroll bar to scroll down through the information about KeyCite.* Notice that the KeyCite symbols, such as the red and yellow colored flags, are defined. Read the definitions.

18. *Click the Westlaw tab* (see Westlaw Exhibit 2). The Welcome to Westlaw screen should now be displayed.

19. *Click Directory on the toolbar.* You should now be at the Westlaw Directory screen. *Click on All Databases in the left of the screen.* There should be a search box at the top of the screen that says **"Search the Westlaw Directory."** Below that it should say **"U.S. Federal Materials."** (If you do not see these items, make sure that you have selected "All Databases" on the left side of the screen under Westlaw Directory.) The Directory is where you can interactively select from a list of Westlaw databases. Notice that there is a wide variety of database categories to choose from.

20. *Click U.S. Federal Materials.* You should now see a list of databases, including Federal Cases & Judicial Materials, Federal Statutes, Dockets (Court Docket Information), Pleadings, Motions, and other selections.

21. *Click the Back button on your browser,* or *click Directory on the toolbar to go back to the Directory.*

22. *Click each of the categories on the directory screen* (U.S. State Materials, International/Worldwide Materials, Topical Practice Areas, and the other categories). Scroll down through the lists. When you are done with each category, *click your browser's Back button* or *click Directory on the toolbar.*

23. *Click the Westlaw tab.*

24. *Click Court Docs on the toolbar.*

25. Notice that to the left of the screen it says **"Court Docs Databases."** This is where you can search for court documents. Notice also that at the left of the screen there are databases for appellate briefs, pleadings, motions, trial court orders, forms, and other items.

26. *Click the Westlaw tab.*

27. *Click Site Map on the toolbar.* The Site Map is a good place to locate a Westlaw feature if you cannot find it anywhere else. Read the selections available under each category.

28. *Click the Westlaw tab.* *Note:* The reason you are clicking the Westlaw tab instead of going directly to each item on the toolbar is that it is helpful to have a central starting place from which to access Westlaw tools and features, at least while you are learning Westlaw.

29. *Click HELP on the toolbar.* A "Westlaw Help Center" window should now be displayed, offering options such as Search for Articles, Advanced Search, and Hot Topics.

30. *Click the link for Hot Topics.* Notice that there are specific help topics for printing documents, using terms and connectors, and many others.

31. *Click the link for some of the Hot Topics.* The specific Hot Topics change from time to time, so be sure to check this area often to keep up with the latest tips and tricks.

32. *Scroll back up to the top of the "Westlaw Help Center" window. Click the Contact Us tab at the top of the "Westlaw Help Center" window.* Notice that toll-free phone numbers are available for Westlaw Technical Assistance, Research Assistance, and other resources.

33. **Click the Close icon** (a red box with a white X) **in the "Westlaw Help Center" window.**

34. **Click the Westlaw tab.**

35. **Click Add a Tab on the far right side of the screen** (see Westlaw Exhibit 2). **Click Add Westlaw Tabs.**

36. **Under the General category, click the box next to Paralegal.** If the Paralegal box already has a green check mark next to it, do not click the box.

37. Scroll down through the list, and notice that you can select from a large number of different tabs. This includes topical tabs by legal specialty, jurisdictional state choices, jurisdictional federal choices, and others.

38. **At the bottom of the screen, click Add to My Tab Set.**

39. **At the In Tab Display, click on Set as Default next to Paralegal.** This selection means that from now on when you start Westlaw, the Paralegal tab will be selected.

40. **Click the Paralegal tab.** The Paralegal tab is a great place to start your research. Throughout the rest of these Hands-On Exercises, you will start at the Paralegal tab. On your screen there should be categories for Federal Cases, State Cases, Statutes and Codes, Court Documents, Forms and Checklists, Information about People, and Information about Companies.

This concludes Lesson 1 of the Westlaw Hands-On Exercises. To exit Westlaw, **click on SIGN OFF on the toolbar,** or stay in Westlaw and go on to Lesson 2.

LESSON 2: FIND BY CITATION, FIND BY PARTY NAME, AND EXPLORING RETRIEVED CASES

In this lesson, you will use the following features: Find by Citation, Find by Party Name, Star Paging, Reporter Image, KeyCite overview, Case Outline, and ResultsPlus. If you did not exit Westlaw after completing Lesson 1, go directly to step 6 in the following instructions.

1. Start Windows.

2. Start your Internet browser. Type **www.westlaw.com** in the browser and press the **[ENTER]** key.

3. Your screen should look similar to Westlaw Exhibit 1. At the Westlaw Password field, enter your Westlaw ID and the Westlaw password supplied by your instructor.

4. In the Client ID field, type **Hands-On Exercise 2** (or whatever your instructor tells you to type).

5. **Click Sign On** to sign on to Westlaw. If you are asked to agree to the terms of use, **click I Agree and then click Go.**

6. You should now be at the Paralegal tab (see Westlaw Exhibit 3). You will now learn how to retrieve a case by entering a citation, using the Find by Citation feature.

7. **Click in the white box under Find by citation:.** Type **189 S.W. 3d 777. Click Go next to the citation you just entered.**

WESTLAW EXHIBIT 3

8. The case of *In re Mays-Hooper* should now be displayed (see Westlaw Exhibit 4). When you know the citation of a case, you can enter it in the Find by Citation feature, and Westlaw will immediately retrieve it without your having to indicate a database or enter a search query.

WESTLAW EXHIBIT 4

9. You will now find a case by entering the name of a party. ***Click the Paralegal tab at the upper left of the screen.*** You should now be back at the Paralegal tab screen (see Westlaw Exhibit 3).

10. On the left side of the screen, just below the Find by citation: field, is the heading **"Finding Tools:."** ***Click Find a Case by Party Name.***

11. The Find a Case by Party Name screen should now be displayed (see Westlaw Exhibit 5). Just below **"1. Enter at least one party name:,"** type **Karen Mays-Hooper** (see Westlaw Exhibit 5).

12. ***Click the circle to the left of State Courts:*** (see Westlaw Exhibit 5). ***Click the down arrow next to All Courts and select Texas.***

Reprinted from Westlaw with permission of Thomson Reuters

HANDS-ON EXERCISES

13. **Click Go** (see Westlaw Exhibit 5).

14. A summary of two cases, both with the title *In re Mays-Hooper*, should now be displayed. **Click In re Mays-Hooper, 189 S.W. 3d 777, 49 Tex. Sup.Ct. J. 502.**

15. The *In re Mays-Hooper* case should now be displayed (see Westlaw Exhibit 4).

16. Notice in the *In re Mays-Hooper* case (see Westlaw Exhibit 4) that a summary and the holding of the case are shown (just under the title of the case). These elements are called the *synopsis* of the case. Case synopses are written by Westlaw research attorneys. This is a value-added feature of Westlaw that many other CALR services do not offer.

17. Read the summary and holding in the *Mays-Hooper* case.

18. Notice the heading **"West Headnotes"** after the holding of the case (see Westlaw Exhibit 4), which shows the Headnotes for the case and several Topic and Key Numbers. The Headnotes, Topic Numbers/Key Numbers are also written by West research attorneys, and are a value-added feature of Westlaw that many other CALR services do not offer. These features are discussed in more detail in later exercises.

19. Skim the case by *scrolling down through it with the vertical scroll bar.*

20. Press the [**HOME**] key on the keyboard to go back to the beginning of the case.

21. You will next learn how to use Westlaw Star Paging. Star Paging is a Westlaw feature that allows you to cite to a specific page of the hard-copy reporter. *Click Tools in the lower right corner of the screen* (see Westlaw Exhibit 4).

22. *Click Go to Star Page. Click Go.*

23. At the Go to Star Page: screen, type 777. (This is the beginning page of the case.) *Click Go.*

24. Notice that the *Mays-Hooper* case is again displayed. Look closely the upper left of the screen and you will see "*777" in purple. This tells you that anything after "*777" is on page 777 of the hard copy. So, if you are going to cite anything on this page, you need to cite to page 777.

25. *Scroll down through the case* to the paragraph that starts with "The Supreme Court found the trial court's order unconstitutional . . ." and notice that on the

third line of the paragraph there is a **"*778"** in purple. This is where page 778 of the hard-copy report starts.

26. ***Scroll to the top of the case and click West Reporter Image (PDF) at the top center of the screen.*** If the window opens and then automatically closes, you may have a pop-up blocker running. Press the **[CTRL]** key on the keyboard while ***clicking Reporter Image*** to bypass the pop-up blocker. At the "File Download" window, ***click Open.*** (*Note:* You may need to press the **[CTRL]** key again while clicking Open.)

27. If you have a version of Adobe Reader or another PDF reader installed on your computer, you should now see an image of the hard-copy reporter where you can confirm what is on page 777. *Note:* Your license may not offer access to this feature.

28. ***Click the Close icon*** (a red square with a white X) ***in the "Adobe Reader" window to close the window.***

29. Notice on the left side of the screen that there are two tabs below the Paralegal tab entitled "Result List" and "Links for" (see Westlaw Exhibit 4).

30. ***Click Result List.***

31. On the left side of the screen, you should now see a short summary of the two cases that were retrieved. The Result List tab allows you to see a summary of the results of your query or search.

32. ***Click Links for.*** Notice that the Links for tab includes a KeyCite section (see Westlaw Exhibit 4). This is where you can find the history of the case. ***Click Graphical View in the KeyCite section on the left side of the screen*** (see Westlaw Exhibit 4).

33. Westlaw Exhibit 6 should now be displayed. This is a graphical chart that shows how the case was appealed from the Fort Worth Court of Appeals to the Texas Supreme Court.

WESTLAW EXHIBIT 6

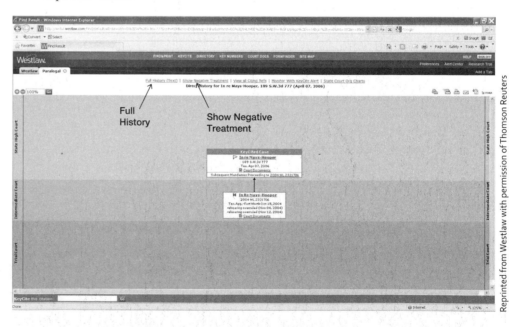

Reprinted from Westlaw with permission of Thomson Reuters

34. ***Click Full History (Text) at the top of the screen.*** You should now see a text-based history of the case.

35. ***Click Graphical View on the left side of the screen*** to go back to the graphical depiction of the history of this case.

36. ***Click Show Negative Treatment.*** (As of the date this exercise was written, there was only one example of negative history.)

37. *Click your browser's Back button to go to the previous screen with the graphical depiction of the case history.*

38. *Click "In re Mays-Hooper"* (just above the case citation) to go back to the case.

39. *Click Citing References in the KeyCite section on the left side of the screen* (see Westlaw Exhibit 4).

40. A screen similar to Westlaw Exhibit 7 should be displayed. (*Note:* The screen may look completely different by the time you read this.) This shows all of the times the case has been cited in other cases. Notice the yellow flag in the upper left of the screen (see Westlaw Exhibit 7). The yellow flag in KeyCite means that there is direct history, and there is negative history, but the case has not been reversed or overruled. Notice in Westlaw Exhibit 4 that the yellow flag is also shown on the first page of the case itself.

WESTLAW EXHIBIT 7

Reprinted from Westlaw with permission of Thomson Reuters

41. *Click your browser's Back button* to go back to the case.

42. *Click Case Outline on the left side of the screen under Full-Text Document* (see Westlaw Exhibit 4). You now should see the sections of the case (Synopsis, Headnote(s), and Opinion(s)). This option is particularly helpful when you are reading an extremely long case, because you can jump between the major sections of the case without having to scroll down through each page.

43. *Click your browser's Back button* to go back to the case.

44. *Click Petitions, Briefs & Filings on the left side of the screen under Case Outline* (see Westlaw Exhibit 4). Notice that a list of the appellate briefs is now shown. If you wanted to read the briefs of the parties, you could do so by clicking the appropriate links. *Note:* Your license may not offer access to this feature.

45. *Click your browser's Back button* to go back to the case.

46. Notice in the lower left of the screen that there is a section entitled **"ResultsPlus."** ResultsPlus is where Westlaw makes suggestions regarding other research that you might find helpful. Three options are listed in the ResultsPlus section.

47. *Click the option under ResultsPlus that says "ALR: 2. Grandparents' Visitation Rights Where Child's Parents Are Living."* You should now see an article from ALR regarding the issue of grandparent visitation rights.

48. *Click your browser's Back button* to go back to the case.

49. *Click the Paralegal tab in the upper left of the screen.*

This concludes Lesson 2 of the Westlaw Hands-On Exercises. To exit Westlaw, *click Sign Off on the toolbar,* or stay in Westlaw and go to Lesson 3.

▶ INTERMEDIATE LESSONS

LESSON 3: NATURAL LANGUAGE SEARCH; EDITING SEARCHES, CHANGING DATABASES; USING THE TERM, DOC, AND BEST FEATURES

In this lesson, you will learn how to select a database; run a Natural Language search; find the scope of a database; edit a search; change to a different database; use the date restriction feature when searching; use the Require/Exclude Terms feature; and use the Term, Doc, and Best features.

If you did not exit Westlaw after completing Lesson 2, go directly to Step 6 in the following instructions.

1. Start Windows.
2. Start your Internet browser. Type **www.westlaw.com** in the browser and press the **[ENTER]** key.
3. Your screen should look similar to Westlaw Exhibit 1. At the Westlaw Password field, type your Westlaw ID and the Westlaw password supplied by your instructor.
4. In the Client ID field, type **Hands-On Exercise 3** (or whatever your instructor tells you to type).
5. *Click Sign On* to sign on to Westlaw.
6. You should now be at the Paralegal Tab (see Westlaw Exhibit 3).
7. You will now look for a federal court case in which an attorney committed fraud by retaining settlement funds of a client in litigation and breached his fiduciary duty to the client.
8. *Under Federal Cases, click Federal Cases.* The database identifier for this database is ALLFEDS.
9. The Search screen should now be displayed (see Westlaw Exhibit 8).

WESTLAW EXHIBIT 8

10. *Click Natural Language* (see Westlaw Exhibit 8). You will now enter a plain English search into the ALLFEDS database using Westlaw's Natural Language feature.

11. In the Search box, type **attorney fraud settlement** and then *click Search Westlaw* (see Westlaw Exhibit 8).

12. Depending on how Westlaw was set up on your computer, your search will most likely return 100 cases. This is the default setting when using Natural Language. As you scroll through the search results, notice that the cases are not in chronological order. Rather, they are presented in the order in which the search terms are used most often and in closest proximity to each other. By doing so, Westlaw is presenting the search results in order of relevance.

13. There are two main problems with the search. First, you are searching in an enormous database; second, you need to list more search terms to limit the search results to cases that are directly on point.

14. *Click Edit Search just under the Paralegal tab in the upper left of the screen.*

15. You should now be back at the Search screen. You will now look at the scope of the ALLFEDS database to see exactly what database you are searching in.

16. *Click the Scope Information for the database symbol,* which looks like a round white ball with a lower-case "i" in the middle of it (see Westlaw Exhibit 8).

17. Notice the information listed about the ALLFEDS database, including the Content Highlights section, which states **"All Federal Cases has all available federal case law with coverage beginning in 1790."**

18. Scroll down to see just how large this database is. In fact, it is huge, containing tens of thousands of cases. When you search in a large database like this, you need more search terms.

19. *Click your browser's Back button* to go back to the Search screen.

20. It can sometimes be more efficient to search in a smaller database than in a larger one. You will now learn how to change your database.

21. *Click Change Database(s) in the upper right of the Search screen* (see Westlaw Exhibit 8).

22. *Click in the white box under* "**Add or Delete database(s):**" and press the **[DELETE]** or **[BACKSPACE]** keys until ALLFEDS has been deleted.

23. Type **DCT4** (see Westlaw Exhibit 9), *then click Run Search.* DCT4 is the database for U.S. District Court Cases for the Fourth Circuit. This is a much narrower database than ALLFEDS.

24. The search will once again retrieve a large number (100) of cases. Although the database is smaller, the search must still be refined and additional search terms added.

25. *Click Edit Search in the upper left portion of the screen.*

26. In the Search box, in addition to "attorney fraud settlement," type **"legal malpractice" "fiduciary duty."** The quotes around "legal malpractice" and "fiduciary duty" force Westlaw to search for these exact phrases (see Westlaw Exhibit 10).

27. Another way to limit the number of cases retrieved is to restrict the dates of the cases retrieved. *Click the down arrow next to* "**Dates: Unrestricted**" *in the Search screen.*

28. *Click After.* In the white box to the right of "After," type **2003** (see Westlaw Exhibit 10).

29. Still another way to limit the number of cases retrieved is to require all of the terms. *Click Require/Exclude Terms in the Search screen* (see Westlaw Exhibit 10).

HANDS-ON EXERCISES

WESTLAW EXHIBIT 9

WESTLAW EXHIBIT 10

30. ***Click the boxes for each of the search terms (attorney, fraud, settlement, "legal malpractice," and "fiduciary duty"), and then click OK.*** Your screen should now look similar to Westlaw Exhibit 10.

31. ***Click Search Westlaw.***

32. A much smaller number of cases should now be returned. One of the cases that should be retrieved is *Hewlette v. Hovis*, 318 F. Supp. 2d 332 (E.D. Va., May 19, 2004). ***Click the* Hewlette v. Hovis case.**

33. The *Hewlette v. Hovis* case should now be displayed (see Westlaw Exhibit 11).

34. Notice that your search terms are highlighted in the synopsis. ***Click the right arrow to the right of Term at the bottom of the screen.*** Each time you click the right arrow next to Term, Westlaw takes you to the next page where your search terms are listed. You can also go backward in the document to look for your search terms, by clicking the left arrow next to Term.

35. ***Click the right arrow to the right of Term to continue to move through the* Hewlette *case.*** Eventually you will move to the next case.

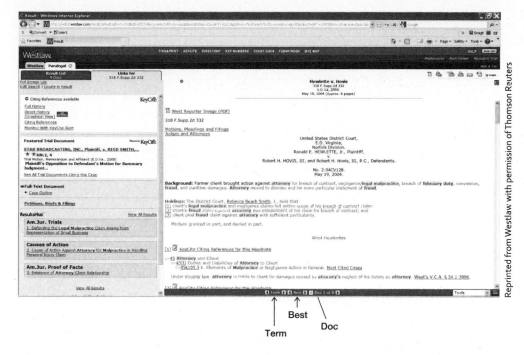

Best

Doc

Term

Reprinted from Westlaw with permission of Thomson Reuters

36. The Best feature allows you to go directly to what Westlaw estimates to be the most relevant part of the case in relation to your search terms. ***Click the left arrow next to Doc at the bottom of the screen*** to go back to the *Hewlette* case. The Doc arrows allow you to move forward and backward through the retrieved cases.

37. You should now be back at the beginning of the *Hewlette* case.

38. Notice that some of the text is in red. ***Scroll down through the case*** and notice that most (but not all) of the Headnotes are in red. The text in red is what Westlaw considers to the "best" part of the case (the part where the majority of your search terms are located).

39. ***Click the right arrow next to Best at the bottom of the screen.*** Westlaw should now have taken you to the best part of the next case.

40. ***Click the right arrow next to Doc at the bottom of the screen.*** You should now be at the next document of the search results. Using the left and right arrows next to Doc, you can move between the search results without returning to the list of results.

41. ***Click the Paralegal tab in the upper left of the screen.***

This concludes Lesson 3 of the Westlaw Hands-On Exercises. To exit Westlaw, ***click Sign Off on the toolbar,*** or stay in Westlaw and go to Lesson 4.

LESSON 4: TERMS AND CONNECTORS SEARCHING

In this lesson, you will learn how to search using Terms and Connectors, use the Thesaurus feature, print a list of cases, use the Locate in Result tool, and use WestClip. If you did not exit Westlaw after completing Lesson 3, go directly to Step 6 in the following instructions.

1. Start Windows.

2. Start your Internet browser. Type **www.westlaw.com** in the browser, and press the **[ENTER]** key.

3. Your screen should look similar to Westlaw Exhibit 1. At the Westlaw Password field, type your Westlaw ID and the Westlaw password supplied by your instructor.

HANDS-ON EXERCISES

4. In the Client ID field, type **Hands-On Exercise 4** (or whatever your instructor tells you to type).

5. *Click Sign On* to sign on to Westlaw.

6. You should now be at the Paralegal tab (see Westlaw Exhibit 3).

7. You will again look for federal court cases in which an attorney committed fraud by retaining settlement funds for a client in litigation and thereby breached his fiduciary duty to the client.

8. Under Search for a database: on the left side of the screen, type **DCT4** and then *click Go.* This is the database identifier for U.S. District Court Cases for the states in the Fourth Circuit.

9. *Click Terms & Connectors.*

10. *Click in the Search box,* type **attorney /p fraud /p malpractice,** and then *click Search Westlaw* (see Westlaw Exhibit 12). The "/p" indicates that the terms should be searched for within a paragraph.

WESTLAW EXHIBIT 12

11. Westlaw should return fewer than 50 cases, but this is still quite a lot, so you should refine your search query. Note that unlike a Natural Language search, there is no preset default number of search results; also, the search results are returned in chronological order (newest to oldest). By using "/s" (search within a sentence) and "/n" (where "n" limits the search within a specific number of words), you can limit the number of cases retrieved.

12. *Click Edit Search in the upper left of the screen just under the Paralegal tab.*

13. In the Search box, delete the current query and type **attorney /s fraud /s legal /3 malpractice /p "fiduciary duty."** Then *click Thesaurus* (which is just under **"Search Westlaw"**). You will use the Thesaurus feature to further refine your search.

14. You should now see a screen similar to Westlaw Exhibit 13. Notice that in the first column, Terms in Search:, the search term "attorney" is highlighted, and that in the second column, Related Terms:, there are synonyms for "attorney."

15. *In the Related Terms: column, scroll down, click "LAWYER," and then click the + (plus sign) next to Add.* Westlaw will then add "*LAWYER*" to the current

Reprinted from Westlaw with permission of Thomson Reuters

search query. There should now be a space between "attorney" and "*LAWYER.*" Westlaw interprets the space to mean OR (e.g., attorney OR lawyer).

16. *In the Terms in Search: column, click "MALPRACTICE." In the Related Terms: column, click "NEGLIGENCE." Next, click on the + (plus sign) next to Add.*

17. *Click OK just below the Terms in Search: column.*

18. The search should now read attorney LAWYER /s fraud /s legal /3 malpractice NEGLIGENCE /p "fiduciary duty" (see Westlaw Exhibit 14).

WESTLAW EXHIBIT 14

Reprinted from Westlaw with permission of Thomson Reuters

19. *Click Search Westlaw.*

20. Westlaw should return fewer than 15 cases, and one of the cases should be the *Hewlette v. Hovis* case.

21. You will now send the results to your printer. ***Click Quick Print in the upper right of the screen.*** The "Quick Print" window will then appear. After a few seconds, the "Print" window will appear. ***Select the printer you would like to print to and click Print.***

HANDS-ON EXERCISES

22. You will now learn how to use the Locate in Result feature. Because your case deals with a settlement, you would now like to search the cases you retrieved for "settlement" to further weed out the cases.

23. ***Click Locate in Result under the tabs at the top of the screen.***

24. Notice that the Search screen is now displayed, but this time the heading says **"Locate Search Terms"** (see Westlaw Exhibit 15).

WESTLAW EXHIBIT 15

25. In the "Locate" box, type **settlement** and then ***click Locate.***

26. The number of cases should now be reduced. Notice that the word **"settlement"** is now highlighted, because it was your search term. The *Hewlette v. Hovis* case should be one of the cases that remains.

27. ***Click Cancel Locate*** to return to the original cases that were retrieved.

28. You will now learn how to add a search to WestClip. WestClip is a feature that allows you to run a search in Westlaw automatically and periodically (on your preset schedule).

29. ***Click Add Search to WestClip.*** (It should be near the top left of the screen, just to the right of the number of documents retrieved.)

30. The WestClip: Create Entry screen should be displayed. Notice that your search appears in this screen. There are just a few things left for you to do. If you were going to actually save this search as a WestClip, you would need to enter a name for the search in the Name of clip: field. You would also want to edit the delivery settings.

31. ***Click Edit in the upper right of the screen to the right of Delivery Settings.***

32. The WestClip: Edit Delivery Settings screen should now be displayed (see Westlaw Exhibit 16).

33. ***Click the down arrow next to Daily in the Frequency: field.*** Notice that you can run the search at several different frequencies. Press the [ESC] key to close the options list.

34. ***Click the down arrow next to the Destination: field.*** Notice that you can have the result faxed to you, emailed to you, or made available to you when you sign on to Westlaw.

Reprinted from Westlaw with permission of Thomson Reuters

35. Press the [ESC] key to close the options list.

36. Notice that there are a number of other options you can set on the right side of the screen.

37. *Click Cancel in the lower left of the screen.*

38. You should now be back at the WestClip: Create Entry screen. *Click Cancel in the lower left of the screen.*

39. You should now be at the Alert Center Directory screen. This is where you can manage a number of different alerts that you can create in Westlaw.

40. *Click the Paralegal tab.*

This concludes Lesson 4 of the Westlaw Hands-On Exercises. To exit Westlaw, *click on Sign Off on the toolbar,* or stay in Westlaw and go to Lesson 5.

LESSON 5: KEYCITE

In this lesson, you will learn how to use Westlaw's research citation tool, KeyCite. You will also learn about depth-of-treatment stars, quotes, citing references, the Limit KeyCite Display tool, and the Research Trail feature. If you did not exit Westlaw after completing Lesson 4, go directly to Step 6 in the following instructions.

1. Start Windows.

2. Start your Internet browser. Type **www.westlaw.com** in the browser and press the [ENTER] key.

3. Your screen should look similar to Westlaw Exhibit 1. At the Westlaw Password field, type your Westlaw ID and the Westlaw password supplied by your instructor.

4. In the Client ID field, type **Hands-On Exercise 5** (or whatever your instructor tells you to type).

5. *Click Sign On* to sign on to Westlaw.

6. You should now be at the Westlaw Paralegal tab (see Westlaw Exhibit 3).

7. *Click KeyCite on the toolbar.* You will now use KeyCite to determine if the *Hewlette v. Hovis* case, which you found in an earlier exercise, is still good law, and you will locate other cases that have cited *Hewlette* in hopes of expanding your research.

WESTLAW EXHIBIT 17

8. The KeyCite screen should now be displayed (see Westlaw Exhibit 17). Take a few minutes and read the narrative in the body of the KeyCite screen. The narrative describes how KeyCite works and what each of the different KeyCite symbols means.

9. In the **KeyCite** this citation: field, type **318 F.Supp.2d 332** (see Westlaw Exhibit 17). This is the citation for the *Hewlette v. Hovis* case. **Click Go.**

10. Your screen should now look similar to Westlaw Exhibit 18. Notice that a green "C" is displayed. In KeyCite, a green "C" means that the case has been cited as a reference but there is no direct history or negative citing references. This means that the *Hewlette v. Hovis* case has, to date, not been overruled or reversed, and that other cases have not negatively referred to it, and that, at least to date, the case is good law in all respects.

11. You will now use KeyCite to find other cases that have cited the *Hewlette v. Hovis* case. This may assist in expanding your research to find other cases that will support your position. However, before you do this, it would be helpful to look at the Headnotes in the *Hewlette v. Hovis* case to know which Headnote

WESTLAW EXHIBIT 18

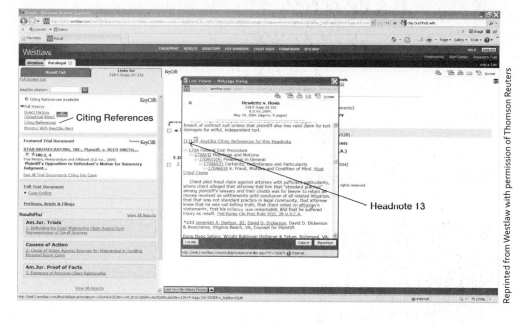

is on point for your purposes. That way, when you look at additional citing references, you can look only at the references that cite *Hewlette* for the issue you are dealing with.

12. ***Click the "1"*** (see Westlaw Exhibit 18); this is the decision itself, 318 F. Supp. 2d 332. Notice that a "Link Viewer" window opens in the middle of the screen, with the decision in it (see Westlaw Exhibit 19).

13. ***Scroll to Headnote 13*** (Federal Civil Procedure 170Ak636; see Westlaw Exhibit 19). This is the issue in the case that you are interested in. You now know that you are looking for any references to Headnote 13.

14. ***Click the Close icon*** (a red square with a white X) ***in the "Link Viewer" window.***

15. ***Click Citing References in the KeyCite section of the page*** (see Westlaw Exhibit 19).

16. Your screen should look similar to Westlaw Exhibit 20. (As of the time of this writing, there were 54 citing references; by the time you read this, there may be more, and they will be shown on your screen).

17. Notice in Westlaw Exhibit 20, just under Positive Cases (U.S.A.), that two stars are shown. These are depth-of-treatment stars. The more stars there are, the more references there are for your case. One star means that your case was merely cited with no discussion, whereas four stars means your case was considered and discussed extensively.

18. Find the seventh case listed in Westlaw Exhibit 20 (*VA Timberline, LLC v. Land Management Group, Inc.*) on your screen. Notice the two purple quotation marks toward the end of the line. This means that in *VA Timberline, LLC* opinion, the court quotes from the *Hewlette v. Hovis* case related to Headnote 4.

19. ***Click the number associated with the* VA Timberline, LLC v. Land Management Group *case (7).*** A "Link Viewer" window should now be displayed that shows where the court in the *VA Timberline* case quoted the *Hewlette* case related to Headnote 4 (see Westlaw Exhibit 21).

WESTLAW EXHIBIT 21

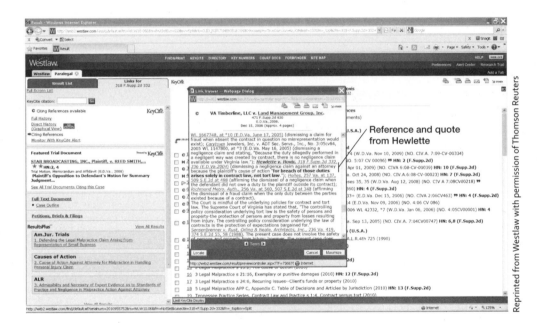

20. Notice in Westlaw Exhibit 21 that the discussion about the *Hewlette* case in the *VA Timberline* case is relatively short. That is why only two depth-of-treatment stars were shown.

21. ***Click the Close icon*** (a red square with a white X) ***in the "Link Viewer" window.***

22. You could continue to go down the list of Citing References in Westlaw Exhibit 20, reading and viewing additional cases related to your Headnote, but there is an easier way to do so if you are looking for a specific Headnote.

23. ***Click Limit KeyCite Display at the bottom of the screen*** (see Westlaw Exhibit 20).

24. The "KeyCite Limits" window should now be displayed (see Westlaw Exhibit 22). You will now tell Westlaw which cites you want to view. If you do not see a list of Headnotes, ***click the Headnotes link on the left side of the screen*** (see Westlaw Exhibit 22). ***Click the box next to [13] Fraud, mistaand condition of mind Key 636(3), then click Apply.***

25. Westlaw will respond by only showing you the citations related to Headnote 13. This is a great tool, particularly if you have an important case that has many, many cites and you want to focus on only one aspect of the case.

WESTLAW EXHIBIT 22

WESTLAW EXHIBIT 23

26. **_Click the Paralegal tab._**

27. Suppose that you didn't mean to click the Paralegal tab and that, for whatever reason, the Back button on your Internet browser didn't work, or you accidentally were kicked off or signed off of Westlaw by mistake. There is a great feature called "Research Trail" that can help you get back to where you were (see Westlaw Exhibit 23).

28. **_Click Research Trail in the upper right corner of the screen._** See Westlaw Exhibit 22. The Research Trail feature shows you where you have been. If you wanted to go back to the _VA Timberline_ case, for example, you could just click it in Research Trail.

29. **_Click the Paralegal tab._**

This concludes Lesson 5 of the Westlaw Hands-On Exercises. To exit Westlaw, **_click Sign Off on the toolbar,_** or stay in Westlaw and go to Lesson 6.

⊙ ADVANCED LESSON

LESSON 6: KEYSEARCH, HEADNOTES, AND KEY NUMBERS

In this lesson, you will learn how to use Westlaw's KeySearch tool, Headnotes and Key Numbers, and Most Recent and Most Cited Cases features. If you did not exit Westlaw after completing Lesson 5, go directly to Step 6 in the following instructions.

1. Start Windows.

2. Start your Internet browser. Type **www.westlaw.com** in the browser and press the [**ENTER**] key.

3. Your screen should look similar to Westlaw Exhibit 1. At the Westlaw Password field, enter your Westlaw ID and the Westlaw password supplied by your instructor.

4. In the Client ID field, type **Hands-On Exercise 6** (or whatever your instructor tells you to type).

5. *Click Sign On* to sign on to Westlaw.

6. You should now be at the Paralegal tab (see Westlaw Exhibit 3).

7. *Click Key Numbers on the toolbar, then click KeySearch* (see Westlaw Exhibit 24). KeySearch is a good place to begin your research because it provides you with a list of legal topics and subtopics; you do not have to know exactly what you are looking for.

WESTLAW EXHIBIT 24

Reprinted from Westlaw with permission of Thomson Reuters

8. *Click Attorneys under Professional Malpractice* (see Westlaw Exhibit 25).

9. *Click Breach of Fiduciary Duty.*

10. Your screen should now look similar to Westlaw Exhibit 26. *Select Cases With West Headnotes, click the down arrow next to All Federal Cases, then select Fourth Circuit Federal Cases. Click in the box next to Fourth Circuit Federal Cases so that it has a green check mark* (see Westlaw Exhibit 26).

11. In the Add Search terms (optional): field, type **Fraud** and then *click Search* (see Westlaw Exhibit 26).

12. Your screen should now look similar to Westlaw Exhibit 27. Notice in the upper left corner of the screen the search query that KeySearch built.

WESTLAW EXHIBIT 25

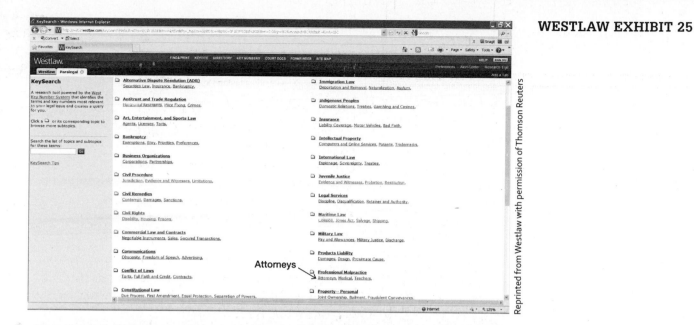

WESTLAW EXHIBIT 26

WESTLAW EXHIBIT 27

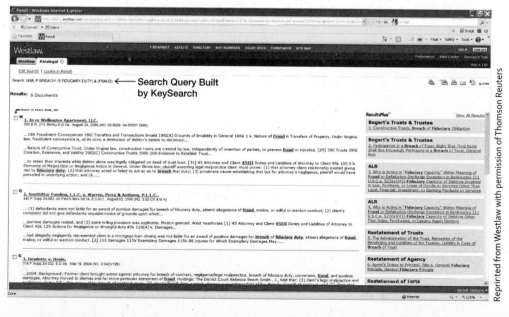

13. *Scroll down the page until you find the* **Hewlette v. Hovis** *case.* In just a few seconds using KeySearch, you were able to find the case you were looking for.

14. *Click the* **Hewlette v. Hovis** *case.* You are now going to find similar cases using the Westlaw Headnote and Key Number system.

15. *In the* **Hewlette v. Hovis** *case, scroll until you come to the first Headnote* (see Westlaw Exhibit 28). Notice in Westlaw Exhibit 28 that the most specific Key Number in Headnote 1 is 45k105.5. You are now going to search for cases that are similar to Headnote 1 using this Key Number.

WESTLAW EXHIBIT 28

16. Click Key Number 45k105.5 in Headnote 1.

17. The Custom Digest screen should now be displayed (see Westlaw Exhibit 29). Under Your digest options:, leave the order as Most Recent Cases. *In the "Your default state jurisdiction is:" section, click Federal and leave All selected.*

18. *Click Search in the bottom left of the screen.* It may take up to a minute for Westlaw to retrieve all the cases.

WESTLAW EXHIBIT 29

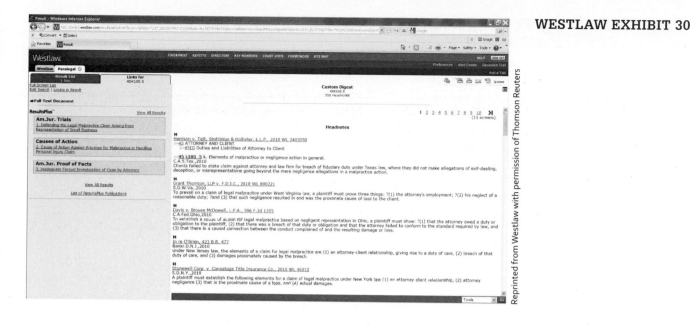

Reprinted from Westlaw with permission of Thomson Reuters

HANDS-ON EXERCISES

19. Your screen should look similar to Westlaw Exhibit 30, but your cases will probably be different. **Scroll down through the list** and notice that you have quite a number of Headnotes from which to expand your research.

20. Remember that the order in which you sorted the cases and Headnotes put the most recent items first. By reading the Headnotes, you can get a good understanding of the elements of a claim for legal malpractice.

21. You will next find the cases and Headnotes that are most cited (the ones that other, similar cases tend to quote or talk about). This can give you a good idea as to which cases are the most important.

22. **Click your browser's Back button twice.** You should now be back at the *Hewlette v. Hovis* case (see Westlaw Exhibit 28). If not, click Research Trail in the upper right of the screen, then click on the *Hewlette v. Hovis* case.

23. **Scroll to the first Headnote again and click Most Cited Cases at the end of Key Number 45k105.5** (see Westlaw Exhibit 28).

24. Notice that this is the same screen as in Westlaw Exhibit 29, except that now Most Cited Cases is selected. **Click Federal and leave All selected.**

25. **Click Search in the lower left of the screen.**

26. Your screen should look similar to (but will probably not include the same cases as) Westlaw Exhibit 30.

27. **Scroll down the first 10 cases or so on your list.** Pay particular attention to the KeyCite colors of the flags. You will want to pay specific attention to red and yellow flags, which point to the negative issues in the cases, so you can evaluate how they might apply to your case. This will help you forecast what your opposing counsel may argue.

28. Once you have found a case on point, always look at the Headnote and Key Numbers, as they can provide you with a wealth of additional information.

29. **Click the Paralegal tab.**

This concludes the Westlaw Hands-On Exercises. To exit Westlaw, **click Sign Off on the toolbar.**

HANDS-ON EXERCISES

LEXISNEXIS COMPUTER-ASSISTED LEGAL RESEARCH

Number	Lesson Title	Concepts Covered
BASIC LESSONS		
Lesson 1	Introduction to LexisNexis	Signing on; introduction to the LexisNexis interface; finding databases; working with LexisNexis tabs
Lesson 2	Get by Citation, Get by Party Name, and Exploring Retrieved Cases	Get by Citation, Get by Party Name, Cite, KWIC, Full, reporter page numbers, distribution options, and a *Shepard's* overview
INTERMEDIATE LESSONS		
Lesson 3	Natural Language Search, Editing Searches, Changing Databases, Using Doc and Term Features	Natural Language searching; editing using date restriction; requiring and excluding terms; using the Doc and Term features
Lesson 4	Terms and Connectors Search	Terms and connectors searching; using the Suggest Terms for My Search feature; printing a list of retrieved cases
ADVANCED LESSON		
Lesson 5	*Shepard's* Citations	Shepardizing; Table of Authorities; Auto-Cite; *Shepard's* Alert

GETTING STARTED

Introduction

Throughout these lessons and exercises, information you need to type into the software will be designated in several different ways:

- Keys to be pressed on the keyboard are designated in brackets, in all caps, and in bold (e.g., press the **[ENTER]** key).
- Movements with the mouse pointer are designated in bold and italics (e.g., ***point to File and click***).
- Words or letters that should be typed are designated in bold (e.g., type **Training Program**).
- Information that is or should be displayed on your computer screen is shown in bold, with quotation marks (e.g., **"Press ENTER to continue."**).
- Specific menu items and commands are designated with an initial capital letter (e.g., click Open).

▶ BASIC LESSONS

LESSON 1: INTRODUCTION TO LEXISNEXIS

This lesson introduces you to LexisNexis. You will learn how to sign on to LexisNexis, take a tour of LexisNexis and the LexisNexis interface, and learn how to find databases and work with LexisNexis tabs. For an overview of the features in LexisNexis, read the LexisNexis section in Chapter 8 of the text.

1. Start Windows.
2. Start your Internet browser. Type **www.lexis.com** in the browser and press the **[ENTER] key.**

3. At the ID field, type the Lexis ID supplied by your instructor.

4. At the Password field, type the Lexis password supplied by your instructor.

5. *Click Sign In* to sign on to LexisNexis.

6. Your screen should now look similar to LexisNexis Exhibit 1 (see LexisNexis Exhibit 1). If your screen does not look like LexisNexis Exhibit 1, *click the Search tab.* LexisNexis is highly customizable, so it is possible that your screens will look different from the screens in the exhibits.

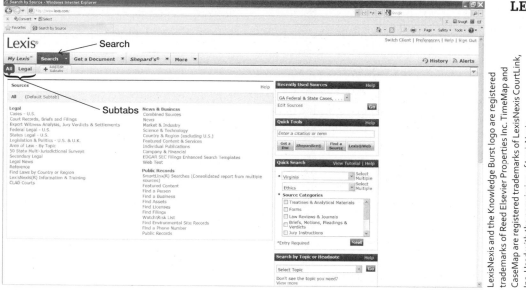

LEXISNEXIS EXHIBIT 1

LexisNexis and the Knowledge Burst logo are registered trademarks of Reed Elsevier Properties Inc. TimeMap and CaseMap are registered trademarks of LexisNexis CourtLink, Inc. Used with the permission of LexisNexis.

7. You will now take a brief tour of LexisNexis. The Search tab (second tab from the left) should be selected. (It should have a red background and **"Search"** should be in white letters; see LexisNexis Exhibit 1).

8. Under the **Search tab**, a number of subtabs should be displayed. The subtabs should, at a minimum, include All and Legal. (See LexisNexis Exhibit 1.)

9. If the Legal subtab is not already selected, *point and click on it.* (See LexisNexis Exhibit 2.)

LEXISNEXIS EXHIBIT 2

LexisNexis and the Knowledge Burst logo are registered trademarks of Reed Elsevier Properties Inc. TimeMap and CaseMap are registered trademarks of LexisNexis CourtLink, Inc. Used with the permission of LexisNexis.

10. The Legal subtab includes sections such as "Cases – U.S." and "Federal Legal – U.S." The Legal subtab is a good place to start your legal research, because you can access many commonly used databases from this screen.

11. *Scroll down and click States Legal – U.S. on the left side of the page.* A list of states should now be displayed.

12. *Click California.* You should now see a list of databases and resources for California. If you wanted to search in one of these databases, you could click the database name and a search window would open where you could enter your search. If you wanted to search multiple databases at the same time, you could click in the check box next to each database and then select Combine sources. A search window would then open that would allow you to search multiple databases at the same time.

13. *Click the Legal subtab* or *click your browser's Back button twice.* You should be back at the Legal subtab (see LexisNexis Exhibit 2).

14. Notice that on the right side of the screen you can access different areas of the law by topic (e.g., "Banking & Financial Services," "Bankruptcy," and "Environment"). If you scroll down the page, you can access briefs, motions, pleadings, verdicts, other secondary legal resources, legal news, and other resources.

15. Press the **[HOME]** key to go back to the top of the page.

16. You can customize the subtabs by adding your own jurisdiction or legal topics that you use a lot.

17. *Click Add/Edit Subtabs,* which is to the right of the Legal subtab (see LexisNexis Exhibit 2).

18. If you scroll down, you will see a list of legal specialty areas and a list of states. You can add subtabs by clicking a selection and then clicking Add. Most users will want to make a tab for their state.

19. Notice that at the top of the screen, under the heading "General," are four subtabs. *Make sure that all four* (Legal, News & Business, Public Records, and Find A Source) *are checked; then click Next.*

20. You should now be on the Preferences screen. Under "Your current subtabs," *click Legal, then click Set as Default, then click Set.*

21. You should now be back at the Legal subtab, but notice that you now have the additional subtabs you selected.

22. *Click the News & Business subtab.*

23. Notice that on the left side of the screen, under Combined Sources, LexisNexis gives you a wide variety of general and legal news databases to search. Also notice that on the right side of the screen, under Individual Publications and Company & Financial, LexisNexis has a number of resources for finding company and financial information.

24. *Click the Source Description icon for News, All (English, Full Text).* (It looks like a lower-case "i" in a square and appears at the end of each source category name. *Note:* If you hover your cursor over an icon for a second, the name of the icon will be displayed.

25. The "Source Information" window should now be displayed. Scroll down through the list using your mouse or the cursor keys on the keyboard. Note all of the publications covered in this database.

26. *Click the Close icon* (a red square with a white X) *in the "Source Information" window.*

27. You can use the Source Description icon (a lower-case "i" in a square) throughout LexisNexis to discover the scope of a database.

28. ***Click the Public Records subtab.*** Notice that a number of public records are available for searching in LexisNexis.

29. ***Click the Find A Source subtab.*** In the Find A Source subtab, you can browse an alphabetical list for a database. Alternatively, you can search for the name of a database. (See LexisNexis Exhibit 3.)

LEXISNEXIS EXHIBIT 3

30. In the Find A Source Option 1: field, type **Harvard Law Review** and then ***click Find*** (see LexisNexis Exhibit 3). A list of resources with "Harvard" in the title, including the *Harvard Law Review,* is displayed. You can access the *Harvard Law Review* database simply by clicking it, but for this exercise it is not necessary.

31. You will now learn about the Get a Document tab. ***Click the Get a Document tab,*** which is at the top of the screen next to the Search tab. (See LexisNexis Exhibit 4.) Notice that there are three subtabs: By Citation, By Party Name, and By Docket Number. You could also access these resources by clicking the drop-down menu to the right of the Get a Document tab.

LEXISNEXIS EXHIBIT 4

HANDS-ON EXERCISES

32. **Click the By Citation subtab.** Using this subtab, you can go directly to a case, statute, or other document by entering its cite.

33. **Click the By Party Name subtab.** Using this subtab, you can retrieve a case by entering a party name.

34. **Click the By Docket Number subtab.** Using this subtab, you can retrieve a case by entering its docket number.

35. You will now learn about the *Shepard's* Citations tab. **Click the Shepard's tab.** (See LexisNexis Exhibit 5.) Notice that there are four subtabs: *Shepard's*, Table of Authorities, Auto-Cite, and LEXCITE. You could also access these resources by clicking the drop-down menu to the right of the *Shepard's* tab.

LEXISNEXIS EXHIBIT 5

36. **Click the Shepard's subtab** (see LexisNexis Exhibit 5). This is where you can enter a cite and get a comprehensive report of the cases, statutes, secondary sources, and annotations that have cited the authority you entered.

37. **Click the Table of Authorities subtab** (see LexisNexis Exhibit 5). Table of Authorities provides an at-a-glance analysis of the cited references within your case and links to in-depth analysis.

38. **Click the Auto-Cite subtab.** Auto-Cite verifies the accuracy of your research and gives you a history of the opinion you are searching on, including cases that refer negatively to your case. Auto-Cite can quickly tell you whether your case or statute is still good law.

39. **Click the LEXCITE subtab.** LEXCITE allows you to find both reported and unreported cases.

40. **Click on the More tab.**

41. This tab provides easy access to other LexisNexis products and services, such as Total Litigator, Transactional Advisor, and Counsel Selector. See LexisNexis Exhibit 6. You could also access these resources by clicking the drop-down menu to the right of the More tab.

LEXISNEXIS EXHIBIT 6

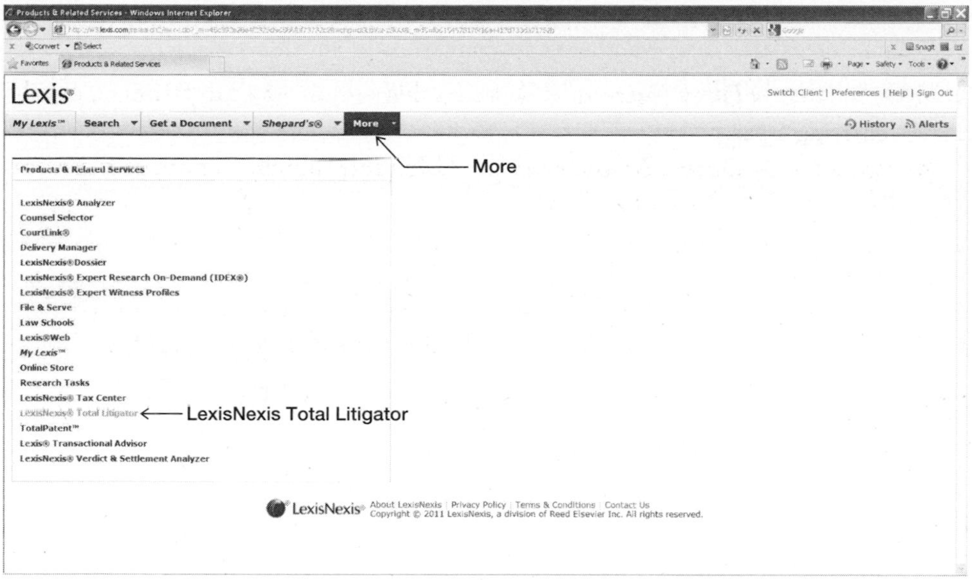

42. You will now learn about the Total Litigator. ***Click LexisNexis Total Litigator.*** The Total Litigator gathers resources for varying stages of litigation (Early Case Assessment; Draft, File & Serve; Discovery; Research; Gather Intel; and Trial Prep.). See LexisNexis Exhibit 7.

LEXISNEXIS EXHIBIT 7

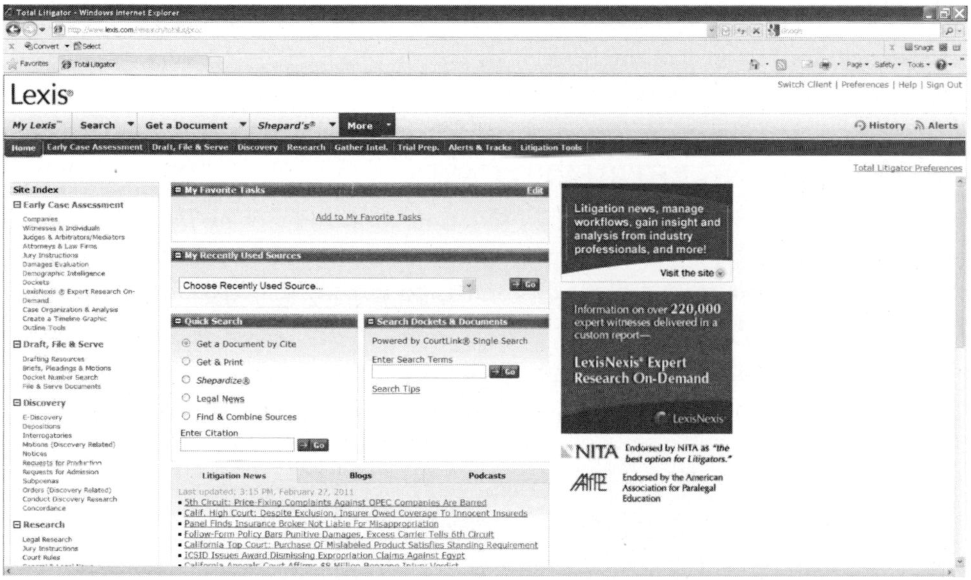

43. ***Click the More tab.***

44. You will now learn about the Transactional Advisor. ***Click Lexis Transactional Advisor.*** The Transactional Advisor provides access to a collection of research links and tools, specifically designed forms, and the latest news on a variety of different areas of the law, such as antitrust, bankruptcy, and tax.

45. You will now learn about the Counsel Selector. ***Click the More tab. Click Counsel Selector.*** This takes you to Martindale.com, a site that facilitates the search for a lawyer or law firm. Attorneys use this site to find attorneys who can assist with a case, whether as co-counsel or in another jurisdiction. See LexisNexis Exhibit 8.

LEXISNEXIS EXHIBIT 8

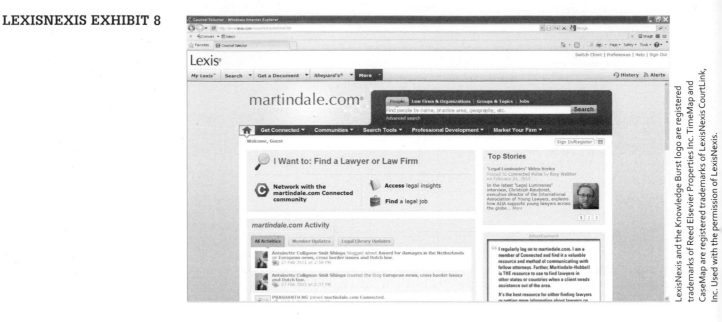

This concludes Lesson 1 of the LexisNexis Hands-On Exercises. To exit LexisNexis, *click Sign Out on the toolbar,* or stay in LexisNexis and go to Lesson 2.

LESSON 2: GET BY CITATION, GET BY PARTY NAME, AND EXPLORING RETRIEVED CASES

In this lesson you will use the Get by Citation tool, the Get by Party Name feature, Cite, KWIC, Full, reporter page numbers, and distribution options. If you did not exit LexisNexis after completing Lesson 1, go directly to Step 6 in the following instructions.

1. Start Windows.
2. Start your Internet browser. Type **www.lexis.com** in the browser and press the **[ENTER]** key.
3. At the ID field, type the Lexis ID supplied by your instructor.
4. At the Password field, enter the Lexis password supplied by your instructor.
5. *Click Sign In* to sign on to LexisNexis.
6. Your screen should now look similar to LexisNexis Exhibit 1. If your screen does not look like LexisNexis Exhibit 1, *click the Search tab* (see LexisNexis Exhibit 1). LexisNexis is highly customizable, so it is possible that your screens will look different from the screens in the exhibits.
7. *Click the Get a Document tab.* Notice that there are three subtabs: By Citation, By Party Name, and By Docket Number. Make sure that the by Citation subtab is selected.
8. In the Get by Citation field, type **189 S.W.3d 777;** *then click Get* (see LexisNexis Exhibit 9).

LexisNexis and the Knowledge Burst logo are registered trademarks of Reed Elsevier Properties Inc. TimeMap and CaseMap are registered trademarks of LexisNexis CourtLink, Inc. Used with the permission of LexisNexis.

9. The case of *In re Karen Mays-Hooper* should now be displayed (see LexisNexis Exhibit 10). If you know the citation of a case, you can enter it in the Get by Citation feature and LexisNexis will immediately retrieve it without your having to indicate a database or enter a search query.

LexisNexis and the Knowledge Burst logo are registered trademarks of Reed Elsevier Properties Inc. TimeMap and CaseMap are registered trademarks of LexisNexis CourtLink, Inc. Used with the permission of LexisNexis.

Page: Select a Reporter

10. You will now learn how to find a case by entering the name of a party.
11. *Click the Get a Document tab.*
12. *Click the By Party Name subtab* (see LexisNexis Exhibit 11).
13. The screen in LexisNexis Exhibit 11 should now be displayed.
14. In the first Party name field, type **Karen Mays-Hooper.**
15. *Click in the circle to the left of State Courts.*

HANDS-ON EXERCISES

LEXISNEXIS EXHIBIT 11

16. *Click the down arrow next to the right of State Courts and select Texas.*

17. *Click Search.*

18. A summary of two cases, each with the title *In re Mays-Hooper*, should now be displayed (see LexisNexis Exhibit 12).

LEXISNEXIS EXHIBIT 12

19. Notice the text **"View: Cite | KWIC | Full | Custom"** in the upper left of the screen (Cite is currently selected). These are the different options for displaying cases in LexisNexis.

20. *Click KWIC.* Notice that only the Case Summary of the first case is shown. To go to the next case, you would need to select **"2 >"** in the Doc section of the Navigation Frame at the bottom of the screen.

21. *Click Cite.* Notice that there are symbols just to the left of the case names. Next to each case is a yellow triangle. This is a *Shepard's Citations* symbol. Scroll to

the bottom of the page, where there is a legend explaining what the symbols mean.

22. ***Click the first case,*** **In re Mays-Hooper,** *No. 04–1040,* ***SUPREME COURT OF TEXAS, 189 S.W.3d 777.***

23. The *In re Mays-Hooper* case should now be displayed (see LexisNexis Exhibit 10).

24. In the *In re Mays-Hooper* case, just under the title of the case, its prior history and a Case Summary appear. The Case Summary is written by LexisNexis research attorneys. This is a value-added service offered by LexisNexis, which many other CALR services do not provide.

25. Read the Case Summary.

26. Notice that after the Core Terms section in the Case Summary are LexisNexis Headnotes. Headnote 1 (*HN1*) states: "So long as a parent adequately cares for his or her children (i.e., is fit), there will normally be no reason for the state to inject itself into the private realm of the family." The Headnotes, which are also written by research attorneys, are another value-added service offered by LexisNexis that many other CALR services do not provide. Headnotes are discussed in more detail in later exercises.

27. Skim the case by ***scrolling down through it using the vertical scroll bar.***

28. When you are finished, press the **[HOME]** key to go back to the beginning of the case.

29. You will next learn how to use the Page command. The Page command in the Navigation Frame allows you to cite to a specific page of the hard-copy (print edition) reporter.

30. ***Click the down arrow next to Page: Select a Reporter in the Navigation frame.*** See LexisNexis Exhibit 10.

31. ***Click 189 S.W.3d 777,*.***

32. Scroll down; just under the listing of the judge and next to Opinion is the term "[*777]." This means that everything after this is on page 777 of the hard-copy reporter, so if you need to cite to the exact page you can do so.

33. Scroll down through the case to the paragraph that starts with "The Supreme Court found the trial court's order unconstitutional . . ." and notice that on the third line of the paragraph the term "[*778]" appears in red. This is where page 778 of the hard-copy report starts.

34. Notice the icons for the options Fast Print, Print, Download, Email, Fax, and View in a printer-friendly format in the upper right of the screen (see LexisNexis Exhibit 10). These are the distribution options, which define the things you can do with the case.

35. ***Click Download.*** The "Deliver Documents—Download" window is displayed.

36. ***Click the down arrow next to Format: Word (DOC)*** and notice that in addition to saving the file in Microsoft Word format, you can save the case to WordPerfect, text-only, Adobe (PDF), or a generic format.

37. ***Click the Close icon*** (a red square with a white X in it) ***in the "Deliver Documents—Download" window.***

38. Press the **[HOME]** key on the keyboard.

39. ***Click Shepardize just under the line "1 of 1" at the top middle of the screen*** (see LexisNexis Exhibit 10). A *Shepard's* Summary for the case is now displayed (see LexisNexis Exhibit 13).

40. ***Click the Search tab in the upper left corner of the screen.***

HANDS-ON EXERCISES

LEXISNEXIS EXHIBIT 13

This concludes Lesson 2 of the LexisNexis Hands-On Exercises. To exit LexisNexis, *click Sign Out on the toolbar,* or stay in LexisNexis and go to Lesson 3.

▶ INTERMEDIATE LESSONS

LESSON 3: NATURAL LANGUAGE SEARCH, EDITING SEARCHES, CHANGING DATABASES, USING DOC AND TERM FEATURES

In this lesson you will learn how to select a database, run a Natural Language search, edit a search, change to a different database, use the Date Restriction feature when searching, use the Require/Exclude Terms feature, and use the Doc and Term features.

If you did not exit LexisNexis after completing Lesson 2, go directly to Step 6 in the following instructions.

1. Start Windows.

2. Start your Internet browser. Type **www.lexis.com** in the browser and press the **[ENTER]** key.

3. At the ID field, type the Lexis ID supplied by your instructor.

4. At the Password field, enter the Lexis password supplied by your instructor.

5. *Click Sign In* to sign on to LexisNexis.

6. Your screen should now look similar to LexisNexis Exhibit 1. If your screen does not look like LexisNexis Exhibit 1, *click on the Search tab* (see LexisNexis Exhibit 1). LexisNexis is highly customizable, so it is possible that your screens will look different from the screens in the exhibits.

7. You will now look for a case in federal court in which an attorney committed fraud by retaining settlement funds of a client in litigation and breached his fiduciary duty to the client.

8. *Click Federal Court Cases, Combined;* this is under the Cases – U.S. section (see LexisNexis Exhibit 2).

9. The LexisNexis search screen (Enter Search Terms) should now be displayed (see LexisNexis Exhibit 14).

10. **Click Natural Language** (see LexisNexis Exhibit 14). You will now type a plain-English search request into the "Federal Court Cases, Combined" database using LexisNexis's Natural Language feature.

11. In the search box, type **attorney fraud settlement**; *then click Search* (see LexisNexis Exhibit 14).

12. Depending on how LexisNexis was set up on your computer, your search will most likely return 20 or more cases. In LexisNexis Exhibit 15, 100 cases were retrieved. This is too many cases to look through.

13. There are two main problems with the search as currently constructed. First, you are searching in an enormous database; second, you need to use more search terms to reduce the number of cases retrieved.

14. **Click Edit Search,** just above the first case that is listed (see LexisNexis Exhibit 15). You should be taken back to the LexisNexis Search screen. You will now look at the scope of the database to see exactly what database you are searching in.

HANDS-ON EXERCISES

15. ***Click the Source Description symbol.*** (It looks like a white square with a lower-case "i" in the middle of it and is just to the left of "Federal Court Cases, Combined," just above the Search field.)

16. Notice the information about the database that is listed, including file name, coverage, and so on.

17. Scroll down to see just how large the database is. This database happens to be extremely large, and contains tens of thousands of cases. When you search in a large database like this, you need more search terms, not less.

18. ***Click the Close icon*** (a red square with a white X) ***in the "Source Information" window.***

19. It can sometimes be more efficient to search in a smaller database than a larger one. You will now learn how to change your database.

20. ***Click Cases – U.S.,*** which is just to the left of Federal Court Cases, Combined.

21. ***Click All Courts – By Circuit on the right side of the screen.***

22. ***Click on 4th Circuit – Federal & State Cases, Combined.*** You will now be searching state and federal cases in the Fourth Circuit only. This is a narrower database than "All Federal Cases."

23. Even with a smaller database, this search would retrieve a large number of cases. You need to refine your search and include additional search terms.

24. In the search box, in addition to "attorney fraud settlement," type the following: **"legal malpractice" "fiduciary duty" conversion** (see LexisNexis Exhibit 16). The quotation marks around "legal malpractice" and "fiduciary duty" force LexisNexis to search for these exact phrases.

LEXISNEXIS EXHIBIT 16

25. Another way to limit the number of cases retrieved is to restrict the dates of the cases retrieved. In the Restrict by Date section at the bottom of the screen, ***click in the From field*** and type **1/1/2003.**

26. Another way to limit the number of cases retrieved is to require some or all of the search terms to appear in the case(s). In the Restrict using Mandatory Terms section, ***click in the Anywhere in retrieved documents: field*** and type **attorney settlement "legal malpractice" "fiduciary duty."**

27. Double-check that there are no misspellings in your search query.

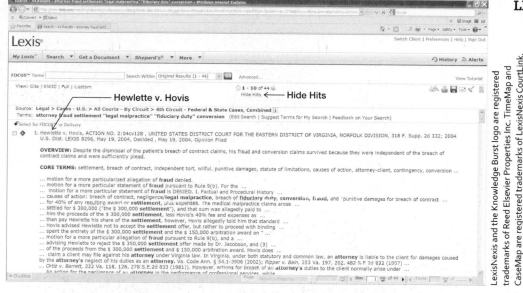

LexisNexis and the Knowledge Burst logo are registered trademarks of Reed Elsevier Properties Inc. TimeMap and CaseMap are registered trademarks of LexisNexis CourtLink, Inc. Used with the permission of LexisNexis.

28. ***Click Search. Click Show Hits in the top middle of the screen.*** Your screen should now look similar to LexisNexis Exhibit 17.

29. LexisNexis should return a much smaller number of cases. One of the cases that should have been retrieved is *Hewlette v. Hovis,* 318 F. Supp. 2d 332 (E.D. Va., May 19, 2004).

30. Scroll down through the cases and notice that all of the search terms are highlighted in these cases (see LexisNexis Exhibit 17). If you have many cases to look through, this level of detail may or may not be helpful. LexisNexis refers to showing the search terms like this as showing the "hits." You will now use the Hide Hits feature to make the search terms disappear so that you see only the Overview and Core Terms sections of the cases.

31. Press the **[HOME]** key to go back to the beginning of the cases.

32. ***Click Hide Hits in the top middle of the screen.*** Notice that now all of the hits have disappeared; they have been replaced with the Overview and Core Terms of the first case.

33. ***Click the* Hewlette v. Hovis *case.***

34. The *Hewlette v. Hovis* case should now be displayed (see LexisNexis Exhibit 18).

35. Scroll down and notice that the search terms are highlighted in the Case Summary.

36. ***Click the right arrow to the right of Term at the bottom of the screen.*** Each time you click the right arrow next to "Term," LexisNexis takes you to the next search term in your case (see LexisNexis Exhibit 18). You could look backward for your search terms in the document by clicking the left (previous) arrow next to "Term."

37. ***Click the right arrow to the right of Term at the bottom of the screen in the Navigation Frame*** to continue to move through the *Hewlette* case.

38. ***Click the right arrow next to Doc to go to the next case.*** The Doc arrows allow you to move forward and backward through the retrieved cases.

39. ***Click the left arrow next to Doc*** to go back to the *Hewlette* case.

40. ***Click the Search tab in the upper left of the screen.***

This concludes Lesson 3 of the LexisNexis Hands-On Exercises. To exit LexisNexis, ***click Sign Out on the toolbar,*** or stay in LexisNexis and go to Lesson 4.

HANDS-ON EXERCISES

LEXISNEXIS EXHIBIT 18

LESSON 4: TERMS AND CONNECTORS SEARCH

In this lesson you will learn how to search using Terms and Connectors, use the Suggest Terms for My Search feature, and print a list of cases. If you did not exit LexisNexis after completing Lesson 3, go directly to Step 6 in the following instructions.

1. Start Windows.
2. Start your Internet browser. Type **www.lexis.com** in the browser and press the **[ENTER]** key.
3. At the ID field, type the Lexis ID supplied by your instructor.
4. At the Password field, enter the Lexis password supplied by your instructor.
5. *Click Sign In* to sign on to LexisNexis.
6. Your screen should now look similar to LexisNexis Exhibit 1. If your screen does not look like LexisNexis Exhibit 1, *click the Search tab* (see LexisNexis Exhibit 1). LexisNexis is highly customizable, so it is possible that your screens will look different from the screens in the exhibits.
7. You will again look for federal court cases in which an attorney committed fraud by retaining settlement funds for a client in litigation and breached his fiduciary duty to the client. This time, however, you will search using Terms and Connectors instead of Natural Language, and you will use the Quick Start option. The Quick Start option is especially useful when you have a clear idea of your search parameters. The Quick Search option is available under the *My Lexis* tab. See LexisNexis Exhibit 19.
8. *Click the My Lexis tab.* See LexisNexis Exhibit 19.
9. In the Quick Search area, *click the radio button next to Terms and Connectors.* In the search box, type **attorney /p fraud /p malpractice.** See LexisNexis Exhibit 19.
10. Next to Select Sources By:, *click the radio button next to Source Type.*
11. *Click the drop-down menu to the right of Jurisdiction and select Virginia.*
12. *Click the drop-down menu to the right of Practice Area and select Ethics.*
13. *Click the box next to Cases from the choices in Source Categories, then click Next Step. In the "Quick Search – Select Sources" window, click the box next to VA Federal & State Cases, Combined; then click Search* (see LexisNexis Exhibit 20).

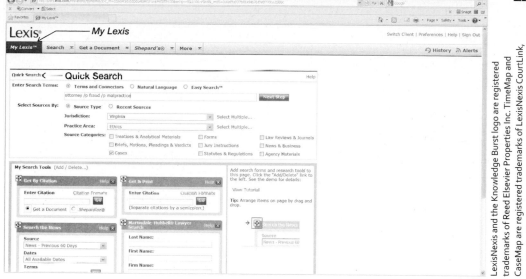

14. LexisNexis should return about 50 cases. Again, this is too many cases to look through. By using "/s" (within a sentence) and adding search terms, you can limit the number of cases retrieved.

15. *Click Edit Search,* just above the first case.

16. In the search box, modify the query to read **attorney OR lawyer /s fraud /p malpractice /p "fiduciary duty" /p conversion.** *Then click Suggest terms for my search* (just to the left of the Search button; see LexisNexis Exhibit 21). You will use this feature to search for synonyms to refine your search.

17. Notice that a number of synonyms are now listed under Suggested Words and Concepts for Entered Terms.

18. *Click in the Search field and delete* "**/p fiduciary duty.**"

19. *Click* "**breach of fiduciary duty**" *under Suggested Words and Concepts for Entered Terms.* Add **/p** in front of "**breach of fiduciary duty.**"

LEXISNEXIS EXHIBIT 21

20. Your Terms and Connectors search should now read **attorney OR lawyer /s fraud /p malpractice /p conversion /p "breach of fiduciary duty"** (see LexisNexis Exhibit 21).

21. *Click Search.*

22. LexisNexis should return fewer than 15 cases, and one of the cases should be *Hewlette v. Hovis.*

23. You will now send the results to your printer. *Click Print* in the upper right corner of the screen.

24. The "Deliver Documents – Print" window should now be displayed. *Select the printer you would like to print to, then click Print.*

25. Scroll down and *click the* **Hewlette v. Hovis** *case.* Notice that this is the same case that was retrieved using the Natural Language search in Hands-On Exercise Lesson 3.

26. Scroll down just below the Case Summary and notice the heading "LEXISNEXIS HEADNOTES." If you do not see the Headnote, *click Show Headnotes,* just to the right of "LEXISNEXIS HEADNOTES."

27. You should see 11 Headnotes for the *Hewlette* case.

28. Look at Headnote 2 ("In Virginia, under both statutory and common law, an attorney is liable to the client for damages caused by the attorney's neglect of his duties as an attorney"; see LexisNexis Exhibit 22).

29. Suppose that this was the issue you were researching. To expand your research, you could click the More Like This Headnote option following the Headnote itself.

30. The More Like This Headnote screen is displayed.

31. *Click the radio button next to Combined Federal Courts: All Federal Courts.*

32. *Click Search* at the bottom of the screen.

33. Notice that additional cases with similar Headnotes are retrieved. Headnotes are a quick and convenient way to expand your research.

34. *Click your browser's Back button twice.* You should now be back to the screen shown in LexisNexis Exhibit 22.

LexisNexis and the Knowledge Burst logo are registered trademarks of Reed Elsevier Properties Inc. TimeMap and CaseMap are registered trademarks of LexisNexis CourtLink, Inc. Used with the permission of LexisNexis.

LEXISNEXIS EXHIBIT 22

HANDS-ON EXERCISES

35. *Click on* **Shepardize:** *Restrict By Headnote at the end of* HN2 (see LexisNexis Exhibit 22). This feature shows cases that have cited *Hewlette* and that have the same Headnote.

This concludes Lesson 4 of the LexisNexis Hands-On Exercises. To exit LexisNexis, *click Sign Out on the toolbar,* or stay in LexisNexis and go to Lesson 5.

▶ ADVANCED LESSON

LESSON 5: *SHEPARD'S CITATIONS*

In this lesson, you will learn how to Shepardize a case, and use the Table of Authorities, Auto-Cite, and *Shepard's* Alert features. If you did not exit LexisNexis after completing Lesson 4, go directly to Step 6 in the following instructions.

1. Start Windows.
2. Start your Internet browser. Type **www.lexis.com** in the browser and press the **[ENTER]** key.
3. At the ID field, type the Lexis ID supplied by your instructor.
4. At the Password field, type the Lexis password supplied by your instructor.
5. *Click Sign In* to sign on to LexisNexis.
6. Your screen should now look similar to LexisNexis Exhibit 1. If your screen does not look like LexisNexis Exhibit 1, *click the Search tab* (see LexisNexis Exhibit 1). LexisNexis is highly customizable, so it is possible that your screens will look different from the screens in the exhibits.
7. *Click the Shepard's tab* at the top of the screen.
8. *Click the Shepard's subtab* (see LexisNexis Exhibit 23). *Click the option Shepard's for Research* (see LexisNexis Exhibit 23). The *Hewlette v. Hovis* case, 318 F. Supp. 2d 332, should already be entered, but if it is not, type **318 F. Supp. 2d 332.**
9. *Click Check.*

LEXISNEXIS EXHIBIT 23

10. A screen similar to LexisNexis Exhibit 24 should be displayed. Notice in LexisNexis Exhibit 24 that *Shepard's* shows the blue diamond with a white "+" (plus sign) symbol for the *Hewlette v. Hovis* case.

11. Scroll down and notice that this symbol means that the *Hewlette* case has had positive treatment.

12. Also in LexisNexis Exhibit 24, notice that 12 other cases have cited the *Hewlette* case.

13. **Click the Shepard's tab** at the top of the page.

14. **Click the Table of Authorities subtab.**

15. The *Hewlette v. Hovis* case, 318 F. Supp. 2d 332, should already be entered, but if it is not, type **318 F. Supp. 2d 332.**

16. **Click Check.**

LEXISNEXIS EXHIBIT 24

17. The Table of Authorities feature allows you to see a summary of all of the law cited by your case, sorted by jurisdiction.

18. **Click your browser's Back button.**

19. **Click the Auto-Cite subtab.**

20. The *Hewlette v. Hovis* case, 318 F. Supp. 2d 332, should already be entered, but if it is not, type **318 F. Supp. 2d 332.**

21. **Click Check.**

22. Auto-Cite gives you the procedural history of your case, the full case name, and other information. For example, for the *Hewlette* case, you can see its procedural history, including whether it was appealed, in addition to other information.

23. **Click the Shepard's tab, then click the Shepard's subtab.**

24. The *Hewlette v. Hovis* case, 318 F. Supp. 2d 332, should already be entered, but if it is not, type **318 F. Supp. 2d 332.**

25. Notice that one of the options just to the left of Check is Set Up *Shepard's* Alert (see LexisNexis Exhibit 23).

26. **Click Set Up Shepard's Alert** (see LexisNexis Exhibit 23).

27. At the Create a New *Shepard's* Alert screen, **click Set Up.**

28. You should now see the Set Up *Shepard's* Alert screen.

29. This feature allows you to monitor changes in cases as they are appealed and work their way through the court system. You can automatically run a *Shepard's* Alert at stated frequencies, such as weekly or monthly, and have the changes emailed to you or made available to you online.

30. **Click Cancel.**

31. **Click the Search tab.**

This concludes the LexisNexis Hands-On Exercises. To exit LexisNexis, **click Sign Out on the toolbar.**

HANDS-ON EXERCISES

CHAPTER 9

The Electronic Courthouse, Automated Courtroom, and Presentation Graphics

HANDS-ON EXERCISES

FEATURED SOFTWARE
TrialDirector
PowerPoint 2007
PowerPoint 2003

TRIALDIRECTOR

INSTALLATION INSTRUCTIONS

I. INTRODUCTION

inData's TrialDirector is case management software that helps you manage transcripts, video depositions, and documents for trial presentations.

II. INSTALLATION INSTRUCTIONS

1. Log in to your CengageBrain.com account.
2. Under "My Courses & Materials", find the Premium Website for Using Computers in the Law Office.
3. *Click "Open" to go to the Premium Website.*
4. Locate "Book Resources" in the left navigation menu.
5. *Click on the link for "TrialDirector 6".*
6. Fill out the form and submit it; a download link will be included in the message to the email address you supplied. *Click on that link and the installer will be automatically downloaded to your computer according to your browser's download settings.*
7. You may get a File Download–Security Warning. *Click Run.* The screen in Installation Exhibit 1 should now be displayed.
8. When the download is complete you will see a screen like TrialDirector Installation Exhibit 2. *Click Run.* The screen in TrialDirector Installation Exhibit 3 should now be displayed. *Click Next.*
9. The screen in TrialDirector Installation Exhibit 4 should now be displayed. *Click the button next to "I accept the terms in the license agreement"* then *click Next.*

File Download - Security Warning

Do you want to run or save this file?

Name: TD6WebSetup.exe
Type: Application, 223MB
From: 69.16.184.144

Run Save Cancel

While files from the Internet can be useful, this file type can potentially harm your computer. If you do not trust the source, do not run or save this software. What's the risk?

TRIALDIRECTOR INSTALLATION EXHIBIT 1

Internet Explorer - Security Warning

Do you want to run this software?

Name: TD6WebSetup
Publisher: **inData Corporation**

More options

Run Don't Run

While files from the Internet can be useful, this file type can potentially harm your computer. Only run software from publishers you trust. What's the risk?

TRIALDIRECTOR INSTALLATION EXHIBIT 2

TrialDirector 6 - InstallShield Wizard

Welcome to the InstallShield Wizard for TrialDirector 6

The InstallShield(R) Wizard will install TrialDirector 6 on your computer. To continue, click Next.

WARNING: This program is protected by copyright law and international treaties.

inData. DISCOVER. MANAGE. PRESENT. WIN.

< Back Next > Cancel

TRIALDIRECTOR INSTALLATION EXHIBIT 3

TrialDirector 6 - InstallShield Wizard

License Agreement

Please read the following license agreement carefully.

inData.

INDATA CORPORATION SOFTWARE LICENSE TERMS

INDATA TRIALDIRECTOR 6 SOFTWARE

These license terms are a legal agreement between you (either an individual or a single entity) and inData Corporation ("inData") and apply to the software product identified above, including any enhancements, derivatives, updates, "online" or electronic documentation, supplements and the media on which you received it (the "Software").

BY INSTALLING, COPYING, DOWNLOADING, ACCESSING OR OTHERWISE USING THE SOFTWARE, YOU ACCEPT THESE TERMS. IF YOU DO NOT AGREE TO THESE TERMS,

○ I accept the terms in the license agreement
○ I do not accept the terms in the license agreement

Print

InstallShield

< Back Next > Cancel

TRIALDIRECTOR INSTALLATION EXHIBIT 4

10. The screen in TrialDirector Installation Exhibit 5 should now be displayed. ***Click the Install button.***

**TRIALDIRECTOR
INSTALLATION
EXHIBIT 5**

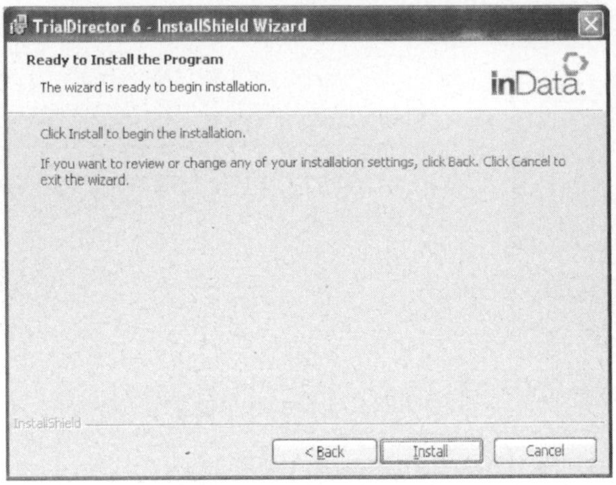

11. When the installation is finished, the screen in TrialDirector Installation Exhibit 6 should be displayed. ***Click Finish.***

**TRIALDIRECTOR
INSTALLATION
EXHIBIT 6**

12. ***Open TrialDirector.*** The TrialDirector 6 Registration window will open. ***Enter your product serial number in the space indicated (this number was included in your email from inData Corporation), then click Next.***

13. Confirm the contact information and ***click Next.***

14. A window will open telling you where the product activation code will be sent. Confirm that the email address is correct and ***click Yes.***

15. Confirm your contact information again and ***click Next.***

16. In the TrialDirector 6 Registration window, you will get a message that says "Your software activation code has been emailed." ***Open your email account, retrieve the activation code and enter the activation code in the space indicated. Click Next, the click OK.***

17. You have now successfully installed TrialDirector 6; however, the program has no data in it for you to manipulate. ***So, go back to the first email you received from inData Corporation. At the end of the Installation Instructions is a section titled Sample Data. Click the link to download the Sample Data, then follow the on-screen instructions.***

Number	Lesson Title	Concepts Covered
BASIC LESSONS		
Lesson 1	Navigating in TrialDirector—Part I	Working with the Case Library and the Workbooks Explorer; Document Manager; and Coding Tools; Playing Video Transcripts; Creating New Workbooks
Lesson 2	Navigating in TrialDirector—Part II	Working with Annotations Tools: Highlighter, Arrow, Line, Rectangle, Ellipse, Freehand Draw, Redaction, Text, Sticky Note, Stamp, Label, and Annotation Selector; Saving Annotations
INTERMEDIATE LESSONS		
Lesson 3	Working with the Transcript Manager	Multimedia Player; Word Index; Closed Captioning; Creating a New Video Clip
Lesson 4	Creating a New Case and Issue Codes	Creating a New Case; Creating New Issue Codes; Assigning Issue Codes to Sections of a Deposition
ADVANCED LESSON		
Lesson 5	Working in Presentation Mode	Opening Presentation Mode; Zones; Loading and Moving Images in Presentation Mode; Creating Enlargements and Callouts; Display Video and Deposition Clips

HANDS-ON EXERCISES

GETTING STARTED

Overview

TrialDirector is a trial presentation graphics program. It allows you to organize and manipulate items of evidence to be used in trial presentations.

Introduction to This Training Manual

Throughout this training manual, information you need to operate the program will be designated in several different ways.

- Keys to be pressed on the keyboard will be designated in brackets, in all caps, in bold and enlarged type (press the **[ENTER]** key).
- Movements with the mouse will be designated in bold and italic type (***point to File on the menu bar and click the mouse***).
- Words or letters that should be typed will be designated in bold and enlarged type (type **Training Program**).
- Information that is or should be displayed on your computer screen is shown in the following style: ***Press ENTER to continue.***

▶ BASIC LESSONS

LESSON 1: NAVIGATING IN TRIALDIRECTOR – PART I

In this lesson you will start TrialDirector.

1. Start Windows. Then, ***double-click on the TrialDirector icon on the desktop*** to start TrialDirector. Alternatively, ***click the Start button, point to***

Programs or All Programs, and then click the TrialDirector icon. If the Trial Registration window appears, *click Continue.* If a Product Bulletin window opens, *click OK.*

2. *In the "Open a Case" window, select TrialDirector 6 Sample Case, then click Open.* Your screen should look like TrialDirector Exhibit 1. TrialDirector opens in the Case Library tab.

**TRIALDIRECTOR
EXHIBIT 1**

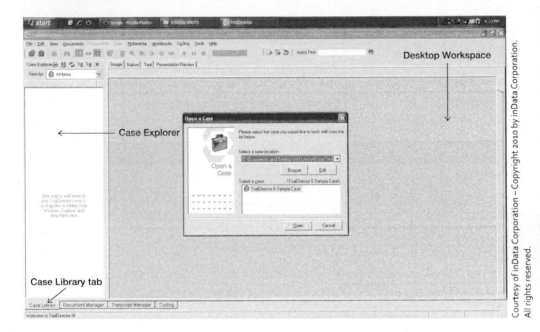

3. The right side of the screen contains the Desktop Workspace. This is where the selected documents, transcripts, images, etc., appear. The left side of the screen contains the Case Explorer and the Workbooks Explorer. The Case Explorer is the main repository of all files in TrialDirector. The default categories in the Case Explorer are Documents, Multimedia and Transcripts. We will now look at each of these.

4. *Click the small plus sign next to Documents to expand this category. Click on DEMO00145.* On the right side of the screen (called the Desktop Workspace) you should now see the image of a letter dated June 23, 1999. (See TrialDirector Exhibit 2.) Notice that the file you just selected also has a plus sign next to it. *Click on the plus sign next to DEMO00145.* Two additional sub-files appear: DEMO00145 and DEMO00146. This allows you to see individual pages of a multi-page document.

5. *Click the small plus sign next to Multimedia to expand this category. Click on VIDEO01.* On the right side of the screen you should now see a video screen and controls. (See TrialDirector Exhibit 3.) *Click on the small green arrow (fourth icon from the left) to play the video.* You can stop it by clicking the square icon. Remember, if you position your cursor over any of the icons you can see its function.

6. *Click the small plus sign next to Transcripts to expand this category. Double click on King, Stacy (Vol. 01) – 11/09/2007 [MPEG-1 Video].* (*Note:* if you

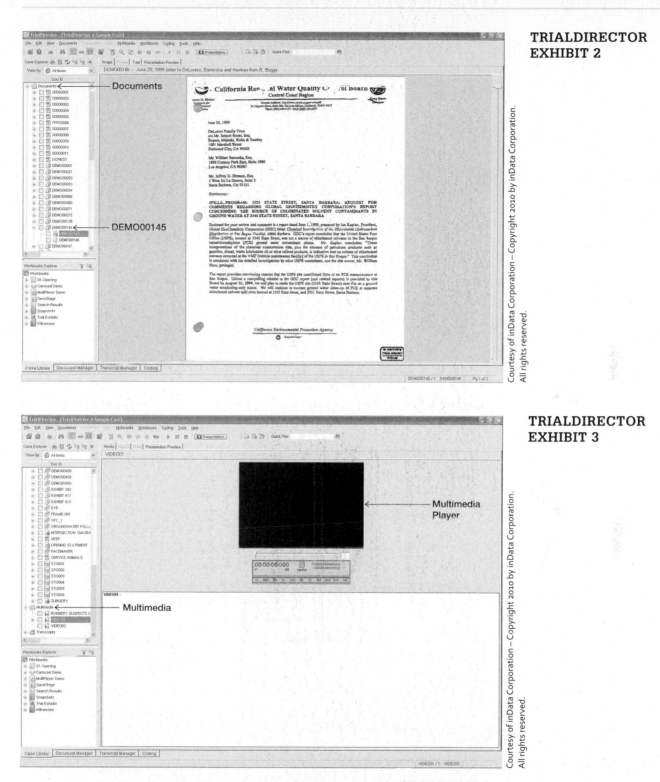

TRIALDIRECTOR EXHIBIT 2

TRIALDIRECTOR EXHIBIT 3

HANDS-ON EXERCISES

cannot read the full name of an item in the Case Explorer, you can expand it by clicking and dragging the border between the Case Explorer and the Desktop Workspace.) On the right side of the screen you should now see the transcript of a deposition and a multimedia player and exhibit preview. (See TrialDirector Exhibit 4.) Notice that a number of sub-files now appear and the Transcript Manager tab opened automatically. ***Click the small green arrow (third***

**TRIALDIRECTOR
EXHIBIT 4**

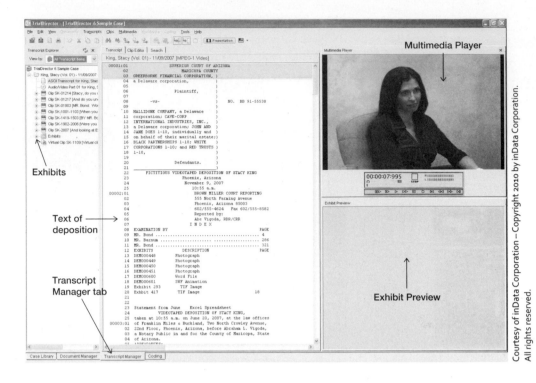

arrow from the left) under the video screen. Notice that as the video plays, the transcript has a rolling scroll simultaneously highlighting the video of the witness' testimony.

7. *Double click the sub-file Clip SK-01217 ["And do you understand that you've been…"].* A new set of sub-files appears; these contain individual segments of the deposition. *Double click the sub-file Page 13:12 to 13:13.* Notice that the video screen now plays this brief segment and that the transcript now shows the corresponding section of the deposition.

8. *Click the plus sign next to Exhibits, then double click the sub-file EXHIBIT 417 [Phone Log].* Notice that the phone log now appears in the Exhibit Preview screen directly under the video player. This allows the user to simultaneously display the audio/visual of the deposition, the transcript and the exhibits as they are discussed in the deposition.

9. *Click the Case Library tab at the bottom left corner of the screen to return to the Case Library.* We previously looked at the Case Explorer. We will now look at the Workbooks Explorer. Workbooks are essentially electronic files in which the user may place specific images for use at trial. Additional workbooks may be created as needed.

10. *Click the plus sign next to 01-Opening to see the exhibits that are to be used during the Opening Statement in this case. Then double click on DEMO00071.* The corresponding exhibit (a document from the California Insurance Group) appears in the Desktop Workspace.

11. We will now add another file to the 01-Opening Workbook. *Click the plus sign next to the Exhibit DCWEST from the Documents file in the Case Explorer.* Notice that a sub-file appears containing the one page of this document. *Place your cursor on this sub-file, then click and drag the file down to the 01-Opening Workbook.* You will need to place the cursor directly over this file. You should now see DCWEST as a sub-file in the 01-Opening Workbook.

12. We will now create a new Workbook. To do so, *click Workbooks in the main toolbar, click Create New Workbook then select Standard.* Notice that a new

workbook appears in the Workbook Explorer. It has the default name of New Workbook. We want this to contain our to do list; to change the name to To Do List, type **To Do List** and *press the [ENTER] key.*

13. *Click on File, then click on Exit. When prompted Quit TrialDirector 6?, click Yes.*

This concludes Lesson 1.

LESSON 2: NAVIGATING IN TRIALDIRECTOR—PART II

In this lesson, you will work with the various annotation tools available in TrialDirector.

1. Start Windows. Then, *double-click on the TrialDirector icon on the desktop* to start TrialDirector. Alternatively, *click the Start button, point to Programs or All Programs, and then click the TrialDirector icon.* If the Trial Registration window appears, *click Continue. In the "Open a Case" window, select TrialDirector 6 Sample Case, then click Open.* Your screen should look like TrialDirector Exhibit 1.

2. TrialDirector opens in the Case Library tab.

3. We will be working in the Document Manager; *click the Document Manager tab at the bottom left corner of the screen.* Your screen should look like TrialDirector Exhibit 5.

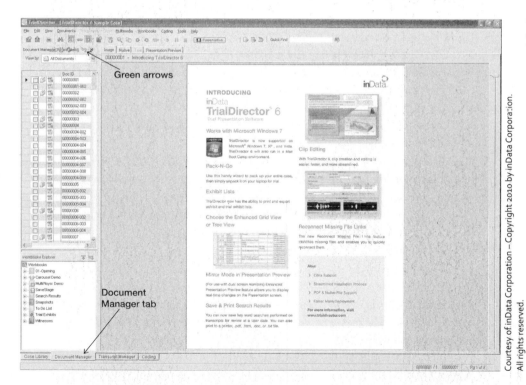

TRIALDIRECTOR EXHIBIT 5

4. The grid view of documents allows you to list just the individual documents in the case or to list every page of each document. *Click the green up arrow above the Case Explorer to show a list of just the individual documents. Click the green down arrow above the Case Explorer to show the list of every page of each document. Now, scroll down and click DEMO00001.* A document titled Notice of Deposition of California Capital Insurance Company should appear in the Desktop Workspace.

**TRIALDIRECTOR
EXHIBIT 6**

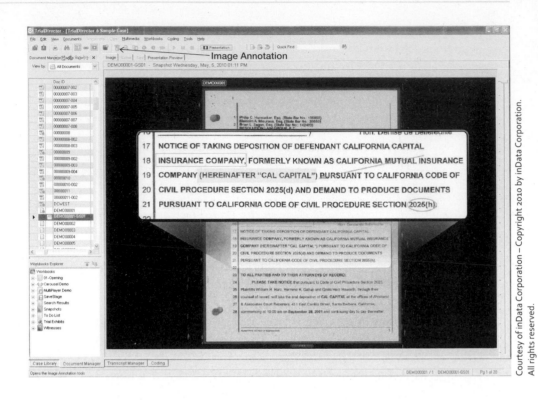

HANDS-ON EXERCISES

5. *Click the next document, DEMO00001-GS01.* Your screen should now look like TrialDirector Exhibit 6. This is an example of how you can select a portion of a document you want to highlight for your audience and add annotations (or "markups") to it. Notice how the user has highlighted a portion of the text and has added an arrow, an ellipse and a rectangle to draw attention to specific portions of the text. We will now explore the various annotation tools available in TrialDirector.

6. *You will now markup some documents so click DEMO00003. Then, click the ninth icon on the toolbar (it looks like a coffee cup with some markers in it) to open the Image Annotation toolbar.* The Annotation Toolbar will open. See TrialDirector Exhibit 7. The first icon from the left is the Annotation Selector. It is used to adjust, move or delete markups. We will use this tool later in this exercise.

7. The second icon from the left is the Highlighter. *Click the Highlighter icon; the default color is yellow.* For now, that is fine. We want to highlight paragraph 1 so *move your cursor over paragraph 1 and then click and drag the cursor over the paragraph until the entire paragraph is highlighted yellow.* See TrialDirector Exhibit 7.

8. On the right hand side of the annotation toolbar is the color selection palette. We will now highlight paragraph 2 in green (or whatever color you prefer). *With the Highlighter tool still selected, click on green on the color selection palatte. Then move your cursor over paragraph 2 and then click and drag the cursor over the paragraph until the entire paragraph is highlighted green.* See TrialDirector Exhibit 7.

9. The third icon from the left is the arrow tool, which can be used to point to an important point on an image. *Click on the arrow tool icon and then move the cursor next to the word "PLAINTIFFS" then click and drag the arrow.* See TrialDirector Exhibit 7.

10. At the far end of the annotation toolbar are tools to adjust the tool line width and the arrowhead. *Use your cursor to move both the tool line width and arrowhead tools to the maximum (all the way to the right).* You can also change the color of the arrow, so *click on the color black from the color selection palette. Then, with the arrow tool still selected, move the cursor next to the words "ENVIRONMENTAL ACTIONS" then click and drag the arrow.* See TrialDirector Exhibit 7.

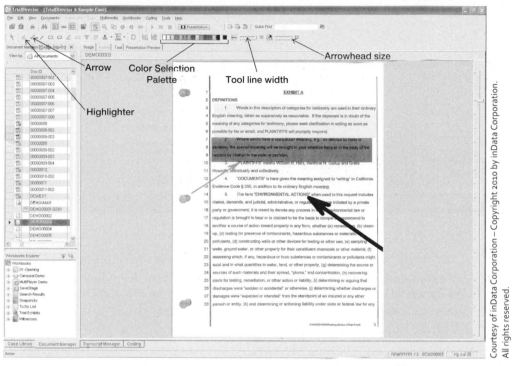

**TRIALDIRECTOR
EXHIBIT 7**

HANDS-ON EXERCISES

11. We will now choose another image (DEMO00005) to markup. *Click on DEMO00005.* Notice that when you do, a small window opens with options for saving the annotations. You can save the image with the markups or you can save a new image with the markups, leaving the original image unaltered. We will save these markups on a new image, so *click Save as New Revision.* Notice that a new file now appears on the grid (DEMO00003 01). **Click on** DEMO00005 and the image will appear in the Desktop Workspace.

12. The fourth icon from the left is the line tool. This is used to underline something on an image. *Click on the line tool icon and then move the cursor under paragraph 10, then click and drag to draw a line under paragraph 10.* See TrialDirector Exhibit 8. Notice that the color and width tools we used with the arrow tool can also be used with the line tool.

13. The fifth icon from the left is the rectangle tool. This is used to draw a box around an important area of an image. We will draw a box around the section of the image titled I. PROCEDURES, GUIDELINES AND POLICIES INFORMATION. *Click on the rectangle tool icon and then move your cursor to the upper left corner of the desired section, then click and drag until the entire section is included within the box.* See TrialDirector Exhibit 8. Notice that the color and width tools we used with the arrow tool can also be used with the rectangle tool.

14. The sixth icon from the left is the ellipse tool. This is used to draw a circle or oval around an important area of an image. We will draw an ellipse around the

**TRIALDIRECTOR
EXHIBIT 8**

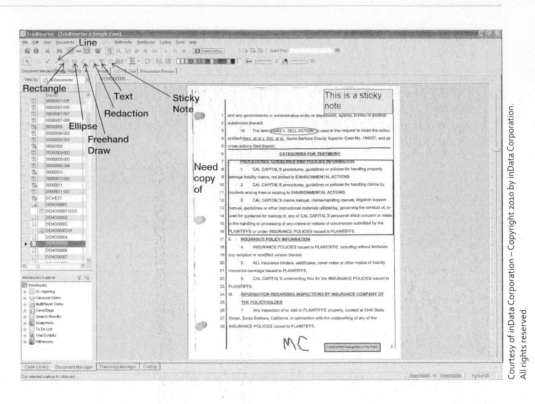

text <u>HARZ v. ZELL ACTION</u> in paragraph 10 at the top of the image. ***Click the ellipse tool icon and then click and drag it around the desired text until it is completely enclosed within the oval.*** See TrialDirector Exhibit 8. Notice that the color and width tools we used with the arrow tool can also be used with the ellipse tool.

15. The seventh icon from the left is the freehand draw tool. This is used to draw a freehand line or other mark on an image. We will use it to place your initials on the image. ***Click the freehand draw icon and then draw your initials at the bottom of the page.*** See TrialDirector Exhibit 8. Notice that the color and width tools we used with the arrow tool can also be used with the freestyle draw tool.

16. The eighth icon from the left is the redaction tool. This is used to redact or cover up a section of an image. We will use it to redact the name of the Word file at the bottom right corner of the image. ***Click on the redaction tool icon and then click and drag the cursor over the Word file name until it is covered by a light gray box.*** The redacted material will remain visible while in Document Manager, but it would be not be visible if the document were viewed in Presentation Mode. See TrialDirector Exhibit 8.

17. The ninth icon from the left is the Text tool. This is used to add text to an image. ***Click on the Text tool icon and move the cursor to the area to the left of the rectangle you drew earlier, then draw a box.*** This is where the text will appear. After you draw the box, type **Need copies of this**. ***Then click somewhere outside of the text box;*** the box will disappear and only the text will remain. See TrialDirector Exhibit 8. It is possible that you may not be able to see all of your text now; you will when we change the font size later. You can also change the color of the text by selecting a color from the color selection palette.

18. The tenth icon from the left is the Sticky Note tool icon. It is used to create an electronic sticky note that looks like and acts like a real sticky note. ***Click on the***

Sticky Note tool icon and move the cursor to the upper right corner of the image, then click and drag the cursor to draw a box similar to the one in TrialDirector Exhibit 8. Inside the box, type **This is a sticky note**, *then click somewhere on the image outside of the sticky note box.* See TrialDirector Exhibit 9.

19. The eleventh icon from the left is the Stamp tool icon. It is used to place a stamp on an image similar to the rubber stamps (and ink pads) that were used on paper documents. First, *click on the down arrow to the right of the Stamp tool icon.* A drop down menu of the available stamps appears.

20. *From the drop down menu click on the Redact icon and then place your cursor over the redacted material at the bottom of the page and click one time.* The word Redacted should now appear over that portion of the image. See TrialDirector Exhibit 9.

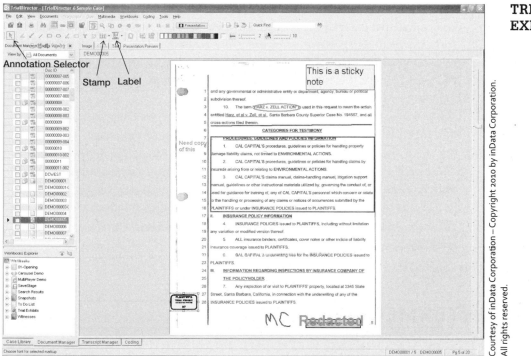

TRIALDIRECTOR EXHIBIT 9

21. The twelfth icon from the left is the Label tool icon. It is used to place an electronic label on an image similar to the sticky labels that are applied to paper documents. *First, click on the down arrow to the right of the Label tool icon.* A drop down menu of the available labels appears.

22. *From the drop down menu click on the PLAINTIFF'S TRIAL EXHIBIT label. A window will open asking for the Exhibit number. Type 07, then click OK. Then move your cursor to the lower left hand corner of the image and click one time.* The label should now appear in that spot. See TrialDirector Exhibit 9.

23. We will now go back to the first icon on the Annotation toolbar, the Annotation Selector tool. The Annotation Selector tool allows you to edit, move, resize or delete an annotation. We will use the Annotation Selector to move the label we just made and placed at the lower left corner of the image to the upper left corner of the image.

24. *Click one time on the Annotation Selector tool icon (the first icon on the left). Then move your cursor over the label and double click.* Notice that the label now has a box around it with handles on the corners and sides.

See TrialDirector Exhibit 9. You can use these handles to move the label to another location on the image. *To move the label, you need to click on the image and drag it to upper left corner of the image.*

25. The Annotation Selector tool can also be used to change the font of text within an annotation. We will change the font of the text within the sticky note at the upper right corner of the image.

26. *With the Annotation Selector tool still selected, move your cursor over the text box and click.* Again, notice that the text box now has a box around it with handles at the sides and corners. *Now right click on the sticky note and a menu of options appears. Click the fifth option, Choose Font,* and the Font dialog box opens.

27. In the Font dialog box, we will change the font to 22, *so scroll down the list of available fonts until 22 appears. Click one time on 22 to select that font.*

28. You can also change the style of the font, add effects (strikeout and underline) and change the color of the font. *Click the down arrow under Color and from the drop down menu, click one time on Red. Then click OK.* The sticky note now has the new font and color. If you need to enlarge the sticky note so you can see all of the text, you can do so by clicking on one of the handles and dragging it to the desired size.

29. We will now close this exercise, but first we will save the changes we made to this page. We will save the changes to a new revision of the image.

30. On the Annotation toolbar, there are two icons that look like floppy discs. *Click on the middle floppy disc to save the markups to a new revision of the image. Then look at the Case Explorer.* There is now a new file DEMO0005-01. This is the new image of this document with the annotations.

31. *Click on File, then click on Exit. When prompted Quit TrialDirector 6?, click Yes.*

This concludes Lesson 2.

▶ INTERMEDIATE LESSONS

LESSON 3: WORKING WITH THE TRANSCRIPT MANAGER

In this lesson, you will work with depositions, the Word Index and create a new clip.

1. Start Windows. Then, *double-click on the TrialDirector icon on the desktop* to start TrialDirector. Alternatively, *click the Start button, point to Programs or All Programs, and then click the TrialDirector icon.* If the Trial Registration window appears, *click Continue. In the "Open a Case" window, select TrialDirector 6 Sample Case, then click Open.* Your screen should look like TrialDirector Exhibit 1.

2. TrialDirector opens in the Case Library tab.

3. We will be working with transcripts in this lesson, so *click on the Transcript Manager tab*. Your screen should like TrialDirector Exhibit 10. The components of the Transcript Manager include the Transcript Explorer, the Transcript Viewer, the Multimedia Player and the Exhibit Preview.

4. *Click the plus sign next to King, Stacy (Vol. 01)-11/09/2007- [MPEG -1 Video], then double click the sub-file ASCII Transcript for King, Stacy (Vol. 1)-11/09/2007- [MPEG -1 Video] (an ASCII file is essentially just a text file).* The text of the King deposition now appears in the Transcript Viewer. Notice that the multimedia controls are now green indicating that they are

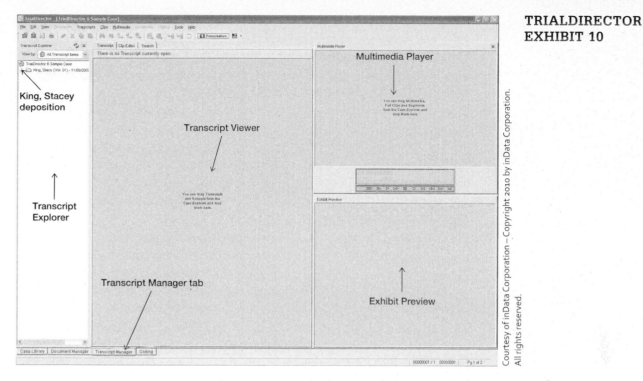

**TRIALDIRECTOR
EXHIBIT 10**

active. ***Click the play button under the Multimedia Player (it is an arrow; the third icon from the left). The audio/video will begin to play in Multimedia Player.*** Notice that the transcript scrolls in time to the audio/video.

5. ***Click the stop button under the Multimedia Player (it is a square; the sixth icon from the left) to stop the audio/visual.***

6. ***Click View on the toolbar and then click on Word Index.*** The Word Index now appears to the left of the Transcript Viewer. See TrialDirector Exhibit 11. The Word Index is a comprehensive of every word (and non-words such as numbers) with links to their specific locations within the transcript.

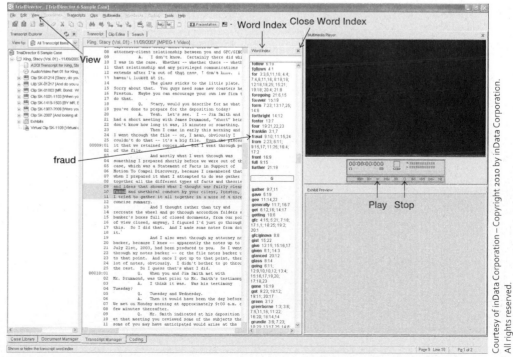

**TRIALDIRECTOR
EXHIBIT 11**

HANDS-ON EXERCISES

7. *Scroll down the Word Index until you see the word "fraud." Click on the link 9:10 to the right of the word fraud.* Notice that the Transcript Viewer now highlights the testimony on page 9, line 10 of the deposition. See TrialDirector Exhibit 11. *Clicking the green multimedia arrow begins the Multimedia Player at that part of the deposition.*

8. *Click the small x at the top of the Word Index to close the Word Index.*

9. A deposition must be indexed in order to be able to create a Word Index. If the deposition you are working on has not been indexed, you can do so within TrialDirector. *Click on Transcripts on the toolbar.* The third item on the drop down menu is Index Transcript. It is greyed out now because the King deposition has already been indexed. *Click somewhere else on the screen to close the drop down menu.*

10. *Click Multimedia on the main menu, then Closed Captioning.* This will enable the closed captioning feature. *Click the green multimedia arrow.* Notice that now as the audio/visual plays, the testimony is presented on the screen. This can be beneficial when it is difficult to understand what the deponent is saying or can assist viewers with impaired hearing.

11. Look at the Transcript Explorer. There are a number of clips listed there. Clips are excerpts of a deposition. They are typically prepared to highlight a brief exchange or admission made at the deposition. There are a number of ways to create a new clip. We will use the one step clip creation method.

12. The first step is to select the portion of the text to be included. *Scroll through the transcript until you come to page 8, line 18. Place your cursor on that line and click and drag the cursor down to page 9, line 25.* See TrialDirector Exhibit 12.

13. *With your cursor on the selected text, right click. From the menu, click on Create New Clip from Selected Text.* See TrialDirector Exhibit 11.

14. The new clip has been created and may now be found in the Transcript Explorer. See TrialDirector Exhibit 12.

TRIALDIRECTOR EXHIBIT 12

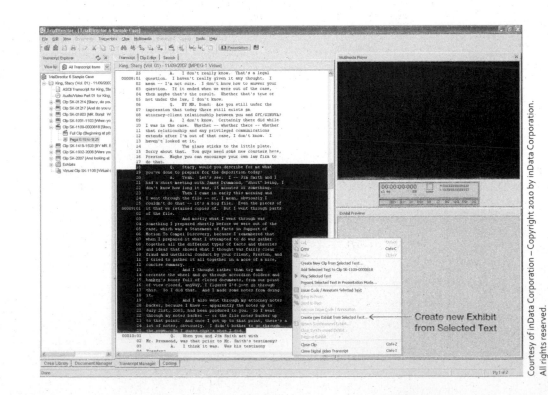

15. *Click on File, then click on Exit. When prompted Quit TrialDirector 6?, click Yes.*

This concludes Lesson 3.

LESSON 4: CREATING A NEW CASE AND ISSUE CODES

In this lesson, you will create a new case and assign issue codes to a deposition.

1. Start Windows. Then, *double-click on the TrialDirector icon on the desktop* to start TrialDirector. Alternatively, *click the Start button, point to Programs or All Programs, and then click the TrialDirector icon.* If the Trial Registration window appears, *click Continue. In the "Open a Case" window, select TrialDirector 6 Sample Case, then click Open.* Your screen should look like TrialDirector Exhibit 1.

2. TrialDirector opens in the Case Library tab.

3. To create a new case in TrialDirector, there are several options. *Click the new case icon (the first icon on the left – it looks like a briefcase).* The "Create a New Case" window opens and asks where the new case should be located in the computer. The default location is fine, so *click Next.*

4. In the next window, you need to enter the name of case. Type **Hatfield v. McCoy** *in the text box under Description.* The Matter Number is the internal file number assigned the case by the law firm. Type **123ABC** in the text box next to Matter number. The text box next to Notes: can be used to include the court's civil action number, the name of the judge assigned to the case and other information. In the text box next to Notes: type **CV-JDC-120429**. See TrialDirector Exhibit 13. *Click Next.*

TRIALDIRECTOR EXHIBIT 13

5. The next window gives the user the opportunity to enable additional layers of security by creating a password which would be required of any users seeking access to this case and enable case encryption to encrypt the case databases.

**TRIALDIRECTOR
EXHIBIT 14**

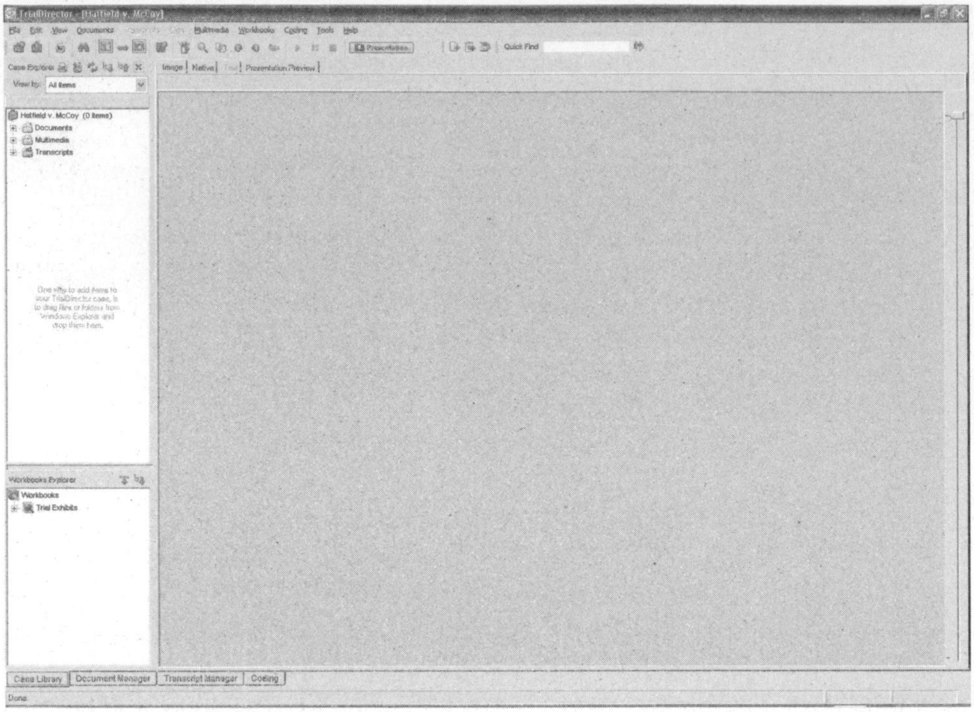

We will not enable security for this case, so **click Create**. Your screen should now look like TrialDirector Exhibit 14.

6. We will now go back to the Transcript Manager and see how issue codes are created and used to facilitate the organization and retrieval of information at trial.

7. Since our new case does not have any files in it, **click the Open Case icon and then select TrialDirector 6 Sample Case. Click Open. Then, click on the Transcript Manager tab.**

8. TrialDirector allows the user to assign issue codes to specific images and sections of depositions. Similar to the way issue codes are used in litigation support software, they organize disparate pieces of evidence into coherent files. (*Note*: it is possible to import issue codes that have already been created in Summation at the same time those files are imported.) Issue codes thus make it easier to retrieve specific pieces of evidence when they are needed. (When you are at a trial or hearing, the judge is not going to wait while you rifle through your notebooks looking for the "smoking gun.")

9. We will assign issue codes to portions of the deposition of Stacy King. **In the Transcript Manager, click the plus sign to the left of King, Stacy (Vol. 01)-11/09/2007-MPEG in the Transcript Explorer. Then double-click ASCII Transcript for King, Stacy (Vol. 1)-11/09/2007-[MPEG - 1 Video].**

10. We will create an issue code for discussions of "fraud" during the deposition. To find these portions of the deposition, we will use the Word Index feature we looked at in an earlier lesson.

11. **Click on View from the toolbar and then click on Word Index.**

12. **At the top of the Word Index is an empty text box. Type fraud in the text box then click on the first entry (9:10).** Notice that the reference to "fraud" occurs towards the end of the answer to a question that appears at page 8, line 18. Generally, when making video clips or assigning an issue code, it is better practice to include more than just the specific line in which the key word is uttered. You want to provide some context for this information, so we will include the question asked of the witness and the entire answer in our issue code.

13. To create an issue code, you must first select the specific portion of the text to which this code is to be assigned. ***So move your cursor to the question beginning at page 8, line 18 and then click and drag the cursor down to page 9, line 25.***

14. ***Then, with the cursor over the selected text, right click and then click on Issue Code / Annotate Selected Text. The Issue Code / Annotate Selected Text box will open. Click Manage….***

15. The Manage Issue Codes… box opens. ***Click New.*** A new issue code (F1) appears next to yellow rectangle. The description currently reads New issue code. ***The cursor should already be at the end of this description, so click the Backspace key one time to clear the text*** and then *type* **Fraud.** See TrialDirector Exhibit 15. ***Click Exit to close this box.***

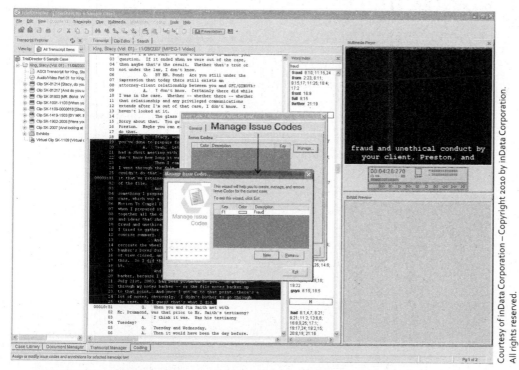

**TRIALDIRECTOR
EXHIBIT 15**

16. You are now back in the Issue Codes / Annotate Selected Text box, but now notice that the new issue code for fraud appears. ***Click the small square at the left of the line on which Fraud appears; a check mark should appear. Then click Apply. The color of the selected text will change. Click Exit to close the Issue Codes / Annotate Selected text box, then click anywhere on the transcript.*** Notice that the selected text is highlighted and that a new sub-file appears under the file Issue Codes and Annotations called Fraud with a reference to specific portion of the text we selected.

17. We will now repeat this process for the two other references to fraud. ***Click on the link to the second reference to fraud at page 11, line 15.*** Again we want to include the complete question and answer with the reference to fraud. ***Place your cursor at page 11, line 4 and click and drag the cursor to page 12, line 5.***

18. ***Then, with the cursor over the selected text, right click and then click on Issue Code / Annotate Selected Text. The Issue Code / Annotate Selected Text***

box will open. Notice that the issue code for fraud already exists, so *click the small square at the left of the line on which Fraud appears; a check mark should appear. Then click Apply.* The color of the selected text will change. *Click Exit to close the Issue Codes / Annotate Selected text box, then click anywhere on the transcript.* Notice that the selected text is now highlighted and that a new sub-file appears under the file Issue Codes and Annotations called Fraud with a reference to the specific portion of the text we selected.

19. *Click on the link to the third reference to fraud at page 11, line 24.* Notice that reference is part of the text selected for the issue code of fraud in the previous step, so there is no further action required.

20. *Click on File, then click on Exit. When prompted Quit TrialDirector 6?, click Yes.*

This concludes Lesson 4.

▶ ADVANCED LESSON

LESSON 5: WORKING IN PRESENTATION MODE

In this lesson, you will explore presentation mode.

1. Start Windows. Then, *double-click on the TrialDirector icon on the desktop* to start TrialDirector. Alternatively, *click the Start button, point to Programs or All Programs, and then click the TrialDirector icon.* If the Trial Registration window appears, *click Continue. In the "Open a Case" window, select TrialDirector 6 Sample Case, then click Open.* Your screen should look like TrialDirector Exhibit 1.

2. TrialDirector opens in the Case Library tab.

3. We will be learning about Presentation Mode, so *click Presentation Preview in the Desktop Workspace.* This tool simulates the screens you would see in Presentation mode but is easier to navigate. You screen should look like TrialDirector Exhibit 16.

TRIALDIRECTOR EXHIBIT 16

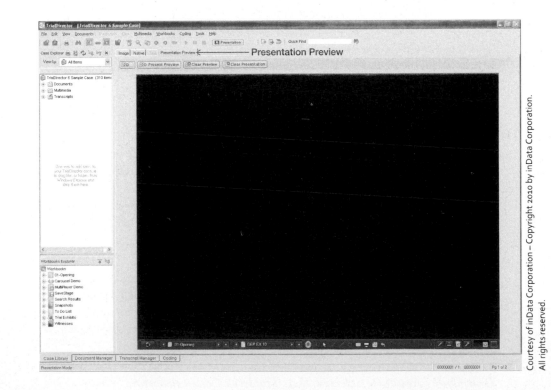

4. There are a number of ways to display images in Presentation Mode. For example, images made by retrieved by creating a script (a set of instructions prepared to load images in a specified order), by using a bar code reader (each image in TrialDirector is assigned a unique bar code) or by entering the exhibit number. We will use exhibit numbers to load images into Presentation Mode.

5. Before loading a document into Presentation mode it is important to understand the concept of zones. It is possible to load images using the full screen or place two sides side by side (or one atop the other) or to place up to four documents in the four quadrants of the screen. In TrialDirector the zones are used as follows:

   Zones 1 & 2 split the display vertically.
   Zones 3 & 4 split the display horizontally.
   Zones 5, 6, 7 & 8 split the display into quadrants.
   Zone 9 uses the full display. This is the default zone. If you do not choose a zone, your images will display using the full screen.

6. Zones may be selected by clicking the corresponding (F) key. For example, to place an image on the left side of the screen (Zone 1), you would click the F1 key. You may also change the zone by using the Select Zone / Zone Indicator at the far right of the Presentation toolbar.

7. There are two drop down menus on the left side of the toolbar at the bottom of the Presentation screen. ***Click the first up arrow and select 01-Opening, then click the second up arrow and select GFC_1. Then click the green up arrow.*** The image of GFC_1 should appear. Since you did not select a zone, the default zone (full screen) was employed. See TrialDirector Exhibit 17.

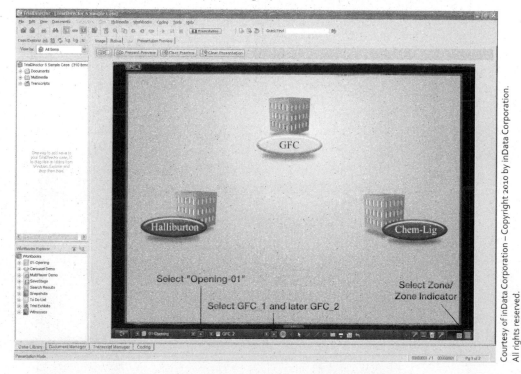

TRIALDIRECTOR EXHIBIT 17

8. ***Then press the [F1] key and click the green up arrow again.*** This loads the next document into the Presentation Preview and, since you selected Zone 1, the next document (GFC_2) will appear on the left side of the screen and the first document will move to the right side of the screen. See TrialDirector Exhibit 18. This method of presenting images would be useful if you wanted to show multiple pages of a document.

**TRIALDIRECTOR
EXHIBIT 18**

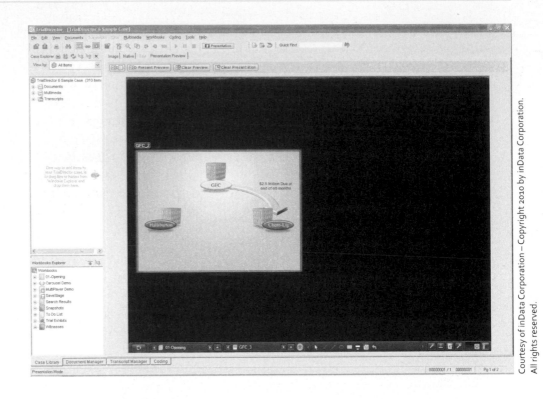

9. It is possible to select a portion of an image and enlarge it to emphasize it to the audience. A callout is an enlargement of a portion of an image displayed over the image of the complete document. You will first select a text document, so *first press the [F9] key so the image will use the full screen, click the second up arrow, then click EX at the top of the menu. Select DEP EX 10, then click the green up arrow. Click the Projection Zoom tool icon and then place it over the portion of DEP EX 10 as noted in TrialDirector Exhibit 19. Click and drag your cursor until the entire section is included within the*

**TRIALDIRECTOR
EXHIBIT 19**

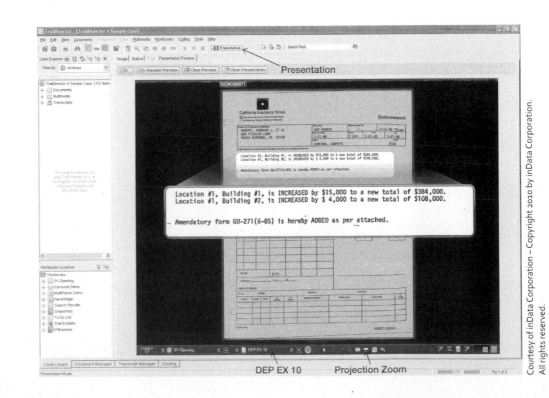

box. When you release, the callout will appear over the image of the complete document. See TrialDirector Exhibit 19. You can move the callout by clicking on it and dragging it to the desired location.

10. You can show other forms of evidence in Presentation Mode. To do so, we need to leave the Presentation Preview and go to Presentation Mode. To do this you may ***click the Presentation button on the main toolbar.*** See TrialDirector Exhibit 19.

11. We want to display deposition testimony in Presentation Mode. ***Click the first up arrow and select MultiPlayer Demo, then click the second up arrow and select SK-1902-2006. Then click the green up arrow and the brief video clip will play on the screen.*** If the video does not play, ***click on the image*** and it will begin.

12. ***Press the [ESC] key twice and when prompted Exit Presentation?, click Yes.***

13. ***Click on File, then click on Exit. When prompted Quit TrialDirector 6?, click Yes.***

This concludes the TrialDirector Hands-On Exercises.

PRESENTATION SOFTWARE

 *Read this first!*

1. Microsoft PowerPoint 2007
2. Microsoft PowerPoint 2003

I. DETERMINING WHICH TUTORIAL TO COMPLETE

To use the PowerPoint Hands-On Exercises, you must already own or have access to Microsoft PowerPoint 2007 or PowerPoint 2003. If you have one of these programs but do not know the version you are using, it is easy to find out. For PowerPoint 2003, start the program, click Help on the menu bar, then click About Microsoft Office PowerPoint. The program should then tell you what version you are using. For PowerPoint 2007, click the Office button in the upper left of the screen, click PowerPoint Options, then click Resources. The program will tell you what version you are using. You must know the version of the program you are using and select the correct tutorial version or the tutorials will not work correctly.

II. USING THE POWERPOINT HANDS-ON EXERCISES

The PowerPoint Hands-On Exercises in this section are easy to use and contain step-by-step instructions. They start with basic skills and proceed to intermediate and advanced levels. If you already have a good working knowledge of PowerPoint, you may be able to proceed directly to the intermediate and advanced exercises. To be truly ready to use presentation software in the legal environment, you should be able to accomplish the tasks and exercises in the more advanced exercises.

III. ACCESSING THE DATA

Some of the advanced PowerPoint Hands-On Exercises use documents on the disk provided with this text. To access these files, put the disk in your computer and click Start. Click My Computer, double-click on the appropriate drive, then double-click the PowerPoint Files folder. You should then see a list of presentations that are available for these exercises.

IV. INSTALLATION QUESTIONS

If you have questions regarding installation of the exercise files data from the disk, you may contact Technical Support at 1-800-648-7450.

Number	Lesson Title	Concepts Covered
BASIC LESSONS		
Lesson 1	Creating a Presentation	Selecting a presentation design; entering text; entering speaker's notes; saving a file
Lesson 2	Creating Additional Slides	Inserting a new slide; selecting a slide layout; viewing a slide in Slide Show, Outline, and Slide Sorter views; creating additional slides
INTERMEDIATE LESSON		
Lesson 3	Creating a Graph	Creating a chart; entering data in a chart
ADVANCED LESSON		
Lesson 4	Finalizing the Presentation	Creating transition effects; creating animation effects; viewing a final presentation

GETTING STARTED

Overview

Microsoft PowerPoint 2007 is a presentation graphics program. It allows you to create presentations, charts, graphs, tables, and much more. PowerPoint 2007 is easy to learn and easy to use. Please note that you will be creating a presentation for an opening statement.

Introduction

Throughout these lessons and exercises, information you need to type into the software will be designated in several different ways:

- Keys to be pressed on the keyboard are designated in brackets, in all caps, and in bold (e.g., press the **[ENTER]** key).
- Movements with the mouse pointer are designated in bold and italics (e.g., ***point to File on the menu bar and click***).
- Words or letters that should be typed are designated in bold (e.g., type **Training Program**).
- Information that is or should be displayed on your computer screen is shown in bold, with quotation marks (e.g., **"Press ENTER to continue."**).
- Specific menu items and commands are designated with an initial capital letter (e.g., click Open).

⏵ BASIC LESSONS

LESSON 1: CREATING A PRESENTATION

In this lesson, you will start PowerPoint 2007, select a background design for the opening statement presentation, enter the first slide, view your slide, and save your presentation.

1. Start Windows. After it has loaded, ***double-click the Microsoft PowerPoint 2007 icon on the desktop*** to start the program. Alternatively, ***click the Start button, point to Programs or All Programs, click Microsoft Office, then point and click on Microsoft Office PowerPoint 2007.***

2. A blank presentation should appear on your screen. ***Click the Office button in the upper left corner of the screen, then click New.*** The "New Presentation" window should now be displayed.

3. ***On the left side, under Templates, click Installed Themes. Scroll down and select Paper. Click Create.***

4. A blank title screen should now be displayed.

5. ***Click "Click to add title."*** Notice that you are now allowed to type your own title. Type **OPENING STATEMENT** (see PowerPoint 2007 Exhibit 1).

6. ***On the Home ribbon tab, click the Center icon in the Paragraph group.***

7. ***Click "Click to add subtitle."*** Type **RICHARDS V. EZ PEST CONTROL** (see PowerPoint 2007 Exhibit 1).

8. ***On the Home ribbon tab, click the Center icon in the Paragraph group.***

9. The slide is now created.

10. To view your slide, ***click the Slide Show icon in the lower right of the screen*** (PowerPoint 2007 Exhibit 1). *Note:* You will see three icons in the lower right of the screen (for Normal view, Slide Sorter view, and Slide Show view). The

**POWERPOINT 2007
EXHIBIT 1**

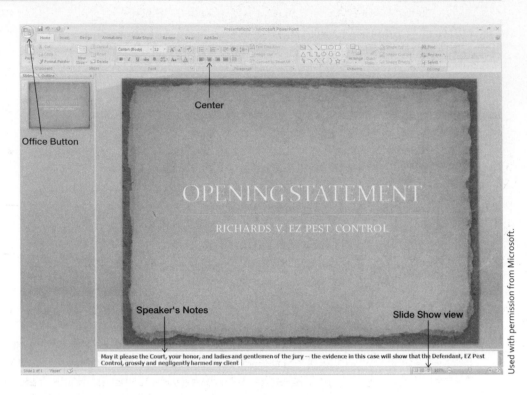

Slide Show icon is all the way to the right. Remember, if you point to any icon and hold the mouse pointer there for a second, the title of the icon will be displayed.

11. You should now see your slide displayed full screen on your computer. Notice that the dark background with the light-colored letters makes your slide very readable. This is how your audience will see your slide.

12. Press the **[ESC]** key to return to editing your presentation.

13. Notice that at the bottom of the screen, under the current slide, it says **"Click to add notes."** This is the speaker's notes section of the screen. Speaker's notes are not shown in Slide Show view, but they can be printed so that the presenter has talking points to which to refer.

14. *Click anywhere in the speaker's notes section.* Type **May it please the Court, your honor, and ladies and gentlemen of the jury—the evidence in this case will show that the Defendant, EZ Pest Control, grossly and negligently harmed my client** (see PowerPoint 2007 Exhibit 1).

15. *Click the Slide Show icon in the lower right of the screen again.* Notice that the speaker's notes do not appear.

16. Press the **[ESC]** key to return to editing your presentation.

17. It is a good idea to save your work often. To save your presentation, *click the Office Button and then click Save.*

18. Type **Richards Opening Statement**, *then click Save* to save the file in the default directory. Be sure to remember where the file is saved so that you can retrieve it for the next lesson.

This concludes Lesson 1. To exit PowerPoint, *click the Office button and then click Exit PowerPoint.* To go to Lesson 2, stay at the current screen.

LESSON 2: CREATING ADDITIONAL SLIDES

In this lesson, you will create additional slides for the opening statement presentation you created in Lesson 1, and you will look at the presentation using several views. If you did not exit PowerPoint from Lesson 1, go to Step 3 in the following instructions.

1. Start Windows. ***Double-click the Microsoft Office PowerPoint 2007 icon on the desktop*** to start PowerPoint 2007 for Windows. Alternatively, ***click the Start button, point to Programs or All Programs, then click the Microsoft PowerPoint 2007 icon*** (or ***point to Microsoft Office and then click Microsoft Office PowerPoint 2007).*** You should be in a clean, blank document.

2. ***Click the Office button, then click Open.*** The "Open" window should now be displayed. Navigate to the folder where the file is located. ***Click Richards Opening Statement, then click Open.*** Alternatively, if you click the Office button, recently used files appear on the right side of the menu. Locate your file, then ***click on it.***

3. You should have the "Opening Statement" slide on your screen. Notice in the lower left of the screen that it says **"Slide 1 of 1."** This shows you what slide number you are on.

4. To create a new slide, ***on the Home ribbon tab, click the down arrow next to New Slide in the Slides group.*** Notice that the program offers a number of different layouts.

5. ***Click the Title and Content option.***

6. A new slide is displayed on your screen. The top part of the slide should say **"Click to add title"** and the bottom section of the slide (next to a bullet) should say **"Click to add text."** There should also be graphics in the center of the screen.

7. ***Click*** **"Click to add title."** Type **Reasons for Lawsuit** (see PowerPoint 2007 Exhibit 2).

8. ***On the Home ribbon tab, click the Center icon in the Paragraph group.***

9. ***Click*** **"Click to add text."** Type **Recovery of damages from EZ Pest for negligence and breach of contract** and press the **[ENTER]** key. Notice that an additional bullet has been created.

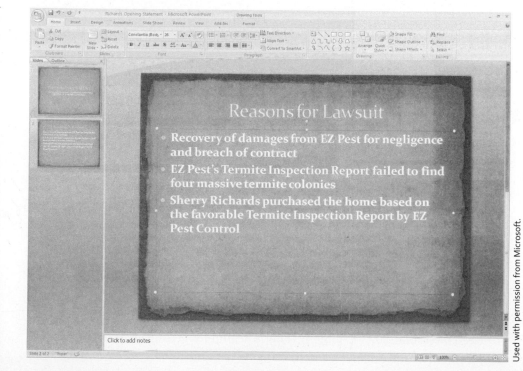

**POWERPOINT 2007
EXHIBIT 2**

10. Type **EZ Pest's Termite Inspection Report failed to find four massive termite colonies** and then press the **[ENTER]** key.

11. Type **Sherry Richards purchased the home based on the favorable Termite Inspection Report by EZ Pest Control** and press the **[ENTER]** key.

12. The slide is now created (see PowerPoint Exhibit 2).

13. To view your slide, *click the Slide Show icon.*

14. You should now see your slide displayed full screen on your computer. With the slide running in Slide Show view, press the **[PAGE UP]** key and notice that the first slide is now shown on your screen. Press the **[PAGE DOWN]** key and notice that you are back at the second slide.

15. Press the **[ESC]** key to return to Normal view.

16. You will now look at your presentation using other views. Notice on the left side of the screen that small versions of both of your slides are displayed (see PowerPoint 2007 Exhibit 2). Notice, just above the slides, that the Slides tab is selected.

17. *Click the Outline tab just to the right of the Slides tab.*

18. The Outline view is now displayed; notice that you can read the words on both of your slides (see PowerPoint 2007 Exhibit 3).

POWERPOINT 2007 EXHIBIT 3

Outline view

Used with permission from Microsoft.

19. *Click the Slides tab just to the left of the Outline tab* to go back to the Slides view.

20. You will now view your slides using the Slide Sorter view. *Click the Slide Sorter view icon.* The Slide Sorter view icon is at the bottom right of the screen; it is the second of the three View icons, and has a picture of four small squares (see PowerPoint 2007 Exhibit 1).

21. Notice that you can now see all of your slides on the screen at the same time (see PowerPoint 2007 Exhibit 4). This is helpful for getting an overview of your presentation and arranging and rearranging the slide order.

Slide Sorter view

**POWERPOINT 2007
EXHIBIT 4**

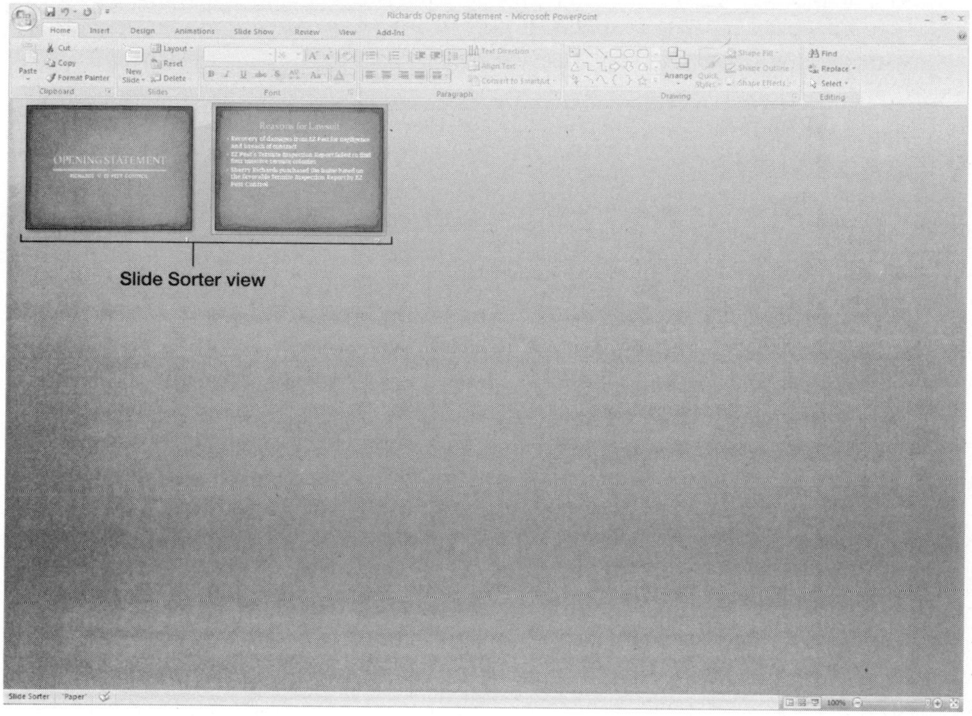

22. While you are in Slide Sorter view, *point to the second slide, click on it, and (holding down the mouse button) drag the mouse pointer to the left of the first slide. Release the mouse button.* Notice that the order of the slides has been changed.

23. Press **[CTRL]+[Z]** to undo the move and put the slides back into their original order.

24. *Click the Normal view icon in the lower right of your screen* (see PowerPoint 2007 Exhibit 1).

25. You should now have the "Opening Statement" slide on your screen. If you are not there, use the **[PAGE DOWN]** key to go there.

26. You are now ready to create another slide. *On the Home ribbon tab, click the down arrow next to New Slide in the Slides group. Click the Title and Content option.*

27. A new slide is displayed on your screen. The top part of the slide should say **"Click to add title"** and the bottom section of the slide (next to a bullet) should say **"Click to add text."** There should also be graphics in the center of the screen.

28. *Click* **"Click to add title."** Type **Undisputed Facts of the Case** (see PowerPoint 2007 Exhibit 5).

29. *On the Home ribbon tab, click the Center icon in the Paragraph group.*

30. *Click* **"Click to add text."** Type **July 2006 – Sherry Richards, age 65, purchases house** and press the **[ENTER]** key.

31. Type **November 2007 – Massive Formosan termite colonies found dating back 5 years** and press the **[ENTER]** key.

32. Type **December 2007 – Cost to repair termite damage $158,000**.

33. Your presentation now has three slides in it.

34. To save your presentation, *click the Save icon on the Quick Access toolbar.* (It looks like a floppy disk and is in the upper left of the screen.)

**POWERPOINT 2007
EXHIBIT 5**

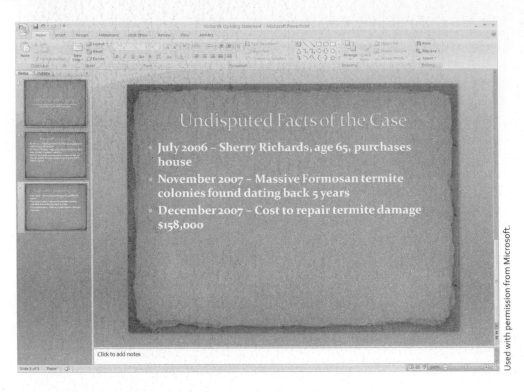

This concludes Lesson 2. To exit PowerPoint, *click the Office button, then click Exit PowerPoint.* To go to Lesson 3, stay at the current screen.

▶ INTERMEDIATE LESSON

LESSON 3: CREATING A GRAPH

In this lesson, you will add a slide with a graph to the opening statement presentation. If you did not exit PowerPoint after completing Lesson 2, go to Step 4 in the following instructions.

1. Start Windows. *Double-click the Microsoft Office PowerPoint 2007 icon on the desktop* to start PowerPoint 2007 for Windows. Alternatively, *click the Start button, point to Programs or All Programs, then click the Microsoft PowerPoint 2007 icon* (or *point to Microsoft Office and then click Microsoft Office PowerPoint 2007*). You should be in a clean, blank document.

2. *Click the Office button, then click Open.* The "Open" window should now be displayed. Navigate to the folder where the file is located. *Click Richards Opening Statement and then click Open.* Alternatively, if you click the Office button, recently used files appear on the right side of the menu. Locate your file and then *click on it.*

3. You should have the "Opening Statement" slide on your screen. Push the **[PAGE DOWN]** key until you are on the third slide, "Undisputed Facts of the Case."

4. You are now ready to create another slide. *On the Home ribbon tab, click the down arrow next to New Slide in the Slides group.*

5. *Click on the Title and Content option.* A new slide is displayed on your screen.

6. The top part of the slide should say **"Click to add title"** and the bottom section of the slide should say **"Click to add text."** In addition, there are a

number of graphical icons in the middle of the screen; one of them is a bar chart.

7. ***Click on "Click to add title."*** Type **Value of Richards Home** and then press the **[ENTER]** key (see PowerPoint 2007 Exhibit 6). ***On the Home ribbon tab, click on the Center icon in the Paragraph group.***

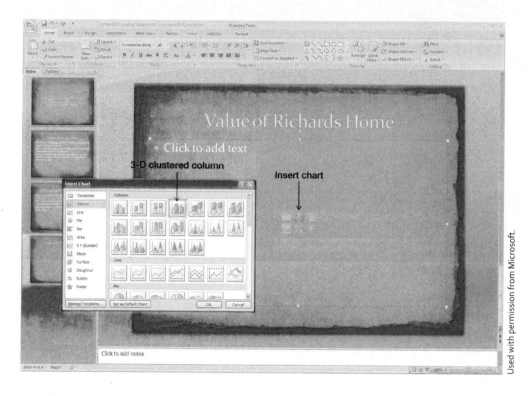

Used with permission from Microsoft.

POWERPOINT 2007 EXHIBIT 6

8. Notice that, in the lower middle of the new slide, there are six graphical icons. ***Click on the Insert Chart icon*** (it is in the middle on the first row—it looks like a multicolored vertical bar chart).

9. The "Insert Chart" window is displayed (see PowerPoint 2007 Exhibit 6). ***Click on Column under Templates on the left side of the window, then click on the 3-D Clustered Column chart*** (e.g., see PowerPoint 2007 Exhibit 6—it is on the first row, fourth chart from the left).

10. ***Click on OK.***

11. A default chart is displayed on the left and a default spreadsheet is displayed on the right (see PowerPoint 2007 Exhibit 7).

12. You will now add some data and new titles, and also delete some data.

13. Type over the existing data in the spreadsheet for columns A and B as follows (do not do anything with columns C and D yet):

	A	B	C	D
	2009	2010	2011	2012
Value	225,000	215,000	175,000	150,000

14. You will now delete columns C and D, because they are not necessary. ***Point to cell C1 and (holding the mouse pointer down) drag to the right so that cell D7 is highlighted.***

15. ***Right-click in the highlighted area, point to Delete, then click Table Columns.***

**POWERPOINT 2007
EXHIBIT 7**

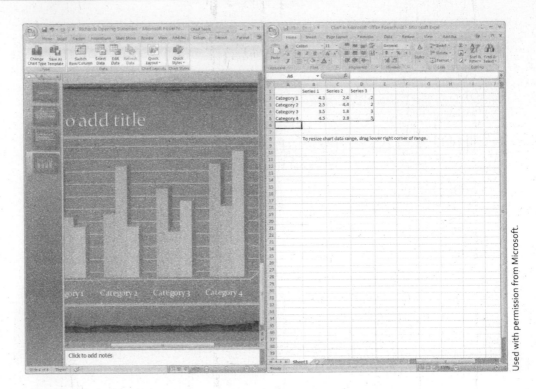

16. A Microsoft Office Excel window will appear saying that the worksheet contains one or more invalid references; ***click OK.***

17. Your spreadsheet and chart should look similar to PowerPoint 2007 Exhibit 8.

**POWERPOINT 2007
EXHIBIT 8**

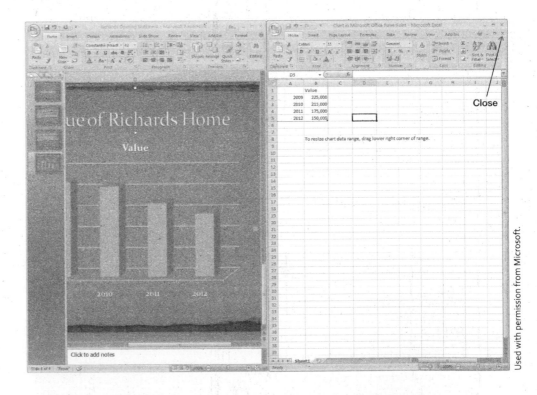

18. ***In the spreadsheet part of the "Chart" window, click the Close icon*** (the X in the upper right corner; see PowerPoint 2007 Exhibit 8).

19. The chart should now be displayed (see PowerPoint 2007 Exhibit 9).

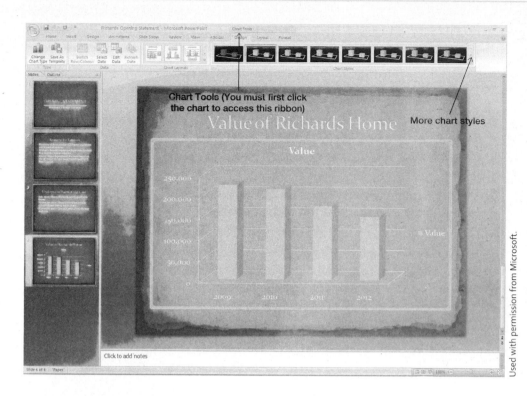

**POWERPOINT 2007
EXHIBIT 9**

20. PowerPoint 2007 offers many premade chart styles and colors to choose from.

21. ***On the Chart Tools – Design ribbon tab, click the More icon in the Chart Styles group*** (see PowerPoint 2007 Exhibit 9). *Note*: You can access the Chart Tools ribbon only when a chart is selected, so ***click the chart if you do not see the Chart Tools ribbon***.

22. A wide variety of chart styles is now displayed. ***Click any of the charts in the last row;*** these are the 3-D sculpted options.

23. The chart is now complete. To view your chart full-screen, ***click the Slide Show icon.***

24. Press the **[ESC]** key.

25. To save your presentation, ***click the Save icon*** (it looks like a floppy disk) ***on the Quick Access toolbar.***

This concludes Lesson 3. To exit PowerPoint, ***click the Office button, then click Exit PowerPoint.*** To go to Lesson 4, stay at the current screen.

▶ ADVANCED LESSON

LESSON 4: FINALIZING THE PRESENTATION

In this lesson, you will add more slides to the opening statement presentation, duplicate a slide, enter slide transition effects, create animation effects, and show your presentation. If you did not exit PowerPoint from Lesson 3, go to step 3 in the following instructions.

1. Start Windows. ***Double-click the Microsoft Office PowerPoint 2007 icon on the desktop*** to start PowerPoint 2007 for Windows. Alternatively, ***click the Start button, point to Programs or All Programs, then click the Microsoft PowerPoint 2007 icon*** (or ***point to Microsoft Office and then click Microsoft Office PowerPoint 2007***). You should be in a clean, blank document.

2. *Click the Office button, then click Open.* The "Open" window should now be displayed. Navigate to the folder where the file is located. *Click Richards Opening Statement and then click Open.*

3. You should have the "Opening Statement" slide on your screen. Push the **[PAGE DOWN]** key until you are at the fourth slide, which is the bar chart.

4. You are now ready to create another slide. *On the Home ribbon tab, click the down arrow next to New Slide in the Slides group.*

5. *Click the Title and Content option.* A new slide should be displayed on your screen.

6. The top part of the slide should say **"Click to add title"** and the bottom section of the slide should say **"Click to add text."**

7. *Click* **"Click to add title"** and then type **7788 SW 52nd Street**.

8. *In the lower box, where it says* **"Click to add text,"** *click on Insert Picture from File.* (It is the first icon on the bottom left; see PowerPoint 2007 Exhibit 10.) You will now add a photograph to the presentation.

**POWERPOINT 2007
EXHIBIT 10**

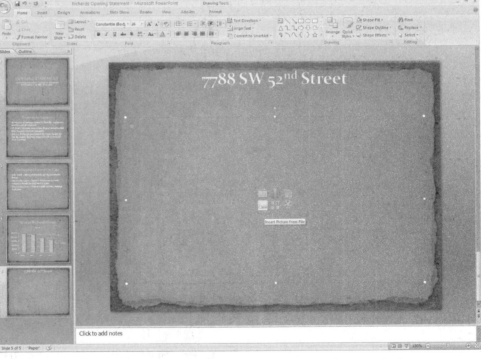

Used with permission from Microsoft.

9. The "Insert Picture" window should now be displayed. Navigate to the drive where the disk that accompanied this text is located.

10. *Double-click the PowerPoint Files folder, double-click the PowerPoint 2007 folder, and then double-click the "Lesson 4 house" (JPEG).*

11. *Click on the photograph of the house, then click Insert.* Your screen should now look like PowerPoint 2007 Exhibit 11. If you need to change the size of the image, *click on one of the sides of the image and drag the image to the desired size.*

12. You will now add another slide. *On the Home ribbon tab, click the down arrow next to New Slide in the Slides group.*

13. *Click the Title and Content option.* A new slide should be displayed on your screen.

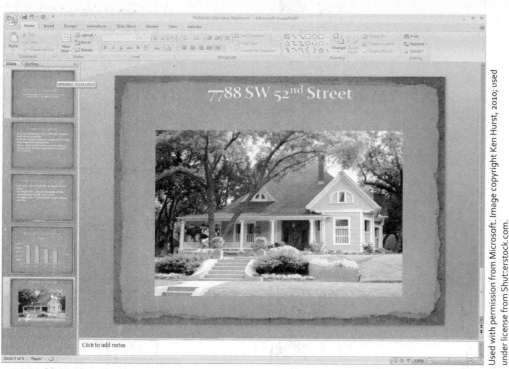

HANDS-ON EXERCISES

14. The top part of the slide should say **"Click to add title"** and the bottom section of the slide should say **"Click to add text."**

15. *Click* **"Click to add title"** and type **Termite Damage**.

16. *In the lower box, where it says* **"Click to add text,"** *click on Insert Picture from File.* (It is the first icon on the bottom left; see PowerPoint 2007 Exhibit 10.) You will now add another photograph to the presentation.

17. The "Insert Picture" window should now be displayed. Navigate to the drive where the disk that accompanied this text is located.

18. *Double-click the PowerPoint Files folder, double-click the PowerPoint 2007 folder, and then double-click the "Lesson 4 termite damage" (JPEG).*

19. *Click on the photograph of termite damage, then click Insert.* Your screen should now look like PowerPoint 2007 Exhibit 12. If you need to change the size of the image, *click on one of the sides of the image and drag the image to the desired size.*

20. Now that you have created all of your slides, you are ready to begin finalizing the presentation. Press **[CTRL]+[HOME]** to go to the first slide in the presentation.

21. *Click the Slide Sorter view icon at the bottom right of the screen.* Notice that you can see all six of your slides on the screen.

22. You will now apply transition effects (effects that take place when you move from one slide to another) and animation effects (effects that take place during display of a single slide).

23. *Click on the first slide, "Richards Opening Statement."*

24. *Click the Animations ribbon tab.* You should see the Transition to This Slide group (see PowerPoint 2007 Exhibit 13). On the left side of the Transition to This Slide group are the various transition choices. To the right are the settings available for each transition.

25. *On the Animations ribbon tab, click the More icon in the Transition to This Slide group.* Notice that many types of slide transitions are available.

**POWERPOINT 2007
EXHIBIT 12**

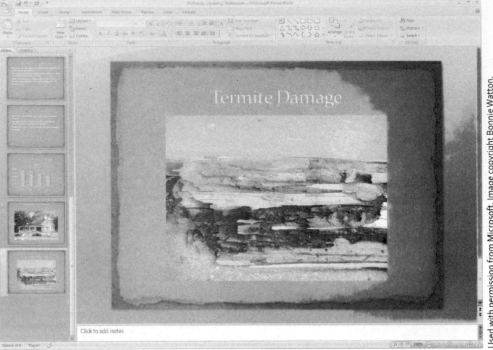

**POWERPOINT 2007
EXHIBIT 13**

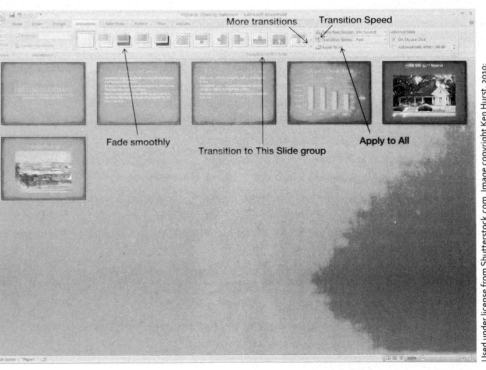

26. Press the **[ESC]** key to make the "More transitions" list disappear.

27. ***On the Animation ribbon tab, click the Fade Smoothly transition effect in the Transition to This Slide group***. Notice that after you selected it, your slide displayed the transition effect. Fade Smoothly is a professional-appearing transition effect that is not distracting, so it is a good one to use in the legal setting.

28. ***On the Animations ribbon tab, click the down arrow next to Transition Speed: Fast and then click Medium.***

29. ***On the Animations ribbon tab, click Apply to All in the Transition to This Slide group.*** This will apply the Fade Smoothly effect to all of the slides in your presentation. Notice that little symbols now appear under all of your slides in the slide sorter; this shows that they have transition effects associated with them.

30. Notice that in the Transition to This Slide group, under Advance Slide, "On Mouse Click" is selected. This means that the presentation will automatically move to the next slide only when the mouse is clicked. You could set it to move to the next slide automatically after a given amount of time, but the current selection is fine for this presentation.

31. ***Click the Slide Show icon at the bottom right of the screen*** to see your presentation, including the transition effects. ***Click the mouse button to proceed through the presentation and go back to the Slide Sorter screen.***

32. You will now create an animation effect that determines how the slides with bullet points appear on the screen.

33. ***Double-click the second slide, "Reasons for Lawsuit."***

34. ***Click anywhere in the lower half of the screen.***

35. ***On the Animations ribbon tab, click the down arrow next to Animate: No Transition in the Animation group*** (see PowerPoint 2007 Exhibit 14).

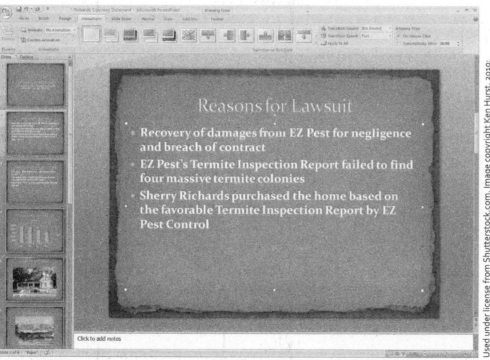

**POWERPOINT 2007
EXHIBIT 14**

36. ***Under Fade, click By 1st Level Paragraphs.*** Notice that the animation effect is then demonstrated.

37. ***Repeat this same process for slide 3.***

38. You are now ready to view your presentation. Press the **[PAGE UP]** key to go to the first slide in the presentation.

39. ***Click the Slide Show icon at the bottom right of the screen.***

40. Your first slide is now shown at full-screen size. To proceed to the next slide, press the **[SPACE BAR]** or ***click the left mouse button.*** Keep pressing

the **[SPACE BAR]** or clicking the left mouse button to proceed with the presentation. Notice on the slides with bullets that you must press the **[SPACE BAR]** or click the mouse to go to the next bullet; this is the animation effect you created.

41. When you get to the end of the presentation, press the **[SPACE BAR]** or *click the left mouse button* to go back to editing the presentation.

42. To print your presentation, *click the Office button, point to Print, and click OK.*

43. To save your presentation, *click the Save icon* (it looks like a floppy disk) *on the Quick Access toolbar.*

44. *Click the Office button and then click Close.*

This concludes the PowerPoint 2007 Hands-On Exercises. To exit PowerPoint, *click the Office button, then click Exit PowerPoint.*

POWERPOINT 2003

Number	Lesson Title	Concepts Covered
BASIC LESSONS		
Lesson 1	Creating a Presentation	Selecting a presentation design; entering text; entering speaker's notes; saving a file
Lesson 2	Creating Additional Slides	Inserting a new slide; selecting a slide layout; viewing a slide in Slide Show, Outline, and Slide Sorter views; creating additional slides
INTERMEDIATE LESSON		
Lesson 3	Creating a Graph	Creating and entering data in a chart
ADVANCED LESSON		
Lesson 4	Finalizing the Presentation	Creating transition effects; creating animation effects; viewing a final presentation

GETTING STARTED

Overview

Microsoft PowerPoint is a presentation graphics program. It allows you to create presentations, charts, graphs, tables, and much more. The PowerPoint program is easy to learn and use. Please note that throughout these lessons you will be creating a presentation for an opening statement.

Introduction

Throughout these lessons and exercises, information you need to type into the software will be designated in several different ways:

- Keys to be pressed on the keyboard are designated in brackets, in all caps, and in bold (e.g., press the **[ENTER]** key).
- Movements with the mouse pointer are designated in bold and italics (e.g., *point to File on the menu bar and click*).
- Words or letters that should be typed are designated in bold (e.g., type **Training Program**).
- Information that is or should be displayed on your computer screen is shown in bold, with quotation marks (e.g., **"Press ENTER to continue."**).
- Specific menu items and commands are designated with an initial capital letter (e.g., click Open).

▶ BASIC LESSONS

LESSON 1: CREATING A PRESENTATION

In this lesson you will start PowerPoint 2003, select a background design for the presentation, enter the first slide, view your slide, and save your presentation.

1. Start Windows. After it has loaded, ***double-click on the Microsoft Office PowerPoint 2003 icon on the desktop*** to start PowerPoint 2003 for Windows. Alternatively, ***click the Start button, point to Programs or All Programs, then click the Microsoft PowerPoint 2003 icon,*** or ***point to Microsoft Office and then click Microsoft Office PowerPoint 2003.*** You should be in a clean, blank document.

2. A blank document should be on your screen. *In the Getting Started task pane on the right side of the screen, under Open, click Create a new presentation…*

3. *Under Templates, click On my computer…*

4. *In the "New Presentation" window, click the Design Templates tab.* Notice that a number of templates are now available.

5. *Click Balance, then click OK.* If **"Balance"** is not displayed on your computer, or if you cannot select it, try selecting another design.

6. A title slide should now be displayed on your screen. The top part of the slide should say **"Click to add title"** and the bottom section of the slide should say **"Click to add subtitle."**

7. *Click* **"Click to add title."** Notice that you are now allowed to type your own title. Type **OPENING STATEMENT** (see Power Point 2003 Exhibit 1).

POWERPOINT 2003 EXHIBIT 1

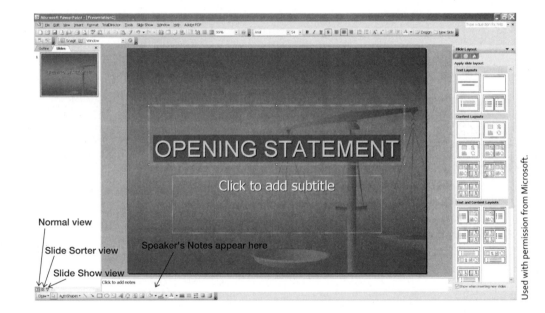

Used with permission from Microsoft.

8. *Click* **"Click to add subtitle."** Type **Richards v. EZ Pest Control**.

9. The slide is now created.

10. To view your slide, *click the Slide Show icon in the lower left corner of your screen*. *Note:* You will see three icons in the lower left corner of the screen for Normal view, Slide Sorter view, and Slide Show. Slide Show is the icon all the way to the right. Remember, if you point to any icon and hold the pointer there for a second, the title of the icon will be displayed.

11. You should now see your slide running full screen on your computer. Notice that the dark background with the white letters makes your slide very readable. This is how your audience will see your slide. Press the **[ESC]** key to go back to editing your presentation.

12. Notice that at the bottom of the screen, under the current slide, it says **"Click to add notes."** This is the speaker's notes section of the screen. Speaker's notes are not shown in the Slide Show view, but they can be printed so that the presenter has talking points to which to refer.

13. *Click anywhere in the Speaker's notes section.* Type **May it please the Court, Your Honor, and ladies and gentlemen of the jury—the evidence in this**

case will show that the Defendant, EZ Pest Control, grossly and negligently harmed my client.

14. *Click the Slide Show icon in the lower left corner of the screen again.* Notice that the speaker's notes do not appear.

15. Press the [**ESC**] key to go back to editing your presentation.

16. It is a good idea to regularly save your work. To save your presentation, *click File on the menu bar.*

17. *Click Save.*

18. Type **Richards Opening Statement** and press the [**ENTER**] key to save the file in the default directory. Be sure to remember where the file is saved so that you can retrieve it for the next lesson.

This concludes Lesson 1. To exit PowerPoint, *click File on the menu bar and then click on Exit.* To go to Lesson 2, stay at the current screen.

LESSON 2: CREATING ADDITIONAL SLIDES

In this lesson, you will enter additional slides into the opening statement presentation you created in Lesson 1, and you will look at the presentation using several views. If you did not exit PowerPoint from Lesson 1, go to Step 3 in the following instructions.

1. Start Windows. *Double-click on the Microsoft Office PowerPoint 2003 icon on the desktop* to start PowerPoint 2003 for Windows. Alternatively, *click the Start button, point to Programs or All Programs, then click the Microsoft PowerPoint 2003 icon,* or *point to Microsoft Office and then click Microsoft Office PowerPoint 2003.* You should be in a clean, blank document.

2. *Click File on the menu bar and then click Open. Select your file and then click Open.* Alternatively, you can *click File on the menu bar and, if your file is shown at the bottom of the drop-down menu, click it.*

3. You should have the "Richards Opening Statement" slide on your screen. Notice in the lower left of the screen that it says "Slide 1 of 1." This shows you what slide number you are on.

4. To enter another slide, *click Insert on the menu bar.*

5. *Click New Slide...*

6. The Slide Layout task pane should be displayed on the right side of the screen. The program gives you a number of different Text Layouts, Content Layouts, and Text and Content Layouts. *Click several of the choices.* Notice that the screen automatically changes.

7. *Click the Title and Text option under Text Layouts.* (In PowerPoint 2003 Exhibit 2, it is second from the top square on the left; it has four bullets in a column with some squiggly lines).

8. A new slide is displayed on your screen. The top part of the slide should say "**Click to add title**" and the bottom section of the slide (next to a bullet point) should say "**Click to add text.**"

9. *Click* "**Click to add title.**" Type **Reasons for Lawsuit** (see PowerPoint 2003 Exhibit 2).

10. *Click* "**Click to add text.**" Type **Recovery of damages from EZ Pest for negligence and breach of contract** and press the [**ENTER**] key. Notice that an additional bullet has been created.

11. Type **EZ Pest's Termite Inspection Report failed to find four massive termite colonies** and press the [**ENTER**] key.

**POWERPOINT 2003
EXHIBIT 2**

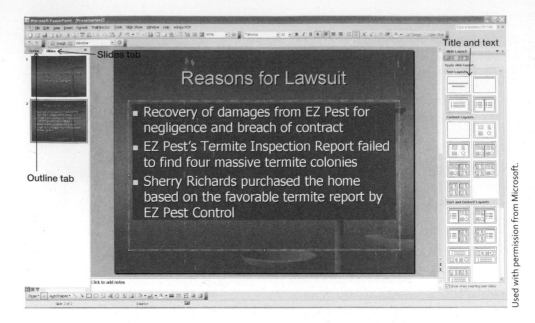

12. Type **Sherry Richards purchased the home based on the favorable termite report by EZ Pest** and press the [**ENTER**] key.

13. The slide is now created. See PowerPoint 2003 Exhibit 2.

14. To view your slide, *click the Slide Show icon.*

15. You should now see your slide running full screen on your computer. With the slide running in Slide Show view, press the [**PAGE UP**] key and notice that the first slide is now shown on your screen. Press the [**PAGE DOWN**] key and notice that you are back at the second slide.

16. Press [**ESC**] to return to Normal view.

17. You will now look at your presentation using other views. Notice on the left side of the screen that small versions of both of your slides are displayed (see PowerPoint 2003 Exhibit 2). Notice just above the slides that the Slides tab is selected.

18. *Click the Outline tab just to the left of the Slides tab* (just under the toolbar in the upper left of your screen).

19. The Outline view is now displayed; notice that you can read the words on both of your slides (see PowerPoint 2003 Exhibit 3).

20. *Click the Slides tab, just to the right of the Outline tab,* to go back to the Slides view.

21. You will now view your slides using the Slide Sorter view. *Click the Slide Sorter view icon.* The Slide Sorter View icon is at the bottom left of the screen; it is the icon in the middle, with a picture of four small squares (see PowerPoint 2003 Exhibit 1).

22. You can now see all of your slides on the screen at the same time (see PowerPoint 2003 Exhibit 4). This is helpful for getting an overview of your presentation and for arranging and rearranging the slide order.

23. While you are in the Slide Sorter view, *click the second slide and drag the mouse pointer (hold down the mouse button) to the left of the first slide, then release the mouse button.* Notice that the order of the slides is now changed.

24. Press [**CTRL**]+[**Z**] to undo the move and put the slides back into their original order.

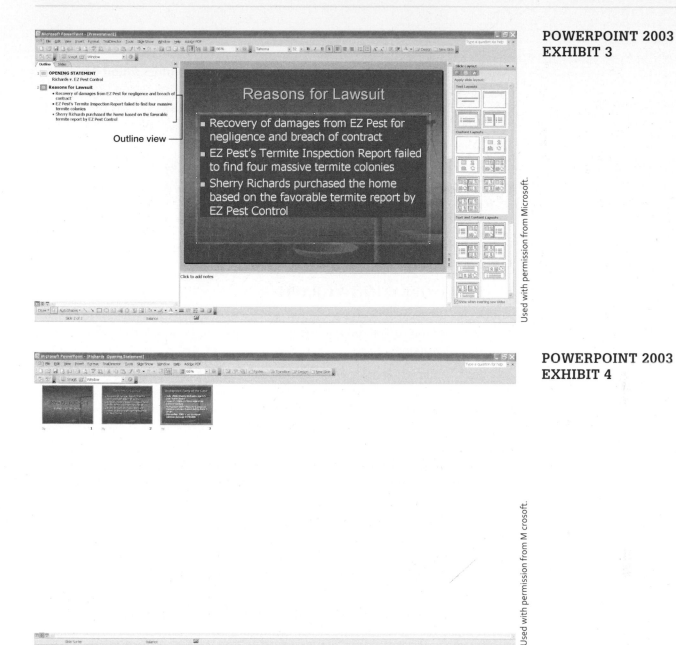

**POWERPOINT 2003
EXHIBIT 3**

Outline view

Used with permission from Microsoft.

**POWERPOINT 2003
EXHIBIT 4**

Used with permission from Microsoft.

25. *Click the Normal View icon in the lower left of your screen* (see PowerPoint 2003 Exhibit 1).

26. You should now have the Opening Statement slide on your screen. If you are not there, use the **[PAGE DOWN]** key to go there.

27. You are now ready to enter another slide. If the Slide Layout task pane is open, *right-click the Title and Text option and then click Insert New Slide.* If the Slide Layout task pane is not open, *click Insert on the menu bar and click New Slide; then select the Title and Text option.*

28. A new slide should now be displayed on your screen. The top of the slide should say **"Click to add title"** and the bottom section of the slide (next to a bullet point) should say **"Click to add text."**

29. *Click* **"Click to add title."** Type **Undisputed Facts of the Case**.

30. *Click* **"Click to add text."** Type **July 2006–Sherry Richards, age 65, purchases house** and press the **[ENTER]** key.

31. Type **June 15, 2006–EZ Pest makes no termite finding** and press the [**ENTER**] key.

32. Type **November 2007–Massive Formosan termite colonies found dating back 5 years** and press the [**ENTER**] key.

33. Type **December 2007–Cost to repair termite damage $158,000** and press the [**ENTER**] key.

34. Your presentation now consists of three slides.

35. To save your presentation, *click the Save icon on the toolbar.*

This concludes Lesson 2. To exit PowerPoint, *click File on the menu bar and then click Exit.* To go to Lesson 3, stay at the current screen.

▶ INTERMEDIATE LESSON

LESSON 3: CREATING A GRAPH

In this lesson, you will insert an additional slide with a graph into the opening statement presentation. If you did not exit PowerPoint from Lesson 2, go to Step 4 in the following instructions.

1. Start Windows. *Double-click the Microsoft Office PowerPoint 2003 icon on the desktop* to start PowerPoint 2003 for Windows. Alternatively, *click the Start button, point to Programs or All Programs, then click the Microsoft PowerPoint 2003 icon,* or *point to Microsoft Office and then click Microsoft Office PowerPoint 2003.* You should be in a clean, blank document.

2. *Click File on the menu bar and then click Open. Select your file and then click Open.* Alternatively, you can *click File on the menu bar and, if your file is shown at the bottom of the drop-down menu, you can click it.*

3. You should have the Opening Statement slide on your screen. Push the [**PAGE DOWN**] key until you are on the third slide, "Undisputed Facts of the Case."

4. To add another slide, *click Insert on the menu bar, then click New Slide.* The Slide Layout task pane should be displayed on the right side of the screen.

5. *Click the Title and Content option.* (In PowerPoint 2003 Exhibit 1, it is the second from the top square on the left under Content Layouts).

6. A new slide should now be displayed on your screen. The top part of the slide should say **"Click to add title"** and the bottom section of the slide should say **"Click icon to add content."**

7. *Click* "Click to add title." Type **Value of Richards Home** and press the [**ENTER**] key (see PowerPoint 2003 Exhibit 5).

8. Notice on the lower portion of the slide, just above **"Click icon to add content,"** that there is a box with six icons in it. *Click the Insert Chart icon.* (It is in the middle of the first row and looks like a multicolored vertical bar chart; see PowerPoint Exhibit 5.)

9. Notice that a default chart with default data is displayed. Also, notice that a window titled "Richards Opening Statement – Datasheet" has appeared.

10. To clear the data in the datasheet, *point to the uppermost cell at the left of the "Datasheet" window. Drag the mouse pointer down and to the right so that all of the data is highlighted,* then press the [**DELETE**] key. (Remember that if you make a mistake at any time, you can press [**CTRL**]+[**Z**] to undo the error.)

11. *Click cell A2. Then, right-click and click Delete.*

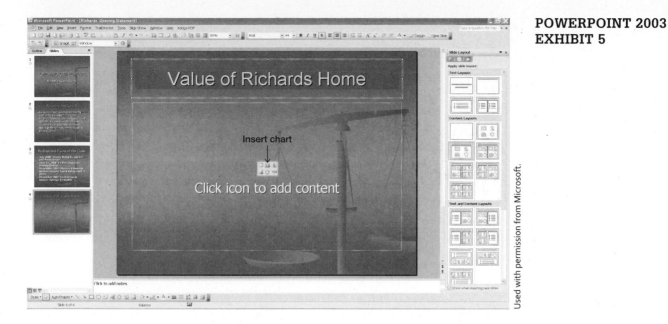

**POWERPOINT 2003
EXHIBIT 5**

12. The "Delete" window should now be displayed. ***Click Entire Row and click OK.*** This will delete that row.

13. Repeat steps 11–12 to delete the next row.

14. Now you are ready to enter the data for your new chart. Enter the following data in the chart exactly as shown:

	A	B	C	D
	2009	2010	2011	2012
Value	225,000	215,000	175,000	150,000

15. Your datasheet and chart should look similar to PowerPoint 2003 Exhibit 6.

16. To see the chart (without the datasheet), ***click anywhere outside of the chart***, such as in the title of the slide "Value of Richards Home." Notice that the chart, including the legend, is properly formatted.

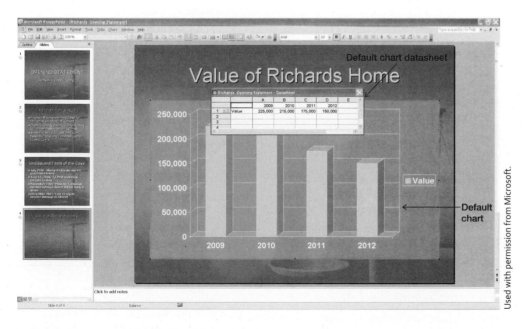

**POWERPOINT 2003
EXHIBIT 6**

17. The chart is now created. To view your chart, *click the Slide Show icon.*

18. Press the [**ESC**] key.

19. To save your presentation, *click Save on the toolbar.*

This concludes Lesson 3. To exit PowerPoint, *click File on the menu bar and then click Exit.* To go to Lesson 4, stay at the current screen.

▶ ADVANCED LESSON

LESSON 4: FINALIZING THE PRESENTATION

In this lesson, you will add more slides to the opening statement presentation, enter slide transition effects, create animation effects, and show your presentation. If you did not exit PowerPoint from Lesson 3, go to Step 3 in the following instructions.

1. Start Windows. *Double-click the Microsoft Office PowerPoint 2003 icon on the desktop* to start PowerPoint 2003 for Windows. Alternatively, *click the Start button, point to Programs or All Programs, then click the Microsoft PowerPoint 2003 icon,* or *point to Microsoft Office and then click Microsoft Office PowerPoint 2003.* You should be in a clean, blank document.

2. *Click File on the menu bar and then click Open. Select your file and then click Open.* Alternatively, you can *click File on the menu bar and, if your file is shown at the bottom of the drop-down menu, you can click it.*

3. You should have the opening statement slide on your screen. Push the [**PAGE DOWN**] key until you are at the last slide, "Value of Richards Home."

4. *Click Insert on the menu bar and then click New Slide.*

5. *From the Slide Layout task pane, click the Title and Content layout under Content Layouts* (the fourth box from the top on the left).

6. *Click in the text box where it says "Click to add title."* Type **7788 SW 52nd Street.**

7. *In the lower box, where it says "Click icon to add content," click on Insert Picture.* (It is the first icon on the bottom left; see PowerPoint 2003 Exhibit 7). You will now add a photograph to the presentation.

POWERPOINT 2003 EXHIBIT 7

8. The "Insert Picture" window should now be displayed. Navigate to the drive where the disk that accompanied this text is located.

9. *Double-click the PowerPoint Files folder, double-click the PowerPoint 2003 folder, then double-click the "Lesson 4 house" (JPEG).*

10. *Click on the photograph of the house, then click Insert.* Your screen should now look like PowerPoint 2003 Exhibit 8. If you need to change the size of the image, you can *click on one of the sides of the image and drag the image to the desired size.*

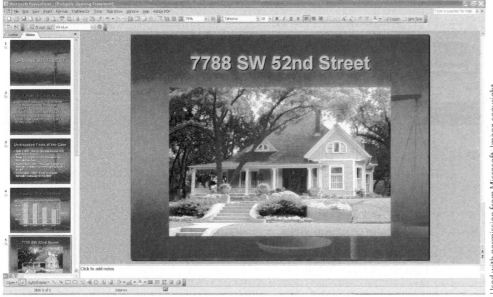

**POWERPOINT 2003
EXHIBIT 8**

HANDS-ON EXERCISES

11. You will now add another slide. *Click Insert on the menu bar and then click New Slide.*

12. *From the Slide Layout task pane, click the Title and Content layout under Content Layouts* (the fourth box from the top on the left).

13. *Click in the text box where it says* "**Click to add title**" and type **Termite Damage.**

14. *In the lower box, where it says "Click icon to add content," click on Insert Picture.* (It is the first icon on the bottom left; see PowerPoint 2003 Exhibit 7.) You will now add another photograph to the presentation.

15. The "Insert Picture" window should now be displayed. Navigate to the drive where the disk that accompanied this text is located.

16. *Double-click the PowerPoint Files folder, double-click the PowerPoint 2003 folder, then double-click the "Lesson 4 termite damage" (JPEG).*

17. *Click on the photograph of the termite damage, then click Insert.* Your screen should now look like PowerPoint 2003 Exhibit 9. If you need to change the size of the image, you can *click on one of the sides of the image and drag the image to the desired size.*

18. You have now created all of your slides, so you are ready to begin finalizing the presentation.

19. Press **[CTRL]+[HOME]** to go to the first slide in the presentation.

20. *Click the Slide Sorter view at the bottom left of the screen.* Notice that you can see all six of your slides on the screen.

**POWERPOINT 2003
EXHIBIT 9**

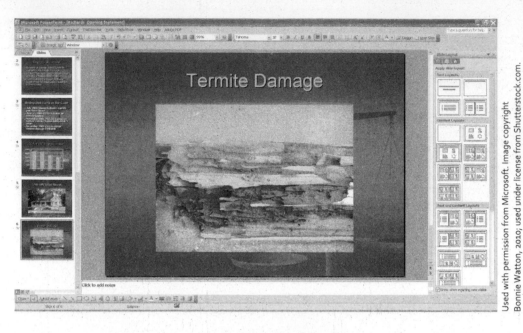

21. You will now enter transition effects (effects that take place when you move from one slide to another) and animation effects (effects that take place during display of a single slide).

22. ***Right-click on the first slide,*** "Richards Opening Statement."

23. ***Click once on Slide Transition....*** (*Note*: There is an icon at the right of the toolbar that says **"Transition."** This icon can also be used to enter transition effects.) Notice that the Slide Transition task pane is now displayed on the right side of the screen, and it lists many transition effects (see PowerPoint 2003 Exhibit 10).

24. ***Scroll down and click the Fade Smoothly transition effect.*** Notice that after you selected it, that slide displayed the transition effect. Fade Smoothly is a professional transition effect that is not distracting, so it is a good one to use in a legal setting.

25. ***In the Slide Transition task pane, under Modify transition, click the down arrow next to Fast and select Medium.***

26. Notice that in the Slide Transition task pane, under Advance Slide, there is a check mark next to **"On mouse click."** This means that the slide will

**POWERPOINT 2003
EXHIBIT 10**

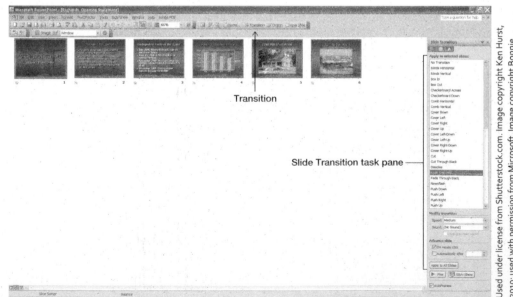

Transition

Slide Transition task pane

automatically move to the next slide when the mouse is clicked. You could set it to move to the next slide automatically after a certain amount of time, but the current selection is fine for this slide.

27. ***In the Slide Transition task pane, click Apply to All Slides near the bottom of the task pane.*** This feature applies the transition effect on this slide to all slides in the presentation.

28. ***Click Slide Show at the bottom of the task pane*** to see your presentation, including the transition effects.

29. ***Click to proceed through the presentation and back to Slide Sorter view.***

30. ***Right-click the second slide,*** "Reasons for Lawsuit."

31. ***Click Animation Schemes.*** Notice that the Slide Design task pane is displayed on the right side of the screen (see PowerPoint 2003 Exhibit 11).

32. ***Click Ascend under Moderate.*** *Note*: When the slide is shown in a slide show, you will need to click the mouse button to get the next bullet to appear.

33. ***Click Apply to All Slides.***

34. You are now ready to view your presentation. ***Click the first slide.***

POWERPOINT 2003 EXHIBIT 11

Slide Design task pane

35. ***Click the Slide Show icon at the bottom left of the screen.***

36. Your first slide is now shown full screen. To proceed to the next slide, press the **[SPACE BAR]** or ***click the left button on the mouse.*** Keep pressing the **[SPACE BAR]** or ***clicking the left mouse button*** to proceed with the presentation.

37. When you have seen the full presentation, PowerPoint will return to Slide Sorter view.

38. To print your presentation, ***click File on the menu bar, click Print, then click OK.***

39. To save your presentation, ***click Save on the toolbar.***

40. ***Click File on the menu bar and then click Close.***

This concludes Lesson 4.

This concludes the PowerPoint 2003 Hands-On Exercises. To exit PowerPoint, ***click File on the menu bar, then click Exit.***